Francis Lieber

Contributions to political science

Francis Lieber

Contributions to political science

ISBN/EAN: 9733742859600

Manufactured in Europe, USA, Canada, Australia, Japa

Cover: Foto ©Suzi / pixelio.de

Manufactured and distributed by brebook publishing software
(www.brebook.com)

Francis Lieber

Contributions to political science

THE MISCELLANEOUS WRITINGS

OF

FRANCIS LIEBER.

II.

CONTRIBUTIONS TO POLITICAL SCIENCE.

CONTRIBUTIONS

TO

POLITICAL SCIENCE,

INCLUDING LECTURES ON THE CONSTITUTION OF THE UNITED STATES

AND

OTHER PAPERS.

BY

FRANCIS LIEBER, LL.D.,

CORRESPONDING MEMBER OF THE INSTITUTE OF FRANCE, AUTHOR OF "POLITICAL ETHICS," "CIVIL LIBERTY," "PRINCIPLES OF LEGAL AND POLITICAL INTERPRETATION," ETC.

BEING

VOLUME II. OF HIS MISCELLANEOUS WRITINGS.

PHILADELPHIA:
J. B. LIPPINCOTT & CO.
LONDON: 16 SOUTHAMPTON STREET, STRAND.
1881.

EDITORIAL NOTE.

THE reader is again requested to bear in mind that in reprinting these essays the rule has been followed to present what Dr. Lieber said, and not what he would have said if he had lived to collect and revise his own writings, in the light of all which has transpired or has been published since the time when he wrote. His own corrections to his publications have, however, been inserted.—(G.)

CONTENTS OF VOLUME II.

LIEBER'S SERVICE TO POLITICAL SCIENCE AND INTERNATIONAL LAW.

BY DR. J. C. BLUNTSCHLI,

PROFESSOR OF POLITICAL SCIENCE AND INTERNATIONAL LAW IN THE
UNIVERSITY OF HEIDELBERG, AND FIRST PRESIDENT OF THE
INSTITUT DE DROIT INTERNATIONAL.

It affords me pleasure to comply with your request for an
expression of my views concerning the importance to science
of our dear departed friend.   His place and influence are not
yet so fully known and appreciated as they ought to be.   If
I can contribute towards making them better understood, I
shall regard it not merely as a discharge of duty, but at once
as a satisfaction and a joy.

Francis Lieber first attained his scientific maturity in
America, the land of his adoption.   His most important
works, " Political Ethics," " Civil Liberty," and " Instructions
for the Government of Armies of the United States in the
Field," had their origin in America, and were first written in
English.   This was likewise the case with his numerous and
able minor treatises.   In so far, then, Lieber belongs to the
United States of America, and has claim to a high rank
among American scholars and authors.

But he was born in Berlin, and obtained his scientific train-
ing and a large part of his intellectual wealth at German
schools and universities, and in the closest intercourse with
representatives of German science.   In so far, then, the German nation also has a share in the merits and fame of the son
whom she bore and educated.

The stormy time of Lieber's youth was passed in a period
when, in Germany, two opposing schools of law and political
science stood over against one another: on the one side, the

7

older and so-called philosophical school, advocating a law of nature; and on the other, the so-called historical school. The latter charged the former with disregarding the safe and solid ground of historical facts and relations; with soaring aloft to the clouds in flights of abstract thought; and with pursuing dreamy ideals, without ever being able to realize them. The philosophical school, on the other hand, blamed the historical school for turning its thoughts entirely towards the past; for yielding slavish obedience to the powers of tradition; for not tolerating progress or improvement; and for being destitute of ideas and genius. If the philosophical method was suspected of revolutionary tendencies, the historical method, on the contrary, had the reputation of being reactionary.

It is characteristic of Lieber, that, in himself, he early triumphed over these opposing tendencies. He was of a decidedly ideal nature. His mind delighted in philosophic contemplation from the heights of human consciousness. In his youth, enthusiasm for national independence and the liberties of the people had brought him into dangerous conflict with a meddlesome and stupid police, and allured him into that philhellenic, wild adventure to Greece. Actual experience in life had somewhat toned him down, but by no means extinguished his love of ideal things. He never lost sight of the highest goal of human destiny. The harmonious development of all moral and intellectual powers, which is the highest kind of liberty, appeared to him the appointed task of individual man and of humanity. All of Lieber's writings are warm and glowing with noble ideas concerning the improvement and development of our race. By a kind of predilection, he draws his arguments from the loftiest principles of divinely created human nature and divinely appointed human destiny. The philosophic, ideal tendencies of his thoughts and aspirations stand everywhere boldly forth. He is a *Liberal* both as man and as scholar.

But he was in no wise a follower of Rousseau, and by no means captivated with those airy systems of the philosophical school in which unwary and unpractical men had allowed themselves to be caught, like flies in cobwebs, by meshes spun out according to mathematical rules. He had brought along from home and school too good a satchel, filled with positive knowledge. He had made too many and too thorough studies in the actual history of nations; and not in vain had been his years of daily intercourse with Niebuhr, a leader in the historical school, who could hardly be charged with a lack of ideas or of genius. Lieber had also suffered various painful experiences which made him keenly sensible of the power which dwells in historic institutions and in the established order. But above all, in America there dawned upon him a full consciousness of the hard realities of life, and the inexpugnable power of facts. Here, better than in Europe, he learned to apply the standard of feasibility and of cautious, calculating experience. On this account all his writings teem with historical proofs and precedents and with useful observations. He knew well the value of hard common sense, and he could harmonize with it his own practical understanding, thus rendering the latter approved. In all these respects he employed the historical method with great advantage.

The settlement of that old-time conflict of schools and the union of the philosophical and historical methods, in contrast to the dangerous one-sidedness of either of the two, was a mark of great progress, effected gradually, and, for the most part, since 1840, in the jurisprudence and political science of Germany; somewhat later, however, in Italy. Lieber belongs to the first representatives of this peaceful alliance, although, indeed, it had been tried by the best politicians long before, by Aristotle, and by Cicero, and recommended by Bacon.

Lieber especially emphasizes in his writings the *moral* side of civil society. He is always inclined to associate *right* and *duty*, not in the sense that a man who has simply a duty stands over against the man who has simply a right, but in the sense that *whoever possesses a right has also a duty to exercise.* It is one of the merits of Rudolf Gneist to have been the first in Germany to advocate and decidedly to promote this idea of the obligatory character of civil right. " Civil rights are civil duties." But even before Gneist, Lieber, although in a somewhat different sense, had stoutly maintained that *duty* is a necessary factor in civil society. To Gneist duty appears to be a necessary quality, a characteristic of civil right; and, in so far, duty is *legal obligation* (*Rechtspflicht*). But, according to Lieber, duty is different from right; the former is *moral obligation*, not legal obligation. For this reason, duty transcends the limits of the legal order, although it is efficacious even within those limits. Duty has a broader basis in the nature of man, which is not governed entirely by law or legally regulated in all lines of its activity. Conscience still urges to the exercise of duty when the laws are silent, and even in political conduct we continue to distinguish between good and evil after the law has ceased to discriminate. For example, an executive officer or a leader in party politics may make a bad use of a legal right which is allowed him by the constitution; and a patriotic citizen may render his country a greater service than the law requires of him.

Lieber, in his Manual of Political Ethics, has laid especial stress upon the immeasurable importance of the moral element in civil life, and he has written a code of civil ethics which is of service at once to science and to morals: to science because he has filled a gap in the branch of politics, to morals because he has encouraged every noble aspiration and every political virtue while manfully combating baseness, even though it vaunt itself in the high places and be masked as holy authority.

Lieber knew that the civil order rests upon the broader and deeper foundation of the moral order, and that the former must sink in ruins if this foundation be destroyed. While showing the connection between the two, he follows the natural inclination of the German to consider, from an ethical stand-point, the world and its progress and to point out their moral worth. The German is fond of moralizing, but it is difficult for him to view things from a political stand-point. Lieber brought to America from over the ocean this German fondness for moralizing, but he also acquired a political cast of thought and developed the same in America. For these reasons, his writings possess a great value for Germans as well as for Americans. Our author represents both nationalities, supplies for both their peculiar wants and defects of education, and enriches each with the peculiar wealth of the other.

Lieber does not always distinguish sharply between law and morals, in the narrow sense. Sometimes a moral right or an ethical demand appears to him like a law. For example, when he is discussing the great and essentially moral force which expresses itself, in political life, as public opinion, he represents the latter as an expression of sovereignty, that is, as public law, which is certainly not the case. True it is, that no one, not even a legitimate king, can permanently withstand the might of public opinion, and true it is, that the latter, if it holds constantly and firmly to a certain course, will finally bring about changes in the constitution itself. And just as the overwhelming power of victory in a war between states decides the fate of nations, so the peaceful but ever-growing moral power of public opinion works on until at last it becomes irresistible.[1] When the mind and heart of the people are fully changed, then becomes inevitable a transformation of the state itself, which is simply a body for the soul of the people to dwell in. But these cases are no operations of sovereignty, no expressions of the supremacy of state, but rather are they radical changes in the conditions and relations upon which the state is founded, or in the situation of its people. We can appreciate the moral worth of public opinion and we should not fail to regard it politically, but we ought never to stamp it as law.

Lieber's work on Civil Liberty is quite in accordance with English and American ideas. And on this account, perhaps, the work was translated into German by Franz Mittermaier, and has become better known in Germany than the Political

---

[1] The latest and best discussion of the subject of Public Opinion is to be found in the article by Holtzendorff (also a friend of Lieber), which was published by the faculty of law at Munich, on the occasion of my doctor's jubilee, August, 1879.

Ethics.   Representative government and self-government are the great works of the English and American peoples.   The English have produced representative monarchy with parliamentary legislation and parliamentary government; the Americans have produced the representative republic.   We Europeans upon the continent, recognized in our turn that in representative government alone lies the hoped-for union between civil order and popular liberty. We found ourselves obliged, therefore, to become students of English and American institutions, although we gradually came to the conviction that mere imitation would be unsuitable and unworthy, an exact reproduction, utterly impossible.   All the more welcome, therefore, were the results which Lieber gave us, of his own experience and personal observations with regard to the workings of representative government.   In his studies concerning the nature of liberty, Lieber again, by a sort of preference, discusses the safeguards which Anglo-American common and statute law have set up and established for the defence of individual freedom against abuse of power.

The Instructions for the Government of Armies of the United States in the Field were drawn up by Lieber at the instance of President Lincoln, and formed the first codification of International Articles of War (*Kriegsvölkerrecht*).   This was a deed of great moment in the history of international law and of civilization.   Throughout this work also we see the stamp of Lieber's peculiar genius.   His legal injunctions rest upon the foundation of moral precepts.   The former are not always sharply distinguished from moral injunctions, but nevertheless, through a union with the same, are ennobled and exalted.   Everywhere reigns in this body of law the spirit of humanity, which spirit recognizes as fellow-beings, with lawful rights, our very enemies, and which forbids our visiting upon them unnecessary injury, cruelty, or destruction. But at the same time, our legislator remains fully aware that, in time of war, it is absolutely necessary to provide for the safety of armies and for the successful conduct of a campaign ; that, to those engaged in it, the harshest measures and most reckless exactions cannot be denied; and that tender-hearted sentimentality is here all the more out of place, because the greater the energy employed in carrying on the war, the sooner will it be brought to an end, and the normal condition of peace restored.

These instructions prepared by Lieber, prompted me to draw up, after his model, first, the laws of war, and then, in general, the law of nations, in the form of a code, or law book, which should express the present state of the legal conscious- ness of civilized peoples. Lieber, in his correspondence with me, had strongly urged that I should do this, and he lent me continual encouragement.

The intimate, personal connection in which I stood with Lieber in his declining years, although, indeed, through in- terchange of letters and not through meetings face to face, was for me a constant stimulus and source of satisfaction. This relation with Lieber was animated and strengthened by great and world-historic events: first of all, the war for the American Union, from 1861 to 1865; then the war between Austria and Prussia, in 1866; and finally, the Franco-Prussian war. From 1860 to 1870, Francis Lieber, in New York, Edward Laboulaye, in Paris, and I in Heidelberg, formed what Lieber used to call a "scientific clover-leaf," in which three men, devoting themselves especially to political science, and at the same time uniting the historical and philosophical methods, combining theory with practical politics, and be- longing to three different nationalities, to three states, and to three peoples, found themselves growing together by ties of common sympathy, and thus, figuratively speaking, represent- ing also the community of Anglo-American, French, and German culture and science. The personal tie, indeed, is now, alas, broken. Lieber is dead. Laboulaye had already vir- tually separated from us, for he could not overcome the bitter- ness caused by his feelings and experience during the Franco- Prussian war. But that community of thought, science, and endeavor, which we represented for three peoples and for three civilizations, is not broken up, but will broaden and deepen and become more fruitful, as surely as the peculiar spirit and individual forms of nationality, existing of their own right, find their true harmony and highest end in the development of humanity.

Lieber had great influence, I may add, in founding the *Institut de Droit International*, which was started in Ghent, in 1873, and forms a permanent alliance of leading international jurists from all civilized nations, for the purpose of working harmoniously together, and thus serving as an organ for the legal consciousness of the civilized world. Lieber was the first to propose and to encourage the idea of professional jurists of all nations thus coming together for consultation, and seeking to establish a common understanding. From this impulse proceeded Rolin-Jaequemyns' circular letter, drawn up in Ghent, calling together a number of men eminent for their learning. This latter proposal to found a *permanent academy for International Law* met with general acceptance, but this was merely a further development of the original idea of Lieber, which was at the bottom of the whole scheme. His notion was now approved and the efficiency of the association was thus assured for the future.

THE RISE OF OUR CONSTITUTION

AND ITS

NATIONAL FEATURES.

SKETCHES OF LECTURES DELIVERED IN THE LAW SCHOOL
OF COLUMBIA COLLEGE, IN NEW YORK.

NOTE.

FROM the condition in which the manuscript pages of the following treatise came under my eye, it is quite clear that Dr. Lieber was considering its publication, but that the copy was not ready for the press at the time of his death. I have not felt at liberty to modify his expressions, even in cases where it is possible he would have made some slight changes. Only a few verbal slips have been corrected. Although these are but Sketches of Lectures (to use his own phrase regarding them), they will recall to his former students his manner, as well as his thoughts, more completely perhaps than if they were elaborated for the press.—G.

16

THE RISE OF OUR CONSTITUTION

AND ITS

NATIONAL FEATURES.

[*An Outline not Completed.*]

MANKIND, but especially the most favored tribes, have spread by migration and colonization, in antiquity as well as in modern times, down to our own days. This is especially true of the Aryan race, and emphatically so of the Cis-Caucasian race—the Europeans and their descendants in other portions of the globe.

The main movement of this kind has been from earliest times from the south of Asia to the northwest, in Europe, in a belt of our globe chiefly between the 30th and 55th degree of northern latitude, until in modern times, when the limits of the zone as well as the northwest direction of the movement are no longer observed, and civilization spreads southward and even moves westward.

Civilization has moved from the Indus northwest to Media, Assyria, Egypt and Palestine, Greece, Rome, Italy, and the west of Europe ; then it passed the Atlantic, and then took a varied direction.

It is not only, however, the change of the course of civilization which is a marked phenomenon in history; another and a more important one is to be observed. When, in antiquity, civilization moved on, it generally left the region from which it moved in a relapse. Nations vanished. In modern times nations multiply, and old ones continue to flourish, while new ones rise and flourish along with them.   Ancient nations were short-lived, and never recuperated their health and strength after once having begun to decline; modern states have a recuperative power utterly wanting in antiquity.   The causes are various and of the last importance for the political philosopher and the intelligent lover of his kind.   In antiquity a state or people began its career, rose, reached its maximum, and once declining, descended never to recover; so that the career of ancient states may be appropriately figured by a parabola, which slantingly rises, has its maximum, and precipitately descends without the power of reascending.   Modern states have their progress and lapses, but may recuperate. Their careers may be symbolized by those lines in mathematics which have their maxima and minima, but recover from the latter, and, wave-like, move on.   This makes national longevity possible, and modern civilization stands in need of enduring national lives.   It is an error, therefore, to ascribe youth, manhood, and old age to modern nations as we acknowledge the fact in the individual, and to reason from this figure of speech.   How long modern nations may last no mortal man can know. England is in her thousandth year, and with what *maxima* and *minima?*   Why not a thousand years more ?   The period of Hellenic civilization, which shines like far the most brilliant diamond in history, lasted but a brief time, and although her intellectual and æsthetic culture influences our civilization to this day, Greece never rose again after her culmination, but was irretrievably lost in absorbing and increasing barbarism.

Closely connected with the constant movement and migration of our movable race is the subject of colonization.   Indeed, colonization is one of its phases.   Colonization is the planting of a community more or less organized and contained within itself in a country or on an isle distant from the state sending forth the colonists.   The etymology of the word leads to no especial understanding of its meaning, although etymologies are always interesting, frequently instructive.

The following points deserve especial attention :

Although movability must be ascribed to our whole Aryan,

and especially to the Cis-Caucasian race, yet it is to be observed that certain portions are far more movable and migratory than others. The Greeks in ancient times were ever emigrating, settling in foreign parts. The whole Mediterranean—that cradle of modern civilization—was bordered by Greek colonies, and Greek colonies were planted in Africa and Asia; while in modern times the Germans literally spread over the whole globe, without planting colonies. Some nations show a peculiar aptitude for colonization. The Greeks in ancient times and the English in modern times may be mentioned as prominent illustrations. The latter have proved the greatest colonizers of all history. Out of their colonies have risen, and are rising, whole empires.

But not only do certain tribes and nations prove themselves peculiarly migratory; there are periods when from manifold causes, many of which remain unknown to us, a migratory urgency—a longing for the distance—seizes with peculiar force the whole community and age. The Migration of Nations at the beginning of the Middle Ages, but most especially the age now properly called by historians the Period of Maritime Discovery, succeeded by the Period of Colonial Policy, and the irresistible outflowing of German population into all regions of the earth at the present time—these are the most memorable instances and illustrations.

The colonies which men have planted at different times are of very various character. Three different kinds are most important to be mentioned here.

All states in which Hellenism flourished were city-states, and when an ancient city of Greece became crowded and overpeopled, the enterprising young men resolved on emigration. When all was ready and the emigrants on board, a lamp was sent to the altar of the chief temple in the mother-city, there lighted by the perennial lamp of the temple, and kept burning if possible during the voyage; and the first flame on the altar in the spot chosen for the colony was lighted by this flame brought from home. It symbolized the feeling of filial piety, of Corcyra, for instance, to Corinth, but there all connection with the mother-state ended. A Greek colony had almost always *autonomy*, which, properly, means independence and "self-government" in our modern sense, although this word is a translation of *autonomy* made by the English theologians at the beginning of the seventeenth century. Marseilles was, in Hellenic times, as self-contained and independent as Athens. A similar state of things prevailed with the Semitic tribes. Carthage, although planted by Tyre, was its own mistress.

It is quite different with modern colonies. They always remain, and until the day of independence has come, are desirous and even anxious to remain part of the general empire. Although the British colonies in America carried along with them a very great aptitude as well as legal provision for self-government, they belonged to the English empire, were proud of calling themselves English, and resisted the encroachments of England on the common constitution, as Washington among many others expressed. A modern colony thus remains part of the state-system or empire which planted it, or whence the colonists came who carried the laws of the mother-country and allegiance along with them.

The third species of colonies to be mentioned here is that which consists in a mixture of conquest and colonization, the latter either by emigration to the conquered region, or by collection and assimilation with the conquerors. The ancient Roman municipal colonies all over Europe, by which the perfected municipal law and city government were spread over Europe, preparatory for a new civilization bridging over the gulf of anarchy to the brink of modern times, were such colonies. The Spanish colonies in Mexico and South America, such as they were, belong to the class of conquests, so much so that their planters of colonies have been called, and now receive the distinctive name of, *conquistadores*—conquerors carrying the Spanish sword among the numerous Indians, but no principle of self-government; they themselves possessed none; no aptitude for evolving, ruling, for they knew nothing at home but rigid absolutism.

The student must make himself acquainted with all systems of colonization which in the course of time have developed themselves—the Greek system, the British system, Colonizing conquest, Government colonies, such as different ones planted by Alexander the Great, Military colonies, such as the Austrian colonies near the frontiers of Turkey, both military and agricultural, the Penal colony, the Commercial colony (including the extended factory), the Agricultural colony, and the modern Missionary colony, including both the Jesuit colonies in South America and other parts, and the Protestant missionary colony. Nor may the Huguenot colony be omitted. When France expelled her Protestant subjects, long after the Massacre of St. Bartholomew, foreign countries gladly received them, and in Protestant Germany they were authorized to form "colonies" within some of the largest towns. These French colonies had their own ecclesiastical government, schools and seminaries, and their own courts of law, even down to the beginning of this century.

Self-Government, both the name and its essence, have been spoken of at length in Lieber's Civil Liberty and Self-Government.

As to Greek colonies, see Grote's History of Greece and Heeren's works.

Within a little more than sixty years four events of the greatest influence in all history happened. In 1453 the Turks conquered Constantinople and scattered the Greek scholars over Europe, greatly aiding the restoration of Letters. Nearly at the same time, in 1454, the art of printing was vouchsafed to man; in 1492, Columbus carried out the prophecy of Seneca by discovering America, after Henry the Navigator (1412) and Portuguese navigators had prepared the vast maritime discoveries awaiting our race; and in 1517, Martin Luther began the Reformation. In 1415, John Huss had been burned by the Council at Constance; and in 1481—sad for Spain, for South America, and for all Christianity—the Spanish Inquisition had been established.

The impulse which had been given to the European mind by the study of Greek, in science and revived theology, through the restoration of letters, was also instrumental in producing that age, now called the Period of Maritime Discoveries, succeeded by what historians call the Period of Colonial Policy. All western and central Europe was seized by an enthusiasm for discovering unknown lands and worlds, and for the science then called cosmography, meaning geography far beyond the limits now given to this science even by Ritter and his followers.

Columbus collected passages which indicated the existence of a western continent or large island—the Atlantis of the ancients. In a book called Libro de las Profecias, published by Navarrete, Coleccion 1ro, tom. ii. No. 114, page 272, we find that the great discoverer had entered the passage with which Seneca lets the Chorus conclude the second Act of Medea, containing a prophecy of the discovery inexplicable to us. It is :

> Venient annis sæcula seris
> Quibus Oceanus vincula rerum
> Laxet, et ingens pateat tellus,
> Thethysque novos detegat orbes,
> Nec sit terris ultima Thule.

This astounding passage was written by the pagan a century or two before some writers of the patristic literature declared the belief in a western land sinful, perhaps heretical, and for two of the worst reasons, namely, because the existence of an Atlantis was a universal heathenish belief, and because the Bible makes no mention of a western continent.

The best book the student can be referred to concerning the noble period of maritime discoveries is Oscar Peschel's History of the Age of Discoveries.

William Robertson's Historical Inquiry concerning the Knowledge of the Ancients of India, and the Progress of Commerce with this Country before the Discovery of the Way thither round the Cape of Good Hope. This work was translated into German by George Forster, the companion of Captain Cook (Berlin, 1792).

The great Age of Maritime Discovery produced also one of the most remarkable and influential facts, profoundly and sadly affecting the history of the American states in general, but that of the United States in particular.

The maritime discoverers, before they launched out into the Atlantic, were literally allured stage after stage along the western coast of Africa, when Prince Henry the Navigator or Sailor, as he is called in history, had planted his admiralty quarters at Sagres, and from a very early time indulged in men-robbery. Negroes were first, as indeed in the times of Carthage, considered of doubtful humanity, and at a later time were considered as fair play for slavery, which would lead them to

Christianity. In the middle of the fifteenth century the first negro captives were brought to Lisbon. Those among them who at home were high personages were ransomed with gold-dust, the others remained slaves. The question of right was not asked. Were they not heathens, unbaptized and black? Thus, then, we meet with the astounding phenomenon in history that while in Europe slavery vanishes everywhere among the Cis-Caucasians, and leaves at the most serfdom behind, it is reproduced in a new form by the discoveries along the shore of Africa, which looks as if it had been made to entice the men of our race to sail from cape to cape. Slavery, even negro slavery, however, was not useful at this time in Europe, and the negro was shipped to America, where slave labor became productive. Thus arose this surprising and instructive fact in the history of law, that a different basis of jural ethics made the foundation of the European law, even for the negro in Europe, though he were a fugitive from a colony belonging to the adjudging country in Europe, and the law of the colonies, where the right of property in a human being was largely and unconditionally acknowledged. This again led to the stupendous crime of our race—the slave-trade from Africa to America, which it required the efforts of the most powerful governments of our race, influenced at length by true religion and philanthropy, to abolish, and in which they have not yet entirely succeeded.

The Catholic church, as church, cannot be said to have promoted slavery; on the contrary, occasionally it favored emancipation. The fathers of the church, most especially Chrysostom, favored emancipation; Pope Eugenius is said to have declared emancipation an act pleasing in the sight of God. Spanish authors and priests of authority declared it wrong to carry the heathen into slavery, even were it to teach him Christianity. Soto, the authority chiefly consulted by Charles V., on occasion of the conference held before him and his confessor concerning the introduction of the negro slave-trade,— Soto declared in his works: "There can be no difference between Christians and Pagans, for the Law of Nations is equal to all nations." Mackintosh, in his General View of the Progress of Ethical Philosophy, says to Soto belongs the signal honor of being the first writer who condemned the African slave-trade. "It is affirmed," says he, "that the unhappy Ethiopians are by fraud or force carried away and sold as slaves. If this is true, neither those who have taken them, nor those who purchased them, nor those who hold them in bondage, can ever have a quiet conscience till they emancipate them, even if no compensation should be obtained."[1]

The general feeling, however, was, especially at the earlier times, that paganism, which meant not being baptized, deprived the individual of those rights which a true jural morality considers inherent in each human being. The fact of being baptized or not being baptized determining a claim to the commonest rights, nay more, to mere sympathy with bodily suffering, lasted down to very recent dates in certain groups of people, and may unfortunately do so to this day.

Peschel, in his History of the Age of Discoveries, relates, on distinct authorities, that the Portuguese discoverers trained dogs to track the negroes, and used the torture to force captives to betray the hiding-places of their comrades. Barros[2] gives the account of an expedition in 1444. When the mariners had suffered from storm and feared shipwreck, "at length," he says, "it pleased God, the rewarder of all good deeds, to give them, after so many sufferings in His service, a victorious day, glory for so many hardships, and compensation for their expenses, for there were captured, men, women, and children, one hundred and sixty-five pieces." This terrible simplicity in 1444 is symbolical, and so is the following of the year 1823. The writer saw in Rome a girl amusing a child in her arms by the contortions of some ten or fifteen chafers spiked on the knitting-needle. When expostulations at this cruelty were made, the girl in innocent amazement said, *Ma non è roba battizata.* She meant: it is unbaptized stuff. The occurrence

---

[1] Soto, De Justitia et Jure, lib. iv. quaest. ii. art. 2. This is quoted from Mackintosh.

[2] Barros, Da Asia, dec. i. liv. i. cap. 13.

sank deep in the writer's heart, and often rose again when he studied the history of our cruel race.

The history and legislation of slavery, one of the most instructive subjects, has its entire literature full of teaching by warning as well as by noble example. Here the student can only be directed to it, but this is the more important because the subject has lost its immediate keenness of interest for an American by the abolition of slavery. It will forever remain a prominent subject in historical psychology.

Concerning the slave-trade and its abolition, the student is directed to Sir Thomas Fowell Buxton's African Slave-Trade and its Remedy, London, 1839, Abridgment, 1840. Also, Complete Historico-Philosophical Representation of all the Changes in the Negro Trade from its Beginning to its Abolition, 2 vols., by Albert Hüne, Göttingen, 1820 (in German).

The Icelanders and other Norwegians visited North America about 1000 after Christ, and probably the ancients had some knowledge or a dim tradition of a western continent or vast island, their Atlantis; but what might be called the firm discovery of America, the conscious discovery retaining a hold on the discovered land, belongs to the western and southern people of Europe, misnamed the Latin races. The Spaniards and Portuguese were the chief discoverers, often led by Italian genius, as was also the case in the Spanish armies of Charles V., and especially of Philip the Second. This was signally the case in the chief discoverer, Christopher Columbus, a Genoese, who discovered, in the service of Ferdinand and Isabella, for the glory, and possibly for the ultimate ruin, of Spain.

The Portuguese settlements and colonies in the western portion of South America, having developed themselves within the last century into the empire of Brazil, have not influenced by any characteristic element the growth or decline of America, as belonging to the history of our race. A similar remark may be made concerning the French. They discovered, they settled, they actually enclosed the English colonies, at one time by a semicircle, from the mouth of the Mississippi to Canada; but the French element has no significance in America. The Quixotic attempt of establishing it, avowedly in the interest of the so-called Latin race, over the whole of Mexico by a Bonaparte fighting for an improvised emperor of the Hapsburgs, was a signal and a tragic failure.

The English settled the eastern portion of North America at a much later period, but remained a living part and portion of it, and grew into the most efficient and ruling people of America.

In speaking, therefore, of the Cis-Caucasians, or European people who seized on America, we shall consider the Spanish and the English exclusively; and in nothing, it may be said at once, do these two nations, differing in almost every important point, distinguish themselves from one another more than by their systems or plans of colonization.

They differed at the outset. All discoverers among western Europeans set out with the idea or pretence that they went for the honor of God, that is to say, for the extension of the Holy Roman Catholic church. The ambition of Columbus was supported by the religious fervor of the sincere Romanist. The idea that Christianity formed a part of humanity, and that paganism or the fact of not being baptized, already mentioned, established a non-jural state, or an existence *sine juribus*, led to the conception of the Right of Discovery, one of the most interesting subjects in the whole history of law. It did not mean what it means in our own days, namely, that the government of a man who discovers an unowned (or nearly unowned) land can fairly claim it as standing under its sovereignty, if it can and does establish its manifest protection and influence, and as far as it establishes this weight and influence. Mere verbal claim of thousands of miles on account of its material connection with the first port of landing, can no longer be admitted.

Discovery in what we will call here for brevity's sake the Spanish sense of the word, meant the first visit of a Catholic to an island or country not peopled at all or peopled by non-Christians, whom it was perfectly fair to conquer or subdue by any means, in which not even the lowest animal sympathy had play. Does this cruel ferocity distinguish the Spaniards of those days? It does, in Spain as well as in the new world, but if it is necessary, in any sense whatever, that we know ourselves, it is well to remind the young, that our whole Cis-Caucasian race has distinguished itself so far by an incomparably higher intellectuality, an insatiable greed for gold, and keen cruelty in this pursuit as well as in political and religious hatred—the latter probably on account of the first, or the more excitable cerebral system which the first presupposes. This is no ineradicable matter of material construction, and on every one belonging to our race rests the obligation of contributing to shape our future course differently.

The idea of Christian right over all the non-Christians, and the sovereignty over the whole earth claimed by the Pope, led Alexander VI., the evil-famed Borgia, to divide the globe by the famous line.

The English and Americans have not wholly discarded the idea that the white man, at least, if not the Christian, is entitled to this earth, if not *cultivated* by the occupier. So our Supreme Court decided by an opinion of the Chief Justice of the United States.

So soon as Columbus returned from America to Spain, Ferdinand and Isabella hastened to have the accomplished discovery, and all future acquisitions on the west by taking possession, confirmed by the Pope. Portugal, jealous of these new discoveries, was anxious to have all African discoveries and possessions exclusively secured to herself. They rested on earlier Papal bulls. In the year 1492, Alexander VI., of the Spanish family Borgia, was elected Pope, by no means to the delight of Ferdinand and Isabella. By the bull, dated May 13, 1493, the Pope gave to the Castilian crown the sovereignty over the islands and continent in the western portion of the ocean, provided this grant should not conflict with the rights previously acquired by a Christian prince. This was in favor of Portugal, and the following day, May 14, in order to avoid all difficulties, the Pope drew " a dividing line from the north pole to the south pole," and granted to the crown of Castile " all territories, islands, and continents westward of this meridian towards India or towards whatsoever country situated. This meridian was to be distant one hundred Spanish miles from any of the Azores or Capperdiac Isles" (Navarrete, ii., Nos. 17, 18). The Papal bull therefore divided the globe into two equal parts, between Spain and Portugal. At present, Peschel says, this division would be very clear; but it was far from being so at that time, where methods and apparatus were wanting to determine meridian distances. History has divided, portioned, and dealt out very differently. It was common in the Middle Ages to call the Pope the earthly God, and never has this blasphemous expression apparently been more truly realized than when this crime-beclotted Pope cleft the globe, happily for mankind, on parchment alone.

Concerning the erroneous name Latin race, the student is directed to a paper originally written for the *Revue de Droit International*, published at Ghent, and translated and printed by a student of the Law School of Columbia College. Mr. Chevalier's book on the French expedition to Mexico, to reduce it to obedience to Maximilian, is mainly founded on the justification that the Latin race must needs acquire power or supremacy again, after having been elbowed out of power all over the globe, except in Europe, by the Germanic race, especially by the Anglo-Saxon branch. This book is small and little mentioned since the French expedition failed so signally. It is mentioned here for this very reason.

As to the change and progress of the right of discovery, reference is made to Henry Wheaton's History of the Progress of the Law of Nations, and to Hugo Grotius's The Rights of War and Peace. It is founded in the modern law of nations on no papal permission, but, first of all, on the principle that what belongs to no one may be appropriated by the finder. A number of limitations present themselves at once. See Lieber's Essays on Labor and Property.

The case decided by the Supreme Court of the United States in the preceding text is Johnson *vs.* McIntosh, 8 Wheaton, 543 ; see also, Fletcher *vs.* Peck, 6 Cranch, 142, 143. See also, Lecture II., vol. iii. of Kent's Commentaries.

Francis Parkman's works give information on the French in North America, and attention is directed to the Jesuits in North America in the Seventeenth Century ; Discovery of the Great West ; and the Pioneers of France in the New World.

When the men, significantly called in history *conquistadores*, left Spain to obtain possession of America, the Spaniards were in a remarkable period of their history, which has steadily gone downward ever since in all national affairs.

Whatever there may be in the reign of Ferdinand and Isabella to elicit the approval of succeeding ages, especially that their reign is the period of Spanish nationalization, Charles V., their dynastic successor, and his son, Philip II., strove to revive the Roman idea of a universal monarchy, and they came near realizing it, perhaps in the worst form, namely, a universal monarchy founded upon the idea of an absolutely exclusive religion, the Roman Catholic church, itself an absolute and universal monarchy in matters of faith, both excluding freedom of thought or action.   Freedom had loomed up, in feudal form indeed, in various portions of Spain, at a very early time.   The Justitia (Chief Justice) of Aragon held an independent position, clad with a remarkable vetoing power over all laws passed by the estates; and the oath of fealty sworn by the nobles to the king of Aragon, which expressed that they would be faithful to him as long as he was faithful to the laws—this oath ended with the words *y si no, no* (and if not, not).   Liberty, however, which resembles erratic bodies, luminous though they be, neither endures nor spreads its blessings.   The principle, the very idea of self-government, may be considered as extinguished after the war with the *communeros* (the commons).   In matters of religion the Inquisition was established, and managed with sinister imperiousness and cruelty—an institution which literally changed the whole character of the nation, and, similar to the French democrats in the first revolution, although in a different way, pursued with dark vindictiveness one who was suspected of a crime.   No science, taking the word even in its medieval sense, flourished in Spain, and literature was neither flourishing nor in an ascending course.   Education in its various branches had not flourished and never flourished in Spain. No comprehensive system of law, especially no common law guarding the rights and privileges of the individual, however uncouth in other respects, had developed itself.   The law was not considered as an independent and substantive element of political society, and the lawyer, so Helps shows, was denounced, as a mischief-working vermin, in colonial papers of high origin.

The whole country was seized with a spirit that none but noblemen, priests, the men of arms, the advocates and government officers, were *cavalieros*, and every man strove to be a *cavaliero* or *gentleman*, as we should be obliged to translate the word in this case.   Roscher, in his Colonies, Colonial Policy and Emigration, an authoritative work, says that as late as 1781 the Academy at Madrid offered a prize for the best essay proving that the pursuit of the useful arts has nothing dishonorable in it, or lowering a man in the social scale.[1]

Of these *cavalieros* consisted the *conquistadores*—haughty, believing in the superior race of the Spaniard, albeit more mixed than any other people; believing or pretending to believe in the exclusive truth and saving power of the Roman Catholic religion, which may therefore be imposed by any even the most cruel means, allowing no other division of Christianity; and, lastly, being driven by unsatiable greed for gold—not by a desire to trade or establish commerce, but to *find* gold by any means whatever. The greed for gold, the fanatic exclusion of any religion or modification of Christian theology but the Roman Apostolic religion; the belief in the superiority of the Spanish gentleman on the one hand, and on the other hand the almost illimitable capacity for cruelty; the absence of all experience in self-government and, therefore, the incapacity of transplanting political societies with the germ of self-support within them; contempt for work and labor, and for commerce; no transplanting of a self-developing common law, no idea of popular school education—these were the characteristics of the Spaniards who conquered Mexico and South America, and claimed it for the fairly idolized crown of Spain.

On the other hand, they found countries thickly peopled and advanced in civilization, a civilization estopped in many cases, without any substitution of European culture. There is in Chili an immense stone, on its way to some of the famous roads or causeways, built by the aborigines, when the conquest overtook it and stopped its way. The stone goes by the melancholy name of the Tired Stone, and sadly symbolizes the character of the Spanish conquest in some, even many respects.

---

[1] See Roscher, second edition of 1856, page 146. The whole from page 183 to 205, on Spanish Colonial Policy, of this same work is here recommended to the student.

There was no Spanish colonization in South America, if we take the word colonization in the sense of planting a distant and new community, but the peopled country was divided, and distributed not quite unlike the feudal way in the early period of the European Middle Ages. *Repartimientos* (distributions) and *encomiendas* became the leading ideas in the taking possession of America.

The home government proclaimed in many cases kind intentions and benevolent theories regarding the Indians in Mexico and South America, but Spain was very far from America; the governors sent from Spain considered it the chief object to fill their coffers during the short time they should be left at their posts, in which it indeed came to be considered proper for poor courtiers to replenish their exhausted wealth; and Spain herself had excluded the whole world from participation in her commerce with the colonies. Commerce was until recent times a government matter, and Humboldt was obliged to solicit permission to visit South America and Mexico from the king himself.

The colonial policy, so far as the laws went, but by no means as to the practice which existed, can best be learned from their official collection or digest called *Recapitulacion de las Leges de los Regnos de las Indias*, last edition of 1774. According to these laws even the Indian, once baptized, was to all intents and purposes a Spaniard; yet there existed down to the time when South America declared herself independent an insurmountable jealousy even against the Creoles, the natives of unmixed Spanish descent.

A general knowledge of the *repartimiento* and *encomiendas* can best be obtained from Arthur Helps, The Spanish Conquest in America.

The student must not omit familiarizing himself with William Robertson's History of America, which never reached as far as English North America. Favorable and very unfavorable judgments have been passed on this work, as can easily be seen from the elaborate article on this English writer in Allibone's Dictionary of English Literature. I shall simply add that a distinguished Mexican scholar and statesman, Mr. Francis G. Palacio, well known in the United States, has given his favorable opinion on the portion of Robertson's work relating to the Spanish colonization of Mexico and South America.

The works of William H. Prescott, not to forget his first and, as the author believed, his best work, Ferdinand and Isabella, require to be studied by the American student, especially his Conquest of Mexico.

Alexander von Humboldt's New Spain, in which many remarks on her history, economy, and social state are contained, deserves full and distinct mention here.

A portion of a prize essay by Mr. Gilbert H. Crawford, a student in the Law School, will be given here. I had given as a subject for the prize in my department : The Different Principles and Methods by which South America and North America were settled, etc. Mr. Crawford obtained the prize, and the following is a portion of this deserving essay, copied with the permission of the successful competitor :

"Although the Spaniards were everywhere well received upon their first arrival, the course which they pursued in conquering the country soon obtained for them the most intense hatred of the natives, who, being unable to cope with the invaders in arms, were easily subjugated, and reduced to a degrading servitude. The land, which was domain of the crown, was divided out to the adventurers in estates, which were called *repartimientos* and *encomiendas*. Although always described by these names, they varied much in form at different times.

" The *repartimiento* in its primitive form was an estate of land, simply. But this was soon changed to land with cultivation by the Indians. An area of land usually measured by the number of cazabi mounds upon it, was allotted to an Indian cacique, who was to till it for whomsoever it was assigned. However, this system of servitude even was not sufficient for all purposes, and Indians were given in gangs to individual Spaniards, for working in the mines and for purposes of transportation.

"Slavery, thus introduced in the Indies, was not approved at the Spanish court, and as early as 1502, when Ovando was sent out as governor of Hispaniola, it was insisted on in his instructions 'that all Indians in Hispaniola should be free from servitude, and be unmolested by any one, and that they should live as free vassals of Castile.' They were to pay tribute and were also to assist in getting gold, but for this they were to be paid daily wages. It was found, however, that unless compelled to do so, the Indians would have no intercourse with the Spaniards, but, as Las Cases graphically says, 'shunned them as naturally as sparrows the sparrow-hawk.' Retiring to the mountains, they adopted the suicidal policy of leaving the land uncultivated, in the hope of starving out the intruders.

" It does not seem very probable that many Indians were released from servitude under the instructions sent out from Spain, but it was brought to the notice of the court that the Indians could not be converted unless compelled to live with the Spaniards. To bring the heathen to a knowledge of the Catholic religion had been one of the main objects of their most Catholic majesties in sending out these adventurers, an object, in fact, which was never forgotten in the many orders sent out from the court, and in this instance, in 1503, orders were sent to the Indies to the effect that the Indians should be compelled to have dealings with the Spaniards; they should work for such wages as the governor thought fit; they were to hear mass and be instructed in their parts, and all this as free persons, ' for so they are.'

" Indians were then distributed in *encomiendas*. This is a term of the military orders, and corresponds to our commandery or preceptory. These *encomiendas* were given by a deed generally in these words : ' To you, such a one, is given an *encomienda* of so many Indians, and you are to teach them the things of our holy Catholic faith.' The colonists considered this last clause inserted merely to please the lawyers, as a matter of form, and little attention was paid to it.

" The *legal* relations between the Indians and the Spaniards were frequently changed, but the former generally suffered by these changes, although often made for the purpose of improving their own condition. Dying from the unaccustomed labor imposed upon them, or massacred by the Spanish in a still more wanton manner, the settlements and their neighborhoods soon became depopulated and it was found necessary to procure laborers from a distance. Under cover of an order from the Spanish court, giving permission to enslave cannibals, if that should be found necessary to convert them, forays were made from time to time, and the captives reduced to slavery, although it does not appear that the cannibals were by any means the only ones who thus suffered. We are told that in this manner forty thousand Lacayans were carried to Hispaniola within five years.

" The repartitions which were sometimes made by rendering the property uncertain in its tenure, contributed much to the severe treatment which the Indians received, each proprietor endeavoring to make his profit at once, not knowing how long the property would remain in his hands.

" No one can read over the instructions from time to time sent out by the Spanish court, in regard to the treatment of the Indians, without seeing how deep and true was the solicitude of the monarchs for the welfare of their newly-acquired vassals. When evil counsels did prevail, they must be attributed to the want of sufficient knowledge of the condition of affairs in the Indies ; and the inadequate means of enforcing, at so great a distance, the well-meant orders frequently repeated, relieve the government at home of much of the blame which attaches to the policy of the Spanish conquest.

" Opposed to the cruelty by which the conquerors everywhere distinguished their victories stands the noble conduct of the priesthood. Las Cases, the Protector, who by his long life of self-sacrificing devotion to the cause of humanity did much to mitigate those evils, was ably supported by many whose devotion was only second to his own. The monks generally who had undertaken the task of converting the Indians openly denounced the injustice of slavery, while they established *missions* and instructed the Indians not only in religious knowledge, but in many things for their temporal advancement. These missions, or as Humboldt calls them *états intermédiaires*, between the colony proper and the domain of the wilderness, form an interesting chapter in the history of the Conquest."

The colonization of the British portion of North America was of a different character in most respects, and forms one of the most instructive subjects of history recommended for faithful and truthful study to every one whom the citizenship of the American republic is awaiting.

Several nations sent settlers to what became known very early as British America—the Swedes, Dutch, and English. We have to do here with the latter only, and of them chiefly, though by no means exclusively, with the New England settlements, because they impressed the institutions and character of this country more than any other section.

The English settlers came to America about a century after the Spaniards had conquered and settled in Mexico, and in that century pregnant events had taken place, and vigorous movements in literature and the general culture of central Europe had shown themselves.

The Reformation, breaking forth in Germany about the same time that the Spaniards conquered Mexico, had vastly changed or stirred central Europe, including England. The Netherlands had torn themselves from the ultra-absolute Spain, in the most protracted and heroic struggle for liberty known to history, and established the Republic of the United States (or Provinces) of the Netherlands, with the assistance of the prince, patriot, and martyr who may be called the one star of the *stella duplex* in the firmament of history, and of which the other star is Washington. Bold books on subjects of political philosophy were written in France, and Hotman and Languet, both Protestants, had dared to claim "sovereignty for the estates." In Scotland significant works on the State were

published; in England the absurd desire of James I. to conduct himself as an absolute monarch, as it was the longing of
all the Stuart successors to follow the brilliant and vicious example of Louis XIV. of France, helped to prepare the great
revolution of the seventeenth century, which has influenced
and continues to influence our race more than any other revolution, but it does so comparatively silently, as all great influences in history as well as in nature ; while destruction is quick
and flaring, like lightning.

When the first English settlers in America left their mother-
country Shakspeare had but just died, and Milton had begun
to lift his wings; and the very time that the Mayflower touched
the American shore the first volume of the immortal work,
called by Hugo Grotius the Law of War and Peace—itself a
blessing to humanity—saw the light, while in neighboring
Germany the direst of all contests—the Thirty Years' War—
was raging.

The Reformation had everywhere darted into existence, with
worship in the vernacular, the translation of the Bible, and the
diffusion of the grammar school—the latter founded by means
obtained from the secularization of monastic and other church
property—and the first English and Dutch settlers may be
said to have leapt on shore with the common school as one of
the elements of their new polity in their minds; so that it may
be correct to say that the three great epochs of that all-important branch of modern civilization—the general school
system, all-pervading and reaching through all spheres of
education from the primary school to the university—are the
grammar school of the Reformation, the free school of New
England, and the Prussian school system organized at the
beginning of this century, after the ruin of Prussia, by men
like William von Humboldt.

The settlers of British America came from a virile race,
having, it is true, adopted in many respects the feudal law,
but far more in form, or rather in terms, than in essence. An
idea of nobility, as on the continent, never prevailed in England, and every son of a peer turned a commoner, except the

eldest. To be a commoner was no lowering of the free man, and, although the English law speaks so much of descent by blood, nowhere has it had less to do with settling rank than in England, where even the spouse of the queen regnant may be a commoner, as was the case with Prince Albert, husband of Victoria. I have treated of this important point in my Civil Liberty.

In England commerce was not considered as derogatory of a gentleman, and to be a gentleman did not require to be of noble blood.

The settlers came from a country, *national* for many centuries, when most other countries had not yet become politically nationalized; they came from the country in which the principle and habit of self-government existed, and where the representative system, and the representative system with two houses had developed itself, in contradiction to the continental system of three estates, or, in recent times, the unicameral system of what may be called the French democracy.

They were imbued with the idea of a self-evolving and independent common law, uncouth in many respects, but instinct with protection of individual rights and personal freedom.

They did not go to America to conquer, and impose their religion on the natives by means of violent absolutism, but they fled from England to enjoy the liberty of conscience, as it was called; they did not come hither with a greed for gold, especially not for the simple metal; they came to settle and remain in the new world, to carry on agriculture and commerce, which the home government did not arrogate as a royal prerogative, but left to the individual; they found here no dense population, but Indians still in the hunter's state—sparse in number and little advanced in civilization. Land was abundant and all the acquirers of land held it, with the rarest exceptions, in fee-simple. They brought with them and established here no titles and aristocratic privileges. They were and remained, and were acknowledged by England as Englishmen (Lord Lyndhurst was a native of Boston, New England), and nearly all the early settlers were Protestants, mostly belonging to that ecclesiastic organization called in England the Independent sect; that is to say, that arrangement according to which each religious society has its own insular existence, loosely and unessentially connected with the others, contra-distinguished to the Episcopal church government and the Presbyterian government.

The student is referred to John G. Palfrey's History of New England during the Stuart Dynasty, and also to the first part of George Bancroft's History of the United States from the Discovery of the American Continent.

John L. Motley's The Rise of the Dutch Republic, and History of the United Netherlands — two of the proudest works of American literature — require to be studied by the American student in conjunction with our own history. His picture of William of Nassau has touched many American hearts. My opinion of this work of Motley's may be seen in the article on Motley in Allibone's Dictionary of English Literature.

Concerning these prominent and weighty subjects—self-government, the representative system, estates, nobility on the continent and its non-existence in England, despite of the general aristocratic spirit in society, and all that appertains to the whole apparatus of Anglo-Saxon liberty and its contra-distinction to Gallican democracy—concerning these subjects the student is referred to Civil Liberty and Self-Government.

The English emigrants and colonists settled in America under various, and especially under three forms or conceptions of colonial government, namely, the Proprietary, Charter, and the Crown or Royal Government. They are of course historically interesting, and no earnest student of the spirit and form of our government will omit making himself acquainted with this portion of our history. It is fortunate that it has found a painstaking and dignified historian.

As, however, the traces of the Swedes as well as of the Dutch were wiped away in these colonies, leaving hardly anything but personal names—no institutions, no system or branch of law, no special polity or legislative organism—so also were the various forms of planting the colonies gradually wiped out, with few exceptions, and everywhere came the essentially English or "Anglo-Saxon" apparatus of government to be established and developed; that is to say, the common law and trial by jury, the bicameral system of legislation, the separation of the three functions of government, the idea that all belong to a supreme national government (an eminently English idea), liberty of the press, and a love of freedom or, as even Frederick the Second of Prussia called it, the "republican nerve" of the English people.

I have said on this subject, in my Lectures on the Constitution of the United States, delivered at the time when the Civil War was breaking out, the following:

" They settled in a portion of the globe marked by a dignified geography—a vast country, with fertile plains and generous rivers, and treasuring mountains before them, and behind them the sea—then still as in the times of Horace, but now so no longer, the *oceanus dissociabilis*. The character and the breeding, and the law those men brought with them, and the great country they settled in—these are essential in our history. The different charters, of various and frequently undignified origin, obscurely and often confusedly partitioning this land, were mere conduits of this great migration. So far as these charters mapped out certain portions of the land they were of little more importance in the great translation of the Anglican race than the ships in which these settlers came to this continent. There was little in the various charters that was inherently essential, historically predisposing, historically presaging; but there was historic prophecy in this noble land, with these great coasts, and in the peopling it by that virile race, with its aptitude for self-government, wedded to freedom, tried by persecution. It was a people with the same language, the same common law, the same political concepts, the same reminiscences and historical associations of ideas, the same mother-country, the same literature, the same religion, the same aspirations, the same domestic economy, the same royalty, centring, indeed, at a distance, but spreading over the entire, well-marked, cohesive, yet almost unbounded land, taking possession of the country by the same *jus divinum* of civilization, expounded at a later period by our great Judge Marshall. They were divided by their charters, but at no time was their removal from one province to another impeded on political grounds. All owed and professed the same and a direct allegiance to one crown; none were ever foreigners as to any of the others; there was never even the incipiency of different nationalities among them. They felt themselves, what they soon came distinctly to express themselves to be, a people. The national current flowed here, as it did in the contemporary ununited countries, in Germany and Italy, that had resisted the providential decree of nationalization."

The historian of our colonial period, alluded to above, is James Grahame. (The History of the Rise and Progress of the United States of North America till the British Revolution of 1688, London, 1827, and various other editions.) Allibone, in his Dictionary, gives the opinions of Prescott, Charles Francis Adams, and Kent. I have found the work of much value and very instructive. No student should fail to familiarize himself with it. Every profound and sound history of the United States must contain a clear account of the Period of Settlement.

The constitution which the Marquis of Shaftesbury, proprietor of South Carolina, gave to that colony in the year 1669, and which is generally ascribed to Locke, the friend of the shifting nobleman, is to be found in the first volume of the statutes at large of South Carolina. It is what mineralogists call a "cabinet piece" in that branch of political philosophy which had better be called utopiology. It met with the fate of all invented constitutions and governments symmetrically laid out on paper— the fate of the dead-born child—like French constitutions. Only Shaftesbury's or Locke's constitution is more strongly marked by an artificial originality and small characteristics than the rest of invented constitutions. It ought to serve as a warning. If Locke or Shaftesbury can trip in such a way as to establish caciques in English colonies, what must not be expected of minor minds? The politics in antiquity ascribed to lawgivers as to inventors, such as that of Lycurgus, were all of collective character, with improvements added. Constitutions which are to last and do good must always be historical collections, strained through the sieve of wisdom and seasoned with simplifying improvement. We can learn much from the failures of this sort.

The letter of Frederick the Great, mentioned in the text, is to be found in vol. i. p. 149 of Ranke's *Die deutschen Mächte und der Fürstenbund*, Leipzig, 1871. It was written in January, 1782, by the king to his favorite nephew, Duke Charles of Brunswick, and contains these words: "The fearful corruption which pervades parliament and penetrates the whole English nation has degraded the feeling of honor and the republican nerve, which formerly called forth manly courage and nobility of feeling."

Although many of the colonies had been settled by Englishmen leaving the mother-country because made uneasy there, either for political or religious reasons, yet, as has been observed, the consciousness, it may be said the pride of being English subjects or members of the great British polity grew so soon as they were at a distance from England, and, at the same time, the feeling that the colonies, though belonging to Great Britain, formed a great subdivision for itself, marked by the sea as a country for itself. The word *Country*, be it remembered, is one of the earliest words or names used for our portion of the globe, for which no noun proper formed itself. Our history fell in a period pressing and critical.

Our country formed, before the great war, called in Europe, the Seven Years' War, in America, the French War, almost what might be called an *enclave*, closed in by French possessions from Louisiana, along the Mississippi and Ohio, to Canada. The French and with them the Indians were constant enemies. France and England considered themselves yet hereditary enemies, according to the erroneous statesmanship of the times. Adam Smith had not yet taught his message of peace, that the welfare of one nation is not the ruin of another, but, on the contrary, that the success of one people redounds to the benefit of the other, even as with individuals in the same town.

Everything conspired to animate the English spirit in the colonists, by which is understood both the spirit of loyalty towards the mother-country and the manly consciousness of partaking in the great system of British liberty. At the same time the sub-national consciousness, if this term may be used, became clearer, until we find a number of delegates assembled at Albany, adopting what is called the Albany Plan of Union, drawn up by Dr. Franklin.[1]

The Plan of Union was adopted unanimously, in the month of June, 1754, by commissioners from New York, New Hamp-

---

[1] The Autobiography of Dr. Franklin, last edition by Hon. John Bigelow, according to an unaltered manuscript of Franklin's, published by Lippincott & Co., Philadelphia.

shire, Massachusetts, Connecticut, Rhode Island, Maryland, and Pennsylvania; but, as Franklin says, in England it was considered too *popular*, and in America too much leaning towards power.

Although it was adopted in Albany by the mentioned colonies, the instrument itself was intended for all the colonies, as the title shows, which is: " Plan of a proposed union of the several colonies of Massachusetts Bay, New Hampshire, Connecticut, Rhode Island, New York, New Jersey, Pennsylvania, Maryland, Virginia, North Carolina, and South Carolina, for their mutual defence and security, and for extending the British settlements in North America."

This sounds national, and is what the Greeks would have called Pan-American.

It remains an important document, nevertheless, for it very clearly expresses the conviction of leading American minds of the necessity of unitedness; it promoted this idea in many; it contains many features which we find again in our Constitution, and it is the precursor of the Declaration of Independence— near at hand as to time—not distant even a quarter of a century.

In the small print which follows this paragraph the plan itself is given, and we observe that:

In it we meet again the word *Union*—of the several colonies, things that belong together.

In the first paragraph " one general government" is spoken of; America is used to designate the totality of the British colonies; and it is declared that each colony may retain its " present constitution," *except*, etc. The general government is repeatedly used. At a later period our forefathers used the term National Government.

A president general is to be appointed by the crown, and a " grand council" to be elected by the people of the several colonies; the members of the grand council for three years.

The number of members from each colony to be determined by the sum of money the colony may contribute to the general government, yet not more than seven nor less than two.

The council to meet once a year, but may be called for

extraordinary meeting by the president, if he has received consent of seven members.

The council cannot be prorogued, etc., without their own consent; the members shall receive pay.

The assent of the president general requisite to all acts, or as we would say, not very correctly, he had the vetoing power.

The president and council hold the power of war and peace with the Indians, and they altogether control the Indian affairs, that is, trade, purchase of land for the crown, etc.

They shall regulate and rule, for the crown, all new lands.

They raise soldiers and build forts for the defence of the colonies.

For the purpose of defence they shall make laws, levy general duties and taxes, "equal and just," not "loading industry with unnecessary burdens."

The general accounts yearly to be settled.

A sort of council of state, to consist of twenty-five members of the grand council (from a majority of the colonies), to act with the president.

If the king in council does not disapprove the laws passed in America within three years, they shall remain in force.

All military commission officers, for land or sea, to act "under this general *constitution*," to be nominated by the president and to be confirmed by the council, while all civil officers to be nominated by the council and confirmed by the president.

That the civil as well as military establishment in each colony remain in the state it was then in, "the general constitution" notwithstanding, etc.

Although this cannot be considered as anything more than a sketch, and an insufficient one at that, it must be observed that, despite of this, the whole is pervaded by a national spirit, or a spirit which would become national so soon as a separation from England should take place. Self-government which existed in a high degree in every colony is left untouched, as far as is admissible with a "general government," and nowhere is a most distant indication of a possible future sovereignty, in the sense in which the word is taken now.

The whole is *general*, that is, for the British-American entirety; a *government* is spoken of, and the plan is called a *constitution*. The framers of this plan, and he who drew it up, knew well the full and accurate meaning of these words. Yet the word government applied to congress was strongly rejected before our Civil War, by those who desired to sever themselves from the "general government" and the nation. I mention it as a historical fact of import that the word government was especially rejected.

THE PLAN.

Plan of a proposed union of the several colonies of Massachusetts Bay, New Hampshire, Connecticut, Rhode Island, New York, New Jersey, Pennsylvania, Maryland, Virginia, North Carolina, and South Carolina, for their mutual defence and security, and for extending the British settlements in North America.

It is proposed—That humble application be made for an act of parliament of Great Britain, by virtue of which one general government may be formed in America, including all the said colonies, within and under which government each colony may retain its present constitution, except in the particulars wherein a change may be directed by the said act as hereafter follows:

That the said general government be administered by a president general, to be appointed and supported by the crown; and a grand council to be chosen by the representatives of the people of the several colonies met in their respective assemblies.

That within   months after the passing such act, the house of representatives that happens to be sitting within that time, or that shall be especially for that purpose convened, may and shall choose members for the grand council, in the following proportion, that is to say—

Massachusetts Bay	7
New Hampshire	2
Connecticut	5
Rhode Island	2
New York	4
New Jersey	3
Pennsylvania	6
Maryland	4
Virginia	7
North Carolina	4
South Carolina	4
	48

who shall meet for the first time at the city of Philadelphia, in Pennsylvania, being called by the president general as soon as conveniently may be, after his appointment.

That there shall be a new election of the members of the grand council every three years, and on the death or resignation of any member, his place shall be supplied by a new choice at the next sitting of the assembly of the colony he represented.

That after the first three years, when the proportion of money arising out of each colony to the general treasury can be known, the number of members to be chosen for each colony shall from time to time, in all ensuing elections, be regulated by that proportion (yet so as that the number to be chosen by any one province be not more than seven, or less than two).

That the grand council shall meet once in every year, and oftener if occasion require, at such time and place as they shall adjourn to at the last preceding meeting, or as they shall be called to meet at by the president general, or any emergency ; he having first obtained in meeting the consent of seven of the members to such call, and sent due and timely notice to the whole.

That the grand council have power to choose their speaker ; and shall neither be dissolved, prorogued, nor continue sitting longer than six weeks at one time, without their own consent or the special command of the crown.

That the members of the general council shall be allowed for their service ten shillings sterling per diem, during their session and journey to and from the place of meeting ; twenty miles to be reckoned a day's journey.

That the assent of the president general be requisite to all acts of the grand council ; and that it be his office and duty to cause them to be carried into execution.

That the president general, with the advice of the grand council, hold or direct all Indian treaties in which the general interest of the colonies may be concerned ; and make peace or declare war with Indian nations.

That they make such laws as they judge necessary for regulating all Indian trade.

That they make all purchases from Indians, for the crown, of lands not now within the bounds of particular colonies, or that shall not be within their bounds when some of them are reduced to more convenient dimensions.

That they make new settlements on such purchases by granting lands in the king's name, reserving a quit-rent to the crown for the use of the general treasury.

That they make laws for regulating and governing such new settlements, till the crown shall think fit to form them into particular governments.

That they raise and pay soldiers and build forts for the defence of any of the colonies, and equip vessels of force to guard the coasts and protect the trade upon the ocean, lakes, or great rivers; but they shall not impress men in any colony without the consent of the legislature.

That for these purposes they have power to make laws, and lay and levy such general duties, imposts, or taxes, as to them shall appear most equal and just (considering the ability and other circumstances of the inhabitants in the several colonies), and such as may be collected with the least inconvenience to the people; rather discouraging luxury than loading industry with unnecessary burdens.

That they may appoint a general treasurer and particular treasurer in each government when necessary; and from time to time may order the sums in the treasuries of each government into the general treasury, or draw on them for special payments, as they find most convenient; yet no money to issue but by joint orders of the president general and grand council, except where sums have been appropriated to particular purposes and the president general is previously empowered by an act to draw for such sums.

That the general accounts shall be yearly settled and reported to the several assemblies.

That a quorum of the grand council impowered to act with the president general do consist of twenty-five members; among whom there shall be one or more from a majority of the colonies.

That the laws made by them for the purposes aforesaid shall not be repugnant, but, as near as may be, agreeable to the laws of England, and shall be transmitted to the king in council for approbation as soon as may be after their passing; and if not disapproved within three years after presentation, to remain in force.

That in case of the death of the president general, the speaker of the grand council for the time being shall succeed, and be vested with the same powers and authorities, to continue till the king's pleasure be known.

That all military commission officers, whether for land or sea service, to act under this general constitution, shall be nominated by the president general; but the approbation of the grand council is to be obtained before they receive their commission. And all civil officers are to be nominated by the grand council, and to receive the president general's approbation before they officiate.

But in case of vacancy by death, or removal of any officer, civil or military, under this constitution, the governor of the province in which such vacancy happens may appoint till the pleasure of the president general and grand council can be known.

That the particular military as well as civil establishments in each colony remain in their present state, the general constitution notwithstanding; and that on sudden emergencies any colony may defend itself, and lay the accounts of expense thence arising before the president general and general council, who may allow and order payment of the same as far as they judge such accounts just and reasonable.

Despite of the intense English feeling, consisting as well in the pride of belonging to the great polity which was the only one in Europe which saved liberty, in the eighteenth century, from the vortex of brilliant centralization, as in a sincere loyalty towards the mother-country—despite of all this we find America rising against England within a few years only after the peace which concluded the Seven Years' War. The peace took place in 1763, and as early as in 1765 the congress at New York issued, in the month of October, that Declaration of Rights which every student of our great commonwealth ought to weigh well, with analytical zeal and comprehensive love of his country. The Report of a Committee on the Subject of Colonial Rights, in the Congress held at New York in October, 1765, must be minutely studied in connection with the Declaration of Rights.

The Stamp Act of 1765, now of high historical importance, roused the indignant opposition of the Americans, because it was passed by parliament largely to tax the American colonies without their being represented in parliament, directly or indirectly. It was distinctly on the ground that Englishmen should not be taxed without representation, and that the commerce of the colonies ought not to be shackled, on which the colonies resisted, petitioned, implored, and plunged into a very doubtful rebellion, soon rising into a revolution. No famine, no religious persecution, no cruelty, no aristocratic insolence to a high-minded burgher's maiden (the *causa causans* of so many risings), no neglect of the mother-country, drove the Americans into their revolution, but a civic manliness which held fast to the British principle, already acknowledged and proclaimed in the Great Charter of 1215, of the twinship between Taxation and Representation, led them on; and while the Stamp Act proves great lack of wisdom and justice, even fairness towards the colonies, in the administration of Great

Britain, and that party which held the helm of the ship of state, the American revolution is, on the other hand, the greatest monument in honor of the English polity of self-government, and its liberality in giving growth to such spirit of manly freedom and independence, as is shown by the rising of our forefathers. This is no figure of speech, but is believed to be fact and truth by one who has compared our revolution with that of all others through which our Cis-Caucasian race, distinguished as it is for its revolutions, has gone. Alfred Tennyson, in a brief poem of his,[1] addresses England in these words:

> "Strong mother of a Lion-line,
> Be proud of these strong sons of thine,
> Who wrenched their rights from thee,"

and, it might be added, who remembered the Forced Loan of 1626, and the Petition of Rights of 1627—Hampden and Pym and all the illustrious patriots.

To proceed quite clearly, a remark on the meaning of the word revolution may be here intercalated. The English language has but one word revolution for two historic processes very distinct the one from the other, and for which several languages, for instance the German, have as distinct names. A revolution may be a violent change of the government or some of its essential features within the country whose government is changed, when it is generally accompanied by civil war; or it may be the rising of a distant portion of the people, especially some colonies, which ultimately separate themselves from the mother-country. This is called in German *Abfall*, the falling off. Revolutions of the first kind are the English and French; of the second, that of the Netherlands and our own. Our revolution was almost wholly unaccompanied by civil war, for it was no internal revolution, but an *Abfall*.

---

[1] The poem "England and America in 1782," by Alfred Tennyson, was published in the New York Ledger of January 6, 1872, and is "supposed to be written or spoken," as the poet writes, "by a liberal Englishman at the time of our recognition of American independence."

These few remarks have been made because our revolution has already been spoken of in approving terms, and will be more so still, and vanity, to which we Americans are not averse, often misleads us in contemplating our revolution, without making the necessary distinction. Yet vanity enervates nations like individuals, and takes the nerve out of the character. The scaffold has played no part in our revolution; true, but we had no class of oppressors among us to fight against us, besides the great calmness in our leaders.

We return to the main subject of this section.

There is no period in our whole history which requires more sincere study than that which, with reference to our Constitution, must be called the period of constitutional genesis. Attention is here directed to the two following great facts, namely:

So soon as the Americans thought and felt that they were oppressed by England, it was a national spontaneity which characterized their actions and continued to characterize them to the end. As one people they felt and rose, and as one people they fought it out. Everywhere committees rose; they understood each other, and ended in the continental congress, which acted with varied and great power, derived from no other source than the general consciousness of what is now called national sovereignty. Everywhere the whole of the soil with the institutions in it was called *the Country* from the beginning. Superior authority was yielded to the self-national congress. The highest of all authorities—the self-sufficient universal consciousness—lifted up that authority and yielded to it; not, indeed, without exceptions and difficulties. Every day's history of those times proves it.

The second point deserving our attention is the comparative ease with which the people, who had struggled against separation, fell into the formation of a new nation, greatly aided in this by geographic separation from the mother-country and geographic union within, and continued and farther developed their precious and inherited self-government. To this must be added, or, perhaps, in this is included the absence of proclaiming abstract ideas, and hoping to enforce them by mere force. Other nations have fared very differently. We were saved this misfortune by our inheritance of a large treasure of political experience and great institutions, at the head of which stands the bicameral representative system. A distinguished French writer, M. Laboulaye, in his work on the American Constitution, says that the American revolution resembles more a great law case decided in court than a bitter and sanguinary contest decided on the battle-field. He means obviously the absence of the civil war, and of the guillotine. Another French writer of much distinction[1] says: " It is then on the 14th of July, 1789, that commences the series of strokes of force which has successively handed over France to so many different governments," monarchical, republican, military, communistic, etc. " Summing up, since '89 to our own days, there have been ten or twelve *coups de force*, and twelve different governments, of which not one, no, not one, let us understand it well, has been the responsible expression of the national will; twelve governments, all of which have been usurpations in the precise and scientific sense of the word, each of which having lasted, on an average, from seven to eight years. Thus every eight years violence upsets in France the legal authority and creates a power of circumstance, thrown over by the same weapons which have elevated it. Such is our history, such is France as the revolution has made her, because Right was confounded with Force, the god with the idol, and because she has apotheosized herself (*divinisée*) and declared herself infallible, even in her most execrable aberrations."

After reigns such as Louis XIV. and Louis XV., it is the most difficult problem for a nation to return to anything like liberty. France has become a political razee, and from Louis XV. to our days every successive government, monarchical or

---

[1] Paul Janet, in an article in the *Revue des Deux Mondes*, August 15, 1872. He is the author of several substantial works, especially of Histoire de la Philosophie Morale et Politique dans l'Antiquité et les Temps Modernes; ouvrage couronné par l'Institut (Academy of Moral and Political Sciences). Paris, 1858.

kingless (with the only exception of the brief constitutional government under Louis Philippe), has become a more stringent centralization.

The following is the Declaration of Rights by Congress at New York, in October, 1765:

The members of this congress, sincerely devoted, with the warmest sentiments of affection and duty, to his majesty's person and government, inviolably attached to the present happy establishment of the Protestant succession, and with minds deeply impressed by a sense of the present and impending misfortunes of the British colonies on this continent; having considered as maturely as time will permit the circumstances of the said colonies, esteem it our indispensable duty to make the following declarations of our humble opinion respecting the most essential rights and liberties of the colonists, and of the grievances under which they labor, by reason of several late acts of parliament.

1. That his majesty's subjects in these colonies owe the same allegiance to the crown of Great Britain that is owing from his subjects born within the realm, and all due subordination to that august body, the parliament of Great Britain.

2. That his majesty's liege subjects in these colonies are entitled to all the inherent rights and liberties of his natural born subjects within the kingdom of Great Britain.

3. That it is inseparably essential to the freedom of a people, and the undoubted right of Englishmen, that no taxes be imposed on them but with their own consent, given personally, or by their representatives.

4. That the people of these colonies are not, and from their local circumstances cannot be, represented in the house of commons of Great Britain.

5. That the only representatives of these colonies are persons chosen therein by themselves, and that no taxes ever had been, or can be constitutionally imposed upon them but by their respective legislatures.

6. That all supplies to the crown being free gifts from the people, it is unreasonable and inconsistent with the principles and spirit of the British constitution for the people of Great Britain to grant to his majesty the property of the colonists.

7. That trial by jury is the inherent and invaluable right of every British subject in these colonies.

8. That the late act of parliament entitled "an act for granting and applying certain stamp duties, and other duties, in the British colonies and plantations in America," etc., by imposing taxes on the inhabitants of these colonies; and the said act, and several other acts, by extending the jurisdiction of the court of admiralty beyond its ancient limits, have a manifest tendency to subvert the rights and liberties of the colonists.

9. That the duties imposed by several late acts of parliament, from the peculiar circumstances of these colonies, will be extremely burdensome and grievous ; and from the scarcity of specie, the payment of them absolutely impracticable.

10. That as the profits of the trade of these colonies ultimately centre in Great Britain, to pay for the manufactures which they are obliged to take from thence, they eventually contribute very largely to all supplies granted to the crown.

11. That the restrictions imposed by several late acts of parliament on the trade of these colonies will render them unable to purchase the manufactures of Great Britain.

12. That the increase, prosperity, and happiness of these colonies depend on the full and free enjoyment of their rights and liberties, and an intercourse with Great Britain mutually affectionate and advantageous.

13. That it is the right of the British subjects in these colonies to petition the king, or either house of parliament.

14. That it is the indispensable duty of these colonies to the best of sovereigns, to the mother-country, and to themselves, to endeavor, by a loyal and dutiful address to his majesty, and humble application to both houses of parliament, to procure the repeal of the act for granting and applying certain stamp duties, of all clauses of any other acts of parliament whereby the jurisdiction of the admiralty is extended as aforesaid, and of the other late acts for the restriction of American commerce.

So far the American Declaration of Rights ; but the student ought not to omit making himself acquainted with the Report of a Committee on the Subject of Colonial rights, in the Congress held at New York in October, 1765. The preceding document can only be fully understood by the study of this report. It can be found in the appendix to the first volume of Pitkin's Political and Civil History of the United States of America, already mentioned. *Also :*

A Representation of the Lords Commissioners for Trade and Plantations, touching the Proceedings and Resolutions of the House of Representatives of Massachusetts Bay with respect to the Act for levying a Duty upon Stamps in America, and other Acts of Parliament of Great Britain.

Resolutions introduced into the House of Commons by General Conway, in February, 1766, and which passed before the repeal of the Stamp Act.

Circular Letter of the House of Representatives of Massachusetts, Province of Massachusetts Bay, February 11, 1768.

These and several other historical documents can be found in the above-mentioned place.

An aid to learn the spirit of those times, both here and in England, is a small work, unpretending but full of nourishing information: Patriotic Eloquence, by the late Mrs. Kirkland.

The reader must not instance the Netherlands in contradiction to what has been said in the large print of this section about the self-government of the English colonies, and the debt they owe to England. It is true that the Spanish crown had killed all self-government in Spain to an odious degree, but Spain never planted the Netherlands. The Netherlands never came from Spain. It was only by the descent of the different crowns that the Netherlands came to the Spanish monarch. There was never any inherent or organic connection between Spain and the Netherlands, and the latter had developed their institutions and freedom long before under Charles V. any political connection took place.

I must refer again to my Civil Liberty and Self-Government for an account of the subject of self-government touched upon in the large print.

The most prominent feature in the American revolution, as will be shown, is the persevering declaration that the colonists are Englishmen, and as such possess the right of declining taxation without representation. This proud consciousness was naturally inherent in all the colonists from earliest times. So soon as the Swedish and Dutch demarcations had faded away, there was an unchecked intercourse by trade or otherwise between the different colonies. It is necessary, however, for the student of history and our public law to make himself acquainted with the exact state of inter-colonial exchange and law.

There was self-government to such a degree existing in each of the colonies that, at the great distance from the mother-country, and as occasions arose, especially defence against hostile Indians, a feeling of a closer union than that which consisted only in the fact of consciousness of having one mother-country manifested itself from earliest times.

Safety against the Indians and protection against the claims and encroachments of the Dutch led the New England colonies, in the year 1643, therefore not quite a quarter of a century after the landing of the first settlers of "New England in America," to conclude a union or confederation, calling themselves the United Colonies of New England, the colonists being familiar with the name and title of the United States or Provinces of the Netherlands. Here the title " United," remaining with us throughout our history, begins, and nothing whatever as to previous utter and sovereign separation can be derived from it, as the opponents of our nationality are in the habit of attempting to do.

As early as 1638 Connecticut and New Haven proposed this union, but it was completed only five years later. The completed confederacy lasted about forty years, and consisted of the colonies of Massachusetts, New Plymouth, Connecticut, and New Haven. The fundamental law or instrument was called Articles of Confederation, and by it the respective colonies entered into a " firm and perpetual league of *friendship and amity,* for offence and defence, mutual advice and succor, upon all just occasions, both for preserving and propagating the truth and liberties of the gospel, and for their own mutual safety and welfare." The different colonies were to retain their own jurisdiction and government. No two confederate colonies were to be united into one jurisdiction, nor was any new plantation to be admitted into the league without the consent of the rest. A body of two commissioners from each colony was to govern the affairs of the league. They had power " to hear, examine, weigh, and determine all affairs of war or peace, leagues, aids, charges, and number of men for war, division of spoils and whatever is gotten by conquest, receiving of more confederates for plantations into combination with any of the confederates ; and all things of a like nature which are the proper concomitants and consequences of such a confederation for amity, offence and defence ; not intermeddling with the government of any of the jurisdictions, which by the third article is preserved entirely to themselves."

The commissioners were to meet annually, or each colony in succession, and when met to choose a president, and the determination of any six (three-fourths therefore) to be binding on all.

The expenses of all just wars to be borne by each colony in proportion to its own number of male inhabitants, of whatever quality or condition, between the ages of sixteen and sixty (white or black, free or slave). In case of any sudden invasion the other confederates were immediately to send aid—Massachusetts, one hundred men, and the other colonies forty-five each, or for a less number in the same proportion.

The commissioners were also authorized "to frame and establish agreements and orders in general cases of a civil nature, wherein all the plantations were interested, for preserving peace among themselves, and preventing as much as may be all occasions of war, or difference with others, as about the free and speedy passage of justice, in every jurisdiction, to all the confederates, equally as to their own, receiving those that remove from one plantation to another without due certificates."

It was, also, very wisely provided in the articles that runaway servants and fugitives from justice should be returned to the colonies where they belonged, or from which they had fled. If any of the confederates should violate any of the articles, or in any way injure any one of the other colonies, "such breach of agreement or injury was to be considered and ordered" by the commissioners of the other colonies.

We have here the foreshadowing of some features in our present Constitution. The number two, now for our senators, runs through our history, as will soon appear.

Besides the works suggesting themselves here—Palfrey's History of New England, and Bancroft—there is an excellent work in its way, truthful and plain, namely, A Political and Civil History of the United States of America from the Year 1763 to the Close of the Administration of President Washington in 1797, including a Summary View of the Political and Civil State of the North American Colonies prior to that Period, by Timothy Pitkin, 2 vols. New Haven, 1828. It was the appearance of this book a year after the author's landing in America that greatly helped his introduction to our history, and he acknowledges it gratefully.

The early rise or introduction of certain political terms and words having been mentioned above as an idea, it may not be improper to copy here the earliest American political covenant.

The so-called Pilgrims landed December 22, 1620, a wilderness before them, destitute of any right to the soil, or any powers derived from government.   Never did the great words, UBI SOCIETAS IBI JUS, more forcibly show their inherent and self-sustaining power than when this handful of fugitives and colonists, call them what we may, entered a solemn civil compact and covenant to the following effect: "In the name of God, amen.   We, whose names are under-written, *the loyal subjects* of our dread sovereign, Lord King James, etc., having undertaken, for the glory of God and advancement of the *Christian faith*, and honor of our *king and country*, a voyage to plant the first *colony* in the northern parts of Virginia, do, by these presents, solemnly and mutually, in the presence of God, *and of one another*, covenant and combine ourselves together, into a civil body politic, for our better ordering and preservation and furtherance of the ends aforesaid; and by virtue hereof to enact, constitute, and frame such just and equal laws and ordinances, acts, constitutions, and officers, from time to time, as shall be thought most meet and convenient for the general good of the colony; unto which we promise all due submission and obedience."

At the close of the seventeenth century we meet with a more comprehensive idea of the colonies forming an entirety or a "whole," to use the Greek political terminology (κοινόν). In 1697, therefore more than half a century after the New England Confederacy, a "plan" was drawn up (supposed on fair grounds to be) by William Penn, which was intended to give a general government of some sort to all the American colonies of Great Britain.   This plan has not received much attention, and the following is given from the work of another, to be mentioned farther on in the small print:

"The original, which is referred to by Chalmers as the scheme of Penn, and which, he says, was not favorably received by the ministers, the peers, or the public, is in the State Paper Office, at London.   Many of the phrases, and some of the objects which, one hundred years afterwards, were set forth in our present Constitution, will arrest the attention of the student of our history.

"'A brief and plain scheme, how the English colonies in the north parts of America, viz., Boston, Connecticut, New Hampshire, Rhode Island, New York, New Jersey, Pennsylvania, Maryland, Virginia, and Carolina, may be made more useful to the crown, and one another's peace and safety, with an universal concurrence.

" ' 1. That the several colonies before mentioned do meet once a year, and oftener, if need be, during the war, and at least once in two years in times of peace, by their stated and appointed deputies, to debate and resolve of such measures as are most advisable for their better understanding, and the public tranquillity and safety.

" ' 2. That in order to it, two persons well qualified for sense, sobriety, and substance be appointed by each province as their representatives or deputies, which in the whole make the congress to consist of twenty persons.

" ' 3. That the king's commissioner for that purpose specially appointed, shall have the chair and preside in the said congress.

" ' 4. That they shall meet as near as conveniently may be to the most central colony for ease of the deputies.

" ' 5. Since that may in all probability be New York, both because it is near the centre of the colonies, and for that it is a frontier and in the king's nomination, the governor of that colony may, therefore, also being the king's high commissioner, preside during the session, after the manner of Scotland.

" ' 6. That their business shall be to hear and adjust all matters of complaint or difference, between province and province.

" ' As 1st. Where persons quit their own province and go to another, that they may avoid their just debts, though they may be able to pay them.

" ' 2d. Where offenders fly justice, or justice cannot well be had upon such offenders in the provinces that entertain them.

" ' 3d. To prevent or cure injuries in point of commerce.

" ' 4th. To consider of ways and means to support the union and safety of their provinces against the public enemies. In which congress the quotas of men, and charges, will be much easier and more equally set than it is possible for any establishment made here to do. For the provinces knowing their own condition, and one another's, can debate that matter with more freedom and satisfaction, and better adjust and balance their affairs in all respects for the common safety.

" ' 7. That in times of war, the king's high commissioner shall be general or chief commander of the several quotas upon service against the common enemy, as he shall be advised for the good benefit of the whole.' "

Such was the sagacious plan by which he (William Penn) proposed to bind the colonies together. He was nearly a hundred years in advance of his age.

The extract just given is from page 29 and the following of an Address delivered at Chester before the Historical Society of Pennsylvania, on the 8th of November, 1851, by Edward Armstrong, at the Celebration of the One Hundred and Sixty-ninth Anniversary of the Landing of William Penn at that Place. Philadelphia, 1852. The entire plan has been published in one of the volumes issued by the trustees of the Publication Fund belonging to the Historical Society of Pennsylvania.

On the 5th of September, 1774, a number of delegates chosen by several colonies and provinces of Great Britain in North America to meet and hold a congress at Philadelphia, assembled at Carpenters' Hall. No legal mandate had been issued or could have been issued. It was the general, and so soon as organized, the national impulse and consciousness which gave the delegates the feeling of sovereign right. There were present on the first day delegates from New Hampshire, Rhode Island and Providence Plantations, " from the city and county of New York and other counties in the province of New York," "from the county of Suffolk in the province of New York," "from New Castle, Kent, and Sussex in Delaware," from Maryland, Virginia, and from South Carolina. On the 10th of September, 1774, this ragged representation, viewing it from a strictly legal point of view, but full of national consciousness, " *resolved unanimously*, that the assembly deeply feels the suffering of their *countrymen* in Massachusetts Bay," etc., and farther, "trusting that the effect of the united efforts of North America in their behalf" (in behalf of Massachusetts Bay), etc.

On September 22, only twelve days later, this congress, however incomplete as to organization, adopted again, unanimously, the following potent resolution, in the full morning light of the rising national independence and sovereignty:

"Resolved unanimously, That the congress request the merchants and others in the several colonies not to send to Great Britain any orders for goods, and to direct the execution of all orders already sent to be delayed or suspended until the sense of the congress on the means to be taken for the preservation of the liberties of *America* is made public."— Journal of Congress, vol. i. page 14.

In the resolutions, adopted September 27, September 30, October 1, and October 10—all but one unanimously adopted America as the name for "the *whole*," not including the West Indies. In the last resolution congress declares that any one who should accept office, etc., under the recent act of parliament, "violating the charter of the province of Massachusetts Bay, ought to be held in detestation and abhorrence by all good men, and considered as the wicked tool of that despotism which is preparing to destroy the rights which God, nature, and compact have given to *America*."—Journal of Congress, vol. i. page 18.

The commission by which Colonel Washington was appointed general, and which was debated paragraph by paragraph on June 17, 1775, directs him "to join the said army for the defence of American liberty." In a resolution passed immediately after, George Washington is declared "chosen to be general and commander-in-chief of such forces as are, or shall be, raised for the maintenance and preservation of American liberty."

The word *liberty* is here used in the singular in all these cases. The liberty of the whole country, not the aggregate of a number of various liberties possessed by different little parts, is meant.

When on Monday, April 26, 1783, Washington was introduced to congress, the president solemnly thanked him for his services, and said among other things that "they deserve the grateful acknowledgments of a free and independent nation." Washington, in his reply, says among other things

"that he cannot hesitate to contribute his best endeavors towards the establishment of the *national security in whatever
manner the sovereign power may think proper to direct*, and the
ratification of the definitive treaty of peace or the final evacu-
ation of *our country* by the British forces," etc. Again he
speaks of his "grateful acknowledgments to my country."
On December 23, 1783, Washington resigned, and in June,
1784, the legislature of Virginia passed a resolution that the
executive be requested to have a statue of General Washington erected with an inscription, which tradition ascribes to
Madison, in which it is said that he did pre-eminent service
in "establishing the liberties of his *country*."—The Constitution of the United States, etc., by W. Hickey, 1847, page
206.

The examination of the Declaration of Independence will
lead us to more reflections on this important subject; here we
observe that what has been given shows that in the earliest days
of the rising revolution we find the words nation, countrymen,
America, country, North America, "United America" used,
to which we may add the word continent, especially in the
adjective form, continental money, troops. All these expressions show the prevailing idea and feeling that this portion of
the globe, separating itself from the empire of Great Britain,
was to enter by this separation into a national existence, and
most of them are used because no name for "America" had
formed itself.

What is the meaning of the words country and countrymen?
Country, in the present sense, means a whole land inhabited
by one people—one by organization, by political and ethnological reasons, opposed to the idea of province or petty independence; and countryman means one who is born in the
same country, or is under the same national protection.
Country has an eminently national meaning, and *nation* means
the whole population of a country considered as one political
organization; and what is very important for us to consider is,
that the word *nation* was altogether little used in England.
It was in our very revolution that the word acquired high

political dignity. It was carried over to France, where it soon acquired great historical importance.[1]

America, still frequently used for our country both here and abroad, and almost always when an adjective is wanted to designate the country, naturally presented itself, because no name existed for our country, yet a designation was wanted. No German emigrant goes to the United States, but simply to America. The same is probably the case with Irish emigrants.

North America, very frequently used by John Adams and other patriots of comprehensive views, must be explained in the same way. The first bank established by the continental congress in Philadelphia, in order to obtain means to carry on the war, was called, and long continued to be called, the Bank of North America. The seal of the United States treasury, adopted during the continental congress, has to this day the scroll containing the four abbreviations, Thesaur. Amer. Septent. Sigil., as may be seen on every five-dollar note. There is an instructive paper on the Seals of the Departments, by Benson J. Lossing, in a number of Harper's Monthly for 1869. Continent came to be used, although no man then thought of the United States ever stretching to the Pacific, because it furnished an adjective very much wanted for what was not yet called national—government, money, troops.

All documents, all events, all private letters, even the earliest, as they become known, more and more every day, show this pervading spirit "from New Hampshire to South Carolina, inclusive," and that "they are perfectly united," with reference to opposing British authority, "as to all *internal* taxation." What is *internal* in this case, if not within the country or nation contra-distinguished to others? Nor was there any distinction of classes as to this feeling. Some rhymes—and pretty indifferent ones—written by a soldier in the winter of 1778, after

---

[1] See my paper on Nationalism.

a fearful march with bloody feet, on "the Old War for Independence," begin :

America is in a most pitiful state.[1]

I conclude my remarks by directing attention to the significant fact that our best authorities from earliest times frequently use United States as a singular, and let it be followed by *it*, and this in the most solemn state papers.

The Journal of the Continental Congress is not sufficiently studied, yet it is the genetic record of our country or nation.

The following are extracts of a lecture on the want of a name for our country :

It is unfortunate that our country has no name. A name in science and in the pursuit of knowledge is the distinction of ideas; in politics it is the highest symbol of unity. The orator, the poet, the statesman, the common songster, the patriot, cling to the name of their country, and again draw inspiration from it, and hope when politically the country is torn. Would Italy have reached unity at all, through the long centuries when she was hacked into pieces, had it not been for the sweet and inspiriting name of *Italia ? Italia mia di dolor castello.*

Nothing ultimately remained of German unity or totality but her language, literature, and the name of Germany. Everything seemed to have been lost, only not the name, and the poet's enthusiasm who sang *Das ganze Deutschland soll es sein,* and the many Sängerfeste which were always pre-eminently German or national, until at last that very name, scarcely saved, inspired the provoked country to conquer German unity in foreign land in the blessed year of 1870.

England, with so many historical favors and advantages not vouchsafed to others, had not only from early times a national government, but also a national name—"Merrie England"—The Laws of England. Would Nelson's signal, "England expects every man to do his duty," had he signalled His Majesty King George III., or the United Kingdom of Great Britain, have had the same effect ?

We all know what powerful effect the name France has on every Frenchman. So also the *Netherlands.* Even *Switzerland* unites people of German, Italian, and French tongues.

No name formed itself with us. Printing, criticism, etc., made it more difficult, and our forefathers were upon the whole a very practical and law-abiding, liberty-loving people, but not imaginative or poetic.

Washington was peculiarly fond of the name America. He says : "I have labored ever since I have been in the service to discourage all

---

[1] See American Historical Record, page 419, September, 1872.

kinds of *local* attachment, and distinction of *country* (using it here for colony of birth), denominating the whole by the great name of AMERICA."
—Maxims of Washington, by Schroeder, page 166.

Country, for the United Colonies, was not only common but universal.

It is most significant that the United States of *America* correspond in name to the United States of the Netherlands.

But America overlaps; it does not sufficiently specify. I have read foolish remarks about American *arrogance* in these United States of America. We had no other name, and the English in parliament always used it. Burke, Chatham, Barré, and their opponents always spoke of " America."

The absence of a specific name gives the great importance to our flag ; that *is* specific and national. Happily it is beautiful and poetic, exclusively national and *fully* national, that is the same for the merchant navy, the government, and all, and it is the only flag that is so.

These remarks are not vain. An American statesman, who united with a character the gravest errors in politics, and the kindest possible protection of his slaves with an uncompromising theory in favor of slavery, and one of the keenest and most unrelenting champions of state sovereignty, said to me, when I had expressed my regret at the absence of a name, that it was as it ought to be ; that we ought not to have a name ; that we have no country, we ought to have no other name but that which indicates a mere political system. I had observed that the name United States expressed only a political system.

No one can possibly say how differently the history of our country would have run had our country had a name, and had Philadelphia been permanently made the nation's capital.

The name America is of so great an interest to us that I will give here a paper which was first published in the American Historical Record in 1872 :

The beautiful, but unjust name of our portion of the globe may be said to be of German origin, in a twofold manner.

Emric or Amric is an old Germanic personal name. *Am* means diligence or activity ; hence *Ameise*, the German for *ant*, the industrious creature by way of excellence ; and *ric* (our rich) signifies strong, abundant. Amric, therefore, meant the very industrious or active. German conquerors of Italy carried thither German names, and Amric was euphonized by the Italians into Amrico or Americo, which in turn was Latinized into Americus. So far the origin of Vespucci's name.

How it came to be applied to our continent was thus :

The Germans, neither among the early discoverers nor *conquistadores*, nevertheless, took the deepest interest in the nascent science of cosmography, the corresponding name for what is now called geography, and through this science they influenced positively and practically that great

Age of Maritime Discovery and geographic expansion which widened commerce from the little, yet wonderfully influential, Mediterranean to the commerce of the Atlantic, the Southern Ocean, and the Pacific. Behaim's Globe and Mercator's (Krämer's) Plan, without which navigation could not have much advanced, sufficiently prove this fact. Lorraine was a German principality at the beginning of the sixteenth century, and the reigning duke had formed, at his court, an academy of cosmography, of which a schoolmaster at Strasburg, then as now again, a German city, was a member, or to which at any rate he proposed the name of America for the Western Hemisphere or for North America. The name of this resolute and sagacious schoolmaster was Waldseemüller (Wood-lake-miller), which he transformed into the Græco-Latin monster of a name, Hylacomilus; and Hylacomilus is the man that first wronged Columbus by immortalizing so grandly the name of one who followed the great proto-euretes at a long distance, and who has been outstripped in the character of a discoverer by very many later navigators. But so it was; a name for North America had become an urgent want, felt by all the thinking men of Europe. A distinct thing or idea must have a distinct name; it is a requisite of things. The West Indies, no good or correct name at all events, had become wholly useless since the northern mainland had become known, and since the vast Pacific has been revealed. Humboldt in his contributions to the history of geography has shown all this. Psychologically or ethically speaking there has never been erected a monument so magnificent, undeserving, and cruelly unjust; as if the Madonna di Sisto were not called by Raphael's name, but by that of a man who framed it first! Phonetically speaking, there could be no more beautiful name with its musically flowing four vowels over only three consonants, and they not rugged; and practically speaking there it is, and never to be changed. The misfortune of our namelessness led the men of our revolution to use America, along with Continent, for our country, and we find it again in the United States of America, not North America, although the seal of our treasury has to this day the Latin scroll, "seal of the treasury of North America," as every dollar note shows.

As *United States* is often very inconvenient to be used in the adjective form, we still use frequently *American* for that which belongs to our country or government. Columbia was seized upon by poets, and ever so many towns and counties are called Columbia, while a republic in South America bears this name, but the continent or continental isle, which, as appears from the Book of Prophecies collected by Columbus himself, he meant to discover, has been forever wrenched, as to its name, from him to whom it most justly belonged.

The Revolution and Declaration of the "Great Continental Congress" of the 15th of May, 1776.

The Mecklenburg declarations of independence deserve a passing notice, even in so brief a work as the present. Mecklenburg, a small place in North Carolina, witnessed twice the proclamation of a cluster of bold freemen that America should not endure any longer the assumption of authority, on the part of Great Britain, of taxing without representation. The Second Mecklenburg Declaration, which had been adopted on May 30, 1775, was presented on the 27th of May, 1776. This declaration is interesting for the following points: it shows in a great measure the spirit of liberty and strictly representative freedom pervading the whole "country"; it breathes the spirit of the "whole" forming naturally a patriotic entirety, and it begins with the words: "The Provincial of each Province, under the direction of the great Continental Congress," etc., that is, national congress.

Province was a common name given to the colonies at the earliest period of the revolution, indicating the idea of the entirety of the country lying at the foundation. Shall we, wrote Washington to the congress, supinely allow the English to tear one province after another from us?

On July 4, 1775, Washington issued an order in which he declares that all troops raised or to be raised "for the support and the defence of the liberties of America," etc., "they are now the troops of the *United Provinces of North America;* and it is hoped that all distinctions of colonies will be laid aside, so that one and the same spirit may animate the whole."[1]

The Mecklenburg declaration was presented to the great continental congress on the 27th of May, that is after the resolution, of which we shall speak presently, had been adopted,

---

[1] These words of the great man include within them, like a seed-corn, a whole and wide-branching tree of the history and philosophy of our polity. They are the spontaneous welling forth of patriotism and wisdom—very different from the artificial formulations of some later American statesmen, reminding us of the verbal artificialities of the schoolmen.

but although presented in May, 1776, it had been adopted in May, 1775, and speaks, therefore, the language of that year and preceding ones. The first resolution of this daring proclamation declares "that whosoever directly or indirectly abetted or," etc., "countenanced the unchartered and dangerous invasion of our rights, as claimed by Great Britain, is an enemy to this country, to America, and the inherent and inalienable rights of man."

The Mecklenburg declaration, of which some of the phrases were transferred to the great Declaration of Independence, is of historical import, and the reader is directed, among the well-known works on our history, to The True Origin and Source of the Mecklenburg and National Declaration of Independence, by Rev. T. Smyth, Columbia, S. C., 1847.

On May 15, 1776, the real separation of these "provinces" from Great Britain took place by the adoption on the part of the continental congress of the following resolution:

"Whereas his Britannic Majesty, in conjunction with the Lords and Commons of Great Britain, has, by a late act of parliament, excluded the inhabitants of these United States from the protection of his crown; and whereas no answer whatever to the humble petition of the colonies for redress of grievances and reconciliation with Great Britain has been or is likely to be given, but the whole force of that kingdom, aided by foreign mercenaries, is to be exerted for the destruction of the good people of these colonies; and whereas it appears absolutely irreconcilable to reason and good conscience for the people of these colonies now to take the oaths and affirmations necessary for the support of any government under the crown of Great Britain, and it is necessary that the exercise of every kind of authority under the said crown should be totally suppressed, and all the powers of government exerted, under the authority of the people of the colonies, for the preservation of internal peace, virtue, and good order, as well as for the defence of their lives, liberties, and properties against the hostile invasions and cruel depredations of their enemies: therefore,

"Resolved, That it be recommended to the respective assemblies and conventions of the United Colonies, where no government sufficient to the exigencies of their affairs hath hitherto been established, to adopt such government as shall, in the opinion of the representatives of the people, best conduce to the happiness and safety of their constituents in particular, and America in general."

The continental congress had not met by a mandate from a high authority; the Declaration of Separation was not a combined provincial act; the states, as the parts of the whole soon came to be called, did not pre-exist as self-existing sovereignties, but the act of separation took place on the same revolutionary and national consciousness of right and sovereignty, and sprang from the same will and feeling, according to which this same continental congress not only raised an army, issued commissions, and appointed a general with attributes of dictatorial powers (in the name of the congress), but borrowed money, made treaties with foreign powers, sent ambassadors to foreign parts, issued letters of marque, punished treason—in short, assumed many of the highest attributes of sovereignty, without being authorized or instructed to do so by any one higher than the congress, or by component parts.

" Before, and for nearly two years subsequent to the Declaration of Independence, the struggle was maintained by union alone."[1]

The Declaration of Justification.

Organic growth, which is almost always slow, is in history as well as in nature the normal state of noble things; while violent and abrupt change is abnormal, rapid, and transitory, if of any beneficial character. "A Commonwealth," says Milton, who was a faithful servant of civil liberty, almost as much as he was a priest of poetry, " ought to be as one mighty growth and stature of an honest man, as compact in virtue as in body."

A revolution is dangerous and exceptional; it is a violent interruption of the lawful and peaceful state of things; it is

---

[1] Reverdy Johnson, Union Speech, Baltimore, January, 1861.

always of doubtful issue, and, if unsuccessful, brings about far greater evils than those which lead to the revolution; and lastly, it is for the revolutionists a step beyond the established laws and government, and a falling back on man's own conscience and responsibility to his Maker.

All high-minded men, when they resort at last to revolution, have considered it due to the nations of their race and becoming to themselves, to give a public account of the reasons why they felt urged and justified to resort to this exceptional means.

The Netherlands concluded the pact of Utrecht in 1579, and, in an apology or vindication, they gave the reasons why they felt compelled to separate from the crown of Spain. Governments, they argue, are for the benefit and blessing of the governed, and if a king persistently refuses to change his oppressive and injurious ways, the people are in duty bound to seek or establish another government. This protestation by William of Orange is one of the noblest and most remarkable documents in all history, with which no cultivated citizen of a free commonwealth ought to be unacquainted.

The Apology is one of those productions which increase in interest, and may be again and again referred to as we go on in life. It is a document important in the history of political philosophy, and was issued in Latin. Motley's History of the Dutch Republic ought to be consulted.

A most surprising argument was that used by one of the most prominent English statesmen in favor of the secessionists during the late Civil War. This late premier of England, all his life in leading positions, said on a public occasion, doubtless for the purpose of its being widely spread, that it was astonishing the Northern people (the United States) should oppose the Southern secessionists, and forget that the whole government of the United States arose out of a revolution. Nor could the English oppose the secessionists, for the English government itself arose out of a revolution. As if a revolution of itself was a desirable thing, and the approval we can bestow on a revolution must not depend upon its cause, and the principles involved in it. According to that statesman the almost permanent revolt of the feudal lords would deserve his favorable consideration. What made the American revolution truly great was the principles of high-minded liberty which induced them to separate, and the instant formation or organization of a new nation which was involved in the separation and proclaimed in the Declaration of Independence. Organic integration, not disintegration, is the prescribed law and end of all life—physical as well as psychologic, individual as well as social.

The psychological history of the separation of America from England, which can only be learned from the secret journals of Congress and the memoirs and correspondence of the early patriots, is not more instructive than touching, from the rising of the conviction that separation was necessary to the "great trust" to Washington, "that the liberties of America receive no detriment," and the modest acceptance of the great man to the very declaration itself. This whole portion of history is full of attraction, in the best sense of the word, besides its political importance.

Washington was appointed, June 15, by the unanimous voice of congress, and, on July 6, they issued a declaration to the world showing the causes which led them to take up arms. There is no vaunting of an abstract right of revolt, no launching on the sea of political abstractions, and no presuming vanity, of which history has since been obliged to note down two unfortunate instances; but the declaration is manly in the last degree, and shining with a patriotic brightness which warms and delights the lover of his kind in the same degree as he is acquainted with the struggles through which our civilization has passed.

Having stated the various acts of the British parliament in violation of their rights, says Pitkin in his history, and the hostile proceedings of the administration to enforce them, the declaration observes: "We are reduced to the alternative of choosing between unconditional submission to the tyranny of irritated ministers or resistance by force. The latter is our choice. We have counted the cost of the contest, and find nothing so dreadful as voluntary slavery. Honor, justice, and humanity forbid us tamely to surrender that freedom which is received from our gallant ancestors, and which our innocent posterity have a right to receive from us. We cannot endure the infamy and guilt of resigning our succeeding generations to that wretchedness, which inevitably awaits them, if we basely entail hereditary bondage upon them."

"Our cause is just, our union is perfect, our internal resources are great," etc.

This document was drawn up, so has tradition come down, by John Dickinson.

I partly repeat and desire to impress the fact that those men, free from vanity, resort to revolt for reasons which at that period would have caused no rising in any other country excepting England herself; that there are no abstractions; that the language of those men is as firm, correct, and free from extravagance as they themselves, and wholly different from modern public style; that the declaration of these bold sentiments was not followed by sanguinary crimes; that this first declaration is thoroughly national, for "our union is perfect;" and that no faint premonition of state sovereignty can be detected. This declaration of justification ushered in the war, which lasted from 1775 to 1783; and it was followed a year later by the Declaration of Independence.

The Declaration of Independence, of July the 4th, 1776.

The title of the declaration is, A Declaration by the Representatives of the United States of America in Congress assembled, and paragraph 33[1] has the words, " We, therefore, the representatives of the United States of America in congress assembled."

Until then the word delegate had been used in congress from the first resolution to this declaration. Now the word representative is used. Our forefathers knew the full value of the word representative freely used in the political literature and terminology as well as in legal discussions of the time and earlier periods. Representative is national and fuller in its meaning than *delegate*.

The two words have a significant meaning in our history, as will be seen farther on. Suffice it here to state delegate is first used; then in the declaration, pervaded by a national spirit, representative is used; then, when a relapse into *separatism* produces the Articles of Confederation, delegate is reinstated and representative discarded; next and last the reverse takes place in the Constitution of the United States, in which the word delegate does not occur once (and sovereignty neither), while representative is used, in the case of house of representatives, in the fullest, national, parliamentary sense.

This whole subject is alike instructive, interesting, and novel; instead, therefore, of detaining the reader here any longer, I refer him to the chapters of Civil Liberty and Self-Government, where the difference has been exhibited, also with reference to the difference between *feudal estates* and *national legislatures*.

The first paragraph of the declaration reads as follows, separating the different portions, for our immediate use, namely:

---

[1] To save time and space I have numbered the different paragraphs of the declaration. There are thirty-four of them.

1. When, in the course of human events, it becomes necessary for *one*[1] people to dissolve the political bands which have connected them with another,

2. And to assume among the powers of the earth the separate and equal station to which the laws of nature and of nature's God entitle them,

3. A decent respect to the opinion of mankind requires that they should declare the causes which impel them to the separation.

Psychologically speaking, this paragraph, portion 3, is modest and manly in a touching degree—a decent respect to the opinion of mankind. They felt and were conscious that should they be successful, they would enter as a full member into the commonwealth of nations, formed by our Cis-Caucasian race. Politically speaking, this head and sign of the declaration is thoroughly *national*. When for *one* people, says portion 1, it becomes necessary to disconnect itself from another, it is plainly putting the two as two nations—so we would express it now—opposite each other. Nor ought we to pass over the fact that, according to the original draft of the declaration by Jefferson, with his own erasures and changes, he had written first *for a people*, but erased *a* and put *one* above it with a caret. Portion 2 strongly confirms this. The subject bears repetition, and the state of things even down to our own times requires it; the first paragraph of the declaration is exclusively as well as emphatically national, but it does not stop there.

Paragraph 28, one item in the enumeration of the wrongs which the declaration lays to the king of England reads thus: " He (the king) has constrained our *fellow-citizens*, taken captive on the high seas, to bear arms against their *country*, to become the executioners of their *friends and brethren*, or to fall themselves by their hands."

---

[1] The italicizing in this or any coming passage is the author's own, simply to direct the student's attention to the words. The declaration is so great a document that even this outward change seemed to require explanation.

Fellow-citizen, country, brethren—these are strong words of exclusively national meaning. If brother is used in a political sense, what else can it mean but a person most closely allied either by birth in the same country, considered in the sense of political organization, or by the polity of the land, or by both? It is but another term for fellow-citizen used in the same paragraph. Men belonging to different sovereignties have never been called, nor can they be called, fellow-citizens. No Bavarian would have called a Prussian, under the late, now happily destroyed, state of Germany, his *Mitbürger.* The real meaning of brethren in this declaration is made clear by the beginning of paragraph 31, which is, " Nor have we been wanting in attentions[1] to our British brethren." They were our brethren when we belonged to the same great polity, but now we call our American fellow-citizens alone brethren.

Paragraph 33 pronounces us again a nation, by declaring the king of England "a prince unfit to be the ruler of *a free people.*"

Throughout the charges against the king of England, which begin with paragraph 3 and go to 31, inclusive, the comprehensive word *our* is used for that of all Americans. Paragraph 26 says, " He has plundered our seas, ravaged our coasts, burnt our towns, and destroyed the lives of our people."

In paragraph 25, where the old and bitter use of the word abdication, first used against James II. in 1688, is taken up, it is said, " He has abdicated government *here* by declaring *us* out of his protection, and waging war against *us.*" *Here* has no other meaning than this side the Atlantic, or America, *our country.*

Paragraph 15 speaks of "jurisdiction foreign to our Constitution."

Paragraph 31 concludes with the words, " We must, therefore acquiesce in the necessity, which denounces *our* separation, and hold *them,* as we hold the rest of mankind, enemies in war, in peace, friends."

---

[1] Not *attention* in the singular, as is even printed in Hickey's Constitution, partly published by congress, in 1847.

The declaration expresses a manly regret at the necessity of separation.

But what is our separation? Did each little colony separate individually, and were the English declared henceforth enemies in war to each colony, or to each individual, or did it mean enemies to us as a whole? The war power has never existed with us except in the whole—as an attribute of national sovereignty. Who are the "rest of mankind"? Individuals or nations? Who are "*them*," the single English or the English people as a political entirety? The whole as quoted here has a national meaning, and a national meaning alone. If the questions put here appear ludicrous, it must be observed that the risible element has not been arbitrarily introduced, but, on the contrary, all that is so contrary to the gravity of truth has been assumed and urged.

After the declaration had been signed, congress adopted the following resolution: " That copies of the declaration be sent to the several assemblies, conventions, and committees or councils of safety, and to the several commanding officers of the continental troops; that it be proclaimed in each of the United States and at the head of the army"—a national trumpet blast, or, if not, an insolent presumption. Which was it? Congress, the representative of the nation, does the highest civil act that can be done; it pronounces the birth of a nation, and orders it to be made known to all political bodies, large or small—assemblies, and councils of safety, civil and military, ordering it to be proclaimed "in each of the United States and at the head of the army"—without previously submitting the potent document to any person or body of persons. It is a sovereign blast of nationality. There was no pre-existing state sovereignty, no self-existing sovereign atom of our polity. The nation was born.

I cannot conclude this section without giving the words of Charles Cotesworth Pinckney, soldier and statesman, "at one time an authority of unbounded reverence in South Carolina." In the South Carolina legislature in 1788, when the futility of the Articles of the Confederation had been proved and the question about the adoption of the Constitution was before the different legislatures, Cotesworth Pinckney said: "This admirable manifesto (the Declaration of Independence) sufficiently refutes the doctrine of the individual sovereignty and independence of the several states. In that declaration the several states are not even enumerated; but after reciting, in nervous language, and with convincing arguments, our rights to independence, and the tyranny which compelled us to assert it, the declaration is made in the following words, etc. The separate independence and individual sovereignty of the several states were never thought of by the enlightened band of patriots who framed this declaration. The several states are not even mentioned by name in any part, as if it was intended to impress the maxim on America that our freedom and independence *arose from our union,* and that without it we never could be free or independent. Let us, then, consider all attempts to weaken this union by maintaining that each state is separately and individually independent as a species of political heresy which can never benefit us, but may bring on us the most serious distresses."[1] The nation and independence are born together. No centralization has ever existed with us; no assumption of petty sovereignty, either, that did not speedily lead to rebellion.

The history of the Declaration of Independence, the growth of the ideas, and the positive facts gained by it are rarely studied with sufficient care and comprehensiveness. Nor must the American suffer himself to be deterred from a profound study of this document by the endless balderdash repeated a hundred thousand times every year. Harper's Weekly of July 3, 1858, has a most interesting *fac-simile* of Jefferson's draft, with all his corrections. It shows that Jefferson drew up the declaration with much care, as it was adopted with like calmness of care. There was no passion or haste in the momentous transaction, no acclamation by a collection of men having degenerated into a vociferous mob. The signers were gentlemen and collected as advocates of a high degree are. They were young men.

---

[1] Debates in South Carolina (Miller), page 43. I quote from the Appendix to The Union, a Sermon delivered on the Day of National Fast, January 4, 1861, by T. H. Taylor, D.D. He was a South Carolinian, and settled in New York.

I have made a calculation of the average of the signers of the Declaration of Independence.   There were

Between 20 and 30 years old .	.	.	.	.	.	2		
" 30 " 40 "	.	.	,	.	.	.	17	} 37
" 40 " 50 "	.	.	.	.	.	.	20	
" 50 " 60 "	.	.	.	.	.	9		
" 60 " 70 "	.	.	.	.	.	6		
Over 70 (Franklin, born in 1706) .	.	.	.	.	1			

One Irishman and one Virginian did not know their age, or rather others did not know it.

The average age of the signers was 44½, reminding us of the passage in the despatch of the Venetian ambassador in France, written in 1561, and given by Leopold Ranke, page 16, vol. iii. of The Popes of Rome. Micheli writes to the doge of Venice these remarkable words from France in 1561: "Your highness be convinced that, excepting the common people, who continue zealously to visit the churches, all the others have fallen off (from the old faith), especially the nobility and the younger men under forty years of age, almost without exception."

The Declaration of Independence as a Bill of Rights.

The Declaration of Independence, besides being considered in its potent national character, may be viewed in the light of political philosophy and as a quasi bill of rights.   Indeed, it has been called the bill of rights of our Constitution; while others, and a most prominent American statesman among them, have declared the paragraph in question mere amiable, useless generality.   The second paragraph begins thus:

"We hold these truths to be self-evident, that all men are created equal; that they are endowed by their Creator with certain inalienable rights; that among them are life, liberty, and the pursuit of happiness.   That to secure these rights, governments are instituted among men deriving their just powers from the consent of the governed; that whenever any form of government becomes destructive to these ends, it is the right of the people to alter or abolish it and to institute new government,[1] laying its foundation on such principles and

---

[1] The original is as here printed, but most editions have *governments* (in the plural).

organizing its powers in such form as to them shall seem most likely to effect their safety and happiness." It is necessary to read the whole paragraph, the longest in the whole declaration.

In order to understand the spirit of this whole passage, it is indispensable to present to our minds the period of the history of political philosophy—and there is no more instructive history—in which this passage was written, or of which it was the effect. It is not only the *usus loquendi* which, according to all hermeneutics, is requisite for truthful interpretation, but the whole political and philosophical spirit of the age of which we ought to have a vivid presentation in our minds. This makes it necessary that the philosophy of the period, say of the latter half of the eighteenth century, should be remembered—a period which in its somewhat jejune, philosophical character might perhaps be called the *happiness-period*, though no one, so far as I know, has ever given a definition, or even at least a general designation of that happiness, ever present in the writings of the period, and out of which arose at the beginning of this century the utilitarian doctrine.

If the outlines given in paragraph 2 lead to no definite legislative conceptions, the spirit which pervades the paragraph is nevertheless the fruit of noble political conceptions, and animates to high legislation. The *jus divinum* of mankind, that governments are for the benefit of men, and not the reverse, is reacknowledged after the Dutch Apology.

The Roman law acknowledged that men are equal by the *jus naturæ*, which means by the disposition of nature—by nature. The scholastic writers of the Middle Ages, imagining, as so many persons still do, that previous to the establishment of governments man lived in what was called the state of nature, also taught the original equality of men. Not only the great writer and man, Thomas Aquinas, canonized by the Romish church, but even Mariana, the prominent Spanish Jesuit writer under Philip II., who strove for universal mundane monarchy, as the Pope was the universal ruler of the church, even Mariana teaches the equality by nature or original equality of men. The Dutch declared the object of governments and the great right of revolution in exceptional cases. Two centuries later the Americans proclaim in a national document that "all men are created equal," and that they possess "certain inalienable rights," and "that among them are life, liberty, and the pursuit of happiness." Whatever this "pursuit of happiness" may mean, so much is certain, and so much we know from him who drew up this paragraph and the whole declaration, that it contained an abjuration of slavery, which was continued merely until the proper period for its abolition should arrive, and the lapse of one hundred years more was necessary before the Thirteenth Amendment abolished slavery in 1865, after astounding phases in the theory of slavery had been run through. At one time it was literally doubted by many whether negroes had immortal souls, and benevolent Methodist preachers, born and bred in the South, who taught the contrary, were harshly, in some cases cruelly, treated; and when presiding over the archive office at Washington, I found the official instruction of the *agent* of the "Confederate government," by the "Confederate" secretary of state, to the effect that he should persuade the king of the Belgians, Leopold I., who had the reputation of being a Nestor among the European monarchs, and a man of the greatest possible weight in the councils of nations, that this agent should use all possible diligence and ingenuity to persuade King Leopold that they (the Confederates) were not the rebels or revolutionists, but the North, and that in the famous passage in the Declaration of Independence, by a Southerner, "that all men are created equal," the word *men* meant *white men*. The despatch is still in the archives at Washington. The most surprising of all is the egregious ignorance which could suppose that Leopold, or any other monarch, or, indeed, any man of sense, could be induced to believe such despicable stuff after religion, law, and philosophy had long established and acknowledged, by bulls, decrees, and whole codes, the humanity of the negro.

Von Raumer, Von Mohl, and Janin furnish the student who knows French and German, with important information on this subject.

Continuation of the Declaration of Independence as a Bill of Rights.

It will be remembered, from my lectures on the English Constitution, that in my opinion there is no subject of greater importance in the whole history of the English constitutional development than the Petition of Rights, the Bill of Rights, and the Declaration of the Rights and Liberties of the subject, adopted on February 13, 1688, by the two houses and accepted by William and Mary.[1] Many of the most specific rules of the Bill of Rights, as well as entire laws, have passed over as fundamental and important principles into our Constitution, for instance, the prohibition of billeting soldiers on citizens in times of peace (French and English history made such a rule seriously necessary); or the Habeas Corpus Act, under Charles II., which passed into our Constitution as "the Habeas Corpus principle," which shall not be abridged except under very peculiar circumstances.

As has been said already, however, the Constitution of the United States has no separate bill of rights.

Some of the amendments, adopted immediately after the adoption of the Constitution, treat of points usually referred to in bills or declarations of rights,—*e.g.*, no established religion, right of the people to bear arms, no soldier shall in time of peace be quartered in any house without the consent of the owner, and nearly all the twelve additional articles.

Most of our state constitutions have declarations of rights. There is a great danger in bills of rights for small bodies, because they give an opportunity of fixing unalterably some ideas which may be new-fangled and owing to provincial vanity. Yet they are sometimes necessary and very important.

The Massachusetts constitution of 1780 (chiefly by John Adams) has a Declaration of Rights of the *Inhabitants* of the

---

[1] See Rowland's Manual of the English Constitution, page 427 et seq.

Commonwealth of Massachusetts. And in it is ordained—it is to be marked well—as a *right of the citizen*, that the judiciary shall be independent, and for that purpose judges, *quam diu se bene gesserint*, have honorable salaries by *standing laws*. All this is in the Bill of Rights. See my Reflections on the Changes which may be considered necessary in the Constitution of the State of New York, 1867.

As to the Declaration of Independence, partially to repeat what has been said before, we may consider it,

1. As containing positive declarations.

2. As to what a ruler or government ought not to do, against which the subject or citizen, therefore, ought to be protected.

As to 1. In paragraph 2 we have found that it is declared that All men are born equal.

That there are certain natural rights called inalienable, and that among the chief of these are the enjoyment and the protection of life, liberty, and the pursuit of happiness (the freedom from molestation as long as others are not injured).

That governments are for the benefit of the governed, and that the people have the right to change them if they do not work for the people's benefit.

That the people have the right and the corresponding duty to throw off a government which works permanently to the injury of the governed, and to provide new guards for their future security.

As to No. 2.

Paragraph 5. The king has refused laws unless the right of representation in the legislature be abandoned.

Par. 6. He has called legislatures to meet at unusual places. This reminds us of Magna Charta.

Par. 7. The king has dissolved representative houses for resisting his invasions on the rights of the people.

Par. 8. Has not called new legislatures for a long time, thus destroying the representative principle and endangering the state, and the legislative power has returned to the people at large.

Par. 9. He has endeavored to prevent growing population, and refused to pass laws to encourage their migrations.[1]

Par. 10. Has prevented good administration of justice.

Par. 11. The king has made judges depend on his will.

Par. 12. King appointed unnecessary number of officers.

Par. 13. Kept standing armies in peace without consent of legislature.

Par. 14. King endeavored to make the army superior to the civil power.

Par. 15. Jurisdiction foreign to our Constitution.

Par. 16. Quartered large bodies of troops among us.

Par. 17. Protecting the soldiers when they had killed citizens.

Par. 18. Interfering with our *free trade*.

Par. 19. Imposing taxes without our consent.

Par. 20. Deprived us of trial by jury.

Par. 21. Has removed us from our natural courts.

Par. 22. And many more, all charging the king with having acted against established law and charters, with introducing foreign mercenaries, and altogether injuring the Americans instead of protecting them.

It is indifferent here whether the king of England represents the British government and the "brethren" of the great polity, from which the Americans now declared themselves forever separate. These charges against the king are important in this place, as indicative of what the patriots of that time considered of elementary importance and fundamental necessity in a sound system of civil liberty, and a polity of freemen founded upon the principles which British experience and patriotism, through good periods and all, had proved necessary.

The word inhabitant was also used in New Jersey. The student will do well to make himself acquainted with the different meaning or the actual history of the words inhabitant, subject, citizen, and exclusion of all, except citizen, in the course of time. It has created injury and mischief, I think, that the Constitution knows the word citizen alone, so that there is no word in our terminology to designate the person who is

---

[1] More about this paragraph in the next section.

affiliated with the government, but not a citizen, as, for instance, those foreigners who have made a solemn declaration that they will become citizens—an affiliation considered so important that the law obliged them to take up arms for the United States against the rebels, an obligation so high that a correspondingly high degree of protection is implied. The relation resembles somewhat the *socii* of the Romans, only in the latter was the additional sense of territory. Whole tribes were *socii*, and as such had duties and enjoyed protection.

I find by a law passed in the republic of Geneva, in 1674, that there existed then, and possibly there exists still, a very different civil status in that confined but influential commonwealth. The law is of March 23, 1674, and runs thus: "By the penalty of death it is prohibited in the city or suburbs to enlist a person or cause him to be enlisted, and subject to this penalty is every one, be he citizen, burgher (*bourgeois*), inhabitant, or subject, who, without permission of the *seigneurie*, allows himself to be enlisted and take part in party." The neighboring kingdoms or other states used to enlist the Swiss, as I have yet seen enlisting sergeants with flowing ribbons, from the Netherlands and the Pope, in Bern and other *cantons*.

The study of the Bill of Rights cannot begin more conveniently than with the Rise and Progress of the English Constitution, by Sir Edward Creasy, Chief Justice of Ceylon. Hallam's Constitutional History may be the second work; De Lolme, last edition, with notes by English barristers, may be read before the professional works, Blackstone, etc., be taken up.

On Immigration, Paragraph 9 in particular.

Paragraph 9 reads thus: He (the king) has endeavored to prevent the population of these states; for that purpose, obstructing the laws of naturalization of foreigners, refusing to pass others to encourage their migrations[1] hither, and raising the conditions of new appropriations of lands.

The early patriots considered a disturbance in immigration, a withholding of means to promote it, of so high an offence in the crown, that it was deemed as one of the reasons warranting to dissolve our connection with England.

To the many remarks about the emigration of our race, and the *jus divinum* of the Cis-Caucasian race of inhabiting other portions of the globe besides Europe, which have already been

---

[1] Again, the original has migrations in the plural, although most reprints, perhaps all, have migration in the singular.

made, it is desired to add at this stage of our subject the following historical and other remarks :

Parliament passed, in 1740, an act, 13 George II., 6, vii., which invites foreigners to settle in the king's American colonies, by declaring, after an anti-Know-Nothing preamble, in sufficiently odd language, that foreigners, having resided seven years in the colonies, on taking the oaths of allegiance, etc., are to be his Majesty's natural-born subjects of the kingdom of Great Britain, etc. The preamble pronounces immigration a most desirable thing, and the report of a committee on the subject of colonial rights in the congress held at New York in October, 1765, contains these words :

" It seems to be agreed on all hands that the common law of England, and the grand leading principles of the British constitution, have their foundation in the laws of nature and universal reason ; it is also certain that the British American subjects, by charters from the crown and other royal instruments, are declared entitled to all the rights and privileges of natural-born subjects within the realm, to all intents, constructions, and purposes. This is also the voice of the common law, and agreeable to the decision of the judges, ancient and modern. By the 13 of George II., even foreigners, having resided seven years in the colonies, on taking the oaths of allegiance, etc., are declared to be his Majesty's natural-born subjects of the kingdom of Great Britain, to all intent, construction, and purpose, as if any of them had been born within the kingdom. The preamble of that act runs thus : ' Whereas the increase of the people is the means of advancing the wealth and strength of any nation and country, and that many foreigners and strangers, from the purity of our religion, the benefit of our laws, the advantages of our trade, and the security of our property, might be induced to come and settle in some of his Majesty's colonies in America, if they were made partakers of the advantages the natural-born subjects there enjoy.' The colonists are by this act considered as natural-born subjects, and entitled to all the essential rights of such, unless it could be supposed that foreigners naturalized by this act are entitled to more than the natives. For foreigners so naturalized are to all intents, constructions, and purposes declared to be natural-born subjects, as if born within the realm, and consequently entitled to personal security, personal liberty, and the free disposal of their private property, the grand security of all which is that the last shall not be taken away without the consent of the owner."

Our forefathers never forgot that they were all immigrants or the sons of immigrants, and wished to see the country peopled as fast as might be, having already among them Dutch, Swedes, French, and Germans. What they would have felt about the immigration of other races, especially that of Mongolians, is not a subject to be discussed here.

Emigration, a subject daily growing in importance and of peculiar interest to America, ought to be examined from the following points of view, deserving candid and penetrating inquiry :

Emigration is a natural right, that is, a claim founded on, and arising from, the nature of man or the very characteristics of humanity. It is one of the so-called " inalienable rights," and is comprehended within the right " of liberty and the pursuit of happiness," and can only be modified exceptionally ; for while emigration is an individual right, the poles of the axis around which all human life is destined by Providence to turn are individualism and sociality.

The State is necessary, but still it is for the individual. The State remains on earth and passes away ; the individual is immortal.[1]

Migration, as has been shown, is, moreover, one of the great means of carrying out the high plans of spreading civilization. The opposite to the migratory disposition is the principle of adhesiveness, equally necessary for the progress of our species, and equally injurious if exclusively adhered to. I have enlarged on this subject in Political Ethics, and may be permitted to refer to Charles F. MacLean's *De Jure Emigrandi*, Dissertatio Inauguralis, Berlin, 1869, furnishing an extensive index of literature, but difficult to obtain.

On the other hand, emigration must be considered as a moral question on the part of those who possess the land, which is the desired dwelling place of the emigrant. What right has he who has settled in a new

---

[1] Let no invidious remark be made here about the prevalence of the Church over the State, and "the Pope's power over the emperor." I, at least, am wholly opposed to this view, and felt obliged to say this little in order not to be misunderstood in this period of renewed mediæval demands.

country, or whose parents were immigrants, to shut the door against new-comers? The earth is given to all mankind, and it is the will of the Creator that it be inhabited. The German in the interior of his country has as good a prospective right to some acres of land in Nevada, if he can lawfully obtain it, as the Puritan had to any land in what was later called Massachusetts Bay. This is the moral view of immigration.

But it must not be left out of view that a state, by the attributes of national sovereignty, retains the right to regulate or, exceptionally, to prohibit immigration in cases of supreme necessity. If, for instance, it is convinced that the mixture of many now distinct races can only work deterioration, and at the same time that the mandate is gone forth for the Cis-Caucasian race to be the bearers of civilization, such nation would have of course the right and corresponding duty to regulate immigration accordingly. This it will be observed has nothing to do with regulating rights according to color or race, which had never been done in the whole history of our race, until, slavery being extinct in Europe, negro slavery was introduced by the gradual advance of discovery along the coasts of Africa, and the carrying of the Ethiopian to America. We Americans are peculiarly situated. We have four races in our country —the aborigines, the Cis-Caucasian race, the negroes, and now also the Mongolian race, which threatens to overrun the world eastward, as it has done repeatedly by a westward course, once getting as far as in a portion of Germany when, by the battle of Liegnitz, as late as in 1241, they were finally repulsed. If under these circumstances the American government should at any future time prohibit the immigration of any peculiar race, or of all except the Aryans of our portion, nothing could be objected to it on the score of right. Most people connect, involuntarily, the idea of extirpation or murder with that of the extinction or absorption of a race. This is a radical error. Prevention of increase is not murder.

Immigration and emigration form no less an important subject in political economy. As to the first, it is remarkable that the protectionists, so vehement against admitting "the products of foreign pauper labor," admit the importation of the pauper labor itself. As to preventing emigration on grounds of political economy, I refer to what has been said on the natural right of emigration. All that is justly said in political economy, on the necessity of free emigration and immigration of capital, if we may call it so, can be said of emigration of human beings. See my Essays on Labor and Property. True patriotism and statesmanship consists in far higher things than in pretenceful artificialities.

Lastly, emigration may be considered in a psychological or, at any rate, in an ethnological point of view. Some tribes are far more given to migration, even to restlessness, than others, at certain periods, for all these things change, and it is a great error to think that the German character, as it existed at all periods and will exist in all futurity, can be found laid down in Tacitus' Germania.

It will not be amiss for the student to read a short paper of mine on Immigration and on the untoward term *native-born* in the *Nation* of March 21, 1872.

Continued investigation has led me to the belief that the book which formed the pabulum on which the minds of the Northern statesmen fed and grew was Algernon Sidney's Discourses concerning Government, while in the South it was probably Montesquieu's Spirit of Laws which impressed or nourished the minds of the nascent statesmen. Montesquieu's work itself is throughout animated with admiration of British liberty, and was undoubtedly the chief, perhaps the exclusive cause that, at the beginning of the first French revolution, the question was officially weighed whether the French (desirous of establishing liberty, yet destitute of every institutional element which might have served for a farther development) should not adopt a polity similar to that of England.

Nevertheless, it must be acknowledged that the theory of compact, according to which the origin of all governments is to be found in compact, that is to say, in an agreement of those who had no government, upon some conditions of a mutual and comprehensive government,—this theory is of great importance in the progress of our race, for it ascribes a certain dignity to man; it is plausible at first glance, and adhered to by many not ill-instructed men to this day, yet it is erroneous and unphilosophical throughout.

There was a long period in the history of error, in the seventeenth and eighteenth centuries, when a definite term, such as government, at once led people, unconsciously, to suppose that a thing, as absolutely defined as the word which designated it, was meant, and that thing had as distinct an origin as the word had. It was the period when the beginning of languages, the beginning of governments, of religions, was discussed, and almost always referred to agreement.

The theory of the initial compact is wrong and even absurd, for the following reasons, which will be merely indicated in all brevity:

Historically viewing the subject, we have no instance showing us the conclusion of such a compact.

Nor could it possibly be concluded by men who could have no inkling of the necessity or benefits of a polity, since they are imagined to have stalked about each a high and mighty sovereign for himself.

Nor could the majority have bound the minority, which can only be done in an existing polity; without it each one must agree, as it is the case now with congresses of ambassadors, of sovereigns.

Nor had any one the right to bind another, much less children and unborn generations.

If sovereigns, they might withdraw again when it seemed good to them.

All sorts of governments are derived from it. Hobbes, in his Leviathan, derives an atrocious despotism from compact; and Locke, in his Essay on Government, derives the constitutional polity from it.

Authority to command and the duty to obey naturally arises out of and within the family, according to a few great and pervading laws. The family is the first society; the greater society called the state develops itself out of it. Never was a government originally voted into existence by men met around a green table. *Ubi societas ibi jus.* Jus, law, government are as natural and unavoidable as the family.

Still it is true that the theory of the compact greatly influenced our public men before and after the Articles of Confederation. Jefferson adhered so strongly to this theory that he maintained—I have never been able to ascertain whether seriously or half in jest—that, properly speaking, the contract ought to be renewed every ten years. Why every ten years and not every five? and suppose the precious contract be not confirmed!

*   *   *   *   *   *   *   *

WHAT IS OUR CONSTITUTION—LEAGUE, PACT, OR GOVERNMENT?

TWO LECTURES

ON THE

CONSTITUTION OF THE UNITED STATES.

DELIVERED IN THE LAW SCHOOL OF COLUMBIA COLLEGE, DURING THE WINTER OF 1860 AND 1861.

———

FOLLOWED BY

AN ADDRESS ON SECESSION.

ADVERTISEMENT.

THE author of these Lectures, emboldened by a friendship which he esteems a high honor, laid the manuscript before the Hon. Horace Binney, with a request that he would make such annotations as might appear necessary. The opinions of the senior member of the American Bar, and of so profound, philosophical, and elevated a jurist, must needs enhance the value of any discourse on the American Constitution. When, therefore, the manuscript was returned, the author could not allow himself to withhold from his readers Mr. Binney's notes, although they were strictly intended as memoranda for himself alone. He obtained permission, not, indeed, without repeated entreaty, to publish these along with the Lectures—a liberality for which he wishes to express his grateful and affectionate acknowledgment. *Apex autem senectutis tanta auctoritas.*

NEW YORK, March, 1861.

[In reprinting the following paper, the editor has inserted a few verbal changes which were found in Dr. Lieber's handwriting upon a copy which was evidently prepared by him for republication. There is another copy to which he has appended a great many notes, and also a great many newspaper cuttings, but they appear to be materials which he hoped to re-cast, or notes to aid his memory, and accordingly (as they are quite voluminous) they are not inserted here.—G.]

88

WHAT IS OUR CONSTITUTION?

The reader will keep in mind, through the perusal of these lectures, that they were delivered in the beginning of the month of January, 1861—that year, which the European will call the Italian Year, and which our historian may have to call the Sad Year. [Written by Dr. Lieber in March, 1861—G.]

FIRST LECTURE.

HAVING classified the constitutions of modern states, and discussed the characteristic features of the most prominent European fundamental laws, we now approach the question, What is the Constitution of the United States? Do the States form a league? Or is the Constitution a pact, a contract—a political partnership of contracting parties? Do we live in a confederacy? and if so, in a confederacy of what degree of unitedness? Or is the Constitution a framework of government for a united country—a political organism of a people, with its own vitality and self-sufficing energy? Do we form a union, or an aggregate of partners at pleasure?

These are momentous questions—not only interesting in an historical or scientific point of view, but important as questions of political life and social existence, of public conscience, of right and truth in the highest spheres of human action and of our civilization. At no time has the very character and essence of the American Constitution been so much discussed as in ours. Never before have measures of such importance been so made to depend, in appearance, upon the fundamental character of the document called the Constitution of the

United States, while never before have those in high authority attended less to its intrinsic history, its contents, and its various provisions, in order to justify actions affecting our entire polity. Never before, either in our own or in the history of our race, have whole communities seemed to make acts of elementary and national consequence depend upon a single term; upon the question whether the Constitution is a mere contract, or whether the word, derived as it is from *constituere*, must be understood in the sense in which Cicero takes it, when he speaks of *constituere rempublicam*—that is, organizing the common weal, putting it in order, and connecting all the parts in mutual organic dependence upon one another.

I have used the words *apparently* and *seemingly*, because it admits of little doubt, if of any, that those among the leaders in the present disturbances who make a world of consequences depend upon the solitary question, Is or is not the Constitution of the United States a contract? argue on a foregone conclusion. Or is there a man living who believes that they would give up their pursuit of disunion if it should be proved, by evidence ever so fair, substantial, and free from embittering passion, that the Constitution is not a compact, or is not a mere contract?

The difference between the attenuated logic of special pleading, drawn like wire through the·draw-plate of technical terms in order to make out a case, on the one hand, and a comprehensive search after truth and loyal adhesion to it when found on the other, becomes more distinct and more important as the sphere of action is more extended or the region of argument higher. It is a rule of fallacy—and fallacy has its rules, too—to seize upon one point, one term, to narrow down the meaning even of this one point, and then keenly to syllogize from that single starting-point, irrespective of all other modifying and tributary truths or considerations. Wherever you find it, be at once on your guard—whether the discussion relates to religion, philosophy, to law, politics, or economy, to science, or to interpreting a document, a treaty of nations, or the last will of an individual. The search after truth may be symbolized by the soaring eagle rising to the regions of light in order to view things from above, and not by the perforating gimlet, which alone would be no useful tool.

You have probably seen in the papers of this week a letter written by a former Senator from Louisiana, in which he accepts the nomination for the convention of his State which is to decide whether his State shall secede from the Union. This gentleman states that, in order to enable the people to vote for or against him understandingly, it is necessary that his views and convictions should be distinctly known. He is for secession, and the course of his argument is this—I state it with punctilious correctness:

The Constitution of the United States is a contract.

Mr. Webster says a contract broken at one end is broken all over.

The Constitution of the United States has been broken.

Therefore the contract is broken all to pieces, and is at an end.

Therefore each component part of the former United States stands for itself. (He does not say where it stood before the adoption of the Constitution, for he speaks of Louisiana.)

Therefore each portion, thus floating for itself, can do what seems best to itself—become a separate empire, join a new confederacy, or become again (I suppose) a French dependency, or else a starting-point for a new government, throwing its net over Mexico.

Now the positions of this argument are scarcely more numerous than its fallacies, which it will be appropriate briefly to exhibit.

Suppose, for argument's sake, that the Constitution is a contract, the important questions remain, What sort of contract?—for every lawyer knows full well that there are many different species of contracts—and, Is it a mere contract? Almost all former publicists of note and weight (not to speak of such as Filmer) have considered, and very many of the present day continue to consider, all government to be founded upon an original pact or contract, as I have amply shown you

in preceding lectures.[1]   This supposed social contract was
formed for the common welfare of all, and every bad law is
doubtless an infringement of the contract, but has any publicist mentioned that thereby each contracting member is
authorized to become a *fuoruscito*, whom I have described to
you?   On the contrary, all publicists have maintained that
the government contract is made in perpetuity.   If I am asked,
Where is the historical proof that this government compact
was made in perpetuity?   I answer, Nowhere; nor is there a
historical proof of the original contract at all.   Those who
founded their theory of the origin of government on a supposed contract were forced by the inherent nature of society
to acknowledge the perpetuity of society, and to make it tally
with their original contract.   They felt, although they did not
formulate, the truth that society is a *continuum*.

The laws of all European countries, and of those that have
been peopled by Europeans, have called monogamic matrimony a contract.   Asiatic law does not.   When we call, however, wedlock a contract, we merely designate a certain aspect
of this varied institution.   Treat the relation of husband and
wife, " for better and for worse," as a mere contract, and a
common contract, and you will speedily and logically make
out a special pleading for licentiousness, and end with what
has been shamelessly called Free Love.   Who would seriously
pretend that he was expressing the whole character or indicating the chief meaning of matrimony,—with its preceding
love and poetry, its exclusive and purifying affection, its school
of unselfishness, its ordained procreation, and the founding of
the family—that feeder of the State—its necessity, material
and moral, for society, its sacred ties and indissolubleness, its
religion and industrial power, its internal communism, and
external individuality, its venerable history and energetic
action,—simply by calling it a contract and nothing more?

Mr. Webster, we are continually told, has said that a con-

---

[1] Even Napoleon III. gave the name of compact to the so-called French Constitution, in his throne-speech of February, 1861.

tract broken at one end is broken all over. The great advocate made this statement when he spoke as counsel for his client. He overstated a certain truth; he was too great a lawyer not to know that this does not apply to all contracts; indeed, that it is applicable to a small class of contracts only. If this statement—which represents contracts like Rupert's drops, shivered into countless fragments by the least crack at one end—is to be applied literally to all contracts and agreements, it is easy to prove, by the same show of logic, that every shortcoming of the fulfilment of a promissory oath amounts to perjury, which, nevertheless, the law of no country admits. Everything depends upon what constitutes the breaking of the contract, and upon its nature. Or, wedlock being a contract, in which the wife promises to obey the husband and the husband to love and honor his wife, is the whole contract irrecoverably broken " all over" by any act of disobedience on the part of the wife, or by the husband's ill humor toward her ?

Therefore—the argument goes on—the contract being broken, each contracting party stands for itself. Suppose, then, the original thirteen States were, at any time, sovereign nations, merely *leagued* together by the Constitution, forming an alliance, and nothing more, such as Prussia, Austria, Russia, and Great Britain formed against France, at the beginning of the present century; and suppose, further, that the Rupert's drop has been broken by a single crack at the pointed end,— under all these suppositions they might be considered as having fallen asunder, and back into their original supposed miniature nationalities. But how can this apply to the State of the Senator to whom I have alluded, and to all those States which the United States as an entirety have formed of the common territory? If the glue of the rickety casket has given way, the component parts are what they were before they were pieced together, and Louisiana must be again a territory for sale. But, we are perhaps answered, Louisiana has become in the mean time a sovereign nation. We ask, How or when? If this argument be adopted, the case would stand thus:

Louisiana is a certain territory, whose people depend upon France—a power which has acquired the territory and government from Spain :

For reasons satisfactory to themselves, the contracting parties of the Constitution break their contract in order to acquire, as a totality, the territory from France ; for you are aware that President Jefferson acknowledged that neither he nor any one had the constitutional power of purchasing foreign territory. But the mouth of the Mississippi was believed to be indispensable for the West, whose future greatness had been acknowledged by Washington,[1] and for the whole country. In England, Jefferson would have gone to Parliament and asked for an act of indemnity for having broken the law; our Constitution allows of no *ex post facto* laws, and all that could be done was to approve by silence; but certainly the Constitution was broken, and, therefore, broken "all over:"

Under this broken contract the United States admit, in due time, Louisiana as a State,—that is, they make her a full participant in the Union, and leave to her the self-government[2] which is enjoyed by the States already existing; for, until the very moment of her being created a participating State, she was territory, no independent nation, enjoying no attribute of a sovereign nation whatever. Nay, more, only a portion of that which had constituted in early times the colony was erected into a State, the other portions going elsewhere :

Yet—so the Senator's letter says—the Constitution is broken once more,—twice, "all over,"—and Louisiana falls back on her original sovereignty, which, nevertheless, has never existed, but has been produced in a mysterious fashion not unlike the procreative commingling of two principles in Hindoo cosmogony, by the genetic embrace of two breaks of the Constitution "all over." The sovereignty is made by the Union, and then ante-dated to make it *original,* as sometimes commissions

---

[1] In the Farewell Address, among other papers.

[2] I use the word self-government in the exact sense in which Mr. Jefferson used it, in a passage which I have quoted in the Civil Liberty and Self-Government.

in the army are ante-dated to give the possessor a speedier chance of promotion.

Nor is there, I think, any more substance in that argument, in favor of the lawfulness of secession, which is founded upon the idea of the Constitution being a mere contract, with the additional idea of Reserved Rights,—implying, in this case, the reserved right of disregarding the contract and leaving the Constitution.   This is the avowed and favorite argument of two most prominent statesmen, which will serve as an excuse for my mentioning a thing so void of meaning.   What contract, even in the commonest spheres of life, can that be, the contracting parties of which reserve the right of not being ruled by it at all?   The very idea of a contract, be it of whatever kind, is that of mutual binding for some common purpose, and how this element is expected to agree with an element of reserved right of mutual injury we cannot see.   Can there be such a thing as a reserved right of not doing at all what contracting parties agree to do?[1]   And, let me add, if this theory of reserved right to break up the contract of government at any time be sound, and asserted in the spirit of truth, it logically follows that not only may a State leave the Union whenever it chooses, and do all sorts of things against the other States, but that, on the strength of reserved rights, each State may nullify any portion of the contract, and " resume" the power of coining money, of adopting a king, of

---

[1] NOTE OF MR. BINNEY.—All this is very sound.——Suppose the Constitution is a contract or compact, or convention, etc., it is a contract of *government*—a *constitution*—and this is in its nature and design *for ever*.——It comprehends the present and the *unborn*—through all generations—posterity—which is as unlimited as time.   That any one can break it up rightfully, or diminish its sphere of operation, is an absurdity.——Burlamaqui says, in describing the essential constitution of a state, that its first covenant is an engagement to join *for ever* in one body. 2 Burl. 22, 28.——The Constitution of the United States was made by the *people*, describing them by *one description* as people of the United States —not confederating—nor tying themselves together—but meaning to form a *union* —a unity—a national congress as a people.   Where does a part of this people get the right to withdraw and renounce?——No sound and intelligent man believes it.——*Secession* is a word to drug the consciences of ignorant men who are averse to treason.

sending ambassadors to foreign powers, of not considering the laws of the United States as the supreme laws of the land, and yet remain in the Union. There is nothing whatsoever in the argument on contract and reserved rights that makes it necessary to use secession in the bulk. Nullification was indeed founded upon the assertion of reserved sovereignty applied to a law—a portion of the government. We would thus logically arrive at the following gradation in our public law: Nullification; Partial Secession from, or resumption of, the attributes of the general government; Temporary Secession; Permanent Secession. Whether a government would be much of a government, or a government at all, under such circumstances, is a question which the youngest among my hearers are perfectly competent to decide.

Let us dismiss these introductory discussions of that which the Constitution is not, and rather inquire into what it is—into its essential character, its genesis, and its substance. In doing so I must, however, first remind you of certain truths which we have considered under various aspects, and have found illustrated in different branches of our great topic—the Modern State.

You will bear in mind, then, that the normal type of modern government is the National Polity, in contradistinction to the ancient city-state, to the medieval feudal system, or the political league—as the Hanseatic League, to the merely agglomerated monarchy, to the fragmentary monarchy, or the so-called universal monarchy, as it appeared last under Charles the Fifth, or was attempted by Napoleon the First, to the provincial separatism, or to the crowns of many little kingdoms crowded on one head, or the breaking up of one country, mapped out by Nature herself as a portion of the earth for a united people, into jarring and unmeaning sovereignties that have not the strength to be sovereign. It is the political organism permeating an entire nation that answers the modern political necessities, and it alone can perform, as faithful handmaid, the high demands of our civilization. The highest type, its choicest development, is the organic union of national and local self-government; not, however, national centralism, or a national unity without local vitality. Our age demands *countries* as the *patria* both of freedom and of civilization, and the greatest political blessing vouchsafed to England was her early nationality, together with her early and lasting self-government. By this combination alone she escaped being drawn into the vortex of centralization, which became almost universal on the continent. Modern patriotism will not be minimized; it will not be restricted to a patch of land carved out by some accidental grant; Lucca or Lippe are not names to inspire it; it will have a portion of the earth with a dignified geographical character, pointing to a noble purpose, and a mission imposed by Him who willed that there should be nations. Is there anything nobler in the range of history than a free nation, conscious of its national dignity and purpose? Is there anything nobler to behold in our own times than the struggle of the Italians for a united Italy after centuries of longing—an Italy for which the aged Bunsen, the German scholar and high officer of a bureaucratic state, prayed with his dying breath? Is there anything more fervent than the yearning of the Germans for one undivided Germany, at any cost, disregarding all the long-sustained but diminutive sovereignties, knowing that the sovereign source of political right, above all assumed sovereignties, is the conscious desire of a great people to be a nation?

We have discussed that great period in the history of our race which I have called the period of nationalization, when countries, national governments, national languages, and national literatures arose from the frittered state of the feudal system, and have seen that many peoples of our Cis-Caucasian race have suffered even despotism to take a wide sweep, provided they saw that national cohesion and a *political country* would be its effect.

The national polity is not only the normal type of our period of civilization: it is also characteristic of it. For, if we can call the Jewish theocracy, in a purely political point of view, a national government composed of tribal elements, it was exceptional in antiquity, and did not endure. After the national reigns of David and Solomon, Israel seceded from Judah, and civil war, disgrace, ruin, servitude, and paganism covered the land, while Isaiah threatened and Jeremiah wept.

When, recently, we treated of the internal and administrative organization of the different governments, you will remember that it was stated that the growth of general governments is various and scarcely ever of a uniform character in each single case. Gradual agglomeration and union, conquest, and a certain uniformity imposed by the conqueror, successive and slow systematizing, social assimilation, or a great revolution with a sudden and entire reorganization according to some distinct plan (as was the case with France in her revolution of the last century), evolution and revolution, force, freedom, and accident, are the different processes or forms of changes we meet with in history. These processes influence more or less the form of internal organization, but do not by any means necessarily constitute its lawful foundation. The national type is the type imposed upon our race, as the great problem to be solved and its great blessing to be obtained. It is sovereign to all else. It is the will of our Maker—the Maker of history.

The instinctive social cohesion,—the conscious longing and self-revealing tendency of the people to form a nation, and to make the minor organization subservient to the great end of the modern polity,—the true public spirit and expanding patriotism, which will not be cramped by some grant given by some king to needy courtiers, or extorted in times of gallant political egotism,—these have their plenary rights too. There is no German who thinks that his heart, throbbing for his country, must be awed into calmness by the sovereign rights of a Duke of Berenburg or Reuss; there is no Italian who— because the Duke of Modena had his historically established rights, or Florence has her noble history, and Tuscany has had her kindly princes—thinks he must not consider it the most nobly symbolic occurrence of his history, since Rome ceased to be Rome, when Garibaldi held out his hand to Victor Emanuel, and breathed the words, *Rè d'Italia!*

And these remarks find their application in treating of the constituting fundamental laws of our race, and of our own until now revered Constitution.

SECOND LECTURE.

THE flowing over of European population and its pouring into America is one of the most momentous facts in the history of the cis-Caucasian spreading over the globe. It is the second Migration of Nations; and in this migration of our race it is a fact of historic mark and moment that the southern European nations of Roman Catholic religion and of Latin despotic imprint, without an institutional character, colonized South America; while those who peopled North America, and who gave it distinct social features, were sent from the Teutonic north of Europe, then in the great struggle of Protestantism with Catholicism—a struggle which extended far beyond the sphere of religion, when Hotman and Languet, bold Protestants, had dared to claim "sovereignty for the estates."[1] These settlers of the North came chiefly from the Netherlands and from England—manly, venturous, clad in the armor of self-government, and belonging to a race with institutional instincts. This fact, and that they left Europe after the tide of nationalization had fairly set in, and national governments had become the great normal type of polity, with the ne-

---

[1] The intimate connection between Protestantism and modern liberty was lately solemnly acknowledged, although deeply deplored, by the highest Catholic authority. Pius IX., in his allocution of December 17, 1860, said, "In fact, we have to deplore the invasion of perverse doctrine which, sprung from the principles of the disastrous Reformation, has acquired almost the force of public law." I quote from the London Times, supposing the translation to be correct.

I have frequently been obliged to point to the great process of nationalization manifest in our race. Whether this will lead to or be connected with the ultimate de-papalization of the Catholic Church, returning to its government by councils, is a speculation not to be indulged in in this place.

cessity of countries large enough for large patriotism, and that they came to a large country—these are essential in history. They settled in a portion of the globe marked by a dignified geography—a vast country with fertile plains and generous rivers and treasuring mountains before them, and behind them the sea—then still, as in times of Horace, but now so no longer, the oceanus dissociabilis. The character, and the breeding, and the law those men brought with them, and the great country they settled in,—these are essential in our history. The different charters, of various and frequently undignified origin, obscurely and often confusedly partitioning this land, were mere conduits of this great migration. So far as these charters mapped out certain portions of the land, they were of little more importance in the great translation of the Anglican race than the ships in which these settlers came to this continent. There was little in the various charters that was inherently essential, historically predisposing, historically presaging; but there was historic prophecy in this noble land, with these great coasts, and in the peopling it by that virile race, with its aptitude for self-government, wedded to freedom, tried by persecution. It was a people, with the same language, the same common law, the same political concepts, the same reminiscences and historical associations of ideas, the same mother country, the same literature, the same religion, the same aspirations, the same domestic economy, the same royalty, centering, indeed, at a distance, but spreading over the entire, well-marked, cohesive, yet almost unbounded land, taking possession of the country by the same jus divinum of civilization, expounded at a later period by our great Judge Marshall.[1] They were divided by their charters, but at no time was their removal from one province to another impeded on political grounds. All owed and professed the same and a direct allegiance to one crown; none were ever foreigners as to any of the others; there was never even the incipiency of different nationalities among them. They felt themselves

---

[1] Johnson *vs*. Mackintosh, 8 Wheaton.

what they soon came distinctly to express themselves to be, a people.[1] The national current flowed here, as it did in the contemporary un-united countries, in Germany and Italy, that had resisted the providential decree of nationalization.

In the middle of last century the common feeling found a distinct enunciation. A convention from the different colonies was held at Albany, in June, 1754, to consider a plan of uniting the colonies. The word *union* was there officially used. " Of this convention Franklin was a member, and a plan of general union, known afterwards as the Albany plan of union, but of which he was the projector and proposer, was conditionally adopted by the unanimous vote of the delegates. The condition was that it should be confirmed by the various Colonial Assemblies."[2]

This was in 1754. Our difficulties with the mother country began : and from that moment the idea of one " America," a " United America," one people, one common cause and interest, one nation, one supreme government, became more and more clearly expressed and more distinctly acted upon. It was not, indeed, without occasional movements to the contrary ; but though a ruffling breeze sometimes sends waves on the surface of our Hudson northward, and though the tide stems the river, its volume steadily flows in the appointed course.

In Parliament and in British state papers, " America," as

---

[1] NOTE.—To this passage, or to the whole page containing the concluding remarks, Mr. Binney added the following memorandum : This is historically true, and the Revolution could never have succeeded without it.——I have examined all the measures of the first Congress of Deputies in 1774, 1775, and they all speak this language. The addresses to the people of Great Britain, to the king, to the people of the colonies, to Canada, to Jamaica, all speak the same thing. The people are everywhere *homologous*, and these papers homologated them. Subjects of Great Britain—people of one blood, one language, one religious faith, one hope, one destination, a common paternity—in fine, a family, *in tribes*. ——The different charters were little more than acts of incorporation, to give facility to political action in particular localities.

[2] I quote from Hon. R. C. Winthrop's address, delivered before the Maine Historical Society, Boston, 1859.

one country, is spoken of; we were attacked as one country, we defended ourselves as one country, and we proclaimed our independence as one country, and called the government of that one country the Union.

Let me read to you the words of Charles Cotesworth Pinckney, the honored soldier and statesman, at one time "an authority of unbounded reverence in South Carolina." In the Legislature of 1788, he said:

" This admirable manifesto [the Declaration of Independence] sufficiently refutes the doctrine of the individual sovereignty and independence of the several States. In that declaration the several States are not even enumerated; but after reciting, in nervous language and with convincing arguments, our right to independence, and the tyranny which compelled us to assert it, the declaration is made in the following words," etc. " The separate independence and individual sovereignty of the several States were never thought of by the enlightened band of patriots who framed this declaration. The several States are not even mentioned by name in any part, as if it was intended to impress the maxim on America that our freedom and independence *arose from our Union ;* and that, without it, we never could be free or independent. Let us, then, consider all attempts to weaken this Union by maintaining that each State is separately and individually independent as a species of political heresy which can never *benefit* us, but may bring on us the most serious distresses."

It seems that the following chronological statement, very imperfect on account of its brevity, will, nevertheless, be instructive with reference to the remarks just made.

In 1765 the Stamp duties create a general indignation, and Thacher, of Massachusetts, the associate of Otis, says of Virginia, which first spoke out in resolutions proposed by Patrick Henry, " Those Virginians are men."

In 1765, October 19th. The Declaration of Rights signed by a number of colonies.

In 1768 Massachusetts calls upon all the colonies to join in one united resistance.

In 1772 England passes acts regarding "America."

In 1773, the year when the tea was destroyed, Franklin, agent for Pennsylvania, Massachusetts, New Jersey, and Georgia, recommends to Massachusetts a General Congress.

In 1774 a convention in Suffolk County, Massachusetts, recommends that the detested acts "should be rejected as the attempts of a wicked administration to enslave America."

At the same time the idea of a Provincial Congress is current. Washington writes, "Shall we supinely sit and see one province after another fall a sacrifice to despotism?" A national spirit shows itself throughout the land, and Virginia votes that an attack upon one colony was an attack upon all British America.

In 1774, September 5th. Congress at Philadelphia, the Continental Congress, "American Association."[1]

After the separation of the Continental Congress, general preparation for war, and pronounced determination to assist one another.

1775. "We, the delegates of the United Colonies," give the commission to Washington, and vest him "with full power and authority to act as you shall think for the good and welfare of the service."

1775, July 4th. Washington issues an order, in which he declares that all the troops raised, or to be raised, "for the support and the defence of the liberties of America" being taken into the pay and service of the Continental Congress, "they are now the troops of the United Provinces of North America; and it is hoped that all distinctions of colonies will be laid aside, so that one and the same spirit may animate the whole."

The first resolution of the Mecklenburg Declaration—that bold and historically naïve instrument—declares, "That whosoever directly or indirectly abetted or," etc., "countenanced the unchartered and dangerous invasion of our rights, as claimed by Great Britain, is an enemy to this country, to America, and to the inherent and inalienable rights of man."[2]

1776, May 15th. Virginia directs her delegates to propose a declaration of independence to Congress.

---

[1] A pamphlet was published at Charleston, South Carolina, in 1859, The Association of 1774, with the well-executed fac-similes of the signers.

[2] The second Mecklenburg Declaration, adopted 30th May, 1775, was presented to the Continental Congress May 27, 1776, six weeks before the adoption of the National Declaration of Independence. The second resolution of this second declaration of Mecklenburg begins with the words, "The Provincial Congress of each Province, under the direction of the great Continental Congress," etc.—The True Origin and Source of the Mecklenburg and National Declaration of Independence. By Rev. T. Smyth, D.D., Columbia, South Carolina, 1847.

1776, July 4th.   Declaration of Independence.

1776, July 9th.   Washington communicates the Declaration of Independence, and, in his order of the day, says that he hopes that "every officer and soldier will act with fidelity and courage, as knowing" . . . "that he is now in the service of a state possessed of sufficient power to reward his merit and advance him to the highest honors of a free country."

The first oath administered by order of the Continental Congress was, that the officers of the army acknowledged each of the United States (enumerating them) to be free, independent, and sovereign *States*, abjuring allegiance to Great Britain, and promising to maintain the United States against George III., etc.[1]

1776, July 12th.   Committee appointed to declare a plan of Confederation.

1776, December 27th.   A sort of dictatorship, with stringent authority "wherever he may be," is given to Washington.

1777, November 15th to 17th.   The Articles of Confederation and Perpetual Union actually adopted by Congress.   State governments formed.

1778.   The oath to be taken by the officers was modified, omitting the words thirteen States, so that it read, "to the United States of America."[2]

1782.   Seal of the United States, with the inscription *E Pluribus Unum*, adopted.

1783.   Washington, in his renowned letter to the Governors of the States, points out "four things essential to the well-being, I may even venture to say to the existence, of the United States as an independent power."   And the first of these four things is, "An indissoluble Union of the States under one Federal head."

1786, March 14th.   The oath of officers is changed, and each one swears that "he owes faith and true allegiance to the United States, and agrees to maintain its freedom, sovereignty, and independence."[3]

1787. July 13th.   The "Ordinance for the government of the Territory northwest of the river Ohio."

1788, September 17th.   Constitution of the United States.

Gentlemen, you may examine the many folios of the Amer-

---

[1] 1 Journals, 525, October 21, 1776.

[2] 2 Journals, 427, February, 1778.

[3] 4 Journals, 463–462, March 14, 1786.   I owe this reference, and those in the two preceding notes, to the research of my colleague, T. W. Dwight, LL.D., Professor in the Columbia Law School.

ican Archives,[1] and, in all the documents and state papers recorded there, you will find the same tone, spirit, and language. The people, the nation, the country, "United America," as Washington used the term, at a later period,[2] in the same sense in which we now hear of United Italy, are the habitual terms used by those who struggled for independence and obtained it. The great Declaration of Independence has not a word of separate independence; not an allusion to it; not one separate complaint. It is the people of the whole country that declare themselves independent, and unitedly complain of wrongs felt by the whole. "Before, and for nearly two years subsequent to the Declaration of Independence, the struggle was maintained by union alone,"[3] by a people conscious of being one, in their formation, their interest, and their destiny.

The Declaration of Independence is headed, A Declaration of the Representatives of the United States of America in Congress assembled. On a previous occasion the term United Colonies had been used. The republic of the Netherlands, whose history and polity, achievements and defects were well known and studied by the statesmen of our revolution, styled itself indifferently the United Provinces, and the United States, of the Netherlands; nor was the meaning of the word *State* distinctly settled, either in Europe or America, at the time of the revolution. It is certain that it was not taken in the most enlarged sense of the different meanings which are, even now, attached to this word, the history of which in all the European languages is remarkable and instructive.

Had there been a compact name for our country, it might

---

[1] By Peter Force, Esq., published under the sanction of Congress.

[2] "That as the All-Wise Dispenser of human beings has favored no nation of the earth with more abundant and substantial means of happiness than United America," etc.—Washington, in a sketch of his Farewell Address. See H. Binney's Inquiry into the Formation of Washington's Farewell Address. Philadelphia, 1859, p. 177; and J. Sparks' Washington's Writings, vol. xii. p. 392.

[3] Hon. Reverdy Johnson's speech. Proceedings at a public meeting of the Friends of the Union, on January 10, 1861. Baltimore, 1861.

have been used; but no name had formed itself. Science invents names; but for the growth of names in practical life a formative *naïveté*, not checked by learning and literature, is requisite, the period of which had already passed when the early settlers left their mother country. This want of a name is to be regretted. In history, names like England, France, Italy, have great effect. They are the greatest national symbols a people can have, far greater even than a flag; and I would frankly say that should really the calamity of sejunction and disintegration fall upon us, it would be wise for those who continue to cohere broadly to adopt in their new national constitution one comprehensive name for the country, whether it be the resumption of the old name, Vinland, which the Norse people gave to our portion of America, or any other sound and simple one. Why not call it FREELAND? Taste and tact must guide in matters of this sort.[1] In no wise, however, would I agree in the opinion of one of the most prominent American statesmen, now dead, who maintained repeatedly, in the intercourse I had with him, that the absence of a name for our portion of America had positive significance, and was indeed the result of the fact that there is no American nation, and that we have no country. The history of the United States, all the debates, letters, and state papers belonging to the transition period, from the Declaration of Independence to the adoption of the Constitution, the language of Washington and his compeers, show that this opinion is without foundation.

The Americans declared themselves independent in the year 1776, and in 1777 the Articles of Confederation were adopted. The union sentiment, which pervaded the whole people, and the necessity of united action, led to this first attempt at forming a united government. The succeeding years proved that it was no successful attempt, but they mark

---

[1] "Columbia" has been invented by poetry, for the poet must have a compact name; but it has remained in the realm of poetry. It is worth noting that in Europe, almost universally, the name "America" is used for the United States.

the transition period, and I invite your attention to the following points :

The title of the Articles of Confederation is : *Articles of Confederation and Perpetual Union between the States of*, etc. Here then we meet, for the second time in our history, with the word *union*—a term the meaning of which was well established, and had been so for many centuries, in the English language. The Union is called *perpetual*. Terms of great force are used, both as to the intensity of combination and as to its duration.

Yet the second article of this instrument runs thus : "Each State retains its sovereignty, freedom, and independence, and every power, jurisdiction, and right which is not by this confederation expressly delegated to the United States in Congress assembled."

What does the word *sovereignty* mean in this article ? You will recollect that I showed, in the lectures on this comprehensive subject at the beginning of this course, how vaguely the term *sovereign* has been used, and to this day continues to be used, and how unsatisfactory many arguments touching our highest interests are, because starting from so ill-defined and yet so ambitious a term. Coke declared in the Commons, when the Bill of Rights was debating, that the English law did not know the word *sovereign*. And it would have been far better had the word never entered our public law : but it has been used. Sovereignty, you remember, always means, nowadays, either complete independence towards other, that is, foreign, states, or it means not only the highest but the overruling power within a state ; or it means, in political metaphysics, that original self-sufficient source of authority and power from which all other authority is derived ; or, lastly, it simply means supreme, in any given sphere, being equivalent to chief. You will remember that the word is derived from the low Latin *superanus*, and that the Italian writers of the middle ages speak of the *sovrani* and the *sottani* (the upperlings and underlings).

We need not occupy ourselves with the last-mentioned two

meanings of the term; and as to the first two, let me observe that, surely, with reference to foreign states, no government in this country, other than the United States collectively, has ever been sovereign. Instead of dwelling on details that bear on this point, I give you an extract of Washington's letter of the 8th of June, 1783—the noble circular to the governors on disbanding the army. "It is," he says, "only in our united character as an empire that our independence is acknowledged, that our power can be regarded, or our credit supported among foreign nations. The treaties of European powers with the United States of America will have no validity on a dissolution of the Union. We shall be left nearly in a state of nature; or we may find, by our own unhappy experience, that there is a natural and necessary progression from the extreme of anarchy to the extreme of tyranny, and that arbitrary power is easily established on the ruins of liberty abused to licentiousness."[1]

---

[1] Sparks' Life of Washington, vol. viii., p. 439. I add an extract from a letter of Mr. Binney, relating to this passage. He refers to 1776.

"Really, and in point of fact, there was at that time no *legal union;* it was a voluntary Congress, and no more. Besides, the declaration that they were independent *States* is necessarily distributive and several. Independence is predicated of the States, and not of the one State or government formed by the Union. No such *Union* then existed as in the language of law to constitute a State. The first treaty with France, 6th February, 1778, is between 'the most Christian King and the thirteen United States of North America, to wit: New Hampshire,' etc., giving all their names in order. At that time the Articles of Confederation were not ratified by a single State. I find the dates of ratification were as follows:

By 8 States on 9th July, 1778.	By 1 State on 26th Nov., 1778.
" 1 State on 21st " "	" 1 " on 22d Feb., 1779.
" 1 " on 24th " "	" 1 " on 1st March, 1780.

This treaty, and the Treaty of Alliance on the same day, say nothing about acknowledgment of our independence. France treated us *as* independent, our plenipotentiaries being appointed by Congress, under the separate resolutions of the States, giving authority to their deputies. But the 8th article of the Treaty of Alliance agrees that neither of the two parties shall conclude truce or peace with Great Britain without consent of the other; and they mutually engage 'not to lay down their arms until the independence of the United States shall have been formally or tacitly assured by the treaty or treaties that shall terminate the war.' "

As to the second meaning of sovereignty, we know, indeed, for history testifies to it on every page, that the colonies exercised a very high degree of self-government at the moment when independence was declared (in some cases even before that period), but never absolute autonomy. The feeling of a union—of mutual dependence—underlies the whole from the beginning. The official letter accompanying the Articles of Confederation, dated Yorktown, November 17, 1777, and in which Congress recommends their adoption to the States, has these words: "In short, the salutary measure can no longer be deferred. It seems essential to our very existence *as a free people.*"[1]

Congress, "supported by the confidence of the people, but without any express powers, undertook to direct the storm, and were seconded by the people and by the colonial authorities,"[2] and after the presentation of the Articles, as late as November 15, 1777, to the States (not adopted by all until the year 1781), Congress proceeded as if invested with the most explicit powers; they even went so far as to bind the nation by treaties with France; nor was it thought necessary that those treaties should be ratified by the State legislatures.[2]

Yet those who incline in their arguments towards sejunction and who seem always to confound nationality with centralization object that, as soon as the colonies had declared themselves independent of the uniting crown of Great Britain, each one was of necessity sovereign in its separate character, and hence the words in the third of the Articles of Confederation,—that the States "severally enter into a firm league of friendship."

These words are indeed in the third article; but the fourth article has, on the contrary, a very national character. It was, as I have called it, a transition period—a period of forming, not of finished formation, with all the contradictions and obscurities natural to such a period. The colonies, it is said,

---

[1] Elliot's Debates, vol. i., p. 70.
[2] Du Ponceau, View of the Constitution.

were sovereign, if for no other reason than that they were independent, and could not be otherwise than sovereign; but sovereignty cannot be predicated, it seems to me, in a purely negative sense. Was Alexander Selkirk, when wholly independent, a sovereign? Were the cities of the kingdom of Westphalia, when Jerome declared that he was no longer their king, and before the conquering allies took possession of them, sovereign? The colonies never fully acted as so many sovereigns; all action was united American action, and it seems that if the distinction between de jure and de facto, or between practical (or, rather, *factal*) and theoretical character is inapplicable to anything, it is to sovereignty.

These Articles, however, to which frequent appeal has been made of late, proved utterly inadequate to the wants of the nation. By their adoption the benefits of a government had been hoped for, without establishing a government. The period from 1777 to the adoption of the Constitution is marked, by the side of the noble deeds that were performed, with mutiny, rebellion, jealousy, extravagant notions of equality in Rousseau's sense, want of organic action, lack of funds, and the despondency of some of the best. Even Madison considered America as almost lost; and Washington, the *justus et tenax*,—even he, at least on one occasion, was near losing hope. The call for a better and firmer system for a government became general, and after infinite toil and anxiety the Constitution of the United States was established. It is impossible to understand this great document as it ought to be understood by every one who aspires to a dignified consciousness of his rights and duties as an American citizen, and to become a guardian of American citizenship, without a minute knowledge of our history and a truthful study of the debates which led to the framing and adoption of the Constitution. I once more recommend to you, then, this earnest study as a matter of good faith, conscience, and true loyalty. In this place you are aware that I can do no more than direct your attention to a few essential points. Let me commence by pointing out, in the preamble of our fundamental law, the three words, Constitution, People, Union, and the total absence of the term Sovereignty from the whole document.

To argue from mere terms, of no definite or of a varying meaning, is dangerous, and frequently indicates faithlessness; but when well-understood terms are carefully used in contradistinction to other terms, they become important. Thus we must observe that the fundamental law is no longer called Articles of Confederation, but a Constitution. The framers of the Constitution knew the meaning of the term. Every one of them had heard and read about the Constitution of England, by which had always been understood the aggregate of all those statutes, customary laws, declaratory acts and decisions, which form the framework of that government and secure the rights of Englishmen. They knew that Constitution well, for they had struggled long to have its benefits secured before they ventured on the Declaration of Independence. The term Constitution was carefully and purposely used. Madison distinguished between the new Constitution and the "union when it was a federal one among sovereign States."[1]

This Constitution begins with the words: "We, the people of the United States,"—to me, the most magnificent words I know of in all history. They seem like an entrance, full of grandeur and simplicity, into a wide temple. It is the whole nation that speaks in its entirety and power; and yet the word People, in its plural sense, gives more life to it. The attempt has often been made, inconsistently enough, by those who call themselves strict constructionists, to show that We, the People, does not mean the people, but means the different States. This is a grave mistake, proved by the history of the Constitution, as well as by its own meaning and provisions; as, for instance, by the national election of the President. The mere *modus* of adopting the Constitution proves nothing.

The People of the United States establish the Constitution "in order to form a more perfect union." The Articles of Confederation had already established a perpetual union; a

---

[1] Elliot's Debates, vol. v. p. 135.

more perfect union, therefore, than a perpetual union, means more perfect in its intrinsic character. Perpetuity does not admit of a greater or less degree.

We meet thus with the word *union* for the third time, and it ought to be remembered that, while the framers of our Constitution were men noted for their idiomatic use of the English language, the meaning of the term has not changed from the times of Shakspeare and Milton, nor, indeed, from the earliest times. It has always meant a close and most intimate connection or inter-combination of parts, forming henceforth a whole. Catholics and Protestants have always called marriage a union of husband and wife, and have termed the relation of the Christian soul to Christ a union. The many attempts of reconciling the Protestant and Catholic Churches were called attempts of union.[1] Shakspeare and Milton use union in the most forcible sense. The framers of the Constitution were acquainted with De Foe's History of the Union, namely—of England and Scotland; Bolingbroke had spoken of the union of the king's subjects, meaning the entire agreement of Jacobites and Whigs,[2] as Vilanni, in his history, speaks of "breaking the union of the holy Church."[3] But it is useless to multiply instances. The word and its full meaning were well known to our Revolutionary men. As early as 1782 they had adopted the inscription on the seal of the United States, *E Pluribus Unum*, and this, upon the report of three, two of whom were South Carolinians.[4]

Throughout the Debates of the Constituent Convention we find it expressed—I wish I had counted how often—that there

---

[1] That of Leibnitz, I believe, was the last.   Union was always given, in Latin, by Concordia.

[2] Lord Bolingbroke, in a letter offering his good services to the Ministry.   Letters, p. 250.

[3] Storia, di G. Vilanni, Giunti 1587, 4, 21, 3.

[4] The inscription had been proposed before.   The three forming the committee were Middleton, Boudinot, and Rutledge.   See Capt. Schuyler Hamilton's History of the National Flag, Philadelphia, 1853, p. 105.   The English flag—"the Union"—was the basis of our national flag.

is the most urgent necessity of establishing a national *government*. This is the standing phrase of all the members. They did not mean to make *a nation*. Nations are not made by man, but he may politically stamp a nation; just as government cannot make money, but it may coin commodities that are already values.

Almost as frequently we meet in the debates with the expression, that unless we have a national government we cannot avoid anarchy and convulsion. Those who, like Franklin, did not approve of every feature in the Constitution, declared themselves nevertheless ready to accept it, in order to prevent anarchy and convulsion. Why anarchy? When sovereigns fail to conclude a league, war may follow, but it is not anarchy. Anarchy is absence of law and government where they ought to exist—that is, among and over a people.

The Constitution declares that there is such a crime as treason against the United States. It defines the crime with distinct lineaments. Treason can only be committed by him who owes allegiance against him to whom he owes it. The Constitution, therefore, acknowledges allegiance to the United States; and allegiance is the faith, fidelity, and loyalty due the sovereign—in our case, the nation or country. If different states claim an allegiance due to their sovereignty, it must be proportioned to that sovereignty. Switzerland is divided into cantons, and although the deputies of the cantons were called ambassadors, before the Helvetic Constitution was somewhat assimilated to that of the United States, the Swiss publicists speak of the sovereignty of Switzerland and the *cantonal* sovereignty of each canton, meaning thereby its self-government with an entire organization of a government;[1] but I believe the idea of a cantonal allegiance is unknown to them.

The Constitution invests the national government with most of the usual attributes of sovereignty—far more than the Netherlands would have conferred on Elizabeth had she been willing to become their "prince." It establishes a gov-

---

[1] Bluntschli, General Public Law, Munich, 1857.

ernment in its entirety, and applies a complete representative government to a confederacy of states with the highest degree of self-government. It does this for the first time in all history. The Constitution gives to the House of Representatives a complete national character, by founding the representation on the population, and making the representatives vote individually. It gives even this representative and national character to the Senate, inasmuch as the Senators also vote individually, and not by States, although each State, by sending two Senators, irrespective of its population or wealth, is so far represented as State. No one in Congress has a deputative character, in the mediæval sense, or is there as attorney, depending upon previously given instructions, as the ambassadors of the German princes in the German Diet.[1]

Extreme States-right men have expressed regret that the Articles of Confederation have been abandoned. Little do they know what they wish for. Had our Constitution not been adopted, the necessary consequence of all real confederacies, or of an absence of general government among those who nevertheless feel that they are destined to be one people, must have taken place. One or the other powerful State must, in the inevitable course of events, have obtained the leadership, as Athens or Sparta obtained the hegemony of Greece, or as, in the proclamation of William I., which reached us a few days ago, Prussia claims the German hegemony. Indeed, was not Virginia actually acquiring the American hegemony? In course of time, New York or Pennsylvania would have struggled for the leadership, and we should have had our American Peloponnesian war, and, like Greece, been buried under it.

The Constitution intrusts the executive power to one officer, and that one of a broad national character, elected as he is by the whole. He is the standard-bearer, the *gonfalonier* of the Union.

---

[1] These subjects have been dwelt upon in the chapter on *Instruction*, in my Political Ethics, second volume.

Washington will be admitted as one of the wisest and most profound witnesses as to the spirit and essence of our Constitution, and I may fitly conclude with some extracts from his Farewell Address, which is not only an affectionate address to the people, but a state paper long meditated upon and written most carefully, with the advice and upon the suggestions of fellow-statesmen. This is admirably shown in Mr. Binney's "Inquiry into the Formation of Washington's Farewell Address;"[1] and European writers on public law, by the quotations from it with which I meet in the course of my reading, show that they by no means consider the address merely as an affectionate advice to his fellow-citizens.

Washington uses such expressions as follow: "the unity of government, which constitutes you one people;"—"the name of AMERICAN, which belongs to you in your national capacity, must always exalt the just pride of patriotism more than any appellation derived from local discriminations;"— "carefully guarding and preserving the union of the whole;" —"these considerations . . . exhibit the continuance of the Union as a primary object of patriotic desire;"—"we are authorized to hope that a proper organization of the whole, with the auxiliary agency of governments for the respective subdivisions, will afford a happy issue of the experiment;"—"to the efficacy and permanency of your Union, a government of the whole is indispensable. No alliances, however strict, between the parts can be an adequate substitute;"—"the adoption of a constitution of government better calculated than your former for an intimate union and for the efficacious management of your common concerns;"—"respect for its authority, compliance with its laws, acquiescence in its measures, are duties enjoined by the fundamental maxims of true liberty;" —"the Constitution which at any time exists, till changed by an explicit and authentic act of the whole people, is sacredly obligatory upon all;"—"to put, in the place of the delegated will of the nation, the will of a party;"—"it will be worthy

---

[1] Philadelphia, 1859.

of a free, enlightened, and, at no distant period, a great nation ;"—" if we remain one people, under an efficient government," etc. Read, I advise you, my younger hearers, the
whole Farewell Address with that pondering attention which
a paper so well-advised, of so experienced, so calm, so pure,
and so universally acknowledged a statesman, demands at the
hands of every one of us,—the document of a patriot who is
daily growing in the affection of our race,[1] and who considered it the greatest blessing vouchsafed to him, in his event-
ful life, " to have been, in any degree, an instrument in the
hands of Providence to promote order and union."[2]

The Constitution of the United States broadly declares and
decrees that all the laws made in pursuance of the same shall
be the supreme law of the land. This provision and many
more, such as that establishing a national citizenship, the organic law of amendment which it contains, and the characteristic features that have been mentioned, as well as the whole
genesis of the Constitution, prove the following points :

The Constitution is a law, with all the attributes essential
to a law, the first of which is that it must be obeyed, and that
there must be an authority that can enforce obedience. It is
a law, not a mere adhortation, not a pastoral letter, not a
" proclamation in terrorem."

It is, as far as it goes, a full and complete law, carefully defining its own limits ; and the provision that the national
government has no rights but those which are granted to it,

---

[1] Such works as Guizot's Essay on the Character and Influence of Washington,
translated from the French, Boston, 1840, and, indeed, many other writings of
European authors, prove that history is pointing more and more frequently to
him as a favorite on that tablet on which the names of Thrasybulus, Doria, and
William the Silent are inscribed beside his own.

[2] I copy these words from a letter of Washington's to his " Fellow-Citizens
and Brothers of the Grand Lodge of Pennsylvania" (without date), which I found
in a hairdresser's shop in New York. When waiting for my turn, and revolving
some points of these Lectures in my mind, my attention was attracted by the gilt
frame surrounding the letter. The genuineness of the manuscript no one acquainted with Washington's handwriting will doubt. I believe the letter is
given in no published work.

cannot mean that it must allow itself to be broken up when
ever it pleases any portion possessing the " reserved rights" to
do so. Logically speaking, it would be absurd ;. morally speaking, wicked.. This interpretation of the doctrine of Reserved
Rights, it seems, would amount to nothing less than to the
well-known Mental Reservation, with this fearful difference,
that we would apply to the consciences of entire States what
the Jesuit used for the purpose of easing the consciences of
private persons.

It is a national law, having proceeded from the fulness of
the national necessity, national consciousness, and national
will, and is expressive of a national destiny.

It is a national fundamental law, establishing a complete
national government,—an organism of national life. It is not
a mere league of independent states or nations ; it allows of
no " Sonderbund." It is an organism with living functions ;
not a string of beads in mere juxtaposition on a slender thread,
which may snap at any time and allow the beads to roll in all
directions.

The more you study history in candor and good faith, and
not in order merely to collect points to make out a case, the
more you will be convinced that, as indeed I have indicated
before, the general government, nationally uniting a number
of States, with the framework of local governments, is that
very thing which America has contributed as her share to the
political history of our race. A great historian has justly
observed that Athens and her many illustrious citizens were
never so great and noble as when they were animated and
impelled by a Pan-Hellenic spirit. And so it is with us.
What is great, what is noble, what is of lasting effect, what is
patriotic, what is inspiriting to behold, in our history and public
men, is Pan-American. Provincialism has neither freed nor
raised this people. On the contrary, every step that is taken,
receding from the Constitution as the government of a nation
and a united people, is a step toward the confused transition
state in which the country was under the Articles of Confederation ; every measure that is taken to lessen its health and

vigor, its lawful and organic action, amounts to a drifting toward the anarchy from which the framers rescued the people with infinite labor and exertion.   Sejunction, State-egotism, envious localism, do not only "hurt men, *sed leges ac jura labefactant.*"

Our system, being neither a pure unitary government[1] nor a pure confederacy, is not without its difficulties.   It has its very great difficulties, as our own times prove, but neither in our case nor in any other whatsoever, be it of practice, theory, or science, is an elementary difficulty overcome by seizing upon one of the contending elements exclusively, and by carrying it out to a fanatical end irrespective of other elements.   Seizing upon the single idea of State-sovereignty—a modern fiction, taken in the sense in which the present extremists take it—denying, as was quite recently done in the Senate of the United States, all allegiance[2] to the United States, and imagining that liberty chiefly consists in denying power and authority to the national government, is very much like an attempt of explaining the planetary system by centrifugal power alone.[3]   It is a fact, which you will mark

---

[1] Lest some readers should misapprehend the term *unitary government*, it may be stated that it does not mean either monarchy or a centralized government, but an undivided government for a given community, be it republican or monarchical; the opposite to a federal government.   The government of England is unitary but not centralized.

[2] The so-called " Allegiance cases," in South Carolina, 2 Hill's So. Car. Rep., p. 1–282, are of great interest.   They have been also separately published with the title, "The Book of Allegiance, or a Report of the Arguments of Counsel and Opinions of the Court of Appeals of South Carolina on the Oath of Allegiance; Determined on the 24th of May, 1834."

[3] The lecturer, according to his custom of pointing out the best writer on the opposite side, cited on this occasion the writings and speeches of Mr. Calhoun's latter period.   The reader may find numerous publications taking the extreme, and, therefore, disjunctive State-rights views, mentioned in an article on " Lieber's Civil Liberty and Self-Government," by the late D. J. McCord, in the April number of the Southern Review, Charleston, 1854.   In addition may be mentioned Judge Henry Baldwin's " General View of the Origin and Nature of the Constitution and Government of the United States, deduced from the Political History and Condition of the Colonies and States, and their Public Acts in Congresses and Conventions from 1774 till 1788, together with their Exposition by the Supreme Court of the United States," etc. : Philadelphia, 1837.

as such for future reflection, that almost all, perhaps actually all, the most prominent extremists on the State-rights side—that is to say, of those statesmen who were most perseveringly bent on coercing the national government into the narrowest circle of helplessness—have been at the same time strongly inclined toward centralization and consolidation of power within their respective States. Secessionists by profession would cry "treason,"[1] indeed, were a portion of a State to intimate a desire to peel off one more skin of the bulb. Yet, suppose Rhode Island to secede, why should not Block Island set up as a nation? I say *suppose.* Have we not had close before our eyes a proposition of secession for our city? And what logical process shall stop us from proceeding to the se-junction of the different wards? One thing seems certain—and I conclude my remarks with this observation—that if ever the American people should be forced to make a choice between a unitary government and an unmitigated confederacy, they would be obliged to select the former type.[2]

---

[1] The charge in such case would be grotesque. The like grotesqueness is illustrated in an incident which came to hand while these sheets were passing through the press, and which deserves being preserved in a note. If the papers report correctly, a Texas judge, whose name is given, of Rusk County, in his charge to the grand jury, " defined treason as a crime to be looked after in the event of the State withdrawing from the Union. After the State has fully and unconditionally severed the connection between the State and the Federal Government, then all who adhere to the Union, and so manifest the fact, are guilty of the crime of treason, subject and liable to indictment by the grand jury under the Constitution as it now exists. After secession, any word, deed, or act against the independence of the State would be treason."—*National Intelligencer*, Washington, March 22, 1861.

[2] I append here the last and fullest note of Mr. Binney.

The confederation came first into action—I should rather say *the Congress of Deputies*—by votes of the legislative bodies in the Colonies before independence was declared; it had been *assumed* for the occasion. Deputies were sent to a Congress by votes of the different legislatures, on various terms, generally to agree upon and do what was needful in the emergency.—*American Archives*, vol. i., 693, 4th and 5th September, 1774.

On the 24th of June, 1776, Congress resolved, That all persons abiding within any of the United Colonies, desiring protection from the laws of the same, owe *allegiance* to the *said laws*, and are members of such colony (2 *Journal of Congress*, 217): that all persons members of, or owing allegiance to, any of the United

Gentlemen, I now conclude this year's course on the Modern State. Not, indeed, that I have gone over the whole

---

Colonies, who shall levy war, etc., or be adhered to the King, etc., are guilty of treason against such colony : that it be recommended to the several United Colonies to pass laws for punishing such persons, etc. *Allegiance* in these resolutions means *obedience* and nothing more. There was no independence,—no State Constitution or government.

On the 10th of May, 1776, Congress recommended Colonies to establish forms of government.—2 *Journal of Congress*, 678.

Articles of Confederation were reported in Congress on 21st of July, 1775, and agreed to by Congress 15th November, 1777 ; but not ratified by all the States until 1st of March, 1781. They were ratified by 11 States in 1778, by 1 in 1779, and by 1 in 1781. Maryland seems to have been the last, on the 1st of March, 1781.

The States adopted their forms of government on different days and in different years. My edition of the first Constitution gives these dates : New Hampshire, 5th of January, 1776, to 19th of September, 1776 ; Massachusetts, 1st of September, 1776, to 2d of March, 1780 ; Rhode Island and Connecticut continued their Royal Charter several years after the Constitution of the United States was adopted ; New York, 20th of April, 1777 ; New Jersey, 2d of July, 1776 ; Pennsylvania, 15th of July, 1776, to 28th of September, 1776 ; Delaware, 20th of September, 1776 ; Maryland, 14th of August, 1776 ; Virginia, 6th of May, 1776, to 5th of July, 1776 ; North Carolina, 19th of March, 1778 ; Georgia, 5th of February, 1777.—*The Constitutions of the United States*, by W. Hickey, 398.

Now, whether some or all of these States were not fully sovereign at some point of time, in their separate character, as far as States can be in an undecided revolution, is the point. Supposing the acknowledgment of their independence to *retroact*, which I think is the law, then some of them were, at some point of time, sovereign and independent. As soon as each had ratified the Articles of Confederation, then such State was no longer fully sovereign,—not any of them after the final ratification on 1st of March, 1781. The articles recite that each State retains its sovereignty and independence, and every power, jurisdiction, and right which *is not expressly delegated to the United States*, in Congress assembled.

How much was both expressly delegated and also expressly prohibited to the States ? Prohibitions were, sending and receiving embassies, or entering into any conference, agreement, alliance, or treaty with any king, power, or State. No two States should enter into any treaty or confederation whatever between them ; nor lay imposts or duties which may interfere with treaties by Congress ; nor keep vessels of war in time of peace, *except*, etc. ; nor keep any body of forces, except, etc. ; nor engage in any war, except, etc. Congress—the United States in Congress—alone had these powers ; and these exceptions held till the more perfect union was made in the Constitution of the United States.

This statement disposes of the point. A sovereign who parts with such material parts of sovereignty is *sub graviori lege*,—not a sovereign in the general ground of this comprehensive topic; but I have done what suggested itself as the best course.   When I prepared it, I

---

sense; sovereign, perhaps, in a *particular function*.   And so, in some particular, is every man.   A sovereign who can neither make war nor peace, nor lay a duty— nor make a treaty—nor keep a ship of war or a soldier in time of peace—nor enter into an alliance with another state—cannot possibly come under the established definition of a sovereign.

Illustration:

Allegiance not due to States *at all*.   The sense and use of the word are abused by giving this name to the *fidelity* owing by a citizen to his State.

In the law of England, which follows the law of nations, allegiance is due only to the supreme protecting power—*fealty* to the lord from whom the tenant derives.   The latter word is not technically applicable to a State, but the substance of it is.

Sovereignty in international law exists solely in the United States.   Foreign states know nothing of our States—our States do not separately represent the nation.   *Independence* cannot be predicated to them separately.   They are restrained and subordinated in many particulars by the Constitution of the United States.   In no one instance is the United States subordinated to a State.   The United States *cover* all—*permeate* all—*defend* all, both within and without, against foreign enemies and domestic insurrections, and against aggression by one upon another.

The *Constitution* of the United States is the SUPREME law of the nation, and so are the treaties by the authority of it, and the laws in pursuance of it.

Allegiance and *protection* are reciprocal.   Who protects a State against a State or a foreign nation?   Who protects the inhabitant and citizen of a State from the same?   Who protects a citizen from the State in which he is domiciled?   Protects him against a monarchical or non-republican constitution,—laws violating obligation of contracts—bills of attainder—*ex post facto* laws—tenders of paper money in payment of debts—against coinage of money—duties on imports or exports—troops, ships of war of a State?   The United States only.   Who naturalizes citizens?   What Constitution do they swear to support?   Their first vow and duty are to the *supreme* law; and the same is the duty of the native born.

Two allegiances to different kings, lords, or nations at the same time, impossible; but two *fidelities* in respect to different obligations, both possible and common.   The irreconcilable hostility *in nature*, of one allegiance to a State and another to the Union, is proved by the manner in which, by false doctrine, the one has devoured the other, in our own case.   *State rights* devouring *United States' rights*, and yet all the weaker for it.   United States' rights cannot devour State rights, because the former are protective of the latter,—not the latter of the former.

The idea of one nation—one people—one allegiance—is indispensable to both the dignity and the freedom of the United States; no other sentiment can protect us against the hatreds, jealousies, and hostilities which merely allied peoples asked myself, Shall I treat of the whole in an encyclopedical method? or shall I treat of the most important topics in detail, and thereby indicate to my hearers how the subjects appertaining to our great argument ought to be studied? I decided in favor of the latter. To learn how to study, and to convey coherent and substantial knowledge, is more important than merely to transmit information. It has ever appeared to me that, in all public instruction, but especially in public instruction of young men, there ought to be four main objects before the eye of the teacher. He ought, as a matter of course, to transmit positive information,—the facts of his science; he ought to infuse and evoke knowledge, by which I understand that he ought to cause his hearers to perceive the connection of things, and to make their essential truth part and parcel of the minds and souls of the hearers, so that it buds forth within their hearts, as wisdom, directness and loftiness of purpose, and rectitude of conduct. The teacher ought, moreover, to lead the kindly hearer to the hill-tops of the border knowledge, and, like a guide into a new country, show the land that lies beyond and the avenues that lead to it, although he may not at the time go farther along with them; and, lastly, the public, as every other teacher, from the master of the primary school to the martyr-teacher of Athens, who taught even when dying, must kindle a love of knowledge, inflame the hearts of his hearers with a sacred zeal for critical truthfulness, a steadfast, an heroic devotion to that which is good and true, and impart to them an inmost delight in tracing the rills and swelling brooks of truth and right, which Providence has marked for the progress of our kind. What is teaching, if it be not the transmission and the cultivation of truth? What is truth, if it include not what is right?

Have I succeeded according to this standard? My own

---

always feel. National *identity* is essential to prevent the selfish principle of our nature from turning to opposition. The *general identification* is that which begets a love of the nation or country. We love it more than all others, *because it is ours.*

Defend us from *State-ishness!*

conscientious zeal, which I have applied to these lectures, and your unflagging, painstaking attention during this arduous course, tell me that we may hold up this standard and honestly say we have not met in vain. We have assembled in this hall evening after evening, in fair and in inclement weather, at a period in our country's history when the news of the grave events happening before us struck our ears like the boom of beginning battles. Often and often have they made it one of the severest tasks of your teacher to concentrate his mind on the topic on which he was to lecture to you, and, when he appeared before you, to restrain his heart from overflowing. Was I not here before you, lecturing on Public Law, on State and Government, much like a man obliged to discourse on navigation, aboard a threatened craft, in foul weather, when the ghastly foam of breakers is espied, and the turmoil on the shoal is heard to the leeward? You, on the other hand, soon to be active citizens of that country which is so rudely threatened from within,—not by gallant and inspiriting enemies from without,—have steadily persevered, in the midst of the storms of passion blowing from afar, and perceiving, at times, the breath of depravity near at hand. I thank you for this perseverance. Let us all hope that our country will still remain our country; but if that be decreed which we do not like even to mention, remember that you, above all, are called upon to be the guardians of the country's rights and freedom; and let us meet, whenever we may meet again, like men with clean hands and clean hearts, that have not helped in their fair country's ruin, but, on the contrary, have done all in their sphere to prevent that from which they avert their countenances with sickening horror.[1]

---

[1] A syllabus of the topics that remained to be discussed was given, but is omitted here as not of sufficient interest to the reader.

AN ADDRESS ON SECESSION.

In the year 1850, after the admission of California as a free state, secession was urged by a strong party in South Carolina; but when a convention was held in Charleston, it was found that the so-called co-operationists—that is to say, those who were in favor of secession, indeed, but only conjointly with other states —were in the majority. The Union men of the state, desirous of doing, on their part, whatever might be in their power to strengthen the Union feeling, resolved, in 1851, to celebrate, by a mass-meeting at Greenville, South Carolina, the Fourth of July, a day already then frequently spoken of with little respect. Many citizens were invited, either to be present or "to give their views in writing at length," should they be prevented from participating in the celebration. The author was among the invited guests; but, being on the point of leaving South Carolina for some months, he wrote the following address, which was read, and published in the papers of the day, from one of which he now copies it, having been requested to do so, and being aware that it touches on subjects connected with the Lectures.

FELLOW-CITIZENS: This is the Fourth of July! There is a fragrance about the month of July, delightful and refreshing to every friend of freedom. It was on the sixth day of this month that Leonidas and his martyr band, faithful "*to the laws of their country*," even unto death, sacrificed themselves, not to obtain a victory—they knew that that was beyond their reach —but to do more—to leave to their state, and their country, and to every successive generation of patriots, to the end of time, the memory of men that could " obey the law," and prepare themselves for a certain death for their country as for a joyful wedding-feast. It was on the ninth day of this month, that the Swiss peasants dared to make a stand, at Sempach, against Austria—then, as now, the drag-chain to the chariot

125

of advancing Europe—that memorable day when Arnold Winkelried, seeing that his companions hesitated before the firm rampart of lances levelled against them by the Austrian knights, cried out: "Friends, I'll make a lane for you! Think of my dearest wife and children!"—grasped, as he was a man of great strength, a whole bundle of the enemy's pikes, buried them in his breast, and made a breach, so that over him and the knights whom he had dragged down with him, his brethren could enter the hostile ranks, and with them victory for Switzerland and liberty; and Arnold's carcass, mangled and trodden down, became the corner-stone of the Helvetic Republic. It was on the fourteenth day of this month that the French, awakened from a lethargy into which an infamous despotism had drugged them, stormed and conquered that castle of tyranny, the ominous keys of which Lafayette sent to our Washington, who sacredly kept them to the last day of his life, so that every visitor could see them, as the choicest presents ever offered to him to whom we owe so much of our liberty and of the existence of our great commonwealth. And it was on this day that our forefathers signed that Independence which many of them sealed with their blood, and which the others, not permitted to die for their cause, soon after raised to a great historical reality, by the boldest conception —by engrafting, for the first time in the history of our kind, a representative and complete political organism on a confederacy of states, nicely adjusted, yet with an expansive and assimilative vitality.

These are solemn recollections. As the pious Christian recounts the sacrifices and the victories of his church with burning gratitude and renewed pledges to live worthy of them, so does the fervent patriot remember these deeds with rekindled affections, and resolutions not to prove unworthy of such examples and unmindful of so great an inheritance, but, on the contrary, to do whatever in him lies to transmit the talent he has received from his fathers, undiminished, and, if God permits, increased, to his successors.

Yet there are those in this country who daringly pretend

to make light of the great boon received from our fathers—
of this, by far the greatest act of our history—of that act by
which we stand forth among the nations of the earth—the
Union. There have been patriots as devoted as ours—there
have been republics besides ours; there have been spreading
nations like ours; there have been bold adventurers pressing
on into distant regions before ours; there have been confederacies in antiquity and modern times besides ours; but there
has never been a union of free states like ours, cemented by
a united representation of the single states and of the people
at large, woven together into a true government like ours;
leaving separate what ought to be separated, and yet uniting
the whole by a broadcast and equal representation, changing
with the changing population, so that we cannot fall into a
dire Peloponnesian war, in which Athens and Sparta struggle
for the leadership,—that internecine war into which all other
confederacies have fallen, and in which they have buried themselves under their own ruins, unless they have slowly glided
into submission to one Holland, or one Austria, or one Berne.
Many federations, indeed, have had to bear the larger part of
both the evils.

There are those who pretend to make light of the Union;
there are those who wilfully shut their eyes to the many positive blessings she has bestowed upon us, and who seem to
forget that the good which the Union, with her Supreme
Court or any other vast and lasting institution, bestows upon
men, consists as much in preventing evils as in showering
benefits into our laps. There are those who will not see or
hear what is happening before our own eyes in other countries—in Germany, for instance—that living, yet bleeding,
ailing, writhing, humbled commentator on Disunion. Ah!
fellow-citizens, you can but fear, and justly fear, *that* of disunion which I *know*. With you, the evils of disunion are
happily but matter of apprehension; with me, unhappily,
matter of living knowledge. I am like a man who knows the
plague, because he has been in the East, where he witnessed
its ravages; you only know it from description—and easily

may it be understood why I shudder when I hear persons speak of the plague with trifling flippancy, or courting the appalling distemper to come and make its pleasant home among us, as a sweet blessing which Providence has never yet vouchsafed to us.

There are those who seem to imagine that the Union might be broken up and a new confederacy be formed with the ease and precision with which the glazier breaks his brittle substance along the line which his tiny diamond has drawn—forgetting that no great institution, and, least of all, a country, has ever broken up or can break up in peace, and without a struggle commensurate to its own magnitude; and that when vehement passion dashes down a noble mirror, no one can hope to gather a dozen well-framed looking-glasses from the ground.

There are those even who think that the lines along which our Union will split are ready-marked like the grooved lines in some soft substance, intended from the beginning to be broken into parts for ultimate use.

There are those who speak of the *remedy* of secession—a remedy, as amputation would be a remedy, indeed, to cure a troublesome corn, or as cutting one's throat would remedy a migraine.

There are those, even, it seems to me, who have first rashly conceived of secession as a remedy, and now adhere to it as the end and object to be attained, when they are shown that it would not cure the evils complained of, but, on the contrary, would induce others, infinitely greater, and infinitely more numerous. They fall into the common error of getting so deeply interested in the means, that the object for the obtaining of which the means was first selected is forgotten. But though the error be of daily occurrence, it is a fearful one in this case, because the consequence would be appalling. They almost remind us of those good people in Tuscany, who had contracted so great a fondness for St. Romualdus, that when the saint had concluded to remove from among them, they resolved, in a grave town-meeting, to slay their patron saint, so that they might have at least his bones, and worship them as sacred relics.

We have heard much of secession. It is still daily dinning in our ears. What is secession? Is it revolution, or is it a lawful remedy to which a state is permitted to resort in right of its own sovereignty? Many persons—and there are some of high authority in other matters among them—maintain that even though it might not be expedient in the present case, it cannot be denied that the right of seceding belongs to every state. I have given all the attention and applied all the earnest study that I am capable of to this subject; and everything—our history, the framing of our Constitution, the correspondence of the framers, the conduct of our country, the actions of our states—all prove to my mind that such is not the case. It has been often asserted that the states are sovereign; and they would not be so could they not, among other things, withdraw from the Union whenever they think fit. This is purely begging the question. The question is what sovereignty is, and what, in particular, it means when the term is applied to our confederated states. No word is used in more different applications than this term sovereign; but in no sense, whatever width and breadth be given to it in this or in any other case, does it mean absolute and unlimitable power, if we speak of men. There is but one absolute ruler, one true sovereign. Unlimited power is not for men; and the legal sage, Sir Edward Coke, went so far as to declare, in the memorable debates on the petition of rights, that "sovereignty is no parliamentary word." This is not the place where so subtle and comprehensive a subject can be thoroughly discussed, but I may be permitted to touch upon a few points which may be examined here without inconvenience.

What is right for one state must needs be right for all the others. As to South Carolina, we can just barely imagine the possibility of her secession, owing to her situation near the border of the sea. But what would she have said a few years ago, or what indeed would she say now—I speak of

South Carolina, less the secessionists—if a state of the interior, say Ohio, were to vindicate the presumed right of secession, and to declare that, being tired of a republican government, she prefers to establish a monarchy with some prince, imported, all dressed and legitimate, from that country where princes grow in abundance, and whence Greece, Belgium, and Portugal have been furnished with ready-made royalties—what would we say? We would simply say, this cannot be and must not be. In forming the Union we have each given up some attributes, to receive, in turn, advantages of the last importance; and we have in consequence so shaped and balanced all our systems that no member can withdraw without deranging and embarrassing all, and ultimately destroying the whole.

But does not the Constitution say that every power not granted in that instrument shall be reserved for each state? Assuredly it does. But this very provision is founded upon the supposition of the existence of two powers—the general and the state governments. The Constitution is intended to regulate the affairs between them; secession, however, annihilates one party—the general government—so far as the seceding state is concerned. The supposition that the Constitution itself contains the tacit acknowledgment of the right of secession would amount to an assumption that a principle of self-destruction had been infused by its own makers into the very instrument which constructs the government. It would amount to much the same provision which was contained in the first democratic constitution of France, namely, that if government acts against the law, every citizen has the duty to take up arms against *it.* This was, indeed, declaring Jacobinical democracy tempered by revolution, as a writer has called Turkey a despotism tempered by regicide.

And can we imagine that men so sagacious, so far-seeing, on the one hand, and so thoroughly schooled by experience on the other, as the framers of our Constitution were, have just omitted, by some oversight, to speak on so important a point? One of the greatest jurists of Germany said to me at Frankfort, when the Constituent Parliament was there assembled, of which he was a member: "The more I study your Constitution, the more I am amazed at the wise forecast of its makers and the manly forbearance which prevented them from entering into any unnecessary details, so easily embarrassing at a later period." They would not deserve this praise, or, in fact, our respect, had they been guilty of a neglect such as has been supposed. Can we, in our sober senses, imagine that they believed in the right of secession when they did not even stipulate a fixed time necessary to give notice of a contemplated secession,—knowing, as they did, quite as well as we do, that not even a common treaty of defence or offence—no, not even one of trade and amity—is ever entered into by independent powers, without stipulating the period which must elapse between informing the other parties of an intended withdrawal and the time when it actually can take place ; and when they knew perfectly well that, unless such a provision is contained in treaties, all international law interprets them as perpetual,—when they knew that not even two merchants join in partnership without providing for the period necessary to give notice of an intended dissolution of the house ? It seems to me preposterous to suppose it. The absence of all mention of secession must be explained on the same ground on which the omission of parricide in the first Roman penal laws was explained—no one thought of such a deed.

Those that so carefully drew up our Constitution cannot be blamed for not having thought of this extravagance, because it had never been dreamt of in any confederacy, ancient, mediæval, or modern. Never has there existed an architect so presumptuous as to consider himself able to build an arch equal to its purpose and use, yet each stone of which should be so loose that it might be removed at any time, leaving a sort of abstract arch, fit to support abstractions only—as useful in reality as the famous knife without a blade, of which the handle was missing. Those that insist on the right of secession from the Union must necessarily admit the correlative right of expulsion on the part of the Union. Are they prepared for this?

If the Constitution says nothing on secession; if it cannot be supposed to exist by implication; if we cannot deduce it from the idea of sovereignty, it may be worth our while to inquire into the common law of mankind on this subject. The common law in this case is history.

Now, I have taken the pains of examining all confederacies of which we have any knowledge. In none of the many Greek confederacies did the right of secession exist, so far as we can trace their fundamental principles. In some rare cases an unfaithful member may have been expelled. But in the most important of all these confederacies, and in that which received the most complete organization, resembling, in many points, our own—in the Achæan League—there existed no right of secession, and this is proved by the following case: When the Romans had obtained the supremacy over Hellas, and Greece was little more than a province of Rome, the Ætolians respectfully waited upon the Roman commissioner, Gallus, to solicit permission to secede from the League. He sent them to the senate, and the secessionists obtained at Rome the permission to withdraw—no "leading case," I suppose, for Americans. The Amphictyonic Council allowed of no secession. It was Pan-Hellenic, and never meant to be otherwise. The mediæval leagues of the Lombard cities, of the Swabian cities, and of the Rhenish cities, permitted no spontaneous withdrawal; but the fortunes of the fiercest wars waged against them by the nobility would occasionally wrench off a member and produce disruptions. The great Hanseatic League, which, by its powerful union of distant cities, became one of the most efficient agents in civilizing Europe, and which, as Mr. Huskisson stated in Parliament, carried trade and manufacture into England, knew nothing of secession until the year 1630, when the princes, greedy for the treasures of her cities, had decreed her destruction, and forced many members to secede. This is no leading case either.

The Swiss Confederacy, the Germanic Federation, knew

and know nothing of secession; nor did the United States of the Netherlands—so much studied by some of our framers, and by Washington among them—admit the withdrawal of any single state.

All these confederacies consisted of a far looser web than ours; none had a federal government comparable to ours; yet they never contemplated such a right. And should we do so —we, with a firmer union, a better understanding of politics, a nobler consciousness of our mission as a nation, and greater blessings at stake? Should we, indeed, of all men that ever united into federations, treat our government, by which we excel all other united governments, as a sort of political picnic to which the invited guest may go and carry his share of the viands or not, as he thinks fit, or the humor may move him? Are all the rights on the side of the states—that is, the individuals—and all the obligations, and obligations only, on the side of the confederacy—that is, the whole? This doctrine is the French theory of excessive individual right and personal sovereignty applied to states, and naught else.

I ask, will any one who desires secession for the sake of bringing about a Southern Confederacy, honestly aver that he would insist upon a provision in the new constitution securing the full right of secession whenever it may be desired by any member of the expected confederacy?

To secede, then, requires revolution. Revolution for what? To remedy certain evils. And how are they to be remedied? It is a rule laid down among all the authorities of international law and ethics, that to be justified in going to war it is not sufficient that right be on our side. We must also have a fair prospect of success in our favor. This rule applies with far greater force to revolutions. The Jews who rose against Vespasian had all the right, I dare say, on their side; but their undertaking was not a warrantable one for all that. We, however—should we have sufficient right on our side for plunging into a revolution—for letting loose a civil war? Does the system against which we should rise contain within its own bosom no peaceful, lawful remedies?

We are often told that our forefathers plunged into a revolution, why should not we? Even if the two cases were comparable, which they are obviously not, I would ask on the other hand, Are we to have a revolution every fifty years? Give me the Muscovite Czar rather than live under such a government, if government it could be called. I am a good swimmer, but I should not like to spend my life in whirlpools. And does the question of right or wrong, of truth and justice, go for nothing in revolutions?

Nor would the probability of success be in our favor, since it is certain that secession cannot take place without war, and this war must end in one or the other of two ways. It must either kindle a general conflagration, or we must suffer, single-handed, the consequences of our rashness—bitter if we succeed in lopping ourselves off from the trunk, bitter if we cannot succeed. Unsuccessful revolutions are not only misfortunes, they become stigmas. And what if the conflagration becomes general? Let us remember that it is a rule which pervades all history, because it pervades every house, that the enmity of contending parties is implacable and venomous in the same degree as they have previously stood near each other, or as nature intended the relation of good will to exist between them. It is the secret of all civil and religious wars: it is the secret of divided families: it is the explanation of unrelenting hatred between those who once were bosom friends. Our war would be the repetition of the Peloponnesian War, or of the German Thirty Years' War, with still greater bitterness between the enemies, because it would be far more unnatural. It would shed the dismal glare of barbarism on the nineteenth century. Have they that long for separation forgotten that England, at first behind Germany, France, Italy, and Spain, rapidly outstripped all, because earlier united, without permitting the crown to absorb the people's rights? The separation of the South from the North would speedily produce a manifold disrupture, and bring us back to a heptarchy, which was no government of seven, but a state of things where many worried all. If there be a book which I would recommend, before all others, to read at this juncture, that book is Thucydides. It reads as if it had been written to make *us* pause; as if the orators introduced there had spoken expressly for our benefit; as if the fallacies of our days had all been used and exposed at that early time; and as if in that book a very mirror were held up for our admonition. Or we may peruse the history of cumbered, ailing Germany, deprived of unity, dignity, strength, wealth, peace, and liberty, because her unfortunate princes have pursued, with never-ceasing eagerness, what is called in that country *particularism*—that is, hostility of the parts to the whole of Germany, and after the downfall of Napoleon preferred the salvation of their petty sovereignties, conferred upon them by Napoleon, to the grandeur, peace, and strength of their common country. The history of Germany, the battle-field of Europe for these three centuries, will tell you what idol we should worship, were we to toss our blessings to the winds, and were we to deprive mankind of the proud example inviting to imitation.

I have already gone far beyond the proper limits of a communication for the purpose for which the present one is intended, and must abruptly conclude where so much may yet be said.

I will only add that I, for one, dare not do anything toward the disruption of the Union. Situated, as we are, between Europe and Asia, on a fresh continent, I see the finger of God in it. I believe our destiny to be a high, a great, and a solemn one, before which the discussions now agitating us shrink into much smaller dimensions than they appear if we pay exclusive attention to them. I have come to this country, and pledged a voluntary oath to be faithful to it, and I will keep this oath. This is my country from the choice of manhood, and not by the chance of birth. In my position, as a servant of the state, in a public institution of education, I have imposed upon myself the duty of using my influence with the young neither one way nor the other in this discussion. I have scrupulously and conscientiously adhered to it in all my teaching and intercourse. There is not a man or a youth that can gainsay this.

But I am a man and a citizen, and as such I have a right, or the duty, as the case may be, to speak my mind and my inmost convictions on solemn occasions before my fellow-citizens, and I have thus not hesitated to put down these remarks. Take them, gentlemen, for what they may be worth. They are, at any rate, sincere and fervent; and, whatever judgment others may pass upon them, or whatever attacks may be levelled against them, no one will be able to say that they can have been made to promote any individual advantages. God save the commonwealth! God save the common land!

AMENDMENTS OF THE CONSTITUTION,

SUBMITTED TO THE CONSIDERATION OF

THE AMERICAN PEOPLE. [1865.]

(PAPER No. 83 OF THE LOYAL PUBLICATION SOCIETY.)

The bantling—I had liked to have said monster—Sovereignty (meaning state sovereignty).
—WASHINGTON.
A nation without a national government is an awful spectacle.—ALEXANDER HAMILTON.
Secession is the legitimate consequence of state sovereignty.—JEFFERSON DAVIS.
The ultimate and absolute sovereignty of each state.—ALEXANDER H. STEPHENS.

PREFACE.

WHEN those cathedrals were building which the Middle Ages have be-
queathed to modern times, every inhabitant of the surrounding country used to
be called upon to contribute his share, and many a poor man, who could give
no money to pay the masons' wages, went himself and paid some weeks of his
own labor, with hod or trowel, as his share toward the rearing of the great
fabric intended for the service of all—high or humble.

When those fairs in behalf of the Sanitary Commission were planned on a
scale, and crowned with a success, which form an ennobling characteristic of
our period of bitter strife, all—the wealthy and the needy—freely gave their
share to these large markets, by which millions upon millions have flowed to the
Commission, to be changed by them into balmy relief for our wounded soldiers
and the bleeding foes who fall into our hands. All have helped to swell this
steady stream of mercy—deep, wide, clear, as Dante calls the stream of Virgil's
eloquence.

We live in a time of necessary and searching reform. We cannot avoid its
duty. Things have already changed. They must be readjusted. The harmony
of the great polity has been rudely disturbed; it must be restored in some way.
The civil war, imperiling the existence of our country, has laid bare the roots
of evils in our polity, and shown what some elementary errors must lead to when
legitimately carried out. We have discovered that a part of our foundation has
given way, and that repairs are needed. Let every one contribute his share to
the reconstruction—be it much or be it little, so that he helps in the great work
of repairing the mansion of freedom. I offer this contribution to my country's
cause.

If what I give does not prove acceptable in the form in which it is proffered,
these pages will, nevertheless, lead to reflections which will not fail to be useful,
and may prove fruitful.

FRANCIS LIEBER.

138

AMENDMENTS OF THE CONSTITUTION.

WHEN, shortly before secession was openly proclaimed by our southern states, the writer of these pages had concluded a lecture on the Constitution of the United States, one of his hearers, a young man, apparently of age, asked him, with modest ingenuousness, whether he did not believe that the Constitution owed its origin to inspiration. The ensuing conversation elicited the remark on the part of the inquirer that he had grown up in the belief that the fundamental law of our country had been inspired, or " very nearly so." The youth was well educated, and the son of a very respectable family; yet the confusion of ideas which he evinced was less startling to the lecturer than it would have been, had the latter not been somewhat accustomed both to the extravagant and unhistorical exaltation of the Constitution, and to the illogical phrase, "all but inspired"—self-contradictory words of no unfrequent use either in England or here.[1]

The framers of the Constitution were probably as wise and resolute a set of men as ever met in high national council. Some of them were stamped with that greatness of mind which enables a man to comprehend the past, to penetrate the connection of things where for the common eye none but detached, though crowded, details present themselves, and to divine with

---

[1] The writer recollects no more surprising instance of this self-contradiction, than that which he met with in one of the leading British reviews. Paley was there called, "that all but inspired Paley." If an English reviewer calls Paley all but inspired, an American youth may be pardoned for considering the framers of our Constitution wholly so.

that gift which sees things unseen, and belongs alike to the great statesman, historian, inventor, philosopher, and poet. Their work is full of dignity, wisdom, and sincerity ; but their greatest act—and, so far, the greatest act of our history—is their manly acknowledgment of the utter failure of the Articles of Confederation, which most of them had adopted only about ten years before, and the glorious engrafting of a complete national representative government on a league which they themselves had deemed sufficient to answer, in the new state of things, the wants of the people and the growing demands of our circumstances and conditions—the requisites, in fine, of our assigned place in the family of nations. They themselves loudly denounced the Articles of Confederation ; and most of those who had taken a leading share in the building up of our Constitution on the ruins of the Articles, expressed a limited satisfaction with it when they recommended it to their respective legislatures. The record of their debates while framing the Constitution shows that they were men as we are ; and the debates in the several state conventions on the adoption of the Constitution prove very forcibly that our forefathers considered the framers far from infallible.[1]

The Constitution itself expresses the probability of necessary amendments, and, far wiser than those who would ascribe matchless perfection to it, prescribes the systematic and lawful means of effecting them, in order to prevent violent eruptions, which needs will always take place when the enclosing and unplastic form is no longer able to contain the swelling life within. In the course of some fifteen years after the adoption of the Constitution twelve amendments of great importance were actually made according to the prescribed method. Some of these were of a novel kind ; others incorporated with the Constitution great principles of the English Bill of Rights,[2]

---

[1] A letter of Josiah Quincy, Sr., to J. A. Stevens, Jr., published in Opinions of Prominent Men concerning the Great Questions of the Times, New York 1863 [Loyal National League], contains a remarkable passage on the opinion entertained by the framers of the Constitution on their own work.

[2] For instance, Articles 3 and 8 of the Amendments.

almost looking, in their place among the amendments, as if they had been forgotten in the original framing of the great instrument. In less than ten years from the same period the Virginia and Kentucky resolutions were promulgated, and proved, at the very least, that their framers, among whom there were statesmen who had been prominent in the general convention at Philadelphia in 1787, thought that the great Constitution was not framed with sufficient clearness, and required solemn declaratory interpretation. If the authors of the Virginia and Kentucky resolutions did not mean this, the only alternative left would be that they intended to impose extra-constitutional amendments on the instrument, which would have been unconstitutional, and indeed revolutionary.

All laws must change in course of time—whether they form the framework of a people's polity, or are strictly municipal laws, or constitute the laws of nations—laws of peace or laws of war; for laws are authoritative rules of action (or rules adopted by common consent and usage) for living men banded, more or less closely, in communities, and the condition of life is change—change for the better or change for the worse. So long as life lasts so long is there change. Cessation of organic change is death. The form of laws may indeed remain the same in the statute-book, or in a fundamental constitution; but if the conditions and relations of life materially change, the force of circumstances renders an application of the same formula in a sense differing from the original intention unavoidable, and in the practical use and application of a law lies its essential character as law, not in the verbal formula in which it was expressed, or in the letters of certain terms. Life will change and must change; and if man does not alter the law according to the altered circumstances, the direct and positive demand of the latter forces him into an avowed or hypocritical change of its application. Reality is sovereign and will allow no master. Montesquieu says, indeed, that we ought to approach the change of laws with a trembling hand, which may perhaps be expressed less figuratively thus, that all conscious and direct change must show distinct and proportionately urgent cause why it should be resorted to; while existence, without this proof of cause, is sufficient warrant for continuance. This alone is wise and truthful conservatism. That conservatism which consists in an unalterable adhesion to that which *is*, merely because it *is* —a conservatism which would bring ruin to every individual in his health and house—is revolutionary in matters of state —rebellion against God's great laws of life, of enlargement and elevation of our kind. It is as unreasonable and destructive as the thirst for change, simply because it is change. Both stolid conservatism and arrogant aggression lead to ruin. The history of our race confirms this on every page. How many communities have been irretrievably lost, how many empires have gone down never to rise again, because changes were attempted when it was too late; and happy, indeed, must that country be called where necessary and fundamental changes can take place without convulsive violence or hazardous revolutions, and whose citizens are sufficiently wise and candid to make these changes while there is yet time for them.

Laws are in this respect like languages. That tongue would not be a living language which could not expand and adapt itself to new relations, things, and wider or minuter thoughts. The lexicographer who thinks that, by his dictionary, he can shut the gate upon his language and imprison it, and the forward and licentious innovator, are alike presumptuous, and equally to be discountenanced. A law, a constitution, however important, remains a means, as government and the state themselves, although indispensable to man, are means to obtain things still higher, and the object must not be sacrificed to the means.

In glancing at the history of England we find that hardly fifty years have elapsed at any period of that old commonwealth without some fundamental change, the pronouncing of some great constitutional principle by the bench, or the passing of some constitutional statute. Within the last and present centuries such constitutional changes have followed each other in even quicker succession. The decision that the king cannot levy imposts on imported commodities without an act of parliament to that end, the union of Scotland with England, and the union of the legislature of Ireland with that of Great Britain, the reform bill, the *habeas corpus* act, and all the acts and decisions from the time of Magna Charta, which English writers exhibit when they desire to present to us the British constitution, are such constitutional changes. Yet England has had her revolution—that is to say, a violent struggle which arose out of the altered state of circumstances, and for the peaceful adjustment of which no means seemed to be at hand. England's life, society, and mind had changed; and this civil struggle took place in spite of the fact that England has a purely cumulative constitution—possibly, some may say, *because* it has a cumulative constitution; by which we mean that that which is called the English constitution consists of the aggregate of those usages, principles, and institutions of the common law, decisions of the highest courts, and statutes or bills of rights as well as pacts with ruling dynasties—which the English consider of fundamental importance in their great polity, every one of which, however, may, according to theory, be changed or abolished by parliament; for parliament, including in this case the king, is omnipotent, as the English political parlance has it.

We, with an enacted Constitution—that is to say, with a Constitution distinctly limited and enacted by a higher authority than congress and president, themselves the creatures of the Constitution—are not thereby freed from changes going on around us and within us, for the law of life and change is even above that national sovereignty which enacts the Constitution, as the law of nature and nature's changes is above the rules, be they ever so wise, which man has adopted to make her administer to his wants. We, with an enacted Constitution, must make amendments of the Constitution itself when necessary, while the English may effect the change by an act of parliament, which is far easier, but, on that account, also occasionally more dangerous. We must take together the advantages and disadvantages of cumulative and enacted (or written) constitutions, and use that which history has given as wisely and as best we can.

The framers of our Constitution were finite and imperfect beings; men like ourselves, to whom the future state of our country was not revealed. Had it been revealed, no laws could have been framed in human language fitted alike for their present and our future state. And if a parliament of heavenly beings had decreed our Constitution, none could have been devised that could have been equally applicable to all periods to come. Saying that changes in our Constitution are necessary is not saying that we are wiser than those who framed it, as little as legislators who amend an act or a charter declare themselves thereby superior beings to those who first enacted the law or charter, while such oft-repeated phrases as "the Constitution is good enough for me," are merely the vulgar expressions of short-sighted indolence or undutiful shrinking from glaring dangers.

The axiom of mechanics, that nothing is stronger than its weakest point, may not wholly apply to laws and constitutions; but the lapse of so long a period, with its wear and tear, has revealed feeble points and flaws in the cast of our fundamental law which demand close attention and timely repair, lest the injury become irreparable. Rights and duties are inseparable correlatives, in whatever sphere the one or the other may exist. Indeed, the idea of the one implies the idea of the other. We cannot imagine rights without corresponding duties, nor can we conceive of duties without corresponding rights; and if the living have the right to frame or alter their laws, they have likewise the bounden duty to do so when necessary. Shall a house not be repaired, though it have become ever so damp, simply because an ancestor built it?

It is a remarkable fact, which the historian will find it difficult to explain, unless he succeed in making himself well acquainted with the psychology of the southern politics— that the strictest "constructionists" have acknowledged, more, probably, than any other Americans, that great changes are actually going on, and have endeavored to infuse their opinions accordingly into our polity, or, worse than all, have justified armed resistance on the ground of such changes.

The Constitution says nothing whatsoever concerning free or slave states, yet Mr. Calhoun endeavored to have the principle acknowledged that there ought to be in the senate an equal representation of slave and free states, after which, once established, states should be admitted into the Union by couples—one free and one slave state at a time. Not to speak of the great oversight that slavery itself has never been a stable institution in our country or elsewhere, but has always melted away before civilization, no more radical or novel change could have been introduced into our Constitution, or no more extraordinary, hyper-constitutional principle could have been adopted.

We have been told by a chief justice on the high bench of the United States, that although colored people joined in our struggle for independence, and although the Constitution and the early laws do not declare that the government of the United States is not made for the descendant of the African, yet such had been the development of ideas that it must now be declared to be the spirit of the Constitution; from which unhistorical, hard, illogical, and illegal decision, so much political cynicism was soon after evolved that, besides holding the unhistorical fact that the government of the United States was established *by* white people alone, the illogical conclusion was also drawn that, therefore, it is *for* white people alone.[1]

---

[1] It does not seem to occur to the proclaimer of this political axiom that the government was not established by whites alone, inasmuch as blacks had the right to vote in some southern states as well as in the north when the conventions were elected to adopt or to reject the Constitution. But let us dismiss this argument—were not all the people who established the government males of age, and is the government, therefore, not for females or minors? Could not the same argument be used with reference to the state constitutions, and most forcibly so the constitutions of slave states? Is, then, the slave a being out of the pale of all law? Is he neither protected nor responsible? The laws of the

It would almost appear as if the idea of a government with limited powers turned, in the heads of these publicists, into the idea of a government for a limited number; and who has ever heard of such a thing as a government for a class, or a limited number, or for one of the races living in the same country, and being subject to the same government? What more radical change of the Constitution can be imagined than the one implied in this exclusion theory?

Mr. Stephens, the vice-president of the so-called Confederacy, declared, at the beginning of the rebellion, that it could not be denied that the universal opinion at the time of our revolution was hostile to slavery, and that a government was established into which this opinion was infused; but that since then negro slavery had come to be acknowledged as a social, moral, and political benefit. The southern states, therefore, were right to separate from the north in order to pursue a civilization founded on slavery.

A distinguished writer on the history of the American Constitution declared, in an elaborate address delivered when our civil troubles began, that although the people as a whole had adopted the Constitution, it could not be denied that the idea of state sovereignty had developed itself since that time, and that, according to this idea, the seceding states had a right to claim—we forget exactly what. He has only been men-

---

slave states contradict this. Even in the feudal age, the very period of privilege and exclusiveness, was justice ever refused to a creature—even to a roaming gypsy—on the ground that his forefathers had no hand in establishing the government? Do not the adherents of this political extravagance see to what enormities their theory would lead in the hundreds of cases in which governments have been established by conquest, conspiracy, or *coup d'état*, and if they abandon the overruling principle that men are inherently destined and ordained to live in society, that *Ubi Societas ibi jus est*, and that a government, no matter what its origin may be, is necessary for all, and finds its right to rule in this primary necessity, and this inherent necessity carries along with it even the obligation of temporary obedience to governments *de facto*? Have they never reflected that their theory, literally followed, would dissolve all society, or carry us back to a state of things even worse than Asiatic despotism, under which, at least according to its theory, every owner of real property is at all events a tenant at will?

tioned as an additional evidence that persons of an opposite opinion to ours have manifested the belief that great changes take place in spite of all theories regarding constitutions and their origin, and that those who maintain most stoutly the matchless perfection of the instrument have generally been given most to unconstitutional theories. This is a noticeable fact, to be kept in mind in all candid and earnest discussions on the Constitution; nor ought the fact to be passed over in silence that the very party which most loudly vociferated for the Constitution, and its friends in the north, habitually rail at the Declaration of Independence, sometimes as a well-meaning manifesto of visionary philanthropists in the spirit of the Utopian philosophy of the century, sometimes, and very vehemently, as an irreligious and pestiferous exhalation from an infidel period. I speak of facts, and might encumber my pages with many citations even of quite a recent date.

Yet, while the Declaration forms no part of the Constitution, it will not be denied that in some and important respects it may be considered as the American Bill of Rights; and remarkable, indeed, would be the commentator who, drawing upon the Articles of Confederation for his comments, should decline going one step farther and including the Declaration as one of the means for right interpretation.

Has then, our country greatly and essentially changed since the adoption of our Constitution? We believe that no country or people of antiquity or modern times has changed in circumstances and condition, in national consciousness, and in a great public opinion, which is " the mother of effects," as this country and this people, within the last sixty years, and after a great rebellion has now lasted several years. ‹ The heat of a civil war of such magnitude would alone be sufficient to ripen thoughts and characteristics which may have been in a state of incipiency before; a contest so comprehensive and so probing makes people abandon many things, to which they had clung by mere tradition without feeling their sharp reality, and causes them suddenly to see rugged ground or deep abysses where from a distant view nothing but level plains had appeared.

The extension of our territory from sea to sea, the magnitude of our commerce, the unparalleled growth of our population, the internal union and mutual necessity of all its parts, our relation to foreign nations, our literature, our school systems, our wealth, and our knowledge of far greater though undeveloped wealth; the consciousness of nationality on the one hand, and the development, on the other, of an extravagant idea of state rights; the outspoken disgust at slavery, its dangerous character here, and its exaltation as a blessing there—who can tell all the changes which have taken place, for weal or woe, within the last half century in this country? Nearness magnifies, but we have endeavored calmly to review the history of other nations, and we can find no instance of so great a change within so short a time, and in so many respects, as ours. No wonder, then, that it is believed necessary to amend in some essential points that law which fundamentally regulates the policy of this altered society. And may not the question be put, whether ever a society has come out of a civil war without material changes in its fundamental law, or whether a civil war is of itself not sufficient proof that practical changes have taken place, and require corresponding changes in the political framework of society?

We cannot allow the confusion of ideas which ascribes the superior experience or wisdom generally possessed by a living father compared to that of his son to be carried over to ancestors and past generations, which, indeed, are with reference to the living ones—the younger and less experienced. There are doubtless ages and periods which a rare combination of circumstances makes peculiarly apt for the development of certain great ideas and the establishment of certain institutions in one or the other great spheres of human action—classical periods of taste, of science, of discovery, of patriotism, of freedom, of literature, and of religion; and the essential progress of civilization depends, in a great measure, upon the cherishing and treasuring of that which has thus been gained for mankind, under peculiarly favorable circumstances, or by great suffering, for further development and wider culture. The age at which our forefathers framed the Constitution, and the state of things in America, were, in some respects, peculiarly propitious; but, as it has been stated before, they had not the power, nor had they the right, if they could have had the power, to forestall the changes which might become necessary in the course of this country's history, as little as Magna Charta has or could have forestalled the constitutional development of England. The living have their rights and duties as great and as binding as the dead had, when they were the living.

The question then presents itself to us, if we have the right to change the Constitution, is there any necessity of altering and of amending it in such a manner as to adapt it to the new state of things? Three facts, it would seem, sufficiently answer this question. The country has changed. Civil war has broken out, amazing both as to its magnitude and the entire absence of any of those causes which have produced civil wars heretofore—no galling tyranny, no oppression of certain classes, no religious persecution or disability, no scaffold for patriotism, no expelled government or exiled dynasty, no hunger or other physical suffering, no disproportion of conscious power and lack of share in the government, no superior yet unrepresented wealth, industry, knowledge, or numbers,— nothing of all this has existed with us or been advanced in justification of so fearful a rebellion. And the third reason: This vast strife has already produced, within three short years, changes which are as comprehensive as they are final. Many great and elementary things are out of joint in our polity;· they must be readjusted; new relations must be defined and settled, and constitutionally encompassed. We cannot shirk the duty, even were we unmanly enough to desire it.

If this is acknowledged, the farther question is, what are the necessary changes? What must be defined that has been left undefined by our ancestors? What must be added?

We cannot discover this in a more direct way than by ascertaining two things: first, what has brought about this contest, unique in history; and, secondly, of what points may it may be said, without contradiction, that the overwhelming majority of our people are agreed upon with the fullest, deepest national conviction, as an unalterable effect of this fiery war?

The rebellion has been brought about by two things—by slavery and by state-rights doctrine—understanding by the latter that disjunctive doctrine according to which each portion of our country, called a state, is sovereign in the highest sense—allowing us no nationality, no country, and, consequently, no national government; but ascribing to that which we call the national government the character, not even of a league, not even of a common partnership, but of a mere temporary agreement from which any one of the partners may withdraw at any moment, even with greater ease than a commercial partnership may be dissolved—a character which has never been ascribed to any confederacy in antiquity or in modern times, not even to the present Germanic Confederacy, which, nevertheless, avowedly consists of many sovereign monarchs, and four politically unimportant cities.

All, without exception, acknowledge that slavery and state-rights doctrine are the causes of this rebellion—all people of the United States, South and North, whether in favor of slavery or abhorring it; whether hugging disjunctive provincialism to their breasts as the most inspiring political idea, or having faith in the grandeur of a national destiny and necessity appointed by Providence for his own great ends in the progress of our kind and the ascending path of history.

So distinctly is slavery felt to be the main cause of this rebellion, and so openly is it acknowledged, that not only has it been claimed as the one dividing mark from the first day of fierce rebellion; so that, despite of this very state-rights doctrine, to this day Kentuckians and Missourians sit in the congress of the so-called Confederacy, although the states of Kentucky and Missouri have never declared themselves for the severing of our country; but the very beginning of the proclamation of the " Congress to the People of the Confederate States," officially issued at the adjournment of congress (February, 1864), is in these words : " Compelled by a long series of oppressive and tyrannical acts, culminating at last in the election of a president and vice-president by a party confessedly sectional and hostile to the South and her institutions, these states withdrew from the former Union, and formed a new Confederate alliance."

" Her institutions," in the plural, means, of course, the one institution of slavery, for the so-called " South" was characterized by no other institution. Nay, more, this institution alone gives a political meaning to the otherwise purely geographical and relative term *South ;* and " being hostile" to this institution (which, by the way, was a gross exaggeration) is called the culmination of a long series of oppressive and tyrannical acts. We may judge, then, of the dire oppressiveness and tyranny of these acts, when the series of their iniquity reaches its highest point in hostility to slavery, which in this case tapers off in the attenuated declaration of the president, before he was elected, that he was in favor of no farther extension of slavery. The American Tarquin, the northern Hippias, the godless Louis XI. of this country, the truculent Gessler of these modern days, had committed the unheard-of enormity of expressing his opinion that slavery had better not be extended; whereupon a " down-trodden" people must rise, break their oaths, tear their own history into shreds, cause torrents of blood to flow, and spread misery and untruth over millions and millions.

The profound student always welcomes the plain and bold enunciation, especially in a documentary form, of an idea or theory of wide effect, whether vile or noble, and in this view there will be many who will acknowledge their obligation to those who issued the latest—may it be the last!—manifesto of the rebel congress.

If slavery is universally felt and acknowledged to be the main cause of the present war, the fact is also to be observed that never before in all history has a single institution been considered possessed of equally distinguishing power; and never before has any institution whatever been declared so intangible by reform, as slavery is held to be by its modern defenders. The monarchial government and the republican government have been allowed to be freely discussed without stigmatizing the advocate of the one or the other as a vile and hateful being. The trial by jury is considered by most of us as essential to our liberty, but we do not denounce a man who declares his preference for other judicial methods in civil cases as an enemy of mankind. So soon as slavery is acknowledged in a state, no matter how few slaves there may be, it is by common consent acknowledged as a society characteristically differing from others which allow no property in living human creatures. Nothing can show more forcibly the damaging and isolating, estranging and embittering character of this deplorable anachronism.

As a third cause of the rebellion, must be stated the deep and, as it turned out, fevering jealousy of the South, at perceiving that civilization, number of population, the arts, education, the ships and trade, schools and churches, literature and law, manufactures, agriculture, inventions, wealth, comfort, and power, were rapidly finding their home at the North, to the great disparagement of the South, weighed down by slavery, which, nevertheless, the South would not recognize as an evil. All periods of such developments or changes of power and influence from one portion of a country to another, or from one class to another, have been periods of heart-burning; but in our case the vaunting pride of the receding or lagging portion forbade them to acknowledge the cause, as has been occasionally done in other countries. This third cause, however, is of a psychological character, and not a directly political cause. It cannot be treated of in connection with the subject of constitutional amendments, although it greatly aids us in seeing the true character of slavery.

As to those points on which our nation is now fully agreed, and which must be taken as past discussion, plainly settled and firmly established, all the occasional, individual, and, therefore, boisterous reclaimants to the contrary notwithstanding, we feel sure that we write calmly, as a truthful man ought to write, and undisturbed by the magnifying effect of that which is near and present, when we say they are the following:

That we form, and ought to form, a nation; and that we will on no account allow the integrity of our country and the nationality of our united people to be broken in upon, cost what it may:

That a portion—a state—is not superior in attributes, or the source of power, to the whole—the country:

That secession is treason, and that this civil war *is* rebellion on the part of the seceders—no matter how those who have rebelled may, for the sake of humanity, have been individually treated; that the adoption of the rules and usages of war in the contest of a rebellion implies, no-ways and in no degree, an acknowledgment of the rebellious government:

That slavery, in a variety of corrupting and estranging ways, is the main cause of this rebellion; that it alone distinguishes the " South" from the " North," otherwise perfectly homogeneous portions; that slavery, therefore, ought to be eradicated, and that the effects of this war have already gone far to extirpate this calamitous institution, received from paganism, abolished by Christianity, renewed by fierce cupidity, and, in latter days, deified by professed Christians:

That it is politically impious to withhold from a race or portion of the population the common benefits for which governments are established—justice and protection; and that it is a fearful rebellion against God's own ends, who made man a social being, to say that because a certain set or class of men established a government, therefore the government is for the benefit of those who established it alone—a theory which would justify the most appalling tyranny in those successful generals who with their hosts have often founded governments—a theory far more appalling than Louis the Fourteenth's *L'état c'est moi;* for he acknowledged, at least, that such was the case because God so willed it for the benefit and protection of all:[1]

---

[1] Developed later in the Politics of the Bible, by Bishop Bossuet, who had been appointed instructor of the Duke of Burgundy, heir apparent to Louis XIV., for whom this work was written.

That military victory, and victory alone, can now decide a *bona fide* overthrow of the opposing forces.

Reviewing, then, these points we shall find that amendments of the Constitution—at least political amendments—are chiefly required concerning slavery and the nationality of our government.

The mischief and ruin produced by the vague adoption of potent and comprehensive terms in spheres of high and vast action or thought have never been illustrated, outside of the ecclesiastical dominion and persecution, so sadly and on so large a scale as the gradual and unauthorized introduction of the term sovereignty has done in the history of our country. Never before has an erroneous theory borne more bitter fruits. The Constitution of the United States does not contain once the word sovereignty, studiously omitting it after it had been used in the Articles of Confederation; and only a few days ago[1] a notable member of congress spoke, in a solemn attack on the nationality of our government, repeatedly of the "local sovereignty" in the United States, reminding the student of history of the oath of fidelity which the stadtholder, in assuming his office, was obliged to take separately to each "sovereign city" of Holland and Friesland, and in other portions of that country, whose glorious career was early cut short by the morbid development of the disjunctive and centrifugal principle, not only of state rights, but of city rights, to the extinction of the national and centripetal principle. The Netherlands have passed through all the phases of state-rights doctrine long before us, but it led them to a change of government, not to a large and protracted civil war, although it plunged them into manifold disorders and civil heart-burnings.

The estates of Holland and West Friesland were displeased with the public prayers for the Prince of Orange, which some high Calvinistic ministers were gradually introducing, in the latter half of the seventeenth century, and in 1663 a decree

---

[1] February, 1864.

was issued ordaining to pray first of all "for their noble high mightinesses, the estates of Holland and West Friesland, as the true sovereign, and only sovereign power after God, in this province; next, for the estates of the other provinces, their allies, and for all the deputies in the assembly of the states general, and of the council of state." Here is our state-rights doctrine in full bloom long before our theorists were born, many of whom, indeed, boast of our state-rights doctrine as of something peculiarly American, new and beautiful.

No one is sovereign within the polity of the United States, taking the term in a practical and legal meaning, and no one ought to be sovereign. The United States are sovereign in an international sense; that is, they are equal to any foreign power or potentate, and have no superior on earth; while in a domestic sense, the people, that is, the totality of the nation, have the sovereign power, if they please to exercise it, to establish that government which they deem most appropriate for their circumstances and most corresponding to their own convictions of rights and freedom; but within the established polity of the United States no one, we repeat, is sovereign; has the right to claim sovereignty, or the power to exercise sovereignty. We should not be free men if any one had. Sir Edward Coke declared in the house of commons, when the Bill of Rights was under discussion, that the English law does not know the word sovereign, and well would it have been for our country if it never had slipped into our political terminology, or, at least, had been properly defined.

The old Articles of the Confederation contain indeed this passage:

" Each state retains its sovereignty, freedom, and independence, and every power, jurisdiction, and right which is not by this confederation expressly delegated to the United States, in congress assembled."

Sovereignty is either used in this case pleonastically to express the independence which had been proclaimed by the Declaration of Independence, or else the framers of the Articles fell into the error of attempting to establish a pure confederacy or league, or did not know how to help themselves after having severed their allegiance from the crown of England, at a time when all confederacies of antiquity and modern times had shown that they are inherently weak governments, inadequate to any one of the large demands of civilization, freedom, and independence, and at a time, too, when the national polity, with whatever variety, had become the normal political type of the existing historic period. When small communal polities impede and harass each other, the foundation of a confederacy is a progressive step in political civilization. Such were the Greek confederacies, inadequate as they soon proved themselves notwithstanding. The confederacy of the Iroquois in our country showed a higher political state in its members than that in which the isolated tribes lived; but it is the principle which *unites* the confederated members, not the principle which keeps them apart as so-called sovereign states, that shows the progress.[1]

When the Articles of Confederation were adopted, many confederacies had found already their grave; the Netherlands were descending; Switzerland was allowed to exist by her neighbors (she has now adopted in her general constitution many important points of union from the American Constitution); and Germany was presenting a deplorable spectacle of weakness by her confederacy of sovereign princes into which the empire had lapsed, and by her doctrine of "separatism," the term used in Germany in the last century for sejunctive state-rights doctrine.

Madison, therefore, wrote to Edmund Randolph, prior to the convention of 1787, under date of April 8, of that year,[2] these memorable words:

---

[1] A very interesting account of the confederacy of the Iroquois (which Mr. Calhoun mentioned, not without approbation, on account of the veto power of each single chief, resembling the individual vetoing power in the ancient Polish diet) was given by Mr. Henry R. Schoolcraft, in Senate Documents No. 24, 1846, separately published as Notes on the Iroquois, etc. New York: Bartlett & Welford, 1846.

[2] Elliott's Debates, etc., vol. v. p. 107, Philadelphia edition of 1859.

"I hold it for a fundamental point, that an individual independence of the states is utterly irreconcilable with the idea of an aggregate sovereignty. I think, at the same time, that a consolidation of the states into one simple republic is not less unattainable than it would be inexpedient. Let it be tried, then, whether any middle ground can be taken, which will at once support a due supremacy of the national authority, and leave in force the local authorities so far as they can be subordinately useful."

There is not a word of that mystic local sovereignty, or sovereignty of states, in this plain and wise passage.

Hamilton, who had expressed himself in the convention very strongly on national sovereignty,[1] uses on one occasion, in the Federalist, the term "residuary sovereignty" of the states, which has been used in favor of the state-rights doctrine by several of its advocates. But Hamilton was a national man, and of too penetrating a mind not to see that if the retaining of a certain amount of power in the states were a proof of their real sovereignty, the vast amount of rights which each free citizen retains in the case of every constitution, and for the protection of which constitutions of free communities are chiefly established, would prove an originally full and later residuary sovereignty in the individual. Sovereignty is inherently an attribute of a society, or of the representing agent of society (as in the case of government when it represents at home the nation; abroad, the independent state); sovereignty is not a sum total of many or a few fractional sovereignties, it is the attribute of an organized or organizing people.

Hamilton, moreover, on June 18, 1787, when the question before the convention was: "That the Articles of Confederation ought to be revised and amended so as to render the government of the United States adequate to the exigencies, the preservation, and the prosperity of the Union," said, in a speech in which he examines the various confederacies and elective governments in antiquity and modern times: "The Swiss cantons have scarce any union at all, and have been more than once at war with one another. How, then, are all these

---

[1] Pages 201 and 212 of the volume cited in the preceding note.

evils to be avoided? Only by such a complete sovereignty in the general government as will turn all the strong principles and passions above mentioned on its side."

Ere seventy-five years had elapsed from the day when these words were spoken, Switzerland had passed through a far graver civil war than was known in her history at Hamilton's time,—a war caused by an attempted Sonderbund or separate league,—and the United States were passing through a far graver civil conflict for the integrity of the country than that from which the Swiss had recently emerged.

More than all this—Washington wrote to John Jay, on March 10, 1787, these words (and it were well if they never passed from the memory of the American people): "My opinion is, that the country has yet to *feel* and *see*" (the italicizing is by Washington) "a little more before it can be accomplished" (viz., a constitution). "A thirst for power, and the bantling—I had like to have said the monster—sovereignty, which have taken such fast hold of the states individually, will, when joined by the many whose personal consequence in the line of state politics will in a manner be annihilated, form a strong phalanx against it." [1]

The colonial charters were, indeed, the only patent and legal fashionings of our early politics, and after the Declaration of Independence they constituted the only lines of demarcation visible to the lawyer's eye, so that a confederacy such as it was attempted to establish under the Articles of Confederation naturally suggested itself, but there were from the earliest times deeper causes at work which steadily led the portion of the Saxon race and the descendants of other European nations to form one nation; and throughout the history of this people the tendency toward the formation of a nation, until the nationality is legally pronounced in the formulation which we call the Constitution, is discernible. The Constitution did not make the people or nation, but the framers strove or felt impelled by necessity to enounce it, and to establish something

---

[1] Jay's Life, vol. i. p. 258.

far higher, more serviceable, and more consonant with modern civilization than "a mere treaty, a league between states," as Madison called depreciatingly the Articles of Confederation.

The causes which were always at work toward the formation of a nation were: first, the descent of the chief settlers, for they came from England, the country in which the people had been organized into a nation far earlier than in any other European country, and which had enjoyed the manifold benefits of a national government, when other countries were harassed by the fragmentary state of things derived from feudal confusion—it was the inherent tendency of the Anglo-Saxon race —the natural effect of the very period in which they came and spread in this country, characterized as our modern period is by the fact that the national polity is its normal type of government, as the feudal system had been the normal type of the Middle Ages, or the city-republic that of free antiquity —secondly, the geography of our country both with reference to its being separated from the mother-country by a wide sea, and to the unitary and inter-supplementing character of the country. The symptoms of nationality, growing distincter as our history advances, may be indicated thus: At no period were the inhabitants of one colony considered as strangers in another, and always could the citizen of one portion settle in another, and the Declaration of Independence calls the inhabitants of all the revolted colonies fellow-citizens; the so-called Albany plan of union (in 1754)—an unsuccessful but very palpable attempt at establishing political unity in this country—preceded the revolution by many years; in this plan the colonies were called, as they were always styled in the revolution, United Colonies, until the term United States (derived from the Netherlands, which called themselves United States and United Provinces indifferently) was adopted; the continental congress, ostensibly acting under distinct powers and instruction, appointed Colonel Washington, in June, 1775, "general and commander-in-chief of such forces as are, or shall be, raised for the maintenance and preservation of American liberty; this congress doth now declare that they will maintain and assist him ; and adhere to him, the said George Washington, with their lives and fortunes in the same cause." This sounds more like a national declaration than the commission of a general-in-chief, and was indeed a breath breathed forth by the coming nationality.

Another symptom is the remarkable fact that this congress exercised all attributes of a national government, and was seconded by the people, without having any distinct authority —it issued paper money, it raised troops by requisitions, issued commissions, and actually declared independence in 1776, while none of the constitutions made in 1776 and 1777, before the Articles of Confederation were adopted—those of New York, Pennsylvania, Maryland, and North Carolina—says aught about the treaty-making power, or that of declaring war, so well was it understood that this belonged to the nation, or to the whole, as the Greeks called it, and not to the parts.

Even the Articles of Confederation indicate in many passages the spirit of unionism or nationality, and the struggle of the revolution was carried through by the American consciousness of one people alone, and not, indeed, by haggling petty jealousy of small communities, or by provincial pomposity. As to the Declaration of Independence it is national, from its Alpha to its Omega ; and as to the great men of our revolution—Washington, Franklin, Adams, Hamilton, Madison, Pinckney—they were national men. Grote, the historian, correctly observes that the distinguished men or states of ancient Greece were always greatest, or truly great, when they were Pan-Hellenic. It was so in our revolution, and has been ever since so in our history. Has there ever been a great American that was not Pan-American, that is, National-American, or who was not great because he was National-American ? National-Government was the name given by all our earlier statesmen, Thomas Jefferson included, to the government of the Union, and the term country was freely used at all periods, while it may be added here, that it was actually made a reproach to the writer, by some state-rights men, that in an address which he delivered in 1851, he had maintained that the

Constitution had established a representative *government* over the whole.

The feeling of the Americans has been, from early times, that they are one people, requiring a country, and whether they consciously expressed it to themselves or not, they felt that modern civilization stands in need of countries, having far outgrown the city-states of old, and the provincial sejunctions of times nearer to their own. They were conscious that socially they formed a nation, and that politically they ought likewise to constitute a nation. Wisely said Hamilton: "A nation without a national government is an awful spectacle;" for it presents the enfeebling pain of protracted labor, and the failure of its high mission among the civilized nations of the earth.

Each great period in political history has its pervading type of government, or political dispensation, as it might be called. Our Cis-Caucasian race has passed through many such types. Neither the city-state, nor the feudal system, nor Asiatic monarchy, consisting of conquests agglomerated but incoherent; nor the government based on castes, nor the league, nor even the pure confederacy, is the form of government characteristic of modern times. Our race has happily passed beyond all these. Be it repeated, the normal type of government in our period of political civilization is the national polity. Whether monarchical or republican, whether imbued with the principle of self-government or centralized, whether of a unitary or federal character, the efficient government of a great nation must be of the national type, and few things have been more propitious for England's welfare and her manly freedom, than that she adopted a national government long before the other European countries gave up the fragmentary feudal system.

The writer of these pages has given, on a former occasion, his views on this subject in a manner as distinct as he is able to express them; he begs permission, therefore, to repeat what he then said:

It is a fact or movement of the greatest significance in the whole history of the human race, that this great continent was colonized by European people, at a period when, in their portion of the globe, great nations had been formed, and the national polity had finally become the normal type of government; and it is a fact equally pregnant with momentous results, that the northern portion of this hemisphere came to be colonized chiefly by men who brought along with them the seeds of self-government, and a living common law, instinct with the principles of manly self-dependence and civil freedom.

The charters under which they settled, and which divided the American territory into colonies, were of little more importance than the vessels and their names in which the settlers crossed the Atlantic; nor had the origin of these charters a deep meaning, nor was their source always pure. The people in this country always felt themselves to be one people, and unitedly they proclaimed and achieved their independence. The country as a whole was called by Washington and his compeers America, for want of a more individual name. Still, there was no outward and legal bond between the colonies, except the crown of England; and when our people abjured their allegiance to that crown, each colony stood formally for itself. The Articles of Confederation were adopted, by which our forefathers attempted to establish a confederacy, uniting all that felt themselves to be of one nation, but were not one by outward legal form. It was the best united government our forefathers could think of, or of which, perhaps, the combination of circumstances admitted. Each colony came gradually to be called a state, and called itself sovereign, although none of them had ever exercised any of the highest attributes of sovereignty; nor did the states ever after do so.

Wherever political societies are leagued together, be it by the frail bonds of a pure confederacy, or by the consciousness of the people that they are intrinsically one people, and form one nation, without, however, a positive national government, then the most powerful of these ill-united portions must needs rule; and, as always more than one portion wishes to be the leader, intestine struggles ensue in all such incoherent governments. It has been so in antiquity; it has been so in the Middle Ages; it has been so and is so in modern times. Athens and Sparta, Castile and Aragon, Austria and Prussia, are always jealous companions, readily turned into bitter enemies. Those of our forefathers who later became the framers of our Constitution saw this approaching evil, and they observed many other ills which had already overtaken the confederacy. Even Washington, the strong and tenacious patriot, nearly desponded. It was a dark period in our history; and it was then that our fathers most boldly, yet most considerately, performed the greatest act that our annals record—they engrafted a national, complete, and representative government on our insufficient confederacy; a government with an exclusively national executive, in which the senate, though still representing the states as states, became nationalized in a great measure, and in which the house of representatives became purely national like the executive. Virginia, which, under the Articles of Confederation, was approaching the leadership over all (in the actual assumption of which she would have been resisted by other rapidly growing states, which would inevitably have led to our Peloponnesian war)—Virginia was now represented according to her population, like every other portion of the country; not as a unit, but by a number of representatives who were bound to vote individually, according to their consciences, as national men. The danger of internal struggle and provincial bitterness seemed to have passed, and our country now fairly entered as an equal among the leading nations, in the course where nations, like Olympic chariot-horses, draw abreast the car of civilization. We advanced rapidly; the task assigned to us by Providence was performed with a rapidity which had not been known before; for we had a national government commensurate to our land and, it seemed, adequate to our destiny. So far our former passage.

Yet, the peaceful history of our country, calling, comparatively speaking, but rarely for energetic action of the national government; the universally observed tendency of the swelling and even arrogating importance of the minor or local powers when the uniting authority is weak or rarely called into action; the constant and, it is feared, occasionally wilful confusion of a national authority with *centralization*, and even with despotism (as if there were no such thing as local absolutism and local oppression!), and, on the other hand, the confusion of self-government (the very pride and honor of our race) with sovereignty; the ultimate, open, and total denial that we form a nation, and have a country,[1] accompanied by a tendency of some of our most gifted men to consider the weakening and the lowering of the national government almost an object of patriotism—all these tendencies, almost always accompanied by a tendency to render the state governments as centralized and absolute within the boundary of each separate state as possible, ultimately led to that theory of state rights which proclaimed the loosest *league* the choicest of polities, if polity, indeed, it can be called, and which has brought this country to the strait in which we now find it.[2]

---

[1] It was stoutly maintained by the nullifiers that we have no country and ought to have none; that the absence of a name for our country was not an accident, but that the fact of our having a name which simply indicates a political system was evidence of our having no country, and that if the term nation could be used at all in the United States, it must apply to the united people of each single state. The nation of South Carolina was frequently spoken of in the times of nullification, and again, in the year 1850, when an attempt at separate secession was made. The writer was denounced as *abominably national*, while William C. Preston called out to him significantly, when he first saw the writer after it had been decided, in 1850, that South Carolina would not secede, " *We have a country yet !*"

[2] A candid opponent of the national government cannot assert that there ever was a tendency toward *centralization*, so often denounced, observable in congress. What has been actually observable, at one period, was the tendency of a portion of Americans toward democratic absolutism at the time when General Jackson was called the tribune of the people, and high-handed measures were asked at his hands by that portion of the people; but this portion consisted of so-called state-rights men. The confusion of a national government with centralization is so wilfully and unfairly persisted in, and has formed so prom-

How, then, are the American people to declare and settle forever, by their fundamental law, that they will not admit of

---

inent a characteristic of nullifiers, state-rights men, and secessionists, and is so illogical withal, that it may be well to say a few words on this subject, even though it be but in a confined note. The centralist desires a government which unites all power, unchecked by any institutions of self-government, and undivided into co-ordinate independent branches of government. Centralization may be, and frequently is, democratic as well as monarchical. Indeed all democratic absolutism has a direct and swift tendency toward monarchical centralism. France and Napoleon I. furnish us with a modern illustration. The federalist (not taking the term as a party name) considers a confederation of independent or nearly independent states the best government. When France exhibited absorbing centralism more and more, since the times of Richelieu and Louis XIV., many political philosophers thought they discovered safety in the opposite—in federalism. Lord Brougham, generally admitted to be the author of the Political Philosophy, published in three volumes by the Society for the Diffusion of Useful Knowledge, goes so far as to praise even the organization of the former German empire! The nationalist believes in the necessity of national or unitary government, as opposed to the mere states general or diet of a league, such as the present diet at Frankfort is, or as the diet of the Swiss confederacy used to be. But a national government may be a centralism, as the French is, or a government with many institutions of liberty and self-government, as the English; it may be monarchical, or republican, as ours is and is intended to be. A general government need not be on that account a national government, which requires a *nation*, and must extend with uniformity over the whole. The ancient Asiatic governments were general governments over vast empires, but there was no Persian or Assyrian nation. It shows either ignorance or a perversion of mind to confound nationalism with centralism; and I am sustained by fact and history, when I say, in the text, that those American statesmen or partisans who most assailed the national government, and who pretended, and actually continue to pretend, that they are fighting for liberty when they attack the national government and declare it to be a mere agent; that those American statesmen who were always bemoaning the " centralization," the " tyranny," the " despotism" of the " general government," were all of them, so far as I can recollect, men who worked to concentrate within their respective states all power in the legislature—the only body offering itself in this country, and at the time, for *centralism*. The whole idea which they have of liberty is the barren idea of opposition to the general government. There were highly distinguished men among them, yet all of them fell into the vulgar error of considering liberty to consist in negativism. As to the national government itself, it was treated by the school of state-rights men as if it had been erected for the sole purpose of being degraded in every possible way—as if it were some unsightly fence or wall run up at the outskirts of the town, seemingly erected for no purpose but to be defaced with caricatures and grotesque placards of the invading bill-sticker.

this calamitous sort of state sovereignty? That they know that modern civilization stands in need of *countries*, and that neither city, nor province, nor petty dominion, is sufficient for the modern *patria?* The Constitution cannot enter into a discussion, and if it did, it would be of no effect.

It is believed that the question can be approached in two distinct practical ways, namely, through the subject of allegiance, and by the definition of treason.

Allegiance is that feeling of pride and adhesion, and that faithful devotion to a person's nation which every generous man is conscious of owing to his country—cast into the highest obligation of obedience to the highest agent politically representing the country or the nation. This definition is given with a perfect recollection of Blackstone's definition to the contrary, and of the fact that acts of parliament have declared that allegiance is due to the person of the king and not to the crown, which latter theory is "damnable."[1] English history sufficiently proves that, despite of the law books, allegiance is essentially due to the crown—that is, to the country, and not "due by nature to the person of the king." How else could it be apparently transferred by a convention or revolution from one monarch to another person wearing the same crown, which means, of course, the representation of the country? The relation of a son to a father is a *natural* one, but no act of parliament can unfather a father.

That phase of state-rights doctrine which acknowledged, at one and the same time, the sovereignty of the states and the sovereignty of the United States, admitted likewise of two allegiances—a contradiction in terms. A double allegiance would be a fearful seesaw for a conscientious citizen, and worse

---

[1] The act called Exilium Hugonis de Spencer Patris et Filii, and the repeals and re-repeals of acts concerning allegiance, with much that interests the publicist and jurist, can be found in the Tryal of Dr. Henry Sacheverell, before the House of Peers, &c., &c. London, 1710.

The fact that allegiance is inherently national, all acts and definitions to the contrary notwithstanding, and that history proves this to be so, is treated of at some length in the writer's Political Ethics.

than the allegiance of the feudal times, which was a graduated allegiance, but not a double or multiplied one. We cannot faithfully serve two masters. We owe, indeed, obedience to the state government, but so we owe obedience to many persons, laws, and institutions without its amounting to allegiance. The so-called double allegiance savors of the barbarous, and now extinct petty treason which the wife could commit in England against her husband, making him a sub-sovereign, to whom the wife owed sub-allegiance. Are such barbaric confusions of ideas to be repeated with us?

The inherent inconsistency of a double allegiance has always shown itself as soon as stern and testing cases have presented themselves—practical cases which call for actions and not only for apparent symmetry of verbal positions; while the other phase of the state-rights doctrine, which declared the states *bona fide* and exclusive sovereigns, leaving to the national government the mere character of an attorney, with certain powers to be taken back at any moment by the party for whom the attorney acts, has led to the direst acts of dishonor and dishonesty.

Thomas J. Jackson, who died, as general of the so-called Confederacy, with the soldierly name of honor and affection, Stonewall Jackson, seems to have been a man of singular directness of mind and purpose. He had all along believed in a double allegiance, but when the testing hour arrived, calling for decision, and showing the impossibility of two allegiances, his night-long prayer to be enlightened in his grievous perplexity showed that we cannot have two sovereigns. For one of the two he must decide, and he decided in favor of state allegiance, doubtless convinced for the rest of his life that an honest acknowledgment of two allegiances is a matter of impossibility for an earnest man. Jackson was a Virginian, and there, on the same soil where he wrestled in prayer, another and a greater Virginian had uttered, long before him, those memorable words: "All America is thrown into one mass—where are your landmarks, your boundaries of colonies? They are all thrown down. The distinctions between

Virginians, Pennsylvanians, New Yorkers, and New Englanders are no more; I am not a Virginian, but an American." Had these words of Patrick Henry never touched a chord in Jackson's heart, or at least showed him that two sovereigns being impossible, the question must be whether the one of the parties, called the country or the United States, had not rights too, and greater ones than Virginia? and had he never asked himself what original cause made Virginia so great and so exclusive a sovereign, and whether it had ever acted as real sovereign?

On the other hand, men who believed, or pretended to believe in state sovereignty alone, when secession broke out, went over with men and ships, abandoning the flag to which they had sworn fidelity; thus showing that all along they had served the United States like Swiss hirelings, and not as citizens, in their military service. They did more; not only did they desert the service of the United States, on the ground that their own individual states, to whom they owed allegiance, had declared themselves out of the Union, but in many cases they took with them, or attempted to take with them, the men who owed no such allegiance, being either foreigners or natives of other American states. In either case they actually called publicly on their former comrades to be equally faithless, and desert with their ships or troops. The Swiss mercenaries used to act more nobly. Once having sold their services, and having taken the oath of fidelity, they used to remain faithful unto death, as they did on many a battle-field, and through long periods of history down to the revolution which dethroned Charles the Tenth of France.

The reader will find, at the end of this paper, in the amendments marked A and B, how it is proposed to provide constitutionally for a national expression on the necessity of the integrity of our country, on allegiance, the treasonable character of elevating so-called state sovereignty above the national government, and for the extinction of the Dred Scott principle.

The easy life, which in the course of history had been our

lot, until the civil war burst upon us, engendered a general spirit of levity with reference to matters of government and laws, of which some persons predicted those calamitous consequences which have now befallen us. A trifling spirit is one of the greatest evils which can beset a nation. Levity has been the spirit of too many sad periods of sacred and profane, of early and recent, history, from which peoples are rescued, if rescued at all, by searching punishments only, that we should oppose to these grave lessons the callous disregard of unimpressionable minds. "He that will not hear must feel," holds good in the school of life and nations as in the schools of children. It is suggested, therefore, to the reader, whether an amendment such as is marked C may not be requisite. God admits of no favorites in history, and things will bear the same consequences with us that they have produced with others. Let us gravely treat grave things, and not pass over serious evils with self-deceiving yet empty words. No honest physician does it; no serious statesman can do it; no citizen who sincerely believes in the greatness of his country's mission can do it.

Regarding slavery, little is to be added here. It is past discussion. The wide history of our whole race and the thousands of laws settle it, and the rapid course of events in our own three pregnant years has settled it. We, who know that negro slavery originated in unhallowed greed, braving at last the long resisting better opinion of the governments, at the very time when Europe had at length succeeded in eliminating slavery from her soil; we who believe that slavery is hostile to true civilization and to the longevity of nations, itself a requisite of high modern civilization; we who know that slavery has always been at best a deciduous institution, and that it has always proved itself a cancer wherever communities have neglected to extinguish it so soon as the humanizing system of wages, which acknowledges that the laborer is worthy of his hire, offers itself—we cannot be expected to allow this malignant virus to poison our system forever.

We who have found, to our bitter cost, how perverting and

estranging in statesmanship and morals the character of this institution is among people who call themselves Christians, so that slavery, and slavery alone, divided, for them, the country, the population, the parties, and their aims and views into two portions, pretended to be more distinct than ever language or religion have divided portions of mankind from one another; we who know from law and history, old and new, and from our Constitution, how futile is the attempt to combine the idea and characteristics of *humanity* or a *person* with those of a *thing* that can be sold and bought; we who have learned how bewildering a curse slavery becomes when rebelliously upheld against experience, against the opinion of nearly all men, and the principles of Christianity, which throughout the existence of the Christian church from its earliest days have steadily wrought the emancipation of the bond—we cannot perpetuate this thing when a rebellion raised for the very purpose of extending and perpetuating it gives us the opportunity of extinguishing it forever.

We who remember that we are bidden to " honor all men," and believe that an auction-table on which families are sundered by the hammer of an auctioneer, albeit that he is white, and that the big tears of the victims roll down on dark cheeks, is not an acceptable sight to a God, merciful and holy; we who believe that comparing the relations subsisting between children and parents, or citizens and their governments, with the relation of slavery is hypocrisy, insulting him to whom the argument is addressed, because supposing him to be possessed of the lowest understanding; we who think that justifying slavery on the ground that other classes in other countries are suffering from want or oppression, or that prostitution, too, is a wide-spread evil, which will not be abolished for centuries to come, is unworthy of any upright man, because no one has ever pretended to raise pauperism or prostitution to the dignity of an unapproachable institution, nor called them of divine origin—we certainly must do away with this arch-mischief as soon as may be.

We who believe that there is no logical link between " the

inferiority of the negro race" and the consequent necessity of enslaving it, any more than stupidity in a white man would " entitle him to slavery;" [1] who believe that it is a heaven-crying iniquity belonging exclusively to our age and our country, to maintain that " Capital is by nature entitled to *own* Labor," asserted at the very age which justly prides itself on the dignity of labor and its wedlock with science ; we who feel ashamed that the Sclavonic race should have outstripped ours in the broad emancipation of the serfs in the Eastern dominion, corresponding in vastness to our Western empire, where saddening wilfulness declared, at the same period, that a new mansion of civilization should be reared on the corner-stone of slavery, and that slavery is a " moral, political, and economical benefit," while we know it to be a moral, political, and economical evil and bane, and while we know that, in our country, it has always been in reciprocal connection with the " state-rights doctrine," acting upon one another as cause and effect ; we who know that the framers of our Constitution considered slavery an evil which would soon die out—which was inconsistent with their Declaration of Independence—and which they felt ashamed to mention in the Constitution when they were forced to touch upon it ; we claim it as a right to mention now, for the first time, the word slavery in the Constitution, in order to abolish it.

We who know that Matrimony, the Family, and Property have been acknowledged from the earliest periods of our race as the very elements of civil society and starting-points of civilization ; so much so that ancient and modern heathens deified those benefactors who " introduced matrimony and property ;" and that slavery makes war upon these elements of humanity; we who know that it was the settled purpose of the slave-owners to re-establish slavery in the North; we who witness daily that solemn and symbolic act in our country's history, of black regiments marching along our streets to their embarkation for the southern battle-fields, and legion after legion of armed negroes receiving our own starry standard at

---

[1] These are the sarcastic words of Henry Clay.

the hands of our own patriotic women; we, of course, must be expected to do our utmost that slavery be forever abolished in our land, and that its fundamental law shall put its seal on the perpetuity of this retarded act of justice, reason, right, and wisdom.

The amendment marked E, in the Appendix, will show the reader how we think that the requisite amendment might best be worded.

If slavery is abolished in the United States, it will be necessary to amend that portion of the Constitution which establishes the basis of representation. At present three-fifths of the slave population are added to the number of free persons, in order to make up the number of persons entitled to a proportionate number of representatives in congress. If, then, slavery is abolished, the number of two-fifths of the present slave population would be added to the number to be represented in congress, without giving them the right to vote for the representative. The few white citizens who have been in rebellion would, therefore, gain by the extinction of slavery, so far as the number of representatives is concerned. The latter portion of amendment E, therefore, is necessary.[1] It will be observed that the words used in this portion of the amendment have been taken, as far as it was feasible, from the Constitution itself, Article I., section 2, paragraphs 1 and 3.

There are other amendments which either seem to be desired by most Americans, or have been pronounced desirable by some of our greatest statesmen, or else, which appear to us highly desirable on practical grounds, such as the extension of the presidential term to six years, and not allowing a second election, or of giving to the president the authority of vetoing single items of the appropriation bills, without thereby vetoing the whole—a change highly desirable, it seems, in the advanced state of our country, with its large, manifold, and tempting appropriations. So may the paragraph of section

---

[1] The reasons which have led the writer to the proposition of this amendment have since been published in a letter to Senator E. D. Morgan.

9 of the Constitution, which begins: "No capitation or other direct tax," require an amendment making it clearer, or else it may be found advisable to omit it altogether. It may be wise to consider the propriety of constitutionally declaring polygamy a crime (including polyandry, for what does not happen in our days!). Those who, like ourselves, believe the presence of cabinet ministers in either house of congress of great importance, and who, nevertheless, think that the spirit of the present Constitution forbids it—in which we do not agree with them—will deem it necessary to provide for the presence of the ministers by some amendment.

We restrict our proposed amendments, however, to those great points which present themselves with painful clearness in the present contest of the American people.

As to the Amendment F, it will suffice to state that that which is proposed to be established by it exists, we believe, in every other country and its colonies, even in Spanish colonies, where slavery continues.

According to the law or usage as it now stands, colored people may freely testify in the courts of the United States in some states, in others they cannot testify against or for a white man; but they may in actions or trials of colored people; yet if they do so, it cannot be done on oath, as though the color of a man invalidated the binding power of the oath, and as if evidence thus acknowledged to be weak and not to be relied upon, was, nevertheless, good enough to decide on property or life and death of a colored person! And all this exists in a system of adjudication and trial in which things and circumstances are allowed as evidence, whose proving efficacy is to be weighed by judge and jury. It indicates a confusion of the ideas of truth and fact, and the means of establishing them —of the absolute character of facts and the importance of the person who establishes it, or with reference to whom it is established, according to which the questions concerning a mathematical problem were not whether it is proved, but whether a Frenchman or a German had proved it—a commoner or a nobleman. We are involuntarily reminded of the barbarous age described by the great bishop, Gregory of Tours, who tells[1] us that in his time persons of a vile condition were obliged to take successively more oaths, each on a different relic, to substantiate the same fact, than persons of a better condition; and that, on the other hand, more witnesses were required to prove an offence against personages, as their rank was higher, so that it took between twenty and thirty witnesses to prove an offence against a cardinal, and we forget how many to substantiate an accusation of misconduct against a queen. In much later, yet still half barbarous times, Jews, whose treatment in the Middle Ages resembles much the treatment which the negroes have received at our hands, were not allowed, in some countries, to testify against Christians, while in others, two or three, or still more, Jewish testimonies were requisite to be equivalent to one Christian testimony, and the same was repeated with reference to natives in portions of Asia which had been colonized by Europeans. The History of Human Folly, if that work is complete in any degree, must have a large chapter on the laws and rules of evidence to which men have resorted;[2] but shall we continue them?

If it be objected that this abuse might be remedied by an act of congress, and does not require an amendment of the Constitution, we would reply that so startling a corruption of the rules of evidence ought not only to be remedied by law, but had better be placed beyond the possibility of relapse, and deserves to receive in a period of reform the stamp of the nation's moral consciousness, and the nation's constitutional frown.

In this latter respect Amendment G resembles the proposed amendment marked F. The foreign slave-trade is declared piracy by act of congress, but a person who had been judge

---

[1] In his Historia Francorum.

[2] In most countries, whose law is founded on the Roman law, the rule used to prevail that two strong suspicions were equivalent to one positive testimony, or, that strong suspicion incurred one-half of the penalty incurred by the offence substantiated by proof positive. But these times are past; jurists feel ashamed of them.

declared in open court in the city of New York, in 1860, when certain persons were tried for having been engaged in the African slave-trade, that the law was, in fact, as the district attorney had stated it, but that the universal opinion of the people regarding the criminality of the act had materially changed. On the other hand, the opinion had spread far and wide in the South before secession broke out, that the act was unconstitutional;[1] while a district judge of the United States declared on the bench, in Charleston, in 1860,[2] after the nefa-

---

[1] See a speech by Wade Hampton, Esq., on The Constitutionality of the Slave-Trade Laws, in the Senate of South Carolina, December 10, 1859. Columbia, South Carolina, 1860.

[2] See The Slave Trade not declared Piracy by the Act of 1820.—The United States *vs.* Wm. C. Corrie. Presentment for Piracy. Opinion of the Hon. A. G. Magrath, District Judge in the Circuit Court of the United States for the District of South Carolina, upon a motion for leave to enter a *Nol. Pros.* in the Case. James Conner, District Attorney, A. H. Brown, F. D. Richardson, W. D. Porter, Defendant's Counsel. Charleston, 1860. The case is The United States *vs.* William C. Corrie, April Term, 1860.

The preface of this pamphlet will interest every lawyer. It is here given, therefore, in full:

"The principles discussed in the opinion of the court, in the case of the United States *vs.* William C. Corrie, have been considered by many persons of that importance which required that they should be preserved in a form more permanent than the columns of our daily papers.

"These principles are: (1) That the act of congress of the 15th May, 1820, entitled 'An act to continue in force an act to protect the commerce of the United States, and punish the crime of piracy, and also to make further provision for punishing the crime of piracy,' is not any part of the laws of the United States passed for the suppression of the slave-trade, but relates to the specific offences which it enumerates; and these specific offences have not been, and are not to be, confounded with the slave-trade. (2) That in the trial of all crimes and offences against the laws of the United States, the place or places for trial are, and must have been, ascertained by law; and no power can be admitted to interfere with the trial at such place or places. The right of the accused to be tried at such ascertained place or places is secured by the Constitution of the United States. (3) That in the United States, the right of a court to take cognizance of a crime or offence must be found in the law; and to the law which creates an office, and prescribes the duties of an officer, is his responsibility to be referred in all cases.

"The ability, research, and luminous discussion of principle by which this opinion is characterized, will recommend it to the careful perusal of all who take an interest in questions which touch the rights and liberties of the citizen."

rious traffic in negroes had actually been resumed, that the slave-trade had not been declared piracy by the act of 1820. Under such circumstances, honest and earnest citizens will think it advisable to engrave as indelibly on our Twelve Tables as we are able to do the people's conviction concerning so dark an international crime, and their will concerning its possible recurrence. It is, indeed, one of the essential rules of wise government not to forestall development by fretful or conceited details in the fundamental laws; but it is also one of the highest duties of civic uprightness to settle doubts and stabilitate rights which have been shaken, concerning the elements of polities, and to prevent the consummation of dangers drawing nigh in threatening clouds.

No person who remembers the open declaration of helplessness in the report of the attorney-general of the United States to President Buchanan, confessing that what then was perpetrated in the South was treason, indeed, but that the president had no power to protect the United States, will judge Amendment D unnecessary. The ancient Romans were said to have omitted providing for the punishment of parricide, because so monstrous a deed had not occurred to their minds. Our forefathers omitted to provide for the place of the trial of treason and rebellion when, apparently, at least, a whole community commits it. The dark deed did not occur to their minds, and it is thus our duty to remedy the omission.

In view, then, of all the foregoing remarks, and in solemn reflection on the needs of our nation, and on the degeneracy which slavery has wrought in the South, and on the pertinacity with which some persons continue to brave the deep conviction of our race, and on the patent effects of this trying and sanguinary struggle, we now respectfully submit the following amendments to the consideration of the American people. Doubtless a far better instrument might be devised, if men of the stamp of the framers, with their boldness and their circumspection, and with the addition of all our experience, could meet in a constituent convention, and revise the whole fundamental law. This cannot be done; the confidence of the whole nation cannot be obtained at a period like this. Neither times nor men would be propitious for so comprehensive a work of so exalted a character. Too many theories have seized on the minds of men, and the present period is plainly not favorable to the creation of a new constitution. The many state constitutions of recent date do not show a general progressive improvement in this respect. Let us build additions to the mansion we dwell in, though perfect symmetry may not be obtained. Indeed, very few periods in the course of history can be called propitious for so great a work, but the necessity of certain amendments is there; it is pressing upon us. We propose nothing of a speculative meaning. We propose measures of a direct and urgent practical character, and for these the times appear as fit as the call for them is direct and begins to be loud. The irons have been heated in the forge of civil war; let us have them on the anvil while it is time yet to fashion them with earnest and with skilful blow in the smithy of the Constitution.

John Hampden's motto was: *Vestigia nulla retrorsum.* So let it be ours in this momentous time. No step backward, but on, on—in the field and in the senate; in our aims, in our acts—in our national rights and duties, calling and justice— in all the work before us and around us.

PROPOSED AMENDMENTS.

Articles in Addition to, and Amendments of the Constitution of the United States of America.

(AMENDMENT A.)

ARTICLE XIII.—Every native of this country, except the sons of aliens whom the law may exempt, and Indians not taxed; and every naturalized citizen, owes plenary allegiance to the government of the United States, and is entitled to, and shall receive, its full protection at home and abroad.

(AMENDMENT B.)

ARTICLE XIV.—Article III., section 3, first paragraph of the Constitution, shall be amended so that it shall read as follows :

Treason against the United States shall consist only in levying war against them, or in adhering to their enemies, giving them aid and comfort, or in assisting them in forcible attempts to separate from the United States any state, territories, or unorganized districts, or any parts thereof; or in applying to foreign governments, or people, for aid or support, whether such separation, or resistance to the United States for the purpose of separation, be intended or is already carried out for the time being.

No person shall be convicted of treason unless on the testimony of two witnesses to the same overt act, or to the same positive act (where the treason consists in applying to foreign states or people), or on confession in open court.

(AMENDMENT C.)

ARTICLE XV.—It shall be a high crime directly to incite to armed resistance to the authority of the United States, or to establish or to join societies or combinations, secret or public, the object of which is to offer armed resistance to the authority of the United States, or to prepare for the same by collecting arms, organizing men, or otherwise. No person shall be convicted of this crime unless on the testimony of two witnesses to the same act, or on confession in open court, and congress shall declare the punishment of this crime.

(AMENDMENT D.)

ARTICLE XVI.—Trials for treason shall take place in the state or district in which the crime shall have been committed, unless the administion of justice shall be interrupted or impeded at the time by rebellion or war. Congress shall provide by law that trials for treason shall be held in places where justice may be administered without hindrance.

(AMENDMENT E.)

ARTICLE XVII.—Slavery shall be forever abolished, after the   day of the year   , in this country, the states, territories, unorganized districts, or any parts or places thereof—and shall never be re-established under whatever form or by whatever authority ; and all persons who are now or shall hereafter come and be within the limits and protection of the United States shall be deemed free, all claims of foreign persons or powers, whether at war or in amity with the United States, to the contrary notwithstanding.

Representatives shall be apportioned among the several states which may be included within this Union according to the respective number of male citizens of age having the qualifications requisite for electing members of the most numerous branch of the respective state legislatures. The enumeration of said citizens shall be made by each census of the United States.

(AMENDMENT F.)

Article XVIII.—Knowingly taking part in any slave-trade, directly or indirectly, shall remain piracy, and shall be punishable accordingly.

Holding a person as a slave or in involuntary servitude (except by authority for crimes duly proved), selling or buying a human being, abducting a human being for the sake of selling him or holding him as a slave, and aiding in taking human beings from one place to another, whether within this country or beyond its limits, for the purpose of selling them, shall be high crimes, and punishable with death or otherwise, as may be directed by acts of congress.

(AMENDMENT G.)

The free inhabitants of each of the states, territories, districts, or places within the limits of the United States, either born free within the same or born in slavery within the same and since made or declared free, and all other inhabitants who are duly naturalized according to the laws of the United States, shall be deemed citizens of the United States, and without any exception of color, race, or origin, shall be entitled to the privileges of citizens, as well in courts of jurisdiction as elsewhere.

REFLECTIONS

ON THE

CHANGES WHICH MAY SEEM NECESSARY

IN THE

PRESENT CONSTITUTION

OF THE

STATE OF NEW YORK,

ELICITED AND PUBLISHED BY THE NEW YORK UNION
LEAGUE CLUB, MAY, 1867.

181

CONSTITUTION OF NEW YORK.

The New York state constitution, of the year 1846, is one of the longest constitutions in existence, and in more than one case passes over from the character of a constitution and form of government, as the universally adopted style used to be, into that of a code of laws. It is difficult even for wise men to avoid, in a constitution, principles and outlines so general, that they lose their practical efficiency, on the one hand, and to escape, on the other hand, details and individual directions with which men, in love with some novel theory, or a theory to them novel, constrain future generations and impede the essential progress of their community. A study of all American state constitutions shows in a striking manner the last-mentioned evil; and a careful perusal of the successive constitutions, as they have followed one another in the different states, exhibits the increasing evil of individual sapiency forcing favorite details of special legislation into the fundamental laws of the states. A written or enacted constitution ought to be like a chart of dykes, protecting the land against the inroads of the element ever ready for mischief and destruction; but it ought not to attempt prescribing the culture of the protected land within. The Constitution of the United States has avoided the difficulty of keeping the mean between useless generalities and embarrassing details, probably, better than any existing enacted constitution, certainly better than any other American fundamental law known to me.

The best military authorities tell us that the orders issued by Napoleon before great battles, in the period of his brilliant successes, were characterized by this feature, that the general plan was marked with precision and genius, while, within these lines, sufficient freedom of action was left to his carefully selected commanders, so as to give free play to them for the many emergencies of the battle. Something similar ought to be observed regarding enacted constitutions. The community gains nothing when the framers of a fundamental law go beyond the limits of a constitution and plan of government, and substitute the character of a code of laws for it. The more the latter is done, the more frequent revising conventions become, until they actually change into what might be called periodical super-parliaments.

The approaching convention, it is to be hoped, will direct its attention to this point of simplification, and to those portions of the existing state constitution which contain embarrassing details ; but it seems that the Union League Club, when it honored me with a call for my views on the revision of the constitution, did not ask for a detailed review of the state instrument, but simply for my opinion on some of the main points connected with this great topic. These I am now going to give, repeating, however, that they are simply given as the writer's own, without any responsibility on the part of the association, and that, indeed, I would not have felt induced to give these views on any other condition. They go forth and will be taken for what they are worth.

Laws ought to be certain, both as to meaning and application ; trials ought to be speedy ; judges ought to be independent ; punitory laws ought to be mild, but undoubted in their execution. These are elementary truths now universally admitted by the publicists and political philosophers of our race, and of special importance to a people who acknowledge no other master than their Self-Made Law. Yet every one of these truths is more or less seriously disregarded and counteracted in our present polity.

Pardon.

The present constitution of New York gives to the governor the unrestricted privilege of pardoning persons[1] who have been convicted, in the due and laborious course of law, of an offence against the laws. The governor can wholly or partially remit the punishment which, by regular sentence, has been decreed to be inflicted on a convict, without being responsible to any person or body of men for so doing. The pardoning power is thus an arbitrary power, and, indeed, the only real vetoing power in our modern law-polities, in the sense of the ancient Roman veto of the tribune, although the term vetoing has been universally but wrongly applied to another act of the executive. Veto, in the Roman sense, meant the entire or partial voiding and nullifying of a *law*, or a special execution of a law, for reasons judged sufficient by the tribune, and this is precisely what the pardon granted by the chief magistrate effects with us. It is an element of arbitrariness and absolutism in the midst of a system which pretends to eschew all arbitrariness, and proclaims to be founded, as far as it is possible for men to do, on law and justice alone, because it aims, above all, at Liberty, and liberty must rest on law and justice.

There is no inherent reason why the pardoning power should belong to the executive. It has come to us traditionally from the monarchies in which very naturally the crown acquired by usage the privilege of pardoning, for the monarch is acknowledged as the "source of honor and of mercy," even in those kingdoms in which he is not supposed

---

[1] The subject of pardon, and most of the main topics touched upon in these pages, have been treated at much greater length, though not always from the same point of view, in several of my works, especially in my Civil Liberty and Self-Government, but it will be understood that I could not continually refer, in the course of such a writing as the present, to that or, indeed, to any other book. Thus, there is in the Appendix to the Civil Liberty a somewhat elaborate paper on pardon; but I ask permission now to refer to the work, once for all, and shall not recur to it.

to unite within himself the judge, the legislator, the commander of the forces, and the executor of all laws. Without this tradition, no political philosopher would have assigned the pardoning power to the executive, and there are many and urgent reasons why it should either be taken from the executive, or at least should be greatly modified.

Although the prince has the sole right of pardoning (in all but very exceptional cases), yet this power is practically modified in modern times. Applications for pardon go through a minister of the crown, frequently called minister of justice and grace; but, with us, the chief magistrates of the states are so accessible to every applicant that it becomes difficult, and for some individuals impossible, to resist the pressure of influence and importune applications, wholly unconnected though they generally are with any comparative innocence in the convict for whom a pardon is sought. That which is revolting to all administration of justice naturally happens—the convict connected with influential people stands a much better chance of getting pardoned, without any resort to bribery, than an obscure and friendless prisoner. There are now from five to six applications for pardon daily presented to our chief magistrate; indeed, nearly every convict, nowadays, tries to obtain a pardon, which is not surprising considering the frivolous ease with which our people sign petitions of any sort, frequently for no better reason than to get rid of the importune agent of the petitioner.

It has long been shown by repeated statistics, that a convict sentenced to ten years' imprisonment or more, or for life, stands a better chance than a criminal who has been sentenced to three years' imprisonment; because the former is very likely to be pardoned after about four years, while the latter is allowed to serve out his term, as convicts express it.

All persons who have made the science of punishment an especial subject of their study—all wardens and superintendents of penitentiaries, as far as my inquiry has gone, agree in this, that in those penitentiary systems in which reform is made an object together with punishment, no reform can be looked for so long as the convict occupies his mind with hopes of a pardon or with schemes how to obtain it. Reform requires first of all a resolute resignation to the assigned punishment; it may be followed by an acknowledgment of its justice, after which real and a penetrative reform may take place. Pardon rarely elicits a feeling of gratefulness in the pardoned person which might temper the feeling of hostility towards the non-penal world of which the criminal population is universally possessed.

The reckless pardoning, as it must be called, has wrought another most serious injury in many portions of our country; it has degraded the woman, by being extended to her almost as a matter of course, even in cases of the most heinous crimes, simply on the ground that she is a woman, thus proceeding for a sexual reason in a case of moral character. The woman is in this manner treated as too weak to expect strict moral responsibility from her, and we are consequently justified in saying that she is degraded. Her moral character is so far effaced.

From whatever point of view we may look at the unrestricted privilege of pardoning and its operation, it is inconsistent with our polity; it unsettles the law, and even administration of justice; it encourages crime by increasing impunity, and helps to efface that moral character of the community, without which no freedom, which we so highly prize, can endure. It is illogical and mischievous.

About a year ago the New York Prison Association addressed a number of questions, in a Circular Letter to Former Chief Magistrates of the Different States, on the subject of Pardoning. It was not considered delicate to address governors in power, on a privilege which, at the time, they were exercising. The following are the questions then propounded, with the exception of the last one, as irrelevant here:

I.—"When you were governor of the state of   and possessed the privilege of pardon, did you consider it a desirable attribute of the executive power, or, on the contrary, a burden, and generally a painful moral responsibility ?   Do you think this *unlimited* authority of pardoning necessary in our political system ; or is it, on the contrary, in your opinion, repugnant to our theory of government, which discountenances irresponsible and arbitrary power ?   Has the privilege of pardon, as it now exists, grown out of the polity, peculiarly our own, or does it exist because we found it when our own governments were established ?

II.—" Is it, in your opinion, possible that, easily accessible as our chief magistrates necessarily are, the privilege of pardoning can be guarded against frequent abuse and serious mistakes ?   Does, or does not, the privilege of pardoning, as it now exists, lead, in many cases, to results wholly unconnected with the degree of guilt or the comparative innocence of the convicts, and does not the obtaining of a pardon very frequently depend upon the influence which can be brought to bear on the petition for the pardon, rather than on the merits of the case itself?

III.—" Is it your conviction that the power of pardoning, as it now exists, leads more frequently to a defeat of the ends of justice than to the furtherance of a wise and even-handed administration of the same ?

IV.—" Do you, or do you not, think that a recommendation for pardon by the jury, who pronounce the culprit guilty, ought to be excluded as incompatible with that verdict, and that the recommendation to a merciful consideration should be restricted to the judge or judges who tried the case ?

V.—" Is it your opinion that the ends of justice and the real interest of the convicts themselves would be better promoted, if the power of pardoning in the executive were modified and circumscribed by a wisely-organized council or board of pardon, as is the case in some states in this country and in some European governments ; or do you regard the power of pardoning as an inherent, absolute, and essential attribute of the executive, so that it ought to continue in the same form in which it now exists in nearly all the states ?

VI.—" If you think that there should be a council, or board of pardon, is it your opinion that, whenever state constitutions are changed, authority ought to be conferred upon the legislature to establish such council or board ?

VII.—" Is there, in your opinion, any other mode, besides that indicated in Questions V. and VI., whereby the power of pardon can be properly limited or regulated ?"

All the answers received from the different ex-governors, with one partial exception, if I remember aright, were in that spirit in which the reader will readily perceive that the questions were drawn up.

But is the privilege of pardon necessary at all ?   A most

distinguished philosopher has actually maintained that laws should be very mild and the pardoning power abolished; but no matter how light soever laws may be, those cases cannot be avoided by any human code, in which a plain and strict *application* of the law—and the law ought to be applied strictly and plainly—militates with essential and intrinsic justice.

The pardoning power ought to exist somewhere, and it ought to be wisely circumscribed and organized. No better way of moderating the pardoning power in republics has been discovered, in America as well as in Europe (for instance in the republic of Geneva), than the establishment of a board of pardon, which acts in conjunction with the executive power. In our state it would probably be found the best to establish, by law, a board of say five members, one or two of them to be judges, without the written report of which board to the governor, no pardon should be permitted, or whose consent, after full investigation of the case, should be necessary for the validity of the governor's pardon. The members of the board of pardon should be appointed for a distinct number of years, by the governor with the consent of the senate, and not be elected for a short time, as, for instance, the prison inspector now is—a mode of appointment which has proved injurious to the penitentiary system in our state, and to the essential interests of the community.

If the convention should fear going into details, it may be possible that the end we have in view may be obtained by adding in the new constitution, granting the pardoning privilege to the executive, these words: *modified and circumscribed as the legislature may direct by law.*

This may possibly suffice, but thus much, at least, is urgently called for, if we mean to be a commonwealth of law and principle, and not to surrender it to arbitrary views and subjective whim.

Recuperation of the Full Civil and Political Status.

Another subject of great injustice connected with the irregular and unrighteous use of the pardoning power, is the fact that as the law now stands, a convict sentenced for the most nefarious crimes, but pardoned, re-enters into the possession of all his political rights, voting and all, while his fellow-convict, sentenced for a less crime to a shorter imprisonment, and, because sentenced to a shorter time, remaining unpardoned to the end of his sentence, loses certain political rights in consequence of having been punished for an infamous crime. The theory undoubtedly is, that the executive pardons because he has found that there was good reason for arresting the full course of the law, but whatever the theory may be, the fact is, as it is daily shown, a crying injustice, and *the constitution ought to establish that no pardon induces perfect recuperation of political or civil rights, unless the pardon mentions this fact according to the law which the legislature may establish;* that is to say, the reinstating in the full political or civil status must be subject to the same restriction or modification to which the pardon in general shall be subject.

Rehabilitation.

At all times, our present ones not excepted, it has happened that persons have been condemned for crimes of which it was proved at a later time that they were wholly innocent. If the victim is still alive, there is no other means of restoring him to the status of which he ought never to have been deprived than *pardoning* him. The English and American law does not know the idea of rehabilitation. But in a case such as has been mentioned, it is the community, or its administration of justice, which ought to crave the pardon of the innocent convict—not, indeed, the convict the pardon of the executive, or of any person or body of persons. Public acknowledgment of the grievous error, and compensation, as far as it is possible (which is never very far), ought then to take place, either to the living victim, or to the memory and surviving family if he is no longer living, or has actually died by execution. It is nothing short of barbarous helplessness when a political community does not know how to escape a difficulty but by a process in which there is no reason—not even verbal logic. We have done grievous wrong to a fellow-citizen; therefore we issue a writ of pardon for the offences which we nevertheless confess he has never committed! *It is necessary, therefore, that the idea of rehabilitation be introduced into our law; and it seems that this can be done effectually and beyond cavil only by a proper provision in the constitution, while the board of pardon would be, probably, the most convenient body to act, not as a court of appeal, but as a board of revision, with the power to authorize the governor to issue, not a pardon, but a proclamation of rehabilitation and compensation, together with one of regret on the part of the community.*

Every reader to whose mind is present the case of the English lawyer who, in 1844, was sentenced to transportation for life for forgery, and who, some two or three years ago, was *pardoned* because it was made patent that a most grievous wrong had been perpetrated against him—every such reader will agree that this subject of honorable rehabilitation is neither subtle nor practically useless, but that it is, on the contrary, a subject of plain and palpable political truth, practical candor, and indispensable justice.

Suspension of Sentence.

A subject not wholly unconnected with that of pardon, and directly opposite to the one just reflected upon, is that of suspending sentence.

In England, as well as here, the usage has crept into the courts of justice of suspending the sentence; that is to say, when in a penal trial, after a laborious and costly process, the indicted person has at length been found guilty, and the judge acknowledges the verdict—not setting it aside—he nevertheless undertakes to suspend sentence, sometimes for one reason, sometimes for another. At times the judge couples a certain condition with this suspension, thus creating, in fact, a new sentence. In a noted case, a highly reputed judge, in a neighboring state, suspended sentence provided the person found guilty would leave the state! Once the sentence suspended, it is hardly ever, if indeed, in this country, ever executed. There are persons in our community against whom successively several verdicts of guilty were found, and over whom a corresponding number of suspended sentences hover, none of which will ever be executed. How is it morally possible that a person should be brought back into court and receive sentence, after having been roaming about for a year with the placard of "guilty" pinned to him?

The very first paragraph of the declaration of rights, contained in the English Bill of Rights, is to the effect "that the pretended power of suspending laws or the execution of laws by regal authority, without consent of parliament, is illegal," and we allow a judge "the suspending of laws, or the execution of laws;" for, to this the suspension of sentence, and defeat of the result of a legal trial, obviously amounts.

In the city of New York, this abuse of judicial power, against all correct idea of a true administration of justice, has become quite common, and, it is believed, far more common than anywhere in America or England; while in no other countries have judges been allowed to arrogate this power. It is not known to me, despite of some research, how early this assumption of discretionary power in the judge took place in England, nor have I been able to ascertain when it became habitual in certain localities in the United States; but the evil does exist, and a most serious evil it is. It increases the already alarming impunity with which crime may be committed; it helps to unsettle the administration of justice and the public sense of justice; it is an uncalled-for and unwarranted power in the judge; it is unnecessary, for we have the pardoning power; it introduces an additional element of arbitrariness, where no arbitrary power ought to have a place. The judge, instead of assuming this power, might declare that he means to ask the board of pardon, or the executive, for a favorable consideration of the case. The jury, on the contrary, ought never to make any recommendation against its own verdict, as is now very frequently done.

The abuse exists, and it is very doubtful whether a mere law abolishing it would be proof against all subterfuges of our cavilling generation. It is suggested, *therefore, to extinguish this serious inconsistency by a provision in the new constitution, and to oblige every court to pronounce sentence within the term in which the respective case has been tried.*

The Independence of the Judiciary.

The principle embodied in the Habeas Corpus Act of 1679, and transplanted into the Constitution of the United States as the privilege of the writ of habeas corpus, on the one hand, and the independence of the judiciary on the other, are two of the greatest acquisitions, we might almost say, of the greatest conquests in the progress of civilization, and two of the greatest guarantees of personal security and civil liberty ever devised by man.

By independence of the judiciary is meant the well sustained impartial position of the judge between the two parties (which our trial in courts of law assigns to him), and the freedom of the judge from any influence, direct or indirect, of the executive, the power-holder, the sovereign, be he one person, or may he consist of many or of all. It requires a variety of means to obtain this important end.

After the English had severely suffered from the dependence of the judges upon the crown when it was worn by the Stuarts —those "Stuart judges" whom Lord Campbell, himself chief justice of England, calls ruffians in ermine—and when the great Bill of Rights of 1688 had settled many constitutional points of elementary importance, it was added, by the Act of Settlement of 1700, completing the Bill of Rights, "That after the said limitation shall take effect as aforesaid, judges' commissions be made *quamdiu se bene gesserint*, and their salaries ascertained and established; but upon the address of both houses of parliament it may be lawful to remove them." At a later period, by the first act under George III., it was established that the death of the monarch should not void a judge's commission, as had been the case theretofore, and thus the independence of the English judge and the independent tenure of the office were firmly established and completed.

The principle that judges shall hold their office during good behavior was incorporated in the constitutions which were adopted by New York, Massachusetts, and some other states, after the Declaration of Independence and before the adoption of the Constitution of the United States. The constitution of New York (adopted in 1777) ordains "that the chancellor, the judges of the supreme court, and the first judge of the county court in every county, hold their offices during good behavior, or until they shall have respectively obtained the age of sixty years."

The first constitution of Massachusetts, of 1780, and chiefly indicted by John Adams, contains as " Part I.," "a declaration of Rights of the Inhabitants of the Commonwealth of Massachusetts," consisting of thirty articles, of which the twenty-ninth reads thus :

" It is essential to the preservation of the rights of every individual, his life, liberty, property, and character, that there be an impartial interpretation of the laws, and administration of justice. It is the right of every citizen to be tried by judges as free, impartial, and independent as the lot of humanity will admit. It is, therefore, not only the best policy, but for the security of the rights of the people, and of every citizen, that the judges of the supreme judicial court should hold their offices as long as they behave themselves well ; and that they should have honorable salaries, ascertained and established by standing laws." [1]

Sounder and more direct language cannot be used by man, and that sterling patriot and hero of independence, to whose warm love of liberty we owe in a great measure our Revolution, as much as great events can be owed to individuals—that bold man in the vigorous age of forty and some years—placed the immovability of the judge and his tenure of office during

---

[1] All these early constitutions, together with the Declaration of Independence, the Articles of Confederation between the said states, the treaties between France and the United States of America, were published by a resolution of December 29, 1780, of the Continental congress, in " two hundred correct copies," " to be bound in boards."

good behavior in the very Bill of Rights of his common-wealth. Let us remember this fact. Civil liberty is never promoted by merely increasing the power of the power-holder, and it is always undermined by increasing absolutism, most especially so by democratic absolutism.

The general mode of appointment of judges used to be by the governor, with the consent of the senate, and during good behavior. In many states the legislature elected the judges by joint ballot. This was the mode adopted in South Caro-lina, and at one period in our own state. The governor had nothing to do with the election. To this election by the legislature the state of Georgia added the tenure of office for a short period of years. The judges, it was observed, at once lost in character. At length our state adopted, in the present constitution, the short term of office of Georgia, and substi-tuted popular election for election by the legislature as in Georgia. Thenceforward the change swept over the country until the convention of Massachusetts, in 1853, refused to approve the proposed amendment of judges appointed by popular election for a limited time. She was the first state whose convention made a stand against this innovation.

In no case, I believe, did this change proceed from dissatis-faction with the merits of the old system. Complaints were uttered nowhere, except, indeed, the dissatisfaction that judges who belonged to an opposite party, before they were appointed, should occupy their places on the bench forever, thus with-holding a chance of appointing a fellow-partisan in their stead. But one of the very objects to be obtained by appointment during good behavior is the divesting of the judge of party or executive influence, and it used to be invariably observed, when the old system obtained, that in placing a citizen on the bench as judge for life, the grave responsibility was so dis-tinctly felt by the incumbent, that no dependence on party or any other power could be looked for.

The greatest judges of America have graced the bench under the former order of things; but it is inherent in frail human nature that he who has power wants more. The greed of power is in every one of us, no matter whether that one be called a king, or the many be called the people. The change of name does not change the character of the individuals. We, as people, are as greedy for power as he who wields it alone, and judges independent of the influence of the sovereign have appeared as disagreeable to the American sovereign as they were offensive to a Louis the Fourteenth. Self-limitation is wonderfully rare.

There prevailed likewise the error that people sought for the essence of liberty in universal electiveness, and unchecked absolute electors, so that universal suffrage exist. Liberty, however, consists in no absolutism or despotism, be it democratic or monarchical, and election should by no means extend to every office or occupation. Our legislators ought to be elected; our governor ought to be elected; but who would trust himself to a pilot or a physician elected for him by the community in which he lives? or to an elective watchmaker, or who would wish his cook to be elected for him?

If liberty required judges dependent on the sovereign people, then consistent reasoning would lead us to the conclusion that the highest liberty exists whère there are no officers at all set apart as judges, but where the people themselves, or a crowd of them assembled in the market, are the judges. A more deplorable administration of justice, however, than that of the people of Athens, assembled in the agora, cannot well be imagined, for a community which aims at liberty. An eminent Frenchman—now banished from France, because too " liberal"—proclaimed, in a sort of manifesto issued from his exile, that liberty consists in equality, and equality demands the abolition of two houses and of immovable judges. *We* consider the representative system necessary for liberty in national polities, and the one house system a grievous error; while we believe an independent judiciary an indispensable element of enduring freedom.

The independent position of the judge is more important in republics—and especially in republics founded on universal suffrage—than in monarchies; for, to resist a monarch imparts dignity to a man; there is something heroic in opposition, but opposing the influence of the people, however mistaken they may be, requires far greater courage, for he who does it is easily stamped with contempt, as an enemy to the people, while those who are opposed present no responsibility. Who can bring the people to an account?

It is not because judges are, forsooth, worse than other people, but it is simply because they are human beings like every one of us that they must necessarily become subject to the sovereign, who stands high above the executive, when they desire re-election or wish to remain on good terms with the prince, as Machiavelli calls the sovereign of a state, whether the sovereign power be in one or in the community. That prince has always his courtiers. It has ever been considered highly despotic when kings have taken the administration of justice into their own hands, and not allowed their own courts of law to decide between them and the subjects; and in a somewhat similar manner is it incumbent upon the popular sovereign to erect an independent judiciary between themselves and single citizens, as well as between citizen and citizen.

Candor will oblige every reflecting citizen to confess that, speaking now of our whole country, the elective appointment and short duration of office has not improved our judicial system in any way, nor is it, probably, the people at large who care much for it—certainly not where they fully understand it. It is rather Impatience which leads to the support of the present system—impatience of a portion of the profession at the little chance there would be to obtain a seat on the bench under the old system, and occasional impatience at judges who may stand in the way of certain favorite ideas. We recollect very clearly how the Washington journal, which was considered the "official paper" under President Jackson, vehemently advocated the abolition of the "good behavior" principle in the supreme court, because this tribunal would not render opinions agreeing in spirit with the party then dominant. We are sometimes told that in a certain place the elective principle has worked well, and then a good judge is pointed out to us who has been elected three times in succession, because his party is in an overwhelming majority in his district; so that, as an evidence of the fair working of the principle the approach to an appointment for life or for a long tenure of the office, is pointed out. But all things in a free country must be calculated for the test of parties nearly balanced and increasing in ardor as they approach to an equality in number and in power. Where this state of things obtains in our country the elective judiciary has decidedly not recommended itself.

Every consideration, therefore—many having not been touched upon—seems *to bid us return to the well-tried bulwark of constitutional life and existence—to the non-electiveness of the judiciary, and the appointment during good behavior, to which it would be wise to add the removal of judges by the concurrent vote of both houses of the legislature, two-thirds of the members present concurring, and the cause of removal being entered in the journal of each house; or by a separate two-thirds vote of each house.*

In England it has been seen a judge *may* be removed upon the address of both houses of parliament—that is to say, it shall be lawful for the crown to remove a judge if the two houses have addressed the king to that effect. It is not obligatory for the crown to do so. In our far more popular governments a two-thirds vote of the legislature ought to be necessary on the one hand, and a two-thirds vote, once given, ought to be tantamount to removal, and not make it merely lawful for the executive to remove the judge, thus having drawn down upon himself the adverse opinion of so large a majority of both houses.

Courts of Peace and Arbitration.

There are, indeed, elective judges, if they can be fairly called judges, who, according to the testimony of statistics, as well as of great lawyers, such as Lord Brougham, in the house of lords, highly recommend themselves, and it will not be inappropriate for the convention to consider whether the revised constitution ought not to leave it permissive for the legislature to introduce them at a future period.

In Prussia, Denmark, and other countries permanent courts of arbitration, or rather courts of peace, as they are called in the native languages, have been introduced. Their characteristic features are the following:

The whole country is divided into districts of courts of peace.

Each district elects periodically several judges of peace, so that parties may have a choice.

Each party must plead his own case, no professional lawyer being allowed.

Submission to these courts is wholly voluntary; but the contending parties must agree upon the judge whom they select, and sign a declaration that they will submit to the decision.

Civil suits, of whatever amount, and suits for small personal offences only, are admitted.

The administration of these courts in public.

The introduction of the principle of conciliation and peace for the litigation in law courts was attempted in France, in the first revolution, but their justices of peace never acquired much importance until, as we understand, within the last decennium or two. Nor will it be necessary to say that these judges and courts of peace and arbitration have anything similar with the justices of the peace in the English system of law, except in name.

The amount of property disposed of by the courts of peace, according to the officially published statistics, is stupendous; and the litigation thus prevented is, of course, proportionate. It occurs even that in great cases before the regular courts— for instance, in will cases of comprehensive magnitude and legal difficulty—portions of the case, concerning which the parties may agree, are taken out of the court, and decided by a freely-selected court of peace, whose decision is taken back to the original court, thenceforth to form an element of the case, and of the ultimate decision, not wholly dissimilar to the sending of a portion of a case in chancery before a jury to have facts decided, and of receiving the decision into the general case.

It appears that these courts of peace really mark a distinct progress in our civilization. They are a partial return to the origin of all administration of justice, as real progress is so often a return not to primitive barbarity, but to an original principle; and it is well to be weighed whether the introduction of the voluntary submission to a permanent court of arbitration, with elective judges, would not be wise and expedient when every consideration of substantial liberty and thorough protection calls for the abolition of an elective judiciary of the regular law-courts. Perhaps we may go farther, and say that these courts and messengers of peace, by the side of, and along with, the law-courts, may be found peculiarly assimilative with a modern republican system, and commendable in our polity, in which a sterling and uncompromising administration of the law is made necessary by, and justly expected to exist parallel with, the highest possible individual liberty.

Be it then repeated, that a place ought to be left open in the new constitution for the possible introduction of the system of courts of peace.

Number of Courts.

Speedy administration of justice is so universally acknowledged as a very element of justice itself, that it would be superfluous to dwell on the subject, were it not that in our state the accumulation of judicial business causes a very serious delay of justice. This is not owing to the courts, to the lawyers, or to the character of our trials, but to the fact that the constitution of '46 establishes a number of judges and courts inadequate to the increasing population and wealth, and to the consequently multiplied transactions of men. Care, therefore, ought to be taken in the revised constitution that sufficient adaptiveness to circumstances be left, and that those fettering details be omitted which are peculiarly inexpedient for communities so rapidly changing and growing as our own.

The legislature ought to have the right to adapt the number of courts and of judges to the exigencies of the times ; and the conditions ought to be pointed out under which the legislature shall be obliged to increase the number of courts or to make redistributions of them.

Appointment of State Officers and their Tenure of Office.

So much for the judges ; as to the appointment of the state officers, such as the canal commission, inspector of prisons, it is well to remember that the first of all requisites for an appointment to office, in a stable, regulated polity of freemen, is fitness, and this fitness can be obtained only when responsibility visibly and pointedly centres in the appointing power, and when sufficient time is given for the incumbent to make the experience of one year bear fruit in the next. The idea of possessing an office like an estate is abhorrent to essential civil liberty, but equally abhorrent is the idea of rotation merely for the sake of rotation. It leads to disregard of fitness and even of character ; to a taking the whole government for a prey to be seized upon by him who can—a state of things worse than the treating of offices like convenient farms; to the sway of a few who without responsibility make out the ticket, all appearances of a general election to the contrary notwithstanding ; and finally it leads to the withdrawal of the fittest men and those of a sterling character from an honorable competition for honorable offices, which is one of the greatest evils that can befall a republic. The idea of rotation ; the idea that no one and nothing is entitled to office, not even talent and virtue ; that the more arbitrarily offices are bestowed, the clearer is shown the unrestricted power of the people, and the more absolute the power of the people, the greater is their liberty—these ideas were most strictly and logically carried out in the Greek democracies ; for there they appointed by the lot. Aristotle says in his Politics, that the true criterion of the democracy (the absolute and unmitigated democracy of his time) is the lot, and we all know what those democracies ended in, after a very short-lived existence. The testimony which we find in history is corroborated by the unanimous condemnation of those contemporaries whose reflections have come down to us—of the philosophers, the poets, the statesmen, and the historians. A short life and a rapid downward career, when once the downward course had begun, without any recuperative power—this was the fate of all of them. Modern civilization requires longevity of political societies or nations, and recuperative powers, such as modern nations have shown them, and such as not one ancient state has exhibited.

The former almost universal mode of appointing by the executive, with the consent of the senate, seems to be far the best; certainly no better one has yet been discovered. The last but one constitution of South Carolina effected all appointments by election and by joint ballot of the legislature, without any co-operation of the governor. It produced a stringent centralism without a sharply-felt responsibility—a state of things by no means inviting imitation; indeed, one of the chief advantages of a uni-executive, now universally adopted in America, is this, that the executive is lifted sufficiently above, or singled out from the rest of the citizens, both to feel somewhat, at least, disentangled from party meshes, and to individualize responsibility.

It would seem, then, advisable that the revised constitution *contain a provision which gives all state appointments, and those more local offices which the legislature may point out by law, to the governor, with the consent of the senate, and which lays down the period of years for which such appointments shall hold—say, for instance, six years—unless the legislature assigns a shorter or longer term to any specific office by a two-thirds vote.*

Suffrage.

Whether for the benefit of the people or the contrary, universal suffrage has become the generally adopted principle on which our political systems are based; that is to say, the right of voting for the members of the legislatures is freely granted to every male citizen of age, with some exceptions, however, and among these the exception based upon color is the most prominent. The constitution of 1846 gives the right of voting to every male citizen of age, excepting the man of color; but this exception again has its exceptions.

The train of reasoning in article II. of the present state constitution is this:

Every male citizen of age has a right to vote, without reference to property, education, birth, or knowledge of the language of the land. It is a right which belongs to the inherent humanity of a man of age.

Nevertheless, this humanity is defeated or invalidated by color. By whatever process this may be effected, the color incapacitates.

Yet, again, if a person of color is " seized and possessed of a freehold estate of the value of two hundred and fifty dollars over and above all debts and encumbrances charged thereon, and shall have been actually rated and paid a tax thereon," in that case he "shall be entitled to vote at such election;" so that the possession of an estate of the value of two hundred and fifty dollars, invalidates, in turn, the effect of color, which had incapacitated the person of African descent from voting. Two hundred and fifty dollars restore his full humanity, or make him white, so to say.

So glaring an inconsistency ought not to continue in our fundamental law. The psychologic principle of humanity is first adopted; it is modified by a physiologic reason; and this modification is modified again by an economic reason. Arguments taken from wholly different spheres are here strung together for sound logic, and it would appear advisable that *no property qualification being adopted in general, it ought also to be omitted with reference to persons of color*, who are here, who cannot be extinguished by law, whatever may be done in the course of time by the process of absorption; whose race was forcibly brought hither by our race, and who do not in our state constitute the least respectable portion of the population.

In connection with the subject of state suffrage, it is believed that the convention ought to consider very thoroughly whether it would not be wise and expedient to adopt the principle that no person shall have the right to vote in state elections, or shall be considered a citizen of the state, as it is generally expressed, who is not a citizen of the United States. It is a subject of the highest importance, a discussion of which would require an extent which cannot be allotted to it in a paper like the present one. It must be dismissed, therefore, with this allusion. Citizenship in America, however frequently it has been the ground of dispute, has not yet received that breadth of discussion which it 'deserves and demands, especially in point of state citizenship and American or United States citizenship, and with reference to the question whether there really are two citizenships in America, as many persons seem to suppose. Is it wise—is it even just to allow foreigners to vote in state elections immediately after their arrival, as is actually the case in some states? And is it right or necessary to allow them a share in the important affairs of state governments before the United States confer upon them the complete legal status? Are, then, our state affairs trifles? Strange indeed! According to the state sovereignty doctrine, the states are the only sovereigns, and the United States a mere temporary partnership, yet the citizenship of the sovereign states was thrown to almost every man, whilst the citizenship of that loose partnership was surrounded with dignity.

Extension of Suffrage to Women.

The adoption of universal suffrage has led many persons to the belief and broad assertion that the right of voting is a natural right, and if it is a natural right, it ought, as a matter of course, to be extended to woman; while, on the other hand, many persons seem to profess that no qualification whatever —neither residence, nor acquaintance with our polity or language, nor untarnished character, nor interest in the commonwealth—should be demanded as a requisite for the right of voting. All these are erroneous conceptions.

A natural right cannot mean anything but a right (that is,

a well-founded claim) directly proceeding from the very attributes of humanity, the nature of men. The right of life,
of property, or exclusive possession of what we have produced
or first appropriated when it belonged to no one—as the fish
in the sea ; the right of communion, of locomotion, of education and self-improvement, or progress and civilization; of the
family, as the social institution prior to all states ; the right of
government, that is, of forming political societies to govern
and be governed; the right of having laws and of association ;
the right of exchanging of what is our own; the right of
roads for intercommunication and locomotion; the right of
worshipping—all these are natural rights, because they are
acknowledgments of the constituents of humanity, and claims
of each on each, and ought to remain unmolested in the pursuit and development of humanity.

The natural rights are always observed, at least in their incipiency ; they become always more developed and intenser
as civilization advances; they are always recuperated when
brutal force or ramified despotism has obscured them or beaten
them down for a time ; and the denial of them is always met
with direct resentment, even in the lowest savage, corresponding to the developed consciousness of these primordial or
natural rights.

But how can so special a right as that of voting for a representative be a natural right, when the representative government itself is something that does not spring directly from
the nature of man, however natural it may be in another sense
of the word—that is to say, consistent with the progress of
civilization ?   It is the latest and the highest of all civilized
governments ; but where was the natural right of suffrage
under the patriarchal government—in the Mosaic commonwealth, founded on a hereditary and priestly nobility ; where
in the Asiatic despotism—types of government necessary in
their season—when nothing and nobody was voted for ?

The national polity is the normal type of modern government or of the political dispensation of our age ; the great
aim of our civilization is the greater and greater development,

and firmer establishment and wider extension of substantial civil liberty; and the only means of obtaining this great end, under the first-mentioned condition, is the representative system. The representative system is the only means of protecting individual liberty, and preventing democratic despotism. The right of suffrage, therefore, is a noble right, or ought to be so; but it is not a natural right. It is a political right, to which Providence has led man in the progressive course of history.

Take from a savage the fruit he has just plucked from the tree, or his child, or prevent him from talking with his friend, or incarcerate him, and you will excite his resentment on the spot; but prevent him from voting where the right to do so may have been extended to him by some wholesale theory, and no resentment will be observable. On the contrary, it is unfortunately a fact that the more you extend suffrage, on a really large scale, the less people care for it, until we discover the humiliating fact that at large elections with universal suffrage, it is no uncommon occurrence that only forty-five out of a hundred qualified voters actually go to the poll; fifty and fifty-five per centum are common; sixty and sixty-five per centum shows a deep interest in the question, and seventy-five a passionate interest. Eighty voters out of a hundred hardly ever go to the poll, outside of large cities. Moreover, a question of law, of principle, of a constitution, of secession itself[1] never brings out as many voters as a question of personal interest. Shall A or C be inspector of the county jail? will bring more ballots to the poll than the question, Shall we adopt a proposed constitution?

If, then, the right of voting is a political, and not a natural right, it cannot be claimed for the female sex as a natural right; but it is claimed at present on several other grounds, which, I believe, may be summed up in the following way:

---

[1] So startling a fact requires authority for its statement; I feel obliged, therefore, to deviate from the rule I laid down for myself at the beginning of my paper, and refer the reader to a paper on election statistics in the Appendix to Civil Liberty.

Withholding suffrage from the women is a degradation of the female sex.

If she cannot vote she is not represented.

Giving the right of voting to the latter would highly improve and even refine our elections, and not un-woman the woman.

Lastly: Why not? Why should they not vote like ourselves? Are they worse than we are?

Every student of civilization knows that the position which woman occupies in society is one of the gages by which we try to ascertain the civilization of that society in general. We all know that every step onward has assigned to woman some important element of civilization which, until then, was withheld from her as unfit or unnecessary for her——even education itself; nay, reading and writing not excluded. Every one knows that women are freely admitted to occupations now which but a short time ago would have been withheld from them. It characterizes the Bible very highly that the woman, in the Old Testament, occupies a far higher place than, at the time, she did in Asia generally, and that women appear as prominent personages in the origin and first spread of Christianity, both at the age of Christ and during the first centuries, when the Roman matron, a noble type even in the pagan times, gave essential aid to the diffusion of that religion for which many women as well as men died the martyr's death. We all recollect what American mothers and sisters and daughters have heroically done in our last struggle for our country, and no nobler type of humanity can be conceived than a patriotic mother or wife who, with the hot tears of affection in the last embrace, still says: Go; or who goes to the hospital and gives herself up to the work of comforting and assuaging, and healing, while her husband or her father may be fighting either near or far away. We have had many, many illustrations of this patriotic type; but, happily, patriotism is not necessarily politics, and we say boldly, that those women who truly know their calling, which lies far beyond politics, do not desire the vote.

Not accepting the votes from women is as little degradation to woman, as women are degraded in those monarchies in which no princess can ascend the throne, or, we may say indeed, as she is degraded in England, because she can there ascend the throne only when no brothers of her, even younger than herself, are left to assume the crown. It is a political law which regulates the succession, and no degradation ensues. The Roman church, which canonizes women as well as men, does not degrade the female sex by excluding it from the priesthood.

Division of labor, as the political economists call the very foundation of our whole economy, begins with the division of the sexes, and expands forth as a physiological and psychologic division and distribution of employment, pursuit, and social relations. According to this distribution the political occupation ought not be assumed by woman.

Man and woman are made to complete one another; to become " one flesh and bone," to establish the family, whence the state arises not only in primeval times, but every day anew; the destiny of the woman is to rely, to be protected, to harmonize in society with her attractions, both physical and psychological, the jarring elements brought by men from the sterner and not unfrequently coarser pursuits of practical life; the influence of woman, in her appropriate province, and which, owing to her living far more in the world of feeling than in that of reasoning and calculation, is so direct and great that a transfer to other spheres is dangerous and of evil effect; she exercises and ought to exercise much of her beneficial influence by her delicacy and modesty, and her legitimate influence in the proper sphere would be lost were she to enter the arena of politics. The inter-completing character of the two sexes, so necessary to us in the plans of Providence, would be lost; she would cease to be a true companion; politics would undoubtedly unwoman her, and her essential character and desirable, nay necessary, influence would be lost. Is she to vote by mere impulse and feeling, or is she to visit public meetings? Who wishes this of his own mother, his wife, his

sister, his daughter? So foreign is political strife or management to her nature, that wherever women have seized upon it,
it seems they have seized upon the worst elements in politics,
from the French fish-women in the revolution to a Pompa-
dour. Female monarchs sometimes form exceptions, owing
to their peculiar position; but how would we like to have a
female president, and what would it lead to? Wherever the
distinction of the sexes is erased, in whatever condition of
life this may be, it excites that regret which all confusion of
primary laws produces. There are exceptions indeed. He
who writes these pages fought by the side of a woman-ser-
geant, so brave that she received successively several orders
of distinction, which graced her breast when, at a later period,
she stood before the altar to be wedded to another sergeant.
Ought I, on the ground of this exceptional case, to propose
the extension of the militia law to all the women of the
state?

Where a high property qualification exists, or where, for
any other reason, there are but few votes to be collected, we
may imagine single women to vote without producing a serious
disturbance in society, whatever the effect on themselves may
be; but so far from allowing that the suffrage of women is
nothing but a consistent extension of the universal suffrage
principle, I hold it to be a well-founded truth, that, of all countries, those in which universal suffrage exists are the very ones
in which woman herself and society at large would suffer most
from such a change. Woman would not carry into politics
grace, amenity, and the element of the beautiful, so important
in all civilization; but she would be infallibly contaminated
by the coarser elements of politics, suffer far more than men,
who can, occasionally, swallow a dose of coarseness without
producing a permeating ill effect in their whole system. Not
that coarseness is indifferent. Far from it, indeed! But
the fact will not be denied, that indelicacy has not the general ruinous effect on man which it infallibly produces in
woman. What effects are those produced in women who
enjoy the turf, or speculate at the bourse, in Paris? The

answer, that these places have no good effect on men either, would be no proper reply, for these places denaturalize the woman; the inconsistency in the case produces a hideous character.

Nor can it be said that she is not represented if she does not vote. A representative is not a thing made up of thousands of bits coming from the voters, as the confectioner makes up his figures of many ingredients. The representative is a living individuality, elected because the majority think he will make a fair law-maker for them, and will sufficiently take care of their interest. In this respect is not the interest of the wife, the daughter, the woman in general, whose destiny and calling are closely intertwined with those of the other sex, represented by the vote of the men? If the positive voting alone procures representation, how, then, am I represented when I vote in the minority? A class, indeed, separated for whatever reason it may be from the rest of the community, is not represented if it cannot make its interests felt by the vote; the peasant was plainly not represented when the three estates of the clergy, nobility, and citizens constituted the government; but to say that a husband does not represent his wife or whole family, is abandoning essential truths and attempting to reduce state affairs to fallacious arithmetical calculations.

Enough has probably been said on a subject which, however, has by no means been exhausted, and it may be sufficient simply to add, *that the convention, it is to be hoped, will not yield to the entreaties which will doubtlessly be made in a spirit which happens to be fashionable just now in our restless period. Female suffrage ought not to be established.*

Number of Representatives.

Corruption, even the corruption of representatives, that is, in plain words, the taking of money for the sacred trust of the vote, has become an alarming evil with us, because our government is republican, and republics can weather corruption probably less easily than monarchies; because this corruption has broken out immediately after the high-toned and heroic period of our recent struggle, when willing sacrifice was the prevailing order of the day; because no direct means of cure offers itself for such a malady, and because, not only does in republics responsibility appear to the evil-disposed to be divided, although moral responsibility, in its very nature, is indivisible, but also injury itself seems to the willing offender to be divided and lose its malignant definiteness. To cheat the public, to defraud the treasury, to be dishonest to a commonwealth, appears vague, and is taken as a somewhat abstract offence. We mortals are so coarse that it requires a certain elevation of character not to feel less repugnance to defraud the people than to cheat the same people through a living individual—by name a king.[1]

Corruption in public men has recently been called the "canker-worm of the Anglo-Saxon," with reference to the peculation which is perpetrated both in England and here. There is, however, nothing either English or American, Saxon or not Saxon, in public corruption, although it may show itself, for aught we know, at this moment more glaringly in England and here than anywhere else, because the pursuit of wealth is carried on here more energetically, the opportunity of obtaining it is greater, and the struggle for the obtaining of certain political institutions, and public liberty, is more finished in the two great English-speaking nations than elsewhere. What a canker-worm of the Gallic race has not corruption been within our own remembrance!

---

[1] The imagined divisibility of crime (as if of three men killing another, each committed a third of a murder only); or the imaginary divisibility of responsibility in a body of men (according to which men have so often voted for wrong or shame, when single they would not have had the daring to do so); and the callousness which is felt in injuring an impersonal victim (as if it were not criminal to rob when to a certainty the victim will never know the injury done him)—these subjects have never received the attention and treatment which would be adequate to their psychologic and historical importance. "Single is each man born; single he dies, and single he must answer for what he has done in this life."

Be this, however, as it may, so much is certain, that the evil cannot be cured by a simple political prescription, and especially not by an extension of the number of representatives, as has been irrationally proposed. A thousand representatives, it has been said, will not be so easily corrupted as three hundred; but moral evils are neither cured by mechanical contrivances nor by arithmetical means. On the contrary, when responsibility is spread over a wide surface it becomes proportionally thin and pervious. Bribery would become cheap; men of high character would wholly decline to be nominated for the legislature, and the public standard would sink low indeed, nor ought the election districts be suffered to remain as small as now.

The smaller an election district is made, the smaller will be the man who is sent to the legislature. Many persons believe liberty to consist in close representation, and close representation to consist in the fact of a representative being taken out of the very midst of the smallest possible cluster of men, as if a representative were a sample, sent to the legislature as one bale of cotton is sent to the custom-house representing a hundred fellow-bales on board a ship which has entered the port. Nor is the modern representative an attorney sent with instructions, such as the members of the Third Estate were in the Middle Ages, who asked for new instructions when those they had received proved insufficient. A modern representative is neither a sample, nor a chemical compound of particles taken from the different constituents, nor an attorney or instructed agent with powers limited by the elected. A representative is a living individuality and un-mysterious human being, elected for his character, knowledge, and interest he feels in the community, to be one of the legislators for the whole nation or state, as the case may be, and one of those who act as trustees of the whole, so as to help breaking the absolutism which necessarily makes itself felt wherever the public power acts directly and unmitigated by intervening trustees or representatives. The election of the representative ought to be left perfectly free, so as to make it honorable to be elected, and to leave to the people a free choice. It seems to have been thought in America agreeable to a high sense of liberty if the choice of representatives was restricted by law, and a residence among the electors was required to be qualified for election. Doubtless this was done on the supposition that the representative is sent to the legislature like a sample; in reality, however, no one ought to limit the choice. If electors prefer a man of their neighborhood, they may choose him; but let freemen enjoy the liberty of electing whom they think proper.

Regarding this subject, then, the convention ought to remember that three hundred—rather less than more—is the number of representatives which experience has suggested to us as the most practical;[1] that election districts ought to have a sufficient extent for liberal action, and that full freedom ought to be left to the constituents to elect any citizen of the state, wherever he may reside.

State Sovereignty, Double Allegiance.

The constitution of New York applies the word "sovereign" to the state. Ought it to be left there after we have just emerged from a terrible conflict caused by this very term being applied to the single states? Is it necessary in any way to retain it?

No word has been used in more different significations than that of sovereign, from the first meaning in its derivation from the mediæval *superanus* (signifying optimate, or one of the upper and ruling class in the city-republics) to the meaning of chief, as when we say sovereign remedy; or as courts from which there lay no appeal, were called sovereign courts; to the proud assumption by Louis XIV. and his puny imitators, the Stuarts; and finally, to the mysterious meaning ascribed to it by the secessionists, according to whom a state was "abso-

---

[1] The English exception to this rule is more apparent than real. The English firmly established parliamentary usage rests on conditions totally different from ours.

lutely sovereign," and yet was subject to a superior constitution and was deprived of most attributes generally recognized as those of sovereignty.

Cardinal Mazarin sent word to the French ambassador at Munster to insist above all things on the different German princes being declared sovereign although the form of the empire was allowed to continue. This was avowedly done to make Germany weak and break up the power of Austria. Only now the Germans have commenced to throw off this virus of petty sovereignty, and now again they are opposed by France.

I have collected some interesting facts and given my thoughts on this subject on a previous occasion. A few additional words may, however, be said on State Allegiance. It has been "decided" by our highest court, when it consisted of the senate, that there exists a double allegiance in this state—one allegiance due to the government of the United States, and one to the state of New York; but if allegiance implies the highest or supreme obedience to some one or some power—and what does it mean if it does not mean that? —a double allegiance is an impossibility and *nemo ad impossibilia obligatur.*

I can only repeat that a "double allegiance" is far worse than the graduated allegiance of the feudal system and allegiance following sovereignty; it would seem advisable that *the word sovereign be omitted in the revised constitution as unnecessary, deceptive, indeterminate, and mischievous, capable of a variety of interpretations, and flattering to puny vanity.*

City Government.

This age has been justly called the Age of Cities, for in no period previous to the present one have so many populous cities existed at one and the same time; and at no former age have the demands for personal and individual liberty been so great as at present. The problem how to harmonize dense and large city populations with the highest demands of political liberty—with universal suffrage, for instance—has no-where been solved, and the least approach to a solution has probably been made with us, especially so in the city in which these pages are now writing.

City populations, enjoying a high degree of liberty, are far more subject to demagoguism than the rural population, as all city democracies of antiquity and the Middle Ages show, and as may be very readily accounted for. It is an evil which is vastly increased in those of our cities into which monthly, almost daily, numbers of foreigners, not trained in our politi-cal and school systems, flow, and soon exercise that right of voting which, in ancient cities, even in the most democratic, such as Athens, was jealously withheld from every man not born to the soil and of citizen parents. Our city governments are mismanaged; they are corrupt; maladministration has become the rule; and proportionately little is obtained by the citizen for the high taxes imposed on him. Everywhere are citizens obliged to have recourse to private means for greater safety and greater public cleanliness.

Here, as elsewhere, it has been proposed to find a remedy in frequently repeated elections of all officers, by universal suffrage. This would simply multiply the evil in proportion to the repetition of the elections, and to the further extension of suffrage. Imagine what government—if government, in-deed, it could be called—would come to in a city like New York, with monthly elections of all officers, and women's suf-frage added to the present general suffrage!

A city government is not and ought not to be like a gen-eral, legislating government. A city government is chiefly a police government, and has to watch over the safety of the inhabitants, over their health, and over public morality. These, with common education and public charity, are the legitimate ends which ought to be before the eyes of city officers. The distribution of money for these objects is one of the main objects, and the sums which are levied to obtain these ends are, in our cities, immense, and induce peculation of a flagrant character, where plain and pointed responsibility is diminished by constant change, and by officers backed by electing majorities, and where the public money is voted away chiefly by those who do not pay city taxes. What remedy can be resorted to against an evil growing with appalling rapidity? Would our people, for instance the people of New York, allow a division of the city into a number of municipal corporations containing populations equal to those of other cities of respectable size, say two hundred thousand? And would this not lead, in all probability, to a city confederacy, with its full share of danger and of mischief? At any rate, experienced mariners will not launch at once on such unknown seas—unknown, yet with well-known breakers.

Even if universal suffrage is retained as a general principle for the general state government, as will be most likely the case, there is no reason why a portion of the suffrage for the city government should not be restricted to the tax-payers,— that is why the authority of spending the large sums should not, in part, be restricted to those who pay the sum to be spent. It is a most republican principle. We do not want a representative of public opinion in general, but cashiers, as it were, and we find suffrage restricted in a hundred cases where the election of a representative is not the object. The comptroller, on the other hand, ought, it seems, to be an officer distinctly disconnected with the city government, an officer appointed by the legislature, or by the governor, with the consent of the senate, with a proper inspection over him ; and lastly, the city government ought to be strictly prohibited from appropriating any money, except plainly for city objects of public necessity—no dinners, no medals, no receptions. This undoubtedly would occasionally appear at first stingy, perhaps even mean ; but we have gotten into such straits that we cannot allow ourselves to be drawn from what is necessary and indispensable. Perhaps after the trial of a rigid régime for twenty years, something milder may be introduced by way of amendment to the constitution ; for the present it seems that a provision of the constitution should establish for cities containing a population above a certain number:

Two houses, one of which representing the tax-payers exclusively;

A superintendent of the finances and disbursing officer appointed by the legislature or the governor, with the consent of the senate, for five years at least;

And a strict inhibition of all expenditure, except such as may be required for direct ends of public necessity.

Such a government would be of a tentative character only; but no wise and experienced statesman will pretend to move in novel cases of great importance, in any other way. It is only the demagogue, or the lover of his own fantastic theories, who can pretend to an infallible sagacity in combinations unknown until now.

Education and Educational Test.

Great efforts are made in the state of New York to promote public education, but it is observed by all who are well acquainted with our school system, that, in many portions of the state, the result is not adequate to the expenditure of money and to the time given up to the important end. One of the reasons is the irregularity of the attendance in the school, and the question has frequently occupied our different school boards, whether attendance could not be made obligatory in our state, as it is in many other communities, where fine, and even imprisonment, awaits the parent who neglects to send his children, of a certain age, to school. No one doubts the right of a government—especially of a government founded on universal suffrage; that is, on supposed general intelligence—to make school attendance obligatory, when that government liberally establishes a public school system throughout the land. The given conditions, however, may make it difficult, sometimes impossible, to introduce this principle. Those who have paid minute attention to the state of things in the city of New York, agree that it would be difficult to introduce a plainly compulsory law of school attendance in this place. Indirect means and legitimate allurements may be devised, but it is doubtful whether, at present, simple compulsion could be resorted to by the people. Would it, then, not be wise on the one hand to leave it optional with each county to adopt compulsory school education, and on the other hand to establish the educational test for the right of voting throughout the state?

The optional principle regarding certain laws has been, of late, adopted with good effect in several countries; and no valid reason can be given against an educational test of suffrage in a polity founded on universal suffrage by ballot, and not by word of mouth.

The same lack of logic which was pointed out in another section of these pages pervades our present suffrage. The case stands thus:

We insist on universal suffrage;

Because we think the people at large sufficiently intelligent, or we take the means to make them sufficiently intelligent to vote understandingly;

Our ideas of individual independence demand the voting by ballot and not by open word of mouth;

Yet we allow every one to vote, whether he can read the ballot which he drops into the urn or not; that is to say, whether he knows for whom or what he is voting or not; so that after all we do not care for the individual independence of the voter or an intelligent vote.

The educational test, which only demands the very minimum of education, is especially requisite where universal suffrage exists; and a man who cannot read his own vote, and cannot read his journal, or reports on public affairs, is so separated from public opinion, public discussion, and public progress, in a time when public information is not obtained in the public market as it was in Athens, that there is no wrong whatever in withholding from him the vote.

In the Swiss republics, each voter must write his ballot at the polling-place before the election officers.

No injustice would be done if we adopt the reading and writing test, especially if it were settled that such a test should go into operation three years from the day of the ratification of the new constitution. A man who cannot learn to read and write in three years had better stay away from the polls.

It seems incumbent, therefore, on the convention, *to consider the propriety of introducing a clause in the revised constitution which allows each county to introduce compulsory school attendance, and which makes the test of reading and writing, to be proved, in cases of challenge at the polling-place—the latter by writing the ballot, or a portion of it—a requisite for the exercise of the right of voting, from the beginning of the fourth year after the adoption of the new fundamental law of this state.*

Two subjects will require the attention of the convention— namely, the impossibility of doing all the legislative business of a community of four millions within one hundred days, and the impropriety as well as inconvenience of allowing every judge and magistrate, however limited his sphere may be, to pronounce on the constitutionality of a law according to his fancy ; but these subjects will undoubtedly induce the framers of our fourth constitution to weigh them well, and to provide remedies where they are found necessary.

FRAGMENTS OF POLITICAL SCIENCE

ON

NATIONALISM

AND

INTERNATIONALISM.

A nation without a national government is an awful spectacle.
ALEXANDER HAMILTON.

The following pages (p. 225, et seq.), contain what I believe to be the latest and fullest revision of an essay on " Nationalism and Internationalism," which was dedicated to General U. S. Grant on the eve of his first election to the presidency (New York, 1868).

Those who are interested in tracing the development of a thought may compare with the fuller essay the following earlier and briefer fragment.—G.

NATIONALISM.

THE NATIONAL POLITY IS THE NORMAL TYPE OF MODERN GOVERNMENT.

A FRAGMENT BY FRANCIS LIEBER.

As the city-state was the normal type of free communities in antiquity, and as the feudal system was one of the normal types of government in the Middle Ages, so is the national polity the normal type of our own epoch—not indeed centralism.

Large nations have been formed out of the fragmentary peoples on the continent of Europe, England alone dating the blessing of a national polity over a thousand years back; others are in the act of forming; others, already existing, are carrying out more distinctly or establishing more firmly the national elements of their polities.   For this reason, and because the existence of many nations deeply influences our civilization, the present period will be called the National Period.   It began plainly when so many other great things began—in the middle of the fifteenth century; but the process of nationalization concerning the languages and the literature of the different countries commenced at an earlier time.

The three main characteristics of the political development which mark the modern epoch are:

The national polity ;

The general endeavor to define more clearly, and to extend more widely, human rights and civil liberty;

And the decree which has gone forth that many leading nations shall flourish at one and the same time, plainly distinguished from one another, yet striving together, with one public opinion, under the protection of one law of nations, and in the bonds of one common moving civilization.

The universal monarchy, whether purely political or coupled with the papacy ; a single leading nation ; confederacies of petty sovereigns ; a civilization confined to one spot, or one portion of the globe—all these are obsolete, insufficient for

222

the demands of advanced civilization, and attempts at their renewal are ruinous. Even the course which civilization has steadily taken for thousands of years, from the southeast to the northwest, has ceased. It now spreads for the first time in all directions, and bends its way back to the Orient. The old historic belt between 30° and 50° northern latitude, within which the great current of events has flown, shall confine history no more.

In ancient times one people always swayed and led. Hence the simplicity of chronologic tables presenting the events of that time; and all ancient states were short-lived. Once declining, they never recovered. Their course was that of the projectile: ascending, a maximum, a precipitate descent, and no more rising. Modern nations are long-lived, and possess recuperative energy wholly unknown to antiquity. They could neither be the one nor possess the other without national existence and comprehensive polities, and without the law of nations, as we know it now, which is the manly idea of self-government applied to a number of independent nations in close relation with one another. The universal law of independence, without which men would never have formed society, and which, like all original principles or characteristics of humanity, increases in intensity and spreads in action as the human species advances—the universal law of interdependence applies to nations as it applies to individuals. This blessed interdependence among nations is becoming daily more cheerfully acknowledged; and the old saying, *Ubi Societas ibi Jus,* finds constantly increasing application to entire nations. The civilized nations have come to constitute a community of nations, and are daily forming more and more a commonwealth of nations, under the restraint and protection of the law of nations, which rules *vigore divino.* They draw the chariot of civilization abreast, as the ancient steeds drew the car of victory.

NATIONALISM AND INTERNATIONALISM.

The National Polity is the normal type of Modern Government; Civil Liberty resting on Institutional Self-Government is the high political calling of this period; Absolutism, whether Monarchical or Democratic, intelligent and brilliant or coarse, its pervading danger; and increasing International Neighborliness with growing Agreement of National Forms and Concepts, its fairest Gage of the Spreading Progress of our Kind.

I.

Normal Types of Government. Nationalization.

As the city-state was the normal type of free communities in antiquity, and as the feudal system must be considered as one of the normal types of government in the forbidding Middle Ages, so is the national polity the normal type of our own epoch—not indeed centralism.

The highest national polity yet developed is the representative national government, equally distant from the market-republic of old and the despotism of Asia or Europe, from absorbing centralism and dissolving communism, so called. Centralism may be intensely national, even to bigotry; it may become a political fanaticism; it may be intelligent and formulated with great precision; but centralism remains an inferior species of government. It is no government of peaceful development, and decentralization becomes necessary as self-government or liberty are longed for and present themselves clearer to the mind of a people waxing in manliness and independence. Centralism may be national, but national polity and centralism are far from being equivalent terms. England, which has enjoyed a national polity long before other European countries, is to this day the least centralized state of Europe, and possesses a far higher degree of self-government than any people of the neighboring continent. Germany, although the Germans were called the German Nation in the early times of the emperors, never acquired a national polity, like the English, which dates from the days of Alfred, and is openly and liberally marked out by Magna Charta. There was an England with unbarred national intercommunication long before there was a national France, Spain, or Italy, or a political, national Germany.

The "Evil Tolls" of which the Great Charter of England speaks, and which included the arrogant extortion of tolls by feudal lords along the roads and rivers, and the custom-lines between the different provinces, were abolished on the continent at a much later period. The journal minutely kept by Albert Dürer, when called by Charles V. from Nuremberg to Ghent, gives an appalling picture of the former, and the latter were abolished in France only by the first revolution. Prussia has been at work ever since the congress of Vienna to abolish the internal evil tolls in Germany, and at last succeeded in a measure. Happy, indeed, are we that our Constitution forbids the "evil tolls" in this country.

Those large communities, which we call nations, were gradually formed on the continent of Europe out of the fragmentary peoples left by the disintegration of the Roman empire. The different processes of nationalization form one of the most instructive subjects in the whole history of civilization. England dates the blessing of a national polity over a thousand years back, and in her alone liberty and nationality grew apace. Other nations are even now in the act of forming; others, already existing, are carrying out more distinctly or establishing more firmly the national elements of their polities. For this reason, and because the existence of many nations at the same time deeply influences our civilization, the present period will be called the National Period. It began plainly when so many other great things began—when great events happened and great ideas burst upon mankind, and when inventions and discoveries were made, which ushered in the modern era—in the middle of the fifteenth century; that age when the conquering Mussulman tore the fairest portion from Europe, and thereby forced the restoration of letters and revival of inquiry upon her; when Europe lost Greece in the East, and sent Columbus to the West to discover our continent, and when, close upon this event, the still greater Reformation began at home.

The process of nationalizing the many dialects and jargons had begun in some countries—geographically marked as countries, but wholly unnationalized otherwise—at an earlier time. Dante, singing in the Tuscan dialect, raised it thus to the dignity of the language for all Italy, as later Luther by his own translation of the Bible, made his dialect the German language; and Dante, the greatest poet of his country, which he calls *Italia mia di dolor ostello* (the very inn of grief), because torn to pieces and lacking her destined nationality, became thus the first nationalizer of Italy in the thirteenth and at the beginning of the fourteenth century—five hundred years before Cavour; and now only has Germany made a vigorous movement towards her political nationalization, in which may Heaven bless her leaders' boldest acts.

II.

What is a Nation in the Modern Sense of the Word?

The word Nation, in the fullest adaptation of the term, means, in modern times, a numerous and homogeneous population (having long emerged from the hunter's and nomadic state), permanently inhabiting and cultivating a coherent territory, with a well-defined geographic outline, and a name of its own—the inhabitants speaking their own language, having their own literature and common institutions, which distinguish them clearly from other and similar groups of people; being citizens or subjects of a unitary government, however subdivided it may be, and feeling an organic unity with one another, as well as being conscious of a common destiny. Organic intellectual and political internal unity, with proportionate strength, and a distinct and obvious demarcation from similar groups, are notable elements of the idea of a modern nation in its fullest sense. A nation is a nation only when there is but one nationality; and the attempt at establishing a nationality within a nationality is more inconsistent and mischievous even than the establishment of "an empire within an empire."

No groupings of human beings, short of nations, are adequate to the high demands of modern civilization. Without a national character, states cannot obtain that longevity and continuity of political society which is necessary for our progress. Even our patriotism has become pre-eminently national. Modern patriotism is not satisfied with the narrow bounds of a city, as of old, or the limits of a province, though it be the fairest. Nothing but a country, that is the dwelling-place of a nation, suffices for the *patria* of modern men. But the noblest sentiments and deeds and victories of sword or mind, even of ancient Greece, were of a Panhellenic character. Greece never got, in her political life, beyond frail confederacies with the unavoidable, undefined, but forcibly asserted hegemony of some one state, but her Hellenism—her nationalism in all other respects—in religion, in literature, in the arts, in language and poetry, in philosophy, in republicanism, in colonization and commercial spirit, and indeed in every branch of high culture, blossomed forth everywhere. She died of crushing state sovereignty, which proved so fatal to Germany; to which Napoleon III. strongly desired to reduce Italy, and which was near to be our grave.

In the organic unity lies the chief difference between the words Nation and People. People generally means the aggregate of the inhabitants of a territory, without any additional idea, at least favorable idea. In all European languages, except the English, the words corresponding to People had acquired the meaning of rabble, populace, the lowest and least respectable class. The French Dictionary of the Academy gave hardly another definition of the word *Peuple;* and in

England alone, to her great honor, did it retain, or at any rate acquire at a very early period, an honorable meaning, as Populus had possessed a dignified meaning in the better times of Rome. While the French Academy thus ignominiously defined the word People, Chatham, when George III. had reluctantly appointed him premier, used to be called the People's Minister for "His Majesty's Secretary of State;" and, on the other hand, it was natural that Louis XV. was startled when first the word Nation came to be heard in the last century, in France. He is reported to have said: "Nation! What is Nation? Is there anything besides myself?" The remark seems to be too profound for a being such as he had sunk to be; but there can be no doubt that this supposed question indicated the sentiment of that portion of the French court which was led by the Jesuits, then as under the Spanish predominance, and as now, hostile to national organic unity and to nationalism in its varied manifestations.

Extensive and organized power over large populations does not suffice to make a nation. The Roman monarchy was no national empire; nor had the vast dominion of Charles the Fifth a national character. Prussia, ever since the Peace of Paris, in 1815, called one of the Five Great Powers, never formed a nation. She herself acknowledged, and still acknowledges, that the nation to which she belongs is the German nation, though not yet politically nationalized, as Martin Luther had called it in 1520, in his grand and inspiriting letter "To the Christian Nobility of the German Nation on the Bettering of the Ghostly Class" (Clergy). Nor does common extraction and demarcating institutions, not even a peculiar religion, necessarily constitute a nation in the modern sense. The modern Jews dispersed over the globe have never consolidated into a nation. The Armenians, with their many characteristics of religion, language, and culture, form no nation. Nor does a common language alone constitute a nation. If Panslavism were ever so successful, there would be no Panslavic nation; nor can we properly speak at present of a Russian nation, however distinct the Russian empire may

be.   The Russian system has rather the tendency to trample
out nationalities and national characteristics for the benefit of
a gigantic bureaucracy, called Russia.

In antiquity and the early Middle Ages there existed no
nations, in the modern sense, this side of China, with the only
exception of the Israelites.   There were Assyrian and Median
and Persian empires, but no nations.   The empires were called
after the conquering and ruling tribe or race.   Hence their
sudden conquests and speedy annihilation.

The Mosaic constitution establishes the Israelites as different yet very closely related tribes wrought into a national
sacerdotal government; but, either the untoward surround-
ings of that people in close propinquity to fully developed,
conquering Asiatic despotism, or the inaptitude for political
development and organic congregation, which seems to be
common to the whole Semitic family, led the Israelites to disruption and secession long before their national government
had fully and comprehensively developed itself.   The history
of the Hebrews is a saddening account of national humiliation
and suicide.

The appointed and historic work of the Hebrews was to
guard, in spite of their pagan pruriency, the idea of one God,
Creator and Sustainer of all things and beings, through centuries of alluring, sensuous, and sometimes æsthetic polytheism around them.   Political nationality was subordinate with
them; yet the fact ought to arrest our grave attention that
the only monotheistic people, and the people for whom Moses
legislated, formed, in the earliest times of history, a nation
in the modern sense.   The same cannot be said of ancient
Egypt.

However striking a characteristic of a nation may be found
in a separate language, and however important a separate
name for a country or a nation may be, neither is absolutely
necessary.   We are an illustration.   We have not our separate language; and more than two distinctly separate nations
may speak the English tongue before the Cis-Caucasian race
passes into the twentieth century.   But are we a nation?

III.

The Americans form a Nation.   The Vein of Nationality crops out from our earliest periods, and the sacrifices of our Civil War have been made for two objects, one of which was to save our indispensable Nationality.

Some American publicists and statesmen consider the states, as now constituted, the pre-existent elements of our comprehensive polity, somewhat as though the present reluctance of Nova Scotia to join the Canadian Union indicated a Nova Scotian sovereignty preordained from the beginning.   This is a radical error.   The first states arose, in a great measure, out of the colonial governments, while the genesis of the later and far greater number of states is absolutely national ; and it is, indeed, a fact of moment in our history that thus comparatively small divisions of the country were formed and became normal, differing from the vice-royalties in Spanish America ; but there was nothing in these demarcations of the colonies, or in the charters or the crown gifts, that had any intrinsic connection with a future sovereignty.   The motives of these charters were often reprehensible, the geographic demarcations frequently indicated by ignorance.   What, however, really became important in the colonization of this portion of the globe are the following things and circumstances, which may be justly called factors of our growth and elements of our public life, in nearly all which our characteristics are the direct opposite to the elements of South American colonization.

The country in which our first colonists settled was an almost unbounded body of land in the temperate zone, with an extensive coast and a dignified geography, a rewarding soil and rich in minerals, thinly peopled by rovers in the hunter's stage of civilization, extending from sea to sea, and situated between the Old and the Older World.   The age at which our settlers came hither was the age marked by two characteristics—the formation of nations and the struggle of fierce Spanish Catholicism against Protestantism.   In the Netherlands freedom had been victorious against sinister absolutism; in Germany the direst of all wars, the Thirty Years' War, was raging, and Hugo Grotius published at the same time the first portion of his immortal work.   It was that period at which in Spain absolutism in politics, and the Inquisition and unlimited persecution, had been fully developed, while in England, whence our settlers came, the people accustomed to freedom were preparing for resistance to rising and tentative absolutism.   Our colonists belonged to the virile branch of the Teutonic race in England; they were Protestants.   They rather fled for peaceful existence than in order to conquer and slaughter populous tribes; they came from a country in which a national government had existed for centuries. The feudal estates had long been shaped into a representative system with two houses, and in which a common, that is, a national, law had evolved itself in a great measure independent of the executive, containing manly principles of individual independence and self-government, with a position of the judiciary and the advocate which soon expanded in the noblest dimensions and led to the independence of the judiciary and to the position of the lawyer in North America, which had, and continues to have, a marked influence on our public life. The colonists brought no feudalism along with them; land was owned almost everywhere in fee-simple; no lords, no peasants; and almost all the original settlers came from the independent middle class, from which nearly all freedom in the history of our race has come; and these settlers brought along with them that marked desire to establish common and higher schools with which the Reformation had everywhere leaped into life (the Bible and worship in the mother-tongue, and grammar schools); they were experts in self-government; their country was in one of those periods which seem profusely gifted in literature—Shakspeare had but just died, and Milton began to lift his wings; and to all this must be added that dark feature in the history of our proud race, that while the people struggled bravely for liberty in many portions, and when Europe had abolished slavery within her bosom, she introduced negro slavery in her colonies in America.[1]

Our Cis-Caucasian race, which has been the keenest of all races in the pursuit of wealth, and the most systematically cruel in this pursuit and in religious persecution, developed this new slavery and slave-trade with a fiendish zeal and deplorable success. Slavery became thus also one of the factors of our public life, and we all know the bitter consequences to which it led—the bitterest of all anachronisms.

Long before the American independence was actually declared, the consciousness of our forming a national entirety was ripening. The Continental congress used the words country and America in its official acts—in resolutions and appointments—before that day of mark, the Fourth of July. The very name Continental congress, Continental army and money, shows that the idea of a national unity was present to the minds of all—at home as well as abroad. Unfortunately, no name had formed itself for our portion of the globe. No one can say in what bed our history would have coursed had there been a distinct name for our country, and had Philadelphia become the national capital. Nothing seemed to offer itself for the formation of a name so fit as Americus, of which the German schoolmaster, Waldseemüller, formed the beautiful but cruelly unjust name for our entire hemisphere.[2] As it was, general names came to be used. North America was not unfrequently used to designate our country, as it is still in Germany and France. The bank which the Continental con-

---

[1] No more astounding fact exists in all history than this, that slavery was recognized as perfectly legal in the colonies, that is at a distance, but declared unable to stand before reason and justice at home. The case of Somerset was anticipated in France under Louis XIV.

[2] Waldseemüller, who barbarously changed his long name by græco-latinizing it into Hylacomilus, was a schoolmaster at Strasburg, and proposed the name America to the cosmographic academy of Lorraine. Happily he showed more taste in making our name than in the transformation of his own.

gress established, May 25, 1781, in Philadelphia, after having received the all but desponding letter of General Washington, was called Bank of North America.   It is called thus to this day.   The seal of the treasury of the United States, probably devised by Alexander Hamilton, as it may be seen on each of our legal tender notes, is: *Thesaur. Amer. Septent. Sigil.* (Seal of the Treasury of North America).   If this seal is not of Hamilton's devising it must come from Robert Morris, but Robert Morris was superintendent of the finances; there was no treasury before the year 1789, and it was in 1781 that the office of the "superintendent of the finances" was created. John Adams, and other writers of that period, frequently use North America.   Chatham and his contemporaries always used the name America; Washington was appointed to the command in order to defend and protect "American liberty," before the Declaration of Independence.   But whether there was a distinct name or not, all felt that we were a nation. United America, as the Italians now speak of United Italy, was another name used at the time, and later by Washington and others, for our country.   John Adams ascribes to the speech of Otis against the writs of assistance, therefore before the outbreak of the Revolution, the power of having "breathed into this nation the breath of life;" and when Dr. Franklin, with Deane and Lee, were received as ministers of the United States of America by the king of France on March 19, 1778, after the conclusion of the treaty between the two governments, the king spoke to Franklin of "the two nations."

The pre-revolutionary speeches, specimens of which are given in a modest but very instructive school book (Patriotic Eloquence, by the late Mrs. Kirkland), show that the leading men of America had at that early period no other idea than that of a country, of our land; and that of a nation, of our people.   The puny provincialism which unfolded itself under the insufficient Articles of Confederation, came into vogue after the heroic period of the Revolution, and it led the country to the very brink of ruin and extinction.   So at least Washington and his contemporaries, who knew the state of the country, with sympathetic patriotism and keen insight thought and wrote.

There were constant partial crystallizations of the colonies, united indeed under the British crown, but here demarcated by geographic lines the one from the other. Towards the end of the first half of the seventeenth century, the New England colonies confederated for common protection. Towards the end of the same century, in 1697, a proposition of union of the different colonies was made, as it is supposed with good reason, by William Penn, in " A brief and plain scheme, how the English colonies in the north parts of America, viz., Boston, Connecticut, New Hampshire, Rhode Island, New York, New Jersey, Pennsylvania, Maryland, Virginia, and Carolina, may be made more useful to the crown and one another's peace and safety, with an universal concurrence."[1] Equality of rights of property, and free ingress, egress, and abode, was proposed to be secured to all. In 1754, again fifty years later, Dr. Franklin drew up and proposed the (now called) Albany Plan of Union, unanimously adopted by the delegates at Albany, but not passed by the different assemblies —a plan which foreshadowed the later Union under the Continental congress.

The time of resistance to England approached, and at every point it is to be observed that it is the " whole," as the Greeks called it, that moved and ultimately resisted; all exertions were instinctively national, or in the spirit of a nation to be born. Of the Declaration of Independence there shall be mentioned here three points only: It begins with calling the Americans *one people*, as contradistinguished to the people of the mother-country, the other people; it calls Americans fellow-citizens, and it is Pan-American throughout. No separate independences, and, after this, no aggregate independence

---

[1] The plan itself, and reasons why it is probable that it comes from William Penn, can be found in an Address delivered at Chester, before the Historical Society of Pennsylvania, on the 8th of November, 1851, by Edward Armstrong, etc., etc., in Celebration of the 169th Anniversary of the Landing of William Penn at that place: Philadelphia, 1852—now of course rare, as pamphlets go.

are spoken of; no separate complaint is even alluded to.[1]   The Americans had always the national comprehensive English Constitution before their eyes—no provincial polity—and repeatedly referred to it.[2]

In 1777 The Articles of Confederation were adopted.   They were called Articles, indeed, yet they are Articles of Confederation and Perpetual Union between the states; and in the official Letter of Congress, dated Yorktown, November 17, 1777, in which the states are advised to adopt the Articles, is this passage: "In short, the salutary measure can no longer be deferred.   It seems essential to our very existence *as a free people.*"   The Articles declare that "each state retains its sovereignty, freedom, and independence," but no state had or has ever since enjoyed what the law and all the world call sovereignty, and, moreover, the Articles themselves contain numerous passages of a plainly national character, some of them directly antagonistic to separate sovereignty; for instance, that provision in Article IX., according to which nine out of the thirteen sovereigns can bind, in the most momentous measures, the four remaining sovereigns of the thirteen. The Articles themselves, having declared each state sovereign, take from the states those powers which are universally considered the main attributes of sovereignty.   Nevertheless, the Articles provided for no national government, no broad and open political formulation of our nationality; yet congress, "supported by the confidence of the people, but without any express powers, undertook to direct the storm, and were seconded by the people and by the colonial authorities;" and after the presentation of the Articles to the states (not adopted by all until the year 1781), congress proceeded as if invested with the most explicit powers; it even went so far as to bind the nation by treaties with France; nor was it thought

---

[1] A notable passage on this subject in Reverdy Johnson's speech, in Proceedings at a Public Meeting of the Friends of the Union, Baltimore, January 10, 1861.

[2] Washington wrote to Congress, July 10, 1776, " that freedom and those privileges which have been and are refused us, contrary to the voice of nature and the British Constitution."

necessary that those treaties should be ratified by state legis-latures.[1] Under the Articles of Confederation, in 1782, the seal of the United States, with *E pluribus unum*, was adopted, and early in the year 1786 the oath of military officers, and each one is made to swear that "he owes faith and true alle-giance to the United States, and agrees to maintain its freedom, sovereignty, and independence."[2]

The period between the adoption of the Articles and the Constitution is the most humiliating in our history. All our leading men acknowledged it, and wellnigh lost hope and con-fidence. It is a period far too little studied. The Articles of Confederation are known by very few. Disorganizing pro-vincialism became more and more active and destructive, until a stop was put to the nuisance by the Constitution of the United States, the genesis of which is at least as important as the instrument itself. It is a national work from beginning to end, conceived by the living national spirit of "one people," in spite of destructive provincialism, and establishing a na-tional government in the fullest sense of the word. The in-strument is called a Constitution, not Articles; the word sovereign does not appear once; a national legislature, the members of which vote individually and personally, not by states, and an eminently national and individual executive, in the person of one man, are established, and a portion of the people or of the states (though it must be a large major-ity) can oblige the smaller portion to adopt amendments to the Constitution. No minority of *sovereigns*, however small, can be made subject to a majority of sovereigns, however large. This single fact would annihilate *sovereignty*. We are a nation. The general government was always called in the earlier years of our present government, the national govern-ment, and justly so. The Constitution makes our polity a national representative republic. Ever since the establish-ment of our government two political schools have existed,

---

[1] Lieber's Two Lectures on the Constitution of the United States.
[2] Journals, 417–462, March 14, 1786.

with varying distinctions, the national one and the provincial one, which has often appeared to consider liberty to consist in a marring opposition to the national government, which rejoiced in our not having a name for our country (which is a deficiency not quite unlike the deficiency of the English language itself in not possessing a word for *Patrie* or *Vaterland*), and openly declared the loosest possible confederacy the best of all governments, while the whole world was agreed to consider it in modern times the worst, and confederations good only in as far as they unite, and not as far as they sever.[1]

We have had state rebellions; we have had nullification, and we had a territorial rebellion fomented by state-rights doctrine, coupled with the dark declaration of the divinity of slavery. Our people have gone through a sanguinary and laborious war in order to save and establish more firmly our nationality. We are a nation, and we mean to remain one.

The magnificent words, We, the People, with which the Constitution begins, have often been denied a national character. This absence of national character it was said was indicated by the words which follow, viz., of the United States. Mr. Calhoun denied even the national character in the president of the United States, and allowed only a joint representation of the many different state sovereignties within his individuality, by what mysterious process it is impossible to see. It seems, however, that the meaning of We, the People of the United States, did not appear to the secessionists so absolutely clear as not to require an alteration in the preamble of their constitution, as the reader will perceive from the following comparison of the preamble of our Constitution and that

---

[1] A prominent and bitter state-rights man and, later, secessionist, praised, within my hearing, in a public speech, returning from a foreign mission, the then existing Germanic Confederacy as the best polity! And the most prominent state-rights man, when I once said to him what a pity it was that no American Nelson ever could signal so stirring an order as " England expects," etc., because we have no name for our country, promptly replied, " We have no country, and need no name for one; we ought to have only a name for a mere political system, as you call it."

of the constitution adopted by "the Congress of the Confederate States of America," March 11, 1861.

Preamble of the Constitution of the United States of America.	*Preamble of the Constitution of the Confederate States of America.*
We, the People of the United States,	We, the People of the Confederate States, each State acting in its sovereign and independent character,
in order to form a more perfect Union,	in order to form a permanent federal government,
establish justice, insure domestic tranquillity,	establish justice, insure domestic tranquillity,
provide for the common defence,	(*Left out.*)
promote the general welfare,	(*Left out.*)
and secure the blessings of liberty to ourselves and our posterity,	and secure the blessings of liberty to ourselves and our posterity, invoking the favor and guidance of Almighty God,
do ordain and establish this Constitution for the United States of America.	do ordain and establish this Constitution for the Confederate States of America.

IV.

Political Characteristics of our Age.

The three main characteristics of the political development
which mark the modern epoch are:

The national polity.

The general endeavor to define more clearly, and to extend
more widely, human rights and civil liberty (not unconnected
as this movement is with the pervading critical spirit of the
age, and the wedlock of Knowledge and Labor, which marks
the nineteenth century).

And the decree which has gone forth that many leading
nations shall flourish at one and the same time, plainly distinguished from one another, yet striving together, with one
public opinion, under the protection of one law of nations,
and in the bonds of one common moving civilization.

The universal monarchy, whether purely political, as that

of the Romans, or like that attempted again by Napoleon I.; or whether coupled with the papacy, as cruelly attempted by Charles V., and especially by Philip II., under whom the war-cry was: "One Pope and One King;" a single leading nation; an agglomeration of states without a fundamental law, with the mere leadership or hegemony of one state or other, which always leads to Peloponnesian wars; regular confederacies of petty sovereigns; a civilization confined to one spot or portion of the globe—all these are obsolete ideas, wholly insufficient for the demands of advanced civilization, and attempts at their renewal have led and must lead to ruinous results, the end of all anachronisms recklessly pursued.

Even the course which civilization has steadily taken for thousands of years, from the southeast to the northwest, has ceased in our times. It now spreads for the first time in all directions, and bends its way back to the Orient. The old historic belt between 30° and 50° northern latitude, within which the great current of events has flown, shall confine history no more.

All great ideas which have set whole periods and entire races in motion, and which ultimately are established in great institutions, have their caricatures—often fierce and sanguinary. Communism is thus a caricature of one of these characteristics, and the recently proclaimed anti-nationalism another. All division into nations is to be done away with; all Europe is to be one ant-hill! But why only Europe? Let it be repeated, every idea in history, even the greatest and the holiest, had its hideous caricature.

V.

Interdependence of Individuals and Nations. The Commonwealth of Nations.

The multiplicity of civilized nations, their distinct independence (without which there would be enslaving Universal Monarchy), and their increasing resemblance and agreement, are some of the great safeguards of our civilization. Modern nations of our family have come to agree in much, and the agreement is growing. We have one alphabet; the same systems of notation, arithmetical and musical; one division of the circle and of time; the same sea-league; the same barometer; one mathematical language; one music and the same fine arts; one system of education, high and low; one science; one division of government; one domestic economy; one dress and fashion; the same manners, and the same toys for our children (Asia and Africa have no toys); we have a united mail system, and uniting telegraphs; we have an extending agreement in measures, weights, coinage, and signals at sea, and one financial conception, so that all merchants' exchanges have become meetings of international import, at least of equal effect with that of international diplomacy; we have a rapidly extending international copyright; perfectly acknowledged foreign individual property; we have a common international law, even during war. Add to this, that we really have what has been, not inaptly, called an international literature, in which a Shakspeare and a Kepler, a Franklin, Humboldt, Grotius, and Voltaire belong to the whole Cis-Caucasian race; we have a common history of civilization; and Columbus and Frederick, Napoleon and Washington, for weal or woe, belong to all.

Formerly the process of nationalization was appearing as one of the novel things; now the process of internationalization is going on; and yet there will be no obliteration of nationalities. If such were the case, civilization would be seriously injured. Civilization always dwelled pre-eminently in ancient times with one people, and one government always swayed and led. Hence the simplicity of chronologic tables presenting the events of that time; and all ancient states were short-lived. Once declining, they never recovered. Their course was that of the projectile: ascending, a maximum, a precipitate descent, and no more rising. Modern nations are long-lived, and possess recuperative energy wholly unknown to antiquity. They could neither be the one nor possess the other without national existence and comprehensive polities, and without the law of nations, in its modern and elevated sense, in which it is at once the manly idea of self-government applied to a number of independent nations in close relation with one another, and the application of the fundamental law of Good Neighborhood, and the comprehensive law of Nuisance, flowing from it, to vast national societies, wholly independent, sovereign, yet bound together by a thousand ties.

The all-pervading law of interdependence, without which men would never have felt compelled to form society, beyond the narrowest family ties—and it is even one of the elementary principles of the family—interdependence which, like all original principles or characteristics of humanity, increases in intensity and spreads in action as men advance—this divine law of interdependence applies to nations quite as much as to individuals.

The individual division of labor is no more impelled by it than the production by territorial and climatic division of labor is quickened by the mutual dependence of the dwellers on the earth. This propitious and civilizing interdependence among nations is becoming daily more freely and willingly acknowledged, and the wise saying, *Ubi Societas ibi Jus*, finds constantly increasing application to entire nations. The civilized nations have come to constitute a community, and are daily forming more and more a commonwealth of nations, under the restraint and protection of the law of nations, which has begun to make its way even to countries not belonging to the Christian community, to which the law of nations had been confined. Our Wheaton's Law of Nations has been translated into Chinese, and is distributed by the government of that empire among its high officials. Soon it will form a subject of the Chinese higher state examination. The leading nations—the French, the English, the German, the American —they draw the chariot of civilization abreast, as the ancient steeds drew the car of victory: and these pages are writing at the time when the imperial chancellor of the German Union has been directed by the Union's parliament to propose to all nations the perfect security of private property on the high seas during war, even though belonging to an enemy; and when a citizen of the American republic has entered our city, at the head of a Chinese embassy, sent to the great western powers in America and Europe, for the avowed purpose of attaching China to that union of nations among whom the law of nations has its sway in peace and in war.

INSTRUCTIONS

FOR THE

GOVERNMENT OF ARMIES

OF THE

UNITED STATES

IN THE FIELD.

REVISED BY A BOARD OF OFFICERS.

GENERAL ORDER No. 100.

WAR DEPARTMENT, ADJUTANT-GENERAL'S OFFICE,
WASHINGTON, April 24, 1863.

The following "Instructions for the Government of Armies of the United States in the Field," prepared by FRANCIS LIEBER, LL.D., and revised by a Board of Officers, of which Major-General E. A. HITCHCOCK is president, having been approved by the President of the United States, he commands that they be published for the information of all concerned.

BY ORDER OF THE SECRETARY OF WAR.

E. D. TOWNSEND,
Assistant Adjutant-General.

INSTRUCTIONS

FOR THE

GOVERNMENT OF ARMIES OF THE UNITED STATES

IN THE FIELD.

SECTION I.

Martial Law — Military Jurisdiction — Military Necessity — Retaliation.

1. A PLACE, district, or country occupied by an enemy stands, in consequence of the occupation, under the martial law of the invading or occupying army, whether any proclamation declaring martial law, or any public warning to the inhabitants, has been issued or not. Martial law is the immediate and direct effect and consequence of occupation or conquest.

The presence of a hostile army proclaims its martial law.

2. Martial law does not cease during the hostile occupation, except by special proclamation, ordered by the commander-in-chief; or by special mention in the treaty of peace concluding the war, when the occupation of a place or territory continues beyond the conclusion of peace as one of the conditions of the same.

3. Martial law in a hostile country consists in the suspension, by the occupying military authority, of the criminal and civil law, and of the domestic administration and government in the occupied place or territory, and in the substitution of

247

military rule and force for the same, as well as in the dictation of general laws, as far as military necessity requires this suspension, substitution, or dictation.

The commander of the forces may proclaim that the administration of all civil and penal law shall continue, either wholly or in part, as in times of peace, unless otherwise ordered by the military authority.

4. Martial law is simply military authority exercised in accordance with the laws and usages of war. Military oppression is not martial law; it is the abuse of the power which that law confers. As martial law is executed by military force, it is incumbent upon those who administer it to be strictly guided by the principles of justice, honor, and humanity—virtues adorning a soldier even more than other men, for the very reason that he possesses the power of his arms against the unarmed.

5. Martial law should be less stringent in places and countries fully occupied and fairly conquered. Much greater severity may be exercised in places or regions where actual hostilities exist, or are expected and must be prepared for. Its most complete sway is allowed—even in the commander's own country—when face to face with the enemy, because of the absolute necessities of the case, and of the paramount duty to defend the country against invasion.

To save the country is paramount to all other considerations.

6. All civil and penal law shall continue to take its usual course in the enemy's places and territories under martial law, unless interrupted or stopped by order of the occupying military power; but all the functions of the hostile government —legislative, executive, or administrative—whether of a general, provincial, or local character, cease under martial law, or continue only with the sanction, or if deemed necessary, the participation of the occupier or invader.

7. Martial law extends to property, and to persons, whether they are subjects of the enemy or aliens to that government.

8. Consuls, among American and European nations, are not diplomatic agents. Nevertheless, their offices and per-

sons will be subjected to martial law in cases of urgent necessity only: their property and business are not exempted. Any delinquency they commit against the established military rule may be punished as in the case of any other inhabitant, and such punishment furnishes no reasonable ground for international complaint.

9. The functions of ambassadors, ministers, or other diplomatic agents, accredited by neutral powers to the hostile government, cease so far as regards the displaced government; but the conquering or occupying power usually recognizes them as temporarily accredited to itself.

10. Martial law affects chiefly the police and collection of public revenue and taxes, whether imposed by the expelled government or by the invader, and refers mainly to the support and efficiency of the army, its safety, and the safety of its operations.

11. The law of war does not only disclaim all cruelty and bad faith concerning engagements concluded with the enemy during the war, but also the breaking of stipulations solemnly contracted by the belligerents in time of peace, and avowedly intended to remain in force in case of war between the contracting powers.

It disclaims all extortions and other transactions for individual gain; all acts of private revenge, or connivance at such acts.

Offences to the contrary shall be severely punished, and especially so if committed by officers.

12. Whenever feasible, martial law is carried out in cases of individual offenders by military courts; but sentences of death shall be executed only with the approval of the chief executive, provided the urgency of the case does not require a speedier execution, and then only with the approval of the chief commander.

13. Military jurisdiction is of two kinds: first, that which is conferred and defined by statute; second, that which is derived from the common law of war. Military offences under the statute law must be tried in the manner therein directed;

but military offences which do not come within the statute must be tried and punished under the common law of war. The character of the courts which exercise these jurisdictions depends upon the local laws of each particular country.

In the armies of the United States the first is exercised by courts-martial; while cases which do not come within the Rules and Articles of War, or the jurisdiction conferred by statute on courts-martial, are tried by military commissions.

14. Military necessity, as understood by modern civilized nations, consists in the necessity of those measures which are indispensable for securing the ends of the war, and which are lawful according to the modern law and usages of war.

15. Military necessity admits of all direct destruction of life or limb of *armed* enemies, and of other persons whose destruction is incidentally *unavoidable* in the armed contests of the war; it allows of the capturing of every armed enemy, and every enemy of importance to the hostile government, or of peculiar danger to the captor; it allows of all destruction of property, and obstruction of the ways and channels of traffic, travel, or communication, and of all withholding of sustenance or means of life from the enemy; of the appropriation of whatever an enemy's country affords necessary for the subsistence and safety of the army, and of such deception as does not involve the breaking of good faith either positively pledged, regarding agreements entered into during the war, or supposed by the modern law of war to exist.   Men who take up arms against one another in public war do not cease on this account to be moral beings, responsible to one another, and to God.

16. Military necessity does not admit of cruelty, that is, the infliction of suffering for the sake of suffering or for revenge, nor of maiming or wounding except in fight, nor of torture to extort confessions.   It does not admit of the use of poison in any way, nor of the wanton devastation of a district.   It admits of deception, but disclaims acts of perfidy; and, in general, military necessity does not include any act of hostility which makes the return to peace unnecessarily difficult.

17. War is not carried on by arms alone.   It is lawful to

starve the hostile belligerent, armed or unarmed, so that it leads to the speedier subjection of the enemy.

18. When the commander of a besieged place expels the non-combatants, in order to lessen the number of those who consume his stock of provisions, it is lawful, though an extreme measure, to drive them back, so as to hasten on the surrender.

19. Commanders, whenever admissible, inform the enemy of their intention to bombard a place, so that the non-combatants, and especially the women and children, may be removed before the bombardment commences. But it is no infraction of the common law of war to omit thus to inform the enemy. Surprise may be a necessity.

20. Public war is a state of armed hostility between sovereign nations or governments. It is a law and requisite of civilized existence that men live in political, continuous societies, forming organized units, called states or nations, whose constituents bear, enjoy and suffer, advance and retrograde together, in peace and in war.

21. The citizen or native of a hostile country is thus an enemy, as one of the constituents of the hostile state or nation, and as such is subjected to the hardships of the war.

22. Nevertheless, as civilization has advanced during the last centuries, so has likewise steadily advanced, especially in war on land, the distinction between the private individual belonging to a hostile country and the hostile country itself, with its men in arms. The principle has been more and more acknowledged that the unarmed citizen is to be spared in person, property, and honor as much as the exigencies of war will admit.

23. Private citizens are no longer murdered, enslaved, or carried off to distant parts, and the inoffensive individual is as little disturbed in his private relations as the commander of the hostile troops can afford to grant in the overruling demands of a vigorous war.

24. The almost universal rule in remote times was, and continues to be with barbarous armies, that the private indi-

vidual of the hostile country is destined to suffer every privation of liberty and protection, and every disruption of family ties. Protection was, and still is with uncivilized people, the exception.

25. In modern regular wars of the Europeans, and their descendants in other portions of the globe, protection of the inoffensive citizen of the hostile country is the rule ; privation and disturbance of private relations are the exceptions.

26. Commanding generals may cause the magistrates and civil officers of the hostile country to take the oath of temporary allegiance or an oath of fidelity to their own victorious government or rulers, and they may expel every one who declines to do so. But whether they do so or not, the people and their civil officers owe strict obedience to them as long as they hold sway over the district or country, at the peril of their lives.

27. The law of war can no more wholly dispense with retaliation than can the law of nations, of which it is a branch. Yet civilized nations acknowledge retaliation as the sternest feature of war. A reckless enemy often leaves to his opponent no other means of securing himself against the repetition of barbarous outrage.

28. Retaliation will, therefore, never be resorted to as a measure of mere revenge, but only as a means of protective retribution, and, moreover, cautiously and unavoidably; that is to say, retaliation shall only be resorted to after careful inquiry into the real occurrence, and the character of the misdeeds that may demand retribution.

Unjust or inconsiderate retaliation removes the belligerents farther and farther from the mitigating rules of a regular war, and by rapid steps leads them nearer to the internecine wars of savages.

29. Modern times are distinguished from earlier ages by the existence, at one and the same time, of many nations and great governments related to one another in close intercourse.

Peace is their normal condition; war is the exception.

The ultimate object of all modern war is a renewed state of peace.

The more vigorously wars are pursued, the better it is for humanity. Sharp wars are brief.

30. Ever since the formation and co-existence of modern nations, and ever since wars have become great national wars, war has come to be acknowledged not to be its own end, but the means to obtain great ends of state, or to consist in defence against wrong; and no conventional restriction of the modes adopted to injure the enemy is any longer admitted; but the law of war imposes many limitations and restrictions on principles of justice, faith, and honor.

SECTION II.

Public and Private Property of the Enemy—Protection of Persons, and especially Women; of Religion, the Arts and Sciences—Punishment of Crimes against the Inhabitants of Hostile Countries.

31. A victorious army appropriates all public money, seizes all public movable property until further direction by its government, and sequesters for its own benefit or that of its government all the revenues of real property belonging to the hostile government or nation. The title to such real property remains in abeyance during military occupation, and until the conquest is made complete.

32. A victorious army, by the martial power inherent in the same, may suspend, change, or abolish, as far as the martial power extends, the relations which arise from the services due, according to the existing laws of the invaded country, from one citizen, subject, or native of the same to another.

The commander of the army must leave it to the ultimate treaty of peace to settle the permanency of this change.

33. It is no longer considered lawful—on the contrary, it is held to be a serious breach of the law of war—to force the subjects of the enemy into the service of the victorious gov-

ernment, except the latter should proclaim, after a fair and complete conquest of the hostile country or district, that it is resolved to keep the country, district, or place permanently as its own, and make it a portion of its own country.

34. As a general rule, the property belonging to churches, to hospitals, or other establishments of an exclusively charitable character, to establishments of education, or foundations for the promotion of knowledge, whether public schools, universities, academies of learning or observatories, museums of the fine arts, or of a scientific character—such property is not to be considered public property in the sense of paragraph 31 ; but it may be taxed or used when the public service may require it.

35. Classical works of art, libraries, scientific collections, or precious instruments, such as astronomical telescopes, as well as hospitals, must be secured against all avoidable injury, even when they are contained in fortified places whilst besieged or bombarded.

36. If such works of art, libraries, collections, or instruments belonging to a hostile nation or government, can be removed without injury, the ruler of the conquering state or nation may order them to be seized and removed for the benefit of the said nation. The ultimate ownership is to be settled by the ensuing treaty of peace.

In no case shall they be sold or given away, if captured by the armies of the United States, nor shall they ever be privately appropriated, or wantonly destroyed or injured.

37. The United States acknowledge and protect, in hostile countries occupied by them, religion and morality; strictly private property; the persons of the inhabitants, especially those of women ; and the sacredness of domestic relations. Offences to the contrary shall be rigorously punished.

This rule does not interfere with the right of the victorious invader to tax the people or their property, to levy forced loans, to billet soldiers, or to appropriate property, especially houses, land, boats or ships, and churches, for temporary and military uses.

38. Private property, unless forfeited by crimes or by offences of the owner, can be seized only by way of military necessity, for the support or other benefit of the army of the United States.

If the owner has not fled, the commanding officer will cause receipts to be given, which may serve the spoliated owners to obtain indemnity.

39. The salaries of civil officers of the hostile government who remain in the invaded territory, and continue the work of their office, and can continue it according to the circumstances arising out of the war—such as judges, administrative or police officers, officers of city or communal governments—are paid from the public revenue of the invaded territory, until the military government has reason wholly or partially to discontinue it. Salaries or incomes connected with purely honorary titles are always stopped.

40. There exists no law or body of authoritative rules of action between hostile armies, except that branch of the law of nature and nations which is called the law and usages of war on land.

41. All municipal law of the ground on which the armies stand, or of the countries to which they belong, is silent and of no effect between armies in the field.

42. Slavery, complicating and confounding the ideas of property (that is of a *thing*), and of personality (that is of *humanity*), exists according to municipal law or local law only. The law of nature and nations has never acknowledged it. The digest of the Roman law enacts the early dictum of the pagan jurist, that "so far as the law of nature is concerned, all men are equal." Fugitives escaping from a country in which they were slaves, villains, or serfs, into another country, have, for centuries past, been held free and acknowledged free by judicial decisions of European countries, even though the municipal law of the country in which the slave had taken refuge acknowledged slavery within its own dominions.

43. Therefore, in a war between the United States and a belligerent which admits of slavery, if a person held in bond-

age by that belligerent be captured by or come as a fugitive under the protection of the military forces of the United States, such person is immediately entitled to the rights and privileges of a freeman. To return such person into slavery would amount to enslaving a free person, and neither the United States nor any officer under their authority can enslave any human being. Moreover, a person so made free by the law of war is under the shield of the law of nations, and the former owner or state can have, by the law of postliminy, no belligerent lien or claim of service.

44. All wanton violence committed against persons in the invaded country, all destruction of property not commanded by the authorized officer, all robbery, all pillage or sacking, even after taking a place by main force, all rape, wounding, maiming, or killing of such inhabitants, are prohibited under the penalty of death, or such other severe punishment as may seem adequate for the gravity of the offence.

A soldier, officer or private, in the act of committing such violence, and disobeying a superior ordering him to abstain from it, may be lawfully killed on the spot by such superior.

45. All captures and booty belong, according to the modern law of war, primarily to the government of the captor.

Prize-money, whether on sea or land, can now only be claimed under local law.

46. Neither officers nor soldiers are allowed to make use of their position or power in the hostile country for private gain, not even for commercial transactions otherwise legitimate. Offences to the contrary committed by commissioned officers will be punished with cashiering or such other punishment as the nature of the offence may require ; if by soldiers, they shall be punished according to the nature of the offence.

47. Crimes punishable by all penal codes, such as arson, murder, maiming, assaults, highway robbery, theft, burglary, fraud, forgery, and rape, if committed by an American soldier in a hostile country against its inhabitants, are not only punishable as at home, but in all cases in which death is not inflicted, the severer punishment shall be preferred.

Deserters—Prisoners of War—Hostages—Booty on the Battle-field.

48. Deserters from the American army, having entered the service of the enemy, suffer death if they fall again into the hands of the United States, whether by capture, or being delivered up to the American army; and if a deserter from the enemy, having taken service in the army of the United States, is captured by the enemy, and punished by them with death or otherwise, it is not a breach against the law and usages of war, requiring redress or retaliation.

49. A prisoner of war is a public enemy armed or attached to the hostile army for active aid, who has fallen into the hands of the captor, either fighting or wounded, on the field or in the hospital, by individual surrender or by capitulation.

All soldiers, of whatever species of arms; all men who belong to the rising *en masse* of the hostile country; all those who are attached to the army for its efficiency and promote directly the object of the war, except such as are hereinafter provided for; all disabled men or officers on the field or elsewhere, if captured; all enemies who have thrown away their arms and ask for quarter, are prisoners of war, and as such exposed to the inconveniences as well as entitled to the privileges of a prisoner of war.

50. Moreover, citizens who accompany an army for whatever purpose, such as sutlers, editors or reporters of journals, or contractors, if captured, may be made prisoners of war, and be detained as such.

The monarch and members of the hostile reigning family, male or female, the chief, and chief officers of the hostile government, its diplomatic agents, and all persons who are of particular and singular use and benefit to the hostile army or its government, are, if captured on belligerent ground, and if unprovided with a safe-conduct granted by the captor's government, prisoners of war.

51. If the people of that portion of an invaded country which is not yet occupied by the enemy, or of the whole country, at the approach of a hostile army, rise under a duly authorized levy, *en masse* to resist the invader, they are now treated as public enemies, and if captured, are prisoners of war.

52. No belligerent has the right to declare that he will treat every captured man in arms of a levy *en masse* as a brigand or bandit.

If, however, the people of a country, or any portion of the same, already occupied by the army, rise against it, they are violators of the laws of war, and are not entitled to their protection.

53. The enemy's chaplains, officers of the medical staff, apothecaries, hospital nurses and servants, if they fall into the hands of the American army, are not prisoners of war, unless the commander has reasons to retain them. In this latter case, or if, at their own desire, they are allowed to remain with their captured companions, they are treated as prisoners of war, and may be exchanged if the commander sees fit.

54. A hostage is a person accepted as a pledge for the fulfilment of an agreement concluded between belligerents during the war, or in consequences of a war. Hostages are rare in the present age.

55. If a hostage is accepted, he is treated like a prisoner of war, according to rank and condition, as circumstances may admit.

56. A prisoner of war is subject to no punishment for being a public enemy, nor is any revenge wreaked upon him by the intentional infliction of any suffering, or disgrace, by cruel imprisonment, want of food, by mutilation, death, or any other barbarity.

57. So soon as a man is armed by a sovereign government, and takes the soldier's oath of fidelity, he is a belligerent; his killing, wounding, or other warlike acts, are no individual crimes or offences. No belligerent has a right to declare that enemies of a certain class, color, or condition, when properly organized as soldiers, will not be treated by him as public enemies.

58. The law of nations knows of no distinction of color, and if an enemy of the United States should enslave and sell any captured persons of their army, it would be a case for the severest retaliation, if not redressed upon complaint.

The United States cannot retaliate by enslavement; therefore death must be the retaliation for this crime against the law of nations.

59. A prisoner of war remains answerable for his crimes committed against the captor's army or people, committed before he was captured, and for which he has not been punished by his own authorities.

All prisoners of war are liable to the infliction of retaliatory measures.

60. It is against the usage of modern war to resolve, in hatred and revenge, to give no quarter. No body of troops has the right to declare that it will not give, and therefore will not expect, quarter; but a commander is permitted to direct his troops to give no quarter, in great straits, when his own salvation makes it *impossible* to cumber himself with prisoners.

61. Troops that give no quarter have no right to kill enemies already disabled on the ground, or prisoners captured by other troops.

62. All troops of the enemy known or discovered to give no quarter in general, or to any portion of the army, receive none.

63. Troops who fight in the uniform of their enemies, without any plain, striking, and uniform mark of distinction of their own, can expect no quarter.

64. If American troops capture a train containing uniforms of the enemy, and the commander considers it advisable to distribute them for use among his men, some striking mark or sign must be adopted to distinguish the American soldier from the enemy.

65. The use of the enemy's national standard, flag, or other emblem of nationality, for the purpose of deceiving the enemy in battle, is an act of perfidy by which they lose all claim to the protection of the laws of war.

66. Quarter having been given to an enemy by American troops, under a misapprehension of his true character, he may, nevertheless, be ordered to suffer death if, within three days after the battle, it be discovered that he belongs to a corps which gives no quarter.

67. The law of nations allows every sovereign government to make war upon another sovereign state, and, therefore, admits of no rules or laws different from those of regular warfare, regarding the treatment of prisoners of war, although they may belong to the army of a government which the captor may consider as a wanton and unjust assailant.

68. Modern wars are not internecine wars, in which the killing of the enemy is the object. The destruction of the enemy in modern war, and, indeed, modern war itself, are means to obtain that object of the belligerent which lies beyond the war.

Unnecessary or revengeful destruction of life is not lawful.

69. Outposts, sentinels, or pickets are not to be fired upon, except to drive them in, or when a positive order, special or general, has been issued to that effect.

70. The use of poison in any manner, be it to poison wells, or food, or arms, is wholly excluded from modern warfare. He that uses it puts himself out of the pale of the law and usages of war.

71. Whoever intentionally inflicts additional wounds on an enemy already wholly disabled, or kills such an enemy, or who orders or encourages soldiers to do so, shall suffer death, if duly convicted, whether he belongs to the army of the United States, or is an enemy captured after having committed his misdeed.

72. Money and other valuables on the person of a prisoner, such as watches or jewelry, as well as extra clothing, are regarded by the American army as the private property of the prisoner, and the appropriation of such valuables or money is considered dishonorable, and is prohibited.

Nevertheless, if *large* sums are found upon the persons of prisoners, or in their possession, they shall be taken from them, and the surplus, after providing for their own support, appropriated for the use of the army, under the direction of the commander, unless otherwise ordered by the government. Nor can prisoners claim, as private property, large sums found and captured in their train, although they had been placed in the private luggage of the prisoners.

73. All officers, when captured, must surrender their side-arms to the captor. They may be restored to the prisoner in marked cases, by the commander, to signalize admiration of his distinguished bravery, or approbation of his humane treatment of prisoners before his capture. The captured officer to whom they may be restored cannot wear them during captivity.

74. A prisoner of war being a public enemy, is the prisoner of the government, and not of the captor. No ransom can be paid by a prisoner of war to his individual captor, or to any officer in command. The government alone releases captives, according to rules prescribed by itself.

75. Prisoners of war are subject to confinement or imprisonment such as may be deemed necessary on account of safety, but they are to be subjected to no other intentional suffering or indignity. The confinement and mode of treating a prisoner may be varied during his captivity according to the demands of safety.

76. Prisoners of war shall be fed upon plain and wholesome food whenever practicable, and treated with humanity.

They may be required to work for the benefit of the captor's government, according to their rank and condition.

77. A prisoner of war who escapes may be shot, or otherwise killed in his flight; but neither death nor any other punishment shall be inflicted upon him simply for his attempt to escape, which the law of war does not consider a crime. Stricter means of security shall be used after an unsuccessful attempt at escape.

If, however, a conspiracy is discovered, the purpose of which is a united or general escape, the conspirators may be rigorously punished, even with death; and capital punishment may also be inflicted upon prisoners of war discovered to have plotted rebellion against the authorities of the captors, whether in union with fellow-prisoners or other persons.

78. If prisoners of war, having given no pledge nor made any promise on their honor, forcibly or otherwise escape, and are captured again in battle, after having rejoined their own army, they shall not be punished for their escape, but shall be treated as simple prisoners of war, although they will be subjected to stricter confinement.

79. Every captured wounded enemy shall be medically treated, according to the ability of the medical staff.

80. Honorable men, when captured, will abstain from giving to the enemy information concerning their own army, and the modern law of war permits no longer the use of any violence against prisoners, in order to extort the desired information, or to punish them for having given false information.

SECTION IV.

Partisans—Armed Enemies not belonging to the Hostile Army —Scouts—Armed Prowlers—War-Rebels.

81. Partisans are soldiers armed and wearing the uniform of their army, but belonging to a corps which acts detached from the main body for the purpose of making inroads into the territory occupied by the enemy. If captured, they are entitled to all the privileges of the prisoner of war.

82. Men, or squads of men, who commit hostilities, whether by fighting, or inroads for destruction or plunder, or by raids of any kind, without commission,without being part and portion of the organized hostile army, and without sharing continuously in the war, but who do so with intermitting returns to their homes and avocations, or with the occasional assumption of the semblance of peaceful pursuits, divesting themselves of the character or appearance of soldiers—such men, or squads of men, are not public enemies, and therefore, if captured, are not entitled to the privileges of prisoners of

war, but shall be treated summarily as highway robbers or pirates.

83. Scouts or single soldiers, if disguised in the dress of the country, or in the uniform of the army hostile to their own, employed in obtaining information, if found within or lurking about the lines of the captor, are treated as spies, and suffer death.

84. Armed prowlers, by whatever names they may be called, or persons of the enemy's territory, who steal within the lines of the hostile army, for the purpose of robbing, killing, or of destroying bridges, roads, or canals, or of robbing or destroying the mail, or of cutting the telegraph wires, are not entitled to the privileges of the prisoner of war.

85. War-rebels are persons within an occupied territory who rise in arms against the occupying or conquering army. or against the authorities established by the same. If captured, they may suffer death, whether they rise singly, in small or large bands, and whether called upon to do so by their own, but expelled, government or not. They are not prisoners of war; nor are they, if discovered and secured before their conspiracy has matured to an actual rising, or to armed violence.

SECTION V.

Safe-Conduct—Spies—War-Traitors—Captured Messengers—
Abuse of the Flag of Truce.

86. All intercourse between the territories occupied by belligerent armies, whether by traffic, by letter, by travel, or in any other way, ceases. This is the general rule, to be observed without special proclamation.

Exceptions to this rule, whether by safe-conduct, or permission to trade on a small or large scale, or by exchanging mails, or by travel from one territory into the other, can take place only according to agreement approved by the government, or by the highest military authority.

Contraventions of this rule are highly punishable.

87. Ambassadors, and all other diplomatic agents of neutral

powers, accredited to the enemy, may receive safe-conducts through the territories occupied by the belligerents, unless there are military reasons to the contrary, and unless they may reach the place of their destination conveniently by another route. It implies no international affront if the safe-conduct is declined. Such passes are usually given by the supreme authority of the state, and not by subordinate officers.

88. A spy is a person who secretly, in disguise or under false pretence, seeks information with the intention of communicating it to the enemy.

The spy is punishable with death by hanging by the neck, whether or not he succeed in obtaining the information or in conveying it to the enemy.

89. If a citizen of the United States obtains information in a legitimate manner, and betrays it to the enemy, be he a military or civil officer, or a private citizen, he shall suffer death.

90. A traitor under the law of war, or a war-traitor, is a person in a place or district under martial law who, unauthorized by the military commander, gives information of any kind to the enemy, or holds intercourse with him.

91. The war-traitor is always severely punished. If his offence consists in betraying to the enemy anything concerning the condition, safety, operations, or plans of troops holding or occupying the place or district, his punishment is death.

92. If the citizen or subject of a country or place invaded or conquered gives information to his own government, from which he is separated by the hostile army, or to the army of his government, he is a war-traitor, and death is the penalty of his offence.

93. All armies in the field stand in need of guides, and impress them if they cannot obtain them otherwise.

94. No person having been forced by the enemy to serve as guide is punishable for having done so.

95. If a citizen of a hostile and invaded district voluntarily serves as a guide to the enemy, or offers to do so, he is deemed a war-traitor, and shall suffer death.

96. A citizen serving voluntarily as a guide against his own country commits treason, and will be dealt with according to the law of his country.

97. Guides, when it is clearly proved that they have misled intentionally, may be put to death.

98. All unauthorized or secret communication with the enemy is considered treasonable by the law of war.

Foreign residents in an invaded or occupied territory, or foreign visitors in the same, can claim no immunity from this law. They may communicate with foreign parts, or with the inhabitants of the hostile country, so far as the military authority permits, but no further. Instant expulsion from the occupied territory would be the very least punishment for the infraction of this rule.

99. A messenger carrying written despatches or verbal messages from one portion of the army, or from a besieged place, to another portion of the same army, or its government, if armed, and in the uniform of his army, and if captured while doing so, in the territory occupied by the enemy, is treated by the captor as a prisoner of war. If not in uniform, nor a soldier, the circumstances connected with his capture must determine the disposition that shall be made of him.

100. A messenger or agent who attempts to steal through the territory occupied by the enemy, to further, in any manner, the interests of the enemy, if captured, is not entitled to the privileges of the prisoner of war, and may be dealt with according to the circumstances of the case.

101. While deception in war is admitted as a just and necessary means of hostility, and is consistent with honorable warfare, the common law of war allows even capital punishment for clandestine or treacherous attempts to injure an enemy, because they are so dangerous, and it is so difficult to guard against them.

102. The law of war, like the criminal law regarding other offences, makes no difference on account of the difference of sexes, concerning the spy, the war-traitor, or the war-rebel.

103. Spies, war-traitors, and war-rebels are not exchanged

according to the common law of war.   The exchange of such persons would require a special cartel, authorized by the government, or, at a great distance from it, by the chief commander of the army in the field.

104. A successful spy or war-traitor, safely returned to his own army, and afterwards captured as an enemy, is not subject to punishment for his acts as a spy or war-traitor, but he may be held in closer custody as a person individually dangerous.

SECTION VI.

Exchange of Prisoners—Flags of Truce—Flags of Protection.

105. Exchanges of prisoners take place—number for number—rank for rank—wounded for wounded—with added condition for added condition—such, for instance, as not to serve for a certain period.

106. In exchanging prisoners of war, such numbers of persons of inferior rank may be substituted as an equivalent for one of superior rank as may be agreed upon by cartel, which requires the sanction of the government, or of the commander of the army in the field.

107. A prisoner of war is in honor bound truly to state to the captor his rank; and he is not to assume a lower rank than belongs to him, in order to cause a more advantageous exchange; nor a higher rank, for the purpose of obtaining better treatment.

Offences to the contrary have been justly punished by the commanders of released prisoners, and may be good cause for refusing to release such prisoners.

108. The surplus number of prisoners of war remaining after an exchange has taken place is sometimes released either for the payment of a stipulated sum of money, or, in urgent cases, of provision, clothing, or other necessaries.

Such arrangement, however, requires the sanction of the highest authority.

109. The exchange of prisoners of war is an act of convenience to both belligerents.   If no general cartel has been

concluded, it cannot be demanded by either of them.   No belligerent is obliged to exchange prisoners of war.

A cartel is voidable so soon as either party has violated it.

110. No exchange of prisoners shall be made except after complete capture, and after an accurate account of them, and a list of the captured officers, has been taken.

111. The bearer of a flag of truce cannot insist upon being admitted.   He must always be admitted with great caution. Unnecessary frequency is carefully to be avoided.

112. If the bearer of a flag of truce offers himself during an engagement, he can be admitted as a very rare exception only.   It is no breach of good faith to retain such a flag of truce, if admitted during the engagement.   Firing is not required to cease on the appearance of a flag of truce in battle.

113. If the bearer of a flag of truce, presenting himself during an engagement, is killed or wounded, it furnishes no ground of complaint whatever.

114. If it be discovered, and fairly proved, that a flag of truce has been abused for surreptitiously obtaining military knowledge, the bearer of the flag thus abusing his sacred character is deemed a spy.

So sacred is the character of a flag of truce, and so necessary is its sacredness, that while its abuse is an especially heinous offence, great caution is requisite, on the other hand, in convicting the bearer of a flag of truce as a spy.

115. It is customary to designate by certain flags (usually yellow) the hospitals in places which are shelled, so that the besieging enemy may avoid firing on them.   The same has been done in battles, when hospitals are situated within the field of the engagement.

116. Honorable belligerents often request that the hospitals within the territory of the enemy may be designated, so that they may be spared.

An honorable belligerent allows himself to be guided by flags or signals of protection as much as the contingencies and the necessities of the fight will permit.

117. It is justly considered an act of bad faith, of infamy or fiendishness, to deceive the enemy by flags of protection. Such acts of bad faith may be good cause for refusing to respect such flags.

118. The besieging belligerent has sometimes requested the besieged to designate the buildings containing collections of works of art, scientific museums, astronomical observatories, or precious libraries, so that their destruction may be avoided as much as possible.

SECTION VII.   .

The Parole.

119. Prisoners of war may be released from captivity by exchange, and, under certain circumstances, also by parole.

120. The term *parole* designates the pledge of individual good faith and honor to do, or to omit doing, certain acts after he who gives his parole shall have been dismissed, wholly or partially, from the power of the captor.

121. The pledge of the parole is always an individual but not a private act.

122. The parole applies chiefly to prisoners of war whom the captor allows to return to their country, or to live in greater freedom within the captor's country or territory, on condition stated in the parole.

123. Release of prisoners of war by exchange is the general rule; release by parole is the exception.

124. Breaking the parole is punished with death when the person breaking the parole is captured again.

Accurate lists, therefore, of the paroled persons must be kept by the belligerents.

125. When paroles are given and received, there must be an exchange of two written documents, in which the name and rank of the paroled individuals are accurately and truthfully stated.

126. Commissioned officers only are allowed to give their parole, and they can give it only with the permission of their superior, as long as a superior in rank is within reach.

127. No non-commissioned officer or private can give his parole except through an officer. Individual paroles not given through an officer are not only void, but subject the individuals giving them to the punishment of death as deserters. The only admissible exception is where individuals, properly separated from their commands, have suffered long confinement without the possibility of being paroled through an officer.

128. No paroling on the battle-field, no paroling of entire bodies of troops after a battle, and no dismissal of large numbers of prisoners, with a general declaration that they are paroled, is permitted, or of any value.

129. In capitulations for the surrender of strong places or fortified camps, the commanding officer, in cases of urgent necessity, may agree that the troops under his command shall not fight again during the war, unless exchanged.

130. The usual pledge given in the parole is not to serve during the existing war, unless exchanged.

This pledge refers only to the active service in the field, against the paroling belligerent or his allies actively engaged in the same war. These cases of breaking the parole are patent acts, and can be visited with the punishment of death; but the pledge does not refer to internal service, such as recruiting or drilling the recruits, fortifying places not besieged, quelling civil commotions, fighting against belligerents unconnected with the paroling belligerents, or to civil or diplomatic service for which the paroled officer may be employed.

131. If the government does not approve of the parole, the paroled officer must return into captivity; and should the enemy refuse to receive him, he is free of his parole.

132. A belligerent government may declare, by a general order, whether it will allow paroling, and on what conditions it will allow it. Such order is communicated to the enemy.

133. No prisoner of war can be forced by the hostile government to parole himself, and no government is obliged to parole prisoners of war, or to parole all captured officers if it paroles any. As the pledging of the parole is an individual

act, so is paroling, on the other hand, an act of choice on the part of the belligerent.

134. The commander of an occupying army may require of the civil officers of the enemy, and of its citizens, any pledge he may consider necessary for the safety or security of his army; and upon their failure to give it, he may arrest, confine, or detain them.

SECTION VIII.

Armistice—Capitulation.

135. An armistice is the cessation of active hostilities for a period agreed upon between belligerents. It must be agreed upon in writing, and duly ratified by the highest authorities of the contending parties.

136. If an armistice be declared, without conditions, it extends no further than to require a total cessation of hostilities along the front of both belligerents.

If conditions be agreed upon, they should be clearly expressed, and must be rigidly adhered to by both parties. If either party violates any express condition, the armistice may be declared null and void by the other.

137. An armistice may be general, and valid for all points and lines of the belligerents; or special—that is, referring to certain troops or certain localities only.

An armistice may be concluded for a definite time; or for an indefinite time, during which either belligerent may resume hostilities on giving the notice agreed upon to the other.

138. The motives which induce the one or the other belligerent to conclude an armistice, whether it be expected to be preliminary to a treaty of peace, or to prepare during the armistice for a more vigorous prosecution of the war, do in no way affect the character of the armistice itself.

139. An armistice is binding upon the belligerents from the day of the agreed commencement; but the officers of the armies are responsible from the day only when they receive official information of its existence.

140. Commanding officers have the right to conclude armis-

tices binding on the district over which their command extends; but such armistice is subject to the ratification of the superior authority, and ceases so soon as it is made known to the enemy that the armistice is not ratified, even if a certain time for the elapsing between giving notice of cessation and the resumption of hostilities should have been stipulated for.

141. It is incumbent upon the contracting parties of an armistice to stipulate what intercourse of persons or traffic between the inhabitants of the territories occupied by the hostile armies shall be allowed, if any.

If nothing is stipulated, the intercourse remains suspended, as during actual hostilities.

142. An armistice is not a partial or a temporary peace; it is only the suspension of military operations to the extent agreed upon by the parties.

143. When an armistice is concluded between a fortified place and the army besieging it, it is agreed by all the authorities on this subject that the besieger must cease all extension, perfection, or advance of his attacking works, as much so as from attacks by main force.

But as there is a difference of opinion among martial jurists, whether the besieged have the right to repair breaches or to erect new works of defence within the place during an armistice, this point should be determined by express agreement between the parties.

144. So soon as a capitulation is signed, the capitulator has no right to demolish, destroy, or injure the works, arms, stores, or ammunition, in his possession, during the time which elapses between the signing and the execution of the capitulation, unless otherwise stipulated in the same.

145. When an armistice is clearly broken by one of the parties, the other party is released from all obligation to observe it.

146. Prisoners, taken in the act of breaking an armistice, must be treated as prisoners of war, the officer alone being responsible who gives the order for such a violation of an

armistice.   The highest authority of the belligerent aggrieved may demand redress for the infraction of an armistice.

147. Belligerents sometimes conclude an armistice while their plenipotentiaries are met to discuss the conditions of a treaty of peace; but plenipotentiaries may meet without a preliminary armistice: in the latter case, the war is carried on without any abatement.

SECTION IX.

Assassination.

148. The law of war does not allow proclaiming either an individual belonging to the hostile army, or a citizen, or a subject of the hostile government, an outlaw, who may be slain without trial by any captor, any more than the modern law of peace allows such international outlawry; on the contrary, it abhors such outrage.   The sternest retaliation should follow the murder committed in consequence of such proclamation, made by whatever authority.   Civilized nations look with horror upon offers of rewards for the assassination of enemies, as relapses into barbarism.

SECTION X.

Insurrection—Civil War—Rebellion.

149. Insurrection is the rising of people in arms against their government, or a portion of it, or against one or more of its laws, or against an officer or officers of the government. It may be confined to mere armed resistance, or it may have greater ends in view.

150. Civil war is war between two or more portions of a country or state, each contending for the mastery of the whole, and each claiming to be the legitimate government.   The term is also sometimes applied to war of rebellion, when the rebellious provinces or portions of the state are contiguous to those containing the seat of government.

151. The term *rebellion* is applied to an insurrection of large

extent, and is usually a war between the legitimate government of a country and portions or provinces of the same who seek to throw off their allegiance to it, and set up a government of their own.

152. When humanity induces the adoption of the rules of regular war towards rebels, whether the adoption is partial or entire, it does in no way whatever imply a partial or complete acknowledgment of their government, if they have set up one, or of them, as an independent or sovereign power. Neutrals have no right to make the adoption of the rules of war by the assailed government towards rebels the ground of their own acknowledgment of the revolted people as an independent power.

153. Treating captured rebels as prisoners of war, exchanging them, concluding of cartels, capitulations, or other warlike agreements with them; addressing officers of a rebel army by the rank they may have in the same; accepting flags of truce; or, on the other hand, proclaiming martial law in their territory, or levying war-taxes or forced loans, or doing any other act sanctioned or demanded by the law and usages of public war between sovereign belligerents, neither proves nor establishes an acknowledgment of the rebellious people, or of the government which they may have erected, as a public or sovereign power. Nor does the adoption of the rules of war towards rebels imply an engagement with them extending beyond the limits of these rules. It is victory in the field that ends the strife, and settles the future relations between the contending parties.

154. Treating, in the field, the rebellious enemy according to the law and usages of war, has never prevented the legitimate government from trying the leaders of the rebellion or chief rebels for high treason, and from treating them accordingly, unless they are included in a general amnesty.

155. All enemies in regular war are divided into two general classes; that is to say, into combatants and non-combatants, or unarmed citizens of the hostile government.

The military commander of the legitimate government, in a

war of rebellion, distinguishes between the loyal citizen in the revolted portion of the country and the disloyal citizen. The disloyal citizens may further be classified into those citizens known to sympathize with the rebellion, without positively aiding it, and those who, without taking up arms, give positive aid and comfort to the rebellious enemy, without being bodily forced thereto.

156. Common justice and plain expediency require that the military commander protect the manifestly loyal citizens, in revolted territories, against the hardships of the war, as much as the common misfortune of all war admits.

The commander will throw the burden of the war, as much as lies within his power, on the disloyal citizens of the revolted portion or province, subjecting them to a stricter police than the non-combatant enemies have to suffer in regular war ; and if he deems it appropriate, or if his government demands of him, that every citizen shall, by an oath of allegiance, or by some other manifest act, declare his fidelity to the legitimate government, he may expel, transfer, imprison, or fine the revolted citizens who refuse to pledge themselves anew as citizens obedient to the law, and loyal to the government.

Whether it is expedient to do so, and whether reliance can be placed upon such oaths, the commander or his government have the right to decide.

157. Armed or unarmed resistance by citizens of the United States against the lawful movements of their troops is levying war against the United States, and is therefore treason.

GUERRILLA PARTIES

CONSIDERED WITH REFERENCE TO THE

LAWS AND USAGES OF WAR.

NOTE.

THE following essay was written in 1862 at the request of Major-General H. W. Halleck. The author's bound copy has many memoranda intended to be included in a future edition, but only a part of them are in such a form as to warrant their republication by the editor.—G.

276

GUERRILLA PARTIES

LAWS AND USAGES OF WAR.

THE position of armed parties loosely attached to the main body of the army, or altogether unconnected with it, has rarely been taken up by writers on the law of war. The term guerrilla is often inaccurately used, and its application has been particularly confused at the present time. From these circumstances arises much of the difficulty which presents itself to the publicist and martial jurist in treating of guerrilla parties. The subject is substantially a new topic in the law of war, and it is besides exposed to the mischievous process, so often employed in our day, of throwing the mantle of a novel term around an old and well-known offence, in the expectation that a legalizing effect will result from the adoption of a new word having a technical sound; an illustration of which occurred in the introduction of the Latin and rarer term repudiation to designate the old practice of dishonestly declining the payment of debts—an offence with which the world has been acquainted ever since men united in the bonds of society. We find that self-constituted bands in the South, who destroy the cotton stored by their own neighbors, are styled in the journals of the North as well as in those of the South, guerrillas; while in truth they are, according to the common law—not of war only, but that of every society—simply armed robbers, against whom every person is permitted, or is in duty bound, to use all the means of defence at his disposal; as, in a late instance, even General Toombs, of Georgia, declared to a certain committee of safety of his

277

state, that he would defend the planting and producing of his cotton at all hazards; though, I must own, *he* did not call the self-constituted committee *guerrillas*, but, if memory serves me right, scoundrels.

The term guerrilla is the diminutive of the Spanish word *guerra*, war, and means petty war, that is, war carried on by detached parties; generally in the mountains. It means, farther, the party of men united under one chief engaged in petty war, which, in the eastern portion of Europe and the whole Levant, is called a *capitanery*, a band under one capitano. The term *guerrilla*, however, is not applied in Spain to a single man of the party; such a person is called *guerrillero*, or more frequently *partida*, which means partisan. Thus Napier, in speaking of the guerrilla, in his History of the Peninsular War, uses, with rare exception, the term partidas for the chiefs and men engaged in the petty war against the French. It is worthy of notice that the dictionary of the Spanish academy gives, as the first meaning of the word *guerrilla*—"A party of light troops for reconnoissance, and opening the first skirmishes." I translate from an edition of 1826, published, therefore, long after the Peninsular War, through which the term guerrilla has passed over into many other European languages. Self-constitution is not a necessary element of the meaning given by the Spaniards or by many writers of other nations to the word guerrilla, although it is true that the guerrilla parties in the Peninsular War were nearly all self-constituted, since the old government had been destroyed; and the forces which had been called into existence by the provisional government were no more acknowledged by the French as regular troops than the self-constituted bands under leading priests, lawyers, smugglers, or peasants: because the French did not acknowledge the provisional junta or cortes. Many of the guerrilleros were shot when made prisoners; as the guerrilla chiefs executed French prisoners in turn. It is the state of things these bands almost always lead to, according to their inherent character; yet, when the *partidas* of Mina and Empecinado had swelled to the imposing number

of twenty thousand and more, which fact of itself implies a
certain degree of discipline, Mina made a regular treaty with
the French for the passage of certain French goods through
the lines, and on these the partisan leader levied regular duties
according to a tariff agreed upon between the belligerents
arrayed against one another in fierce hostility.[1]

What, then, do we in the present time understand by the
word guerrilla? In order to ascertain the law or to settle it
according to elements already existing, it will be necessary
ultimately to give a distinct definition; but it may be stated
here that whatever may be our final definition, it is universally
understood in this country at the present time that a guerrilla
party means an irregular band of armed men, carrying on an
irregular war, not being able, according to their character as
a guerrilla party, to carry on what the law terms a *regular* war.
The irregularity of the guerrilla party consists in its origin,
for it is either self-constituted or constituted by the call of a
single individual, not according to the general law of levy,
conscription, or volunteering; it consists in its disconnection
with the army, as to its pay, provision, and movements, and it
is irregular as to the permanency of the band, which may be
dismissed and called again together at any time. These are,
I believe, constituent ideas of the term guerrilla as now used.
Other ideas are associated with the term, differently by different persons. Thus many persons associate the idea of
pillage with the guerrilla band, because, not being connected
with the regular army, the men cannot provide for themselves,
except by pillage, even in their own country—acts of violence
with which the Spanish guerrilleros sorely afflicted their own
countrymen in the Peninsular War. Others connect with it
the idea of intentional destruction for the sake of destruction,

---

[1] The Whigs and Tories in South Carolina in the Revolution—Marion's men
and Butler's men—came to murder their prisoners even contrary to agreements
of surrender, although General Marion, the partisan leader of the patriots, and
a guerrilla chief as he would now be called, was a man of a peculiarly gentle
disposition, who expressed his indignation at murders when committed even by
way of retaliation. Simms's Life of Francis Marion, p. 165.

because the guerrilla chief cannot aim at any strategic advantages or any regular fruits of victory. Others, again, associate with it the idea of the danger with which the spy surrounds us, because he that to-day passes you in the garb and mien of a peaceful citizen, may to-morrow, as a guerrilla-man, fire your house or murder you from behind the hedge. Others connect with the guerrillero the idea of necessitated murder, because guerrilla bands cannot encumber themselves with prisoners of war; they have, therefore, frequently, perhaps generally, killed their prisoners, and of course have been killed in turn when made prisoners, thus introducing a system of barbarity which becomes intenser in its demoralization as it spreads and is prolonged. Others, again, connect the ideas of general and heinous criminality, of robbery and lust with the term, because the organization of the party being but slight and the leader utterly dependent upon the band, little discipline can be enforced, and where no discipline is enforced in war a state of things results which resembles far more the wars recorded in Froissart or Comines, or the Thirty Years' War, and the Religious War in France, than the regular wars of modern times. And such a state of things results speedily too; for all growth, progress, and rearing, moral or material, are slow; all destruction, relapse, and degeneracy fearfully rapid. It requires the power of the Almighty and a whole century to grow an oak-tree; but only a pair of arms, an axe, and an hour or two to cut it down.

History confirms these associations, but the law of war as well as the law of peace has treated many of these and kindred subjects—acts justifiable, offensive, or criminal—under acknowledged terms, namely: the freebooter, the marauder, the brigand, the partisan, the free-corps, the spy, the rebel, the conspirator, the robber, and especially the highway robber, the rising *en masse*, or the "arming of peasants."[1]

---

[1] Using guerrilla for all this is doing violence to the language. I found this day, 6th October, 1862, this paragraph in the Evening Post, New York, first using guerrilla and then highway robber:

"SANTA FÉ MAIL CAPTURED BY GUERRILLAS.—The coaches of the Kansas

A few words on some of these subjects will aid us in coming to a clearer understanding of the main topic which occupies our attention.

Freebooter is a term which was in common use in the English language at no very remote period; it is of rare use now, because the freebooter makes his appearance but rarely in modern times, thanks to the more regular and efficient governments, and to the more advanced state of the law of war. From the freebooter at sea arose the privateer, for the privateer is a commissioned freebooter, or the freebooter taken into the service of the government by the letter of marque. The Sea-Gueux, in the revolution of the Netherlands, were originally freebooters at sea, and they were always treated, when captured, simply as freebooters. Wherever the freebooter is taken, at sea or on land, death is inflicted upon him now as in former times; for freebooters are nothing less than armed robbers of the most dangerous and criminal type, banded together for the purposes of booty and of common protection.

The brigand is, in military language, the soldier who detaches himself from his troop and commits robbery, naturally accompanied in many cases with murder and other crimes of violence. His punishment, inflicted even by his own authorities, is death. The word brigand, derived as it is from *briguer*, to beg, meant originally beggar, but it soon came to be applied to armed strollers, a class of men which swarmed in all countries in the Middle Ages. The term has, however, received a wider meaning in modern military terminology. He that assails the enemy without or against the authority of

---

stage company were attacked on the night of the 16th of September, near the crossing of the Smoky Hill, by a party of fifteen highwayman. The passengers were robbed of all their valuables and the mail-bags were rifled of their contents. Fourteen mules were also stolen. A reward of one hundred dollars is offered for every authenticated scalp of the robbers."

Any persons committing an act of violence, directly or indirectly connected with the present war, or merely committed during this period, are called guerrillas. This illustrates our unfortunate catching at new words, yet always using few words of the dictionary.

his own government, is called, even though his object should be wholly free from any intention of pillage, a brigand, subject to the infliction of death, if captured.[1] When Major von Schill, commanding a Prussian regiment of hussars, marched, in the year 1809, against the French, without the order of his government, for the purpose of causing a rising of the people in the north of Germany, while Napoleon was occupied in the south with Austria, Schill was declared by Napoleon and his brother *a brigand*, and the king of Westphalia, Jerome Bonaparte, offered a reward of ten thousand francs for his head. Schill was killed in battle; but twelve young officers of his troop, taken prisoners, were carried by the French to the fortress Wesel, where a court-martial declared them prisoners of war. Napoleon quashed the finding, ordered a new court-martial, and they were all shot as brigands. Napoleon is not cited here as· an authority in the law of war; he and many of his generals frequently substituted the harshest violence for martial usages. The case is mentioned as an illustration of the meaning attached to the word brigand in the law of war, and of the fact that death is the acknowledged punishment for the brigand.

The terms partisan and free-corps are vaguely used.[2] Sometimes, as we shall see farther on, partisan is used for a self-constituted *guerrillero;* more frequently it has a different meaning. Both partisan-corps and free-corps designate bodies detached from the main army; but the former term refers to the action of the troop, the latter to the composition. The partisan leader commands a corps whose object is to injure the enemy by action separate from that of his own main army; the partisan acts chiefly upon the enemy's lines of connection and communication, and outside of or beyond the lines of operation of his own army, in the rear and on

---

[1] It is very remarkable that the Romans most strenuously insisted upon the military oath. The sacrament was in order to enable a soldier legally to fight with the enemy. See Cicero de Officiis, bk. i. ch. ii., the latter part, and ch. xiii.

[2] Ed. De La Barre Duparcq, Eléments d'Art et d'Histoire Militaires, Paris, 1858, has a chapter on partisans.

the flanks of the enemy. Rapid and varying movements and surprises are the chief means of his success; but he is part and parcel of the army, and, as such, considered entitled to the privileges of the law of war, so long as he does not transgress it. Free-corps, on the other hand, are troops not belonging to the regular army, consisting of volunteers, generally raised by individuals authorized to do so by the government, used for petty war, and not incorporated with the *Ordre de bataille.* They were known in the Middle Ages. The French *compagnies franches* were free-corps; but this latter term came into use only in the eighteenth century. They were generally in bad repute, given to pillage and other excesses; but this is incidental. There were many free-corps in Germany opposed to Napoleon, when that country rose against the French, but the men composing them were entitled to the benefits of the law of war, and generally received them when taken prisoner. These free-corps were composed, in many cases, of high-minded patriots. The difficulty regarding free-corps and partisans arises from the fact that their discipline is often lax, and used to be so especially in the last century, so that frequently they cannot cumber themselves with prisoners; and that, even for their own support, they are often obliged to pillage or to extort money from the places they occupy. They are treated, therefore, according to their deserts, on the principle of retaliation; but there is nothing inherently lawless or brigand-like in their character.

The spy, the rebel, and conspirator deserve notice in this place simply with reference to persons acting as such, and belonging to the population of the country or district occupied by a hostile force. A person dwelling in a district under military occupation, and giving information to the government of which he was subject, but which has been expelled by the victorious invader, is universally treated as a spy—a spy of a peculiarly dangerous character. The most patriotic motives would not shield such a person from the doom of the spy. There have been high-minded and self-sacrificing spies, but, when captured, even if belonging to the armies themselves, they have never been treated otherwise than as common hired spies. Even mere secret correspondence of a person in an occupied district with the enemy, though the contents of the correspondence may have been innocent, has subjected the correspondent to serious consequences, and sometimes to the rigor of martial law, especially if the offence was committed after a proclamation to the contrary. Prince Hatzfeld was appointed by the king of Prussia, on his leaving the capital after the battle of Jena, to conduct public affairs in Berlin, until the city should be occupied by the French, and to send a report to the king every morning until the occupation by the enemy should have taken place. Prince Hatzfeld sent such a report to his own government, giving the number of the French who had arrived at Potsdam on the 24th of October, at five o'clock A.M.—that is, seven hours before the French vanguard entered Berlin. The letter fell into the hands of Napoleon. It is well known that the emperor, at the supplication of the princess, allowed her husband to escape the penalty of a spy. Whatever may be thought of the question, whether the prince, by sending the letter at the hour mentioned, became a spy or not, no one has ever doubted that, had he secretly corresponded with his government after the occupation of Berlin by the French, giving information of the occupants, the French would have been justified in treating him as a spy. The spy becomes, in this case, peculiarly dangerous, making hostile use of the protection which, by the modern law of war, the victor extends to the persons and property of the conquered. Similar remarks apply to the rebel, taking the word in the primitive meaning of *rebellare*—that is, to return to war after having been conquered (*debellatum*) ; and to conspiracies—that is, secret agreements leading to such resumption of arms in bands of whatever number, or, which is still worse, plans to murder from secret places.

This war-rebel, as we might term him, this renewer of war within an occupied territory, has been universally treated with the utmost rigor of the military law. The war-rebel exposes the occupying army to the greatest danger, and essentially interferes with the mitigation of the severity of war, which it is one of the noblest objects of the modern law of war to obtain. Whether the war-rebel rises on his own account, or whether he has been secretly called upon by his former government to do so, would make no difference whatever. The royalists who recently rose in the mountains of Calabria against the national government of Italy, and in favor of Francis, who had been their king until within a recent period, were treated as brigands and shot, unless, indeed, pardoned on prudential grounds.

The rising *en masse*, or "the arming of peasants," as it used to be called, brings us nearer to the subject of the guerrilla parties. Down to the beginning of the first French revolution, towards the end of the last century, the spirit which pervaded all governments of the European continent was, that the people were rather the passive substratum of the state than an essential portion of it. The governments were considered to be the state; wars were chiefly cabinet wars, not national wars—not the people's affairs.

Moser, in his Contributions to the latest European Law of Nations in Times of War (a German work, in 3 vols., from 1779–1781), gives remarkable instances of the claims which the conqueror was believed to have on the property and on the subjects of the hostile country. They were believed to be of so extensive a character that the French, when in Germany, during the Seven Years' War, literally drafted Germans for the French army, and used them as their own soldiers— although it must be added that loud complaints were made, and the French felt themselves obliged to make some sort of explanation. The same work contains instances of complaints being made against arming the peasants, or of levies *en masse*, as contrary to the law of nations; but Moser also shows that the Austrians employed the Tyrolese (always familiar with the use of the rifle) in war, without any complaint of the adversary; and in many countries there are no longer peasants. That separate class we find in the Peasant War in Germany, in the Jacquerie in France, etc. England and the United

States have no peasants proper—that is, a separate class of men, ignorant, barbarous, coarse, wild, etc., such as we have seen in quite recent time in Galicia, when the Austrians called on them to rise against the nobles.

Since that time most constitutions contain provisions that the people have a right to possess and use arms; everywhere *national* armies have been introduced, and the military law of many countries puts arms into the hands of all. Austria armed the people, as militia, in 1805; Russia, in 1812; and Prussia introduced the most comprehensive measure of arming the people in 1813. The militia proper was called *Landwehr;* and those who were too old for service in the Landwehr were intended to form the *Landsturm*—citizens armed as well as the circumstances might permit, and to be used for whatever military service within their own province they might be found fit. It is true that the French threatened to treat them as brigands—that is to say, not to treat them as prisoners of war if captured. The French, however, were expelled from Germany, and no opportunity was given to test their threat.[1]

I believe it can be said that the most recent publicists and writers on international law agree that the rising of the people to repel invasion entitles them to the full benefits of the law of war, and that the invader cannot well inquire into the origin of the armed masses opposing him; that is to say, he will be obliged to treat the captured citizens in arms as prisoners of war, so long as they openly oppose him in respectable numbers, and have risen in the yet uninvaded or unconquered portions of the hostile country.

Their acting in separate bodies does not necessarily give them a different character. Some entire wars have been carried on by separate bands or capitaneries, such as the recent war of independence of Greece. It is true, indeed, that the

---

[1] Yet Napoleon, after having taken Vienna, in 1809, ordered the dissolution of the Austrian Landwehr, and threatened all officers that if they should not return to their homes within a fortnight, their houses should be burned and their property confiscated. Buchholz, vol. iii. p. 541. This was when the Austrians were on the opposite bank of the Danube, and the Landwehr with the army.

question of the treatment of prisoners was not discussed in that war, because the Turkish government killed or enslaved all prisoners; but I take it that a civilized government would not have allowed the fact that the Greeks fought in detached parties and carried on mountain guerrilla to influence its conduct towards prisoners.

I may here observe that the question how captured guerrilleros ought to be treated was not much discussed in the last century, and, comparatively, the whole discussion in the law of war is new. This will not surprise us when we consider that so justly celebrated a publicist as Bynkershoeck defended, as late as the beginning of last century, the killing of common prisoners of war.

It does not seem that, in the case of a rising *en masse*, the absence of a uniform can constitute a difference. There are cases, indeed, in which the absence of a uniform may be taken as very serious *prima facie* evidence against an armed prowler or marauder, but it must be remembered that a uniform dress is a matter of impossibility in a levy *en masse;* and in some cases regulars have had no uniforms, at least for a considerable time. The Southern prisoners made at Fort Donelson, whom I have seen at the west, had no uniform. They were indeed dressed very much alike, but it was the uniform dress of the countryman in that region. Yet they were treated by us as prisoners of war, and well treated too. Nor would it be difficult to adopt something of a badge, easily put on and off, and to call it a uniform. It makes a great difference, however, whether the absence of the uniform is used for the purpose of concealment or disguise, in order to get by stealth within the lines of the invader, for destruction of life or property, or for pillage, and whether the parties have no organization at all, and are so small that they cannot act otherwise than by stealth. Nor can it be maintained in good faith, or with any respect for sound sense and judgment, that an individual—an armed prowler (now frequently called a bushwhacker)—shall be entitled to the protection of the law of war, simply because he says that he has taken up his gun in defence of his country, or because his government or his chief has issued a proclamation by which he calls upon the people to infest the bushes and commit homicides which every civilized nation will consider murders. Indeed, the importance of writing on this subject is much diminished by the fact that the soldier generally decides these cases for himself. The most disciplined soldiers will execute on the spot an armed and murderous prowler found where he could have no business as a peaceful citizen. Even an enemy in the uniform of the hostile army would stand little chance of protection if found prowling near the opposing army, separate from his own troops at a greater than picket distance, and under generally suspicious circumstances. The chance would, of course, be far less if the prowler is in the common dress worn by the countryman of the district. It may be added here, that a person proved to be a regular soldier of the enemy's army, found in citizens' dress within the lines of the captor, is universally dealt with as a spy.

It has been stated that the word guerrilla is not only used for individuals engaged in petty war, but frequently as an equivalent of partisan. General Halleck, in his International Law, or Rules regulating the Intercourse of States in Peace and War, San Francisco, 1861, page 386, et seq., seems to consider partisan troops and guerrilla troops as the same, and seems to consider " self-constitution" a characteristic of the partisan ; while other legal and military writers define partisan as I have stated, namely, a soldier belonging to a corps which operates in the manner given above. I beg the reader to peruse that passage, both on account of its own value and of the many important and instructive authorities which he will find there. They are collected with that careful industry which distinguishes the whole work.

Dr. T. D. Woolsey, page 299, seq., of his Introduction to the Study of International Law, Boston, 1860, says : " The treatment which the milder modern usage prescribes for regular soldiers is extended also to militia called out by public authority. Guerrilla parties, however, do not enjoy the full benefit of the laws of war.   They are apt to fare worse than either regular troops or an armed peasantry.   The reasons for this are, that they are annoying and insidious, that they put on and off with ease the character of a soldier, and that they are prone, themselves, to treat their enemies who fall into their hands with great severity. ''

If the term partisan is used in the sense in which I have defined it, it is not necessary to treat of it specially.   The partisan, in this sense, is, of course, answerable for the commission of those acts to which the law of war grants no protection, and by which the soldier forfeits being treated as a prisoner of war, if captured.

It is different, if we understand by guerrilla parties self-constituted sets of armed men, in times of war, who form no integrant part of the organized army, do not stand on the regular pay-roll of the army, or are not paid at all, take up arms and lay them down at intervals, and carry on petty war (guerrilla) chiefly by raids, extortion, destruction, and massacre, and who cannot encumber themselves with many prisoners, and will therefore generally give no quarter.

They are peculiarly dangerous, because they easily evade pursuit, and by laying down their arms become insidious enemies ; because they cannot otherwise subsist than by rapine, and almost always degenerate into simple robbers or brigands. The Spanish guerrilla bands against Napoleon proved a scourge to their own countrymen, and became efficient for their own cause only in the same degree in which they gradually became disciplined.   The royalists in the north of France, during the first revolution, although setting out with sentiments of loyal devotion to their unfortunate king, soon degenerated into bands of robbers, while many robbers either joined them or assumed the name of royalists.   Napoleon states that their brigandage gave much trouble, and obliged the government to resort to the severest measures.

For an account of the misdeeds and want of efficiency of the Spanish guerrilleros, the reader is referred to Napier's Peninsular War, and especially to chapter ii., book xvii.;

while he will find, in Guizot's Memoirs, vol. iv., page 100, seq., that in the struggle between the Cristinos and Carlists, the guerrilla parties under Mina and Zumalacarreguy regularly massacred their mutual prisoners, until the evil became so revolting to the Spaniards themselves that a regular treaty was concluded between the parties, stipulating the exchange of prisoners immediately after being made. How the surplus on the one or the other side was dealt with, I do not know; but the treaty, concluded after the butchering of prisoners had been going on for a long time, is mentioned in all the histories of that period.

But when guerrilla parties aid the main army of a belligerent, it will be difficult for the captor of guerrilla-men to decide at once whether they are regular partisans, distinctly authorized by their own government; and it would seem that we are borne out by the conduct of the most humane belligerents in recent times, and by many of the modern writers, if the rule be laid down, that guerrilla-men, when captured in fair fight and open warfare, should be treated as the regular partisan is, until special crimes, such as murder, or the killing of prisoners, or the sacking of open places, are proved upon them; leaving the question of self-constitution unexamined.

The law of war, however, would not extend a similar favor to small bodies of armed country people, near the lines, whose very smallness shows that they must resort to occasional fighting and the occasional assuming of peaceful habits, and to brigandage. The law of war would still less favor them when they trespass within the hostile lines to commit devastation, rapine, or destruction. Every European army has treated such persons, and it seems to me would continue, even in the improved state of the present usages of war, to treat them as brigands, whatever prudential mercy might decide upon in single cases. This latter consideration cannot be discussed here; it does not appertain to the law of war.

It has been stated already, that the armed prowler, the so-called bushwhacker, is a simple assassin, and will thus always be considered by soldier and citizen; and we have likewise

seen that the armed bands that rise in a district fairly occupied by military force, or in the rear of an army, are universally considered, if captured, brigands, and not prisoners of
war. They unite the fourfold character of the spy, the brig-
and, the assassin, and the rebel, and cannot—indeed, it must
be supposed, will not—expect to be treated as a fair enemy
of the regular war. They know what a hazardous career
they enter upon when they take up arms, and that, were the
case reversed, they would surely not grant the privileges of
regular warfare to persons who should thus rise in their rear.

I have thus endeavored to ascertain what may be considered the law of war, or fair rules of action toward so-called
guerrilla parties. I do not enter upon a consideration of their
application to the civil war in which we are engaged, nor of
the remarkable claims recently set up by our enemies, de-
manding us to act according to certain rules which they have
signally and officially disregarded towards us. I have simply
proposed to myself to find a certain portion of the law of war.
The application of the laws and usages of war to wars of insurrection or rebellion is always undefined, and depends upon
relaxations of the municipal law, suggested by humanity or
necessitated by the numbers engaged in the insurrection.
The law of war, as acknowledged between independent belligerents, is, at times, not allowed to interfere with the municipal law of rebellion, or is allowed to do so only very
partially, as was the case in Great Britain during the Stuart
rebellion, in the middle of last century ; at other times, again,
measures are adopted in rebellions, by the victorious party or
the legitimate government, more lenient even than the international law of war. Neither of these topics can occupy us
here, nor does the letter prefixed to this tract contain the request that I should do so. How far rules which have formed
themselves in the course of time between belligerents might
be relaxed, with safety, towards the evil-doers in our civil war,
or how far such relaxation or mitigation would be likely to
produce a beneficial effect upon an enemy who in committing
a great and bewildering wrong seems to have withdrawn him-

self from the common influences of fairness, sympathy, truth, and logic—how far this ought to be done, at the present moment, must be decided by the executive power, civil and military, or possibly by the legislative power. It is not for me, in this place, to make the inquiry. So much is certain, that no army, no society, engaged in war, any more than a society at peace, can allow unpunished assassination, robbery, and devastation, without the deepest injury to itself and disastrous consequences, which might change the very issue of the war.[1]

---

[1] In the new edition must be brought in that paroling privates, now daily, yet never before done, creates a new difficulty in the guerrilla baseness. How can small and unauthorized bands be paroled and afterwards watched whether they keep the parole, without any authority to resort to in case the paroles are broken?

In the new edition the distinction between defending and attacking bands must be more insisted upon. It is very important. (*Author's MS. note*, written during the Civil War.)

THE STATUS OF REBEL PRISONERS OF WAR.[*]

WHAT is the precise status of the paroled rebel when the civil war shall be concluded? Does the cartel which admits him as a paroled prisoner of war clothe him with impunity as a citizen? Is he protected against trial while prisoner of war, and unexchanged, for any and every crime he may have committed while in arms against the United States? Are the laws and usages of public war sufficient to guide us in the solution of these questions, and are there sufficiently established precedents in the history of war to lay out for us the plain road we have to travel, in honesty and honor, to reach a satisfactory end?

These and many similar questions are now constantly asked, after Lieutenant-General Grant has received Lee's capitulation; after other portions of the rebel army have surrendered on the same terms, and when similar surrenders in distant regions of our country are daily expected. The writer of this communication has been repeatedly called upon to give his opinion on this grave topic, and he can see no reason why he should withhold it.

The laws and usages of modern public war, so far as they concern the present inquiry, are few, and simply arise out of the nature and necessity of the conditions. A belligerent is not a criminal, and the imprisonment of a captured belligerent is not a punishment. A prisoner of war is no convict; his imprisonment is a simple war measure. The prisoner of war

[*] Published in The Independent, New York, May 10, 1865.

enjoys, as such, great privileges; but he enjoys them only as a prisoner of war, that is to say, as a person taken prisoner when fighting in the service and by command of a belligerent acknowledged as a sovereign government, or taken prisoner in public war. If such person has committed crimes, that is to say, acts of injury not covered by the laws of war, he remains answerable to the captor for the same, and will be punished accordingly. The Instructions for the Government of Armies of the United States in the Field, commanded by President Lincoln to be published as General Order No. 100, 1863, paragraph 59, has these words on the section on prisoners of war: "A prisoner of war remains answerable for his crimes committed against the captor's army or people before he was captured, and for which he has not been punished by his own authorities." Thus, it was reported in the Crimean War that French and English soldiers accused a Russian officer, then prisoner of war, of having encouraged his men in battle to kill or mutilate wounded enemies lying on the field, and that the captured officer was thereupon tried by court-martial, found guilty, and executed. Careful inquiry has not led to satisfactory information regarding the fact, but it is a fact that the account of the transaction was published in the European journals of different countries, and nowhere was any disapprobation expressed against the procedure or the principle, as indeed no one could raise any well-founded objections. So, if it were discovered that a prisoner of war had been concerned in the poisoning or other assassination of an enemy, before his capture, he would plainly remain answerable for the crime, and would be wholly unprotected by his status as prisoner of war. The same would be the case if it were discovered that a prisoner of war had been guilty of cruelty against prisoners, before his capture. As to the punishableness of crimes committed by a prisoner of war, while he is in that state, it is unnecessary to say anything about it.

The law and usages of war, it may be further observed, allow officers only to be paroled and singly dismissed on their parole; make no distinction as to obligations or status between the paroled prisoner of war and the prisoner of war in custody; and, lastly, all parole or imprisonment of prisoners of war is naturally at an end with the conclusion of peace. It cannot be otherwise. When there are many prisoners of war in the hands of the one or the other belligerent at the time when peace is concluded, a separate arrangement is agreed upon how the prisoners shall be marched from the one country to the other, and where they shall be received; but the restoration of the prisoners is always considered as a natural consequence of peace. Russia, during the war with Napoleon I., had sent a certain number of prisoners of war to Siberia, and when, at the conclusion of the Peace of Paris, they were not forthcoming as fast as many persons believed they ought to be sent to France, a general European disapproval made itself heard. In this case the student of the law of war will observe the additional fact that these returning prisoners had to pass through the whole of Germany before they could reach the frontiers of France, and the writer well remembers having seen squads of these French soldiers pass through Germany, of course by government arrangements, long after the conclusion of the great European peace.

These usages are sufficiently simple, but the difficulty, if there be any, arises out of the fact that we are obliged to apply, as far as may be, these rules of war between sovereign governments to a rebellion; in other words, we must apply rules, made for the intercourse of warring parties who commit no crime by warring with one another, to rebels, that is, to men who, by the very fact that they war against us, and call for the application of rules of war, prove that they commit a crime—*i.e.*, treason or armed rebellion against their lawful government. This radical contradiction, inherent in all cases of rebellion against a humane and civilized government, creates those doubts and difficulties which never appeared to the Romans, to Asiatic despotism, or to some ruthless governments even within this century, and which we must endeavor to solve, not only according to the principles of justice and earnest truth, but also of manly fairness, and of honorable candor, not to speak of wisdom and highest expediency, as points not lying within our present scope.

Those jurists of the law of nations who endeavor, in times of peace, calmly and without the bias of strife, to lay down the rules to be observed in times of passion, agree that humanity and wisdom require the application of the laws of public war to rebellions as far as it is possible to do so, and that no consequences with reference to the legal and ultimate status of those who have risen in rebellion can be deduced from the application of military rules applied for the sake of humanity to the fighting parties in a rebellion or civil war.

Our General Order No. 100, 1863, already quoted, has the following on the subject:

[See paragraphs 152, 153, 154, *ante*, p. 273.]

We have fought on this proclamation. We have communicated this General Order No. 100 to the enemy at the time it was issued, and said: Here are the rules which we mean to follow. There has been no misunderstanding on this point.

Considering the laws of regular war, the rules adopted by humane governments in rebellions, and our own code of the laws of war, as well as the principles of law in general, the following results appear plain and just:

1. Any cartel or military agreement remains military in its character, and the general to whom an army surrenders cannot go, or be considered to go in what he grants, beyond his own military power. He cannot, as a military commander, determine anything regarding the rights, or forfeiture of rights in a civil point of view, of those who surrender.

2. When a war ceases, prisoners of war return to their homes, and paroles are at an end. So soon as the rebellion is at an end, the power of parole ceases with it, and the paroled person becomes again simply a citizen or subject, with undiminished responsibility to the law of the land. If an amnesty has been declared in the mean time, that amnesty is not a military but a civil act.

3. No immunity whatever results from a military conven-

tion, beyond the stipulated military points ; and the fact that a written agreement has been entered into by two conflicting parties, in a rebellion, does not by any means imply a pardon of the offences committed up to the time of the agreement.

4. Prisoners of war remain always responsible for penal crimes committed before the capture.

5. All that, in a rebellion, a formal and stipulated surrender implies, and can imply in good faith, is that the act of appearing in arms against the other contracting party shall not be visited as a crime, so far as the articles of surrender go, and so long as they, in their nature, can last.

6. Those who rebelliously have taken up arms cannot enjoy greater immunities than the civilians who have joined the rebellion, and all the privileges they can enjoy are those only which arise out of the stipulated conditions, distinctly laid down in the agreement of surrender, and thereby consented to by the captor.

7. Prisoners may be paroled on different conditions, with a wider or narrower extent of liberty, and " breaking the parole is punished with death when the person breaking the parole is captured again." (General Order No. 100, 1863, paragraph 124.) There is no change of this rule in case of rebellion, when the " home" to which the paroled prisoner is consigned by the parole lies within or is the country of both parties. Nor can the conditions of the parole, be they light or severe, effect any difference.

The subject of an amnesty, of its necessary limits in the present rebellion, and all that is connected with this momentous question, lies outside of the present discussion, the exclusive topic of which was : How far does General Grant's convention with Lee affect the civil status and the legal responsibility of the surrendered and now paroled rebels ?

SOME POINTS IN INTERNATIONAL LAW.

A. ON THE VALUE OF PLEBISCITES IN INTERNATIONAL LAW.

B. ON THE IDEA OF THE "LATIN RACE" AND ITS REAL VALUE IN INTERNATIONAL LAW.

C. SUGGESTIONS ON THE SALE OF ARMS BY THE U. S. GOVERNMENT DURING THE FRANCO-PRUSSIAN WAR.

D. ON INTERNATIONAL ARBITRATION.

E. ON INTERNATIONAL COPYRIGHT.

NOTE.

THREE of the communications which follow were printed in French in the *Revue de Droit International et de Législation Comparée*, 1871 and 1872.

The first appeared also in the New York Evening Post under the signature *Americus*, and was reprinted in Littell's Living Age. A translation by W. W. S. of the second article (on the Latin race), was printed for private circulation in November, 1871, but Dr. Lieber's own language is here given. An English version of the third article, apparently from Dr. Lieber's own pen, appeared in an American journal, and is here reprinted.

The fourth paper, addressed to Hon. Wm. H. Seward, U. S. Secretary of State, was originally published in the New York Daily Times, September 22, 1865.

The fifth letter was addressed to Hon. Wm. C. Preston, U. S. Senator from South Carolina, in 1840.—G.

SOME POINTS IN INTERNATIONAL LAW.

A. THE PLEBISCITUM.

A German American View of the New German Nationality.

THAT portion of the American population which takes a lively interest in the present war between France and Germany is by this time pretty well divided, according to the sympathies for the one or the other country, and those whose affections incline towards France, for whatever reason, maintain that, according to good faith and international honor, no acquisition of French territory by Germany ought to take place without the inhabitants of the respective territories having expressed themselves in a *plebiscitum* favorable towards annexation to Germany. Even leading Germans, at least one of them, Dr. Jacoby, has publicly and strongly expressed this idea. It is with this question that I intend to occupy your readers for a short time. I leave the question aside—Is it wise for Germany to take a single foot of French territory? For argument's sake, we suppose that it is in harmony with profound statesmanship and necessary for the safety of Germany, as well as for the peace of Europe, that Alsace and Lorraine, or a portion of the latter, be incorporated with the German empire ; and here only ask whether this ought to be done by a high-minded people without a *plebiscitum*—whether Americans, professedly lovers and cultivators of freedom, must not naturally be expected to side with the French. Let us judge of the question with manly calmness and just sincerity. Sentimentalism does no good; pretended sentimentalism does harm in every way.

Of the Roman *plebiscitum* nothing need be said here but that it does not fall within the limits of the present discussion. The *plebiscitum* of antiquity was a resolution of the *plebs* as distinguished from the senate, and the *plebs* were not a nation, but simply the non-patrician population of Rome and its immediate vicinity.

The modern *plebiscitum* is exclusively a French, nay, more, a recent Bonaparte innovation. *Plebiscite*, in the modern public law, designates a resolution or decree pretended to be adopted by the nation at large; that is, by the majority of votes of all Frenchmen twenty-one years old and above. They furnish good handles for the time, but are singularly untrustworthy, as every man, learned in election practice, sees at once, when he considers that these *plebiscites* allow no vote but yes or no; that no discussions, no meetings, no party formations are allowed; that the chief of the state has the whole army, all the officers, the entire administration, and the whole election apparatus, before and after the voting, in his hand. Consider this, and see what becomes of *l'Elu du Peuple*. So far as history goes it must be laid down that the modern *plebiscite* is singularly untrue and hollow, and the reasons can be readily discovered. It was the predominant desire of the emperor, now captive in Germany, to proclaim his so-called democratic absolutism as being the result of, and pre-eminently founded upon, the national decision. He adopted the official style: We, Napoleon, by the grace of God and the national will, Emperor of the French. Napoleon the First styled himself by the grace of God and the constitutions of France. The last *plebiscite* had appended to it by the emperor what in parliamentary slang is called a *rider* concerning the confidence which the nation has in the Bonapartes and the necessary continuance of their dynasty. More than seven millions voted yes; yet in no more than four months after, the Bonaparte

empire, *plebiscite* and all, tumbled down, no better than an isolated mountain-house with rotten rafters, in a somewhat blus-
tering wind. The empire, *le système*, as Napoleon I. was so
fond of calling it, broke together. And the breaking came ·
from within. Compare it to Prussia, cut down, exhausted, in
1807, almost to nothing; yet in less than six years she rises
into one of the five great powers of Europe. Give the army
and all civil power over a people unpractised in civil affairs
and untutored in self-government, into the hands of an absolute power-holder, and he must be a singular being if he does
not turn the weathercock the way he wishes it to stand.

International *plebiscites* have not fared better; at least the
more we learn about the details of the vote by which Savoy
and Nice were annexed to France, the more bitterly has the
friend of men to regret the contradiction of the liberal form
and the essential illiberality of a *plebiscite* under such circumstances. It becomes a mockery, and a very bitter farce. This
was a peaceful cession. As to conquests, France, the author
of the resuscitated *plebiscite* (at least of the name), has never
asked the people of territories conquered by her whether they
would like to become French; on the contrary, she has again
and again disposed of land and people at a distance, and on
amity with her, in treaties with other powers, as was proposed
in the Benedetti transactions.

We Americans have five times extended our territory. The
annexation of Texas was the admission of a state, considered
independent, to our Union by treaty. The acquisition of California, however, was by conquest. After we had been victorious over Mexico, Upper California was ceded to us, and
no one ever asked for a *plebiscitum* by which the Californians
should express their willingness to become citizens of the
United States, or the contrary; or for a *plebiscitum* on the part
of the remaining Mexicans, by which their willingness might
have been expressed to part with Upper California. The logic
of the case, it seems, would require the latter as well as the
former. New Mexico was acquired later by mere buying and
selling. No one thought of a vote at the hands of the New

Mexicans, whether they would or would not be Americans. The most important American case, however, is that of Louisiana. The almost boundless territory of Louisiana was acquired by purchase; a Bonaparte ceded it in 1803 for fifteen million dollars, and the president, of all American presidents, most inclined towards French democratic ideas, transcended, as he himself acknowledges, the Constitution, in order to obtain the whole valley of the Mississippi and its mouth, considered, and justly so, a necessity for the development of the United States. And was a single inhabitant of Louisiana, then citizen of the republic of France, called upon to express his idea about the transfer of his allegiance, or was it considered against the honor of France or her first consul that French territory, having been such longer than Alsace, should be ceded to another power?

When our government directed General Jackson, in July, 1821, to take possession of Florida, according to a treaty with Spain, no Spaniard resident in Florida, and no other inhabitant, was asked for his vote about the cession of that country.

So far for the American practice and all but universal history of annexations. The law of nations cannot be cited in favor of *plebiscites* in cases of annexation, for no such rule or custom exists. In many, perhaps in most cases, the *plebiscite* would be impossible; in no case can it be relied upon; nor can an annexation *plebiscite* be demanded from the highest philosophical point of view. An annexation *plebiscite* is, touching the question of transferring allegiance, a most elementary question, beyond the established law of the land; and who, we must ask at once, has decreed, or on what reason is it founded, that a mere majority of men of a certain age shall determine the allegiance of all, the minority, which may be imagined to be large, included? Why not demand two-thirds? Why not three-fourths? But still more difficult to be answered is the question, Who established, in a case of so elementary a character, the right of the living to determine the allegiance of the unborn generations?

The whole idea of annexation *plebiscites* is novel; has been set a-going by the people among the least expert of all nations in matter of popular politics; it may be resorted to if people can agree about it; so far there can be no reliance placed in large *plebiscites*, or in annexation *plebiscites ;* there is no general moral obligation to resort to the latter in cases of war or purchase ; an annexation *plebiscite* does not do away with the odiousness of force, since no one could resort even to the *plebiscite* if territory had not already been conquered; and, lastly, we Americans place ourselves in an awkward position if we demand in the name of liberty or liberality a *plebiscite* for Alsace. We had better follow our much-vaunted Monroe doctrine, and leave Europe to herself.

It is not necessary to discuss now the question of dishonor involved in the cession of territory. Other people, besides the French, possess the feeling of honor, but they have never been asked concerning that point by the French. Paying money, ceding vessels, one would think would touch the honor too.

POSTSCRIPT.

To the Editors of the Evening Post :

The editors of Littell's Living Age have republished my paper on the question whether a *plcbiscite* is necessary concerning the proposed annexation of Alsace and Lorraine, first given in the Evening Post. Although I know that you and I, agreeing almost on every subject of public importance, do not hold the same opinion on the necessity of a *plcbiscite*, I beg you to let me state in your journal the following fact, and merely as a remarkable historical fact, complementary to what I have said on the great changes of allegiance, in American history, without *plebiscites* or people's votes.

It is simply this, that in the year 1790, comparatively speaking a classical age of American politics, shortly after the adoption of the Constitution, a portion of Maryland and Virginia, that is to say, portions of territory with free inhabitants and their own laws, were ceded by the legislatures of two states to the United States, without one voice being lifted to demand, on principles of public law, the vote of the people inhabiting the ceded portions, whether they, or rather whether a majority of them—a majority of those who happened at the time to live and be of twenty-one or more—agreed to this change. And what a change! Not ten years had elapsed since our forefathers plunged into a very doubtful revolution, because the English denied the American colonies the old *Magna Charta* principle of taxation and consent of the taxed going together; while here a number of free people were deprived of these precious rights of freemen without a question being asked by any one. Friends of mine, as well as myself, have made the closest possible inquiry, and the naked fact appears that in December, 1788, the state of Maryland, and in December, 1789, the state of Virginia, ceded certain land to the national government, and that, July 16, 1790, the president of the United States approved the bill accepting the ceded portions of the two states to form the District of Columbia, and that this completed and concluded the whole transaction. I speak of the fact, and not of its justice, simply to show that the men of 1790 assuredly did not believe that a change of the political status required in all cases the so-called consent of the people, which means simply the consent (and that even generally an apparent consent) of the majority. It further proves that those are mistaken who think that the doctrine of a necessary *plebiscite* is peculiarly American. I have shown, I think, that it is peculiarly non-American. For the rest I beg to refer the reader to the article in Littell's Living Age.

B. THE LATIN RACE.

To the Editors of the Evening Post:

Much has been heard within the last fifteen years of the Latin race, and great has been the endeavor to utilize this novel idea on the part of Napoleon III. and his adherents. M. Chevalier's book on Mexico is almost exclusively founded upon the idea that the Latin race—that is, France—ought to be strengthened against the Teutonic race, which has assumed a general sway by its representative power, Great Britain. Closely connected with the erroneous term Latin race was the word Cæsarism, first used in a pamphlet ascribed to the present Bonaparte, and published when he was president of the so-called French republic, and desirous of preparing the public mind (if, indeed, we can speak of a public mind in press-bound France), for the Empire; an imitation also of the Latin idea of the fiercest democratic monarchy. And now, when France has challenged the German hosts, it has been loudly uttered again that it is a "war of races"; meaning, of course, of the Germanic and Latin races.

Thus the attempt is made to carry Latinism into international politics, as it has long been applied to religion. The term Latin race had not been used, but it was an error accepted even by many Protestants that Roman Catholicism was better adapted for the more imaginative southern races than "cold Protestantism." A strange delusion! Was the syllogism of the cold Frenchman, Calvin, more imaginative than the poetic, soulful, fervent German, Martin Luther? Nowhere has the difference between the so-called Latin race and the Germanic race decided between Catholicism and Protestantism. It is the dragoon, the torture of the inquisition; it is bloodshed, and not difference of races, which forced so many people in Europe back into the Roman church or prevented them from publicly leaving it. Italy, France, and Spain were as ripe for the Reformation as England and Germany, and the south of Germany quite as much as the northern portion.

Thus Micheli, the Venetian ambassador in France, wrote to the Doge of the republic in 1561, that many bishops and priests, most monasteries and nunneries have been tainted by the new faith, and adds "with the exception of the very lowest people, the whole nobility and the young men under forty years, almost without exception, have fallen from the old faith."

Leopold Ranke has shown this simply in his work, The Roman Popes, etc., in the Sixteenth and Seventeenth Century. Not the differences of races, but fire, sword, and torture, have stopped the further development of the Reformation—the sinister pomp and power which the Petrine Monarchy had acquired and into which the " Holy Church and Republic of God," as the church was styled at the times of Pepin, had changed.

It is always dangerous, and has often proved in the last degree mischievous, to act on arbitrary maxims, vague conceits, or metaphorical expressions—the more mischievous and tragical the higher the sphere of thought or action may be. Let us inquire then, briefly, into the meaning of this often-used term Latin race.

Much has been said of races and their predetermining character, as if the whole history of countries and portions of the earth were flowing in the veins of each individual; just as others believe that the whole character of a people's history is foreshadowed or predestined in the geography of the land and islands occupied by it. The doctrine of races has recently expanded into the discussion of the Aryan and Semitic races. For this subject we must refer the reader to Disraeli's Lothair. Our inquiry lies within narrower limits.

The word race has probably been abused in modern times more than any other. The rebels told us and each other again and again that they were a race totally different from the race of the North; Buckle finds the history of Spain natural, and in accordance with the race inhabiting Spain; yet there is no race, or at least a mixture of some twenty races.

We are all aware that there are certain races in Europe—the Sclavonic, the Celtic, and the Germanic race, with numerous remnants of important and unimportant races. In looking at these races of the present time and at those of the past, certain pregnant reflections force themselves on our minds.

Some great and eminently leading nations—such as the Greek and the English—have been and are a mixture of varied tribes and races. There are, unquestionably, distinct characteristics belonging to different races; but it must never be forgotten that the tendency of all our civilization is to the greater and greater assimilation of these Cis-Caucasian races, and that all the noblest things—religion, truth, and science, architecture, sculpture, and civil liberty—are not restricted to races. To all these the mandate is given: Go into all the world.

Lastly, races are very often invented from ignorance, or for evil purposes. The pitiful attempt of inventing a separate race on the part of the rebels has been mentioned. The fictitious Latin race is another instance, but of far greater import and far more dangerous.

We know what the Latin language means; we know that the Roman church is frequently called the Latin church; we know that lateen sail means the triangular sail, which is common to this day in the Mediterranean, and which people were obliged to distinguish from the Dutch square sail when this came into use; but what is the meaning of Latin race? It has no ethnographic meaning. There are no Latin people by birth; and, although language does not necessarily decide anything as to races, there is no Latin race were it otherwise, for there is no people now that speaks Latin or a language partly Latin. Neither Italian, nor Spanish, nor French is more than a language mixed with a more or less predominant element of totally changed or corrupt Latin.

Thus it comes to this, that the totality of nations whose different languages have some portion—say from one-fourth to one-fifteenth—of corrupt Latin admixture, are called the Latin race, in order to separate them from the common advance of civilization, and to keep them apart from the noble self-government which first showed itself, rudely but strongly, with the Germanic nations; and to make them look upon the Roman imperialism and the senate of imperial Rome with complacency, and even admiration, while mankind had learned from Tacitus and Suetonius to shudder at those institutions as degradations of our kind. This period, in which cupidity, gastronomy, licentiousness, and cruelty flourished in the palaces of those who make the labels of history, was held up for admiration.

We must be much mistaken if the great mischief-maker who invented the word "Cæsarism," and the oily term "personal government" for what used to be called despotism or tyranny, did not also invent the term "Latin race." He utilized it to his heart's content until of late. France was of course represented as the first of the Latin nations. Strange! The German element preponderates, or is very strong, in the most industrious and densest-peopled portion of France, including the Franche-Comté, Alsatia, Lorraine, Flanders, Artois, as far as Normandy; and a greater proportion of genius for pen or sword has come from this portion of France than from the other parts of this proud and, unfortunately, presuming country.

Let the term "Latin race" be forever banished from church, state, or any other sphere of thought or action as unmeaning, full of mischief, unscientific, and intended to mislead.

C. ON THE SALE OF ARMS.

The report of the select committee appointed by the senate of the United States "to investigate all sales of ordnance stores made by the government of the United States during the fiscal year ending June 30, 1871," has been submitted to the senate, and now lies before that body in the shape of a volume of some 600 pages. To this must be added the report on the same subject to the house of representatives (Report No. 46; 42d congress, 2d session) by the committee on the expenditures in the war department. The United States—at least Congress—is what Bacon would have called very liberal of printing.

Two occurrences have taken place in our times, regretted by every earnest international jurist, and which ought not to be allowed to pass without a signal and lasting improvement of the law of nations under which we are appointed by Providence to develop our civilization—we mean, of course, the infraction of the law of nations on the part of England in the case of the Alabama, and the sales of arms by the United States to one of the belligerents during the late European, and far the greatest war of all history.

The Alabama case is thoroughly known by this time, and there is perhaps an opinion, all but, if not indeed fully, unanimous, among the jurists of the continent of Europe and America, that England did not act according to the dictates of the *jus* which in right and fairness ought to exist among nations, when she allowed Southern rebels to fit out predatory vessels against the United States in her own harbors. She has acknowledged this in the Washington treaty, and whatever doubt may yet exist, let us hope it may be settled by the time this paper is published.

As to the sales of arms, let it be observed that the reports alluded to do not investigate the question whether the sales of ordnance were lawful according to the laws of neutrality or the law of nations, at least not profoundly, but only whether the action of the government was wrong, according to the municipal laws of the United States.

We follow the reports in the subsequent remarks.

An act of congress, approved March 3, 1825, authorizes the president to sell injured arms, and prescribes who shall declare them injured.

In 1865, when the civil war had at length been closed, the government found itself possessed of a large amount of muskets and other arms, not damaged or otherwise unserviceable within the meaning of the act of 1825, and congress passed in 1868 an act, under which the secretary of war is " authorized and directed to cause to be sold, after offer at public sale on thirty days' notice, in such manner and at such times and places at public or private sale as he may deem most advantageous to the public interest, the old cannon, arms, and other ordnance stores, now in possession of the war department, which are damaged or otherwise unsuitable for the United States military service or for the militia of the United States, and to cause the net proceeds of such sales, after paying all proper expenses of sale and transportation to the place of sale, to be deposited in the treasury of the United States." (15 Stat. at L., 259.)

The war between Germany and France broke out in 1870, and on August 22, 1870, President Grant issued a proclamation " enjoining neutrality in the present war between France and the North German Confederation and its allies."

In it is this passage :

Now, therefore, I, Ulysses S. Grant, President of the United States, in order to preserve the neutrality of the United States and of their citizens and of persons within their territory and jurisdiction, and to enforce their laws, and in order that all persons being warned of the general tenor of the laws and treaties of the United States in this behalf, and of the law of nations, may thus be prevented from an unintentional violation of the same, do hereby declare and proclaim that by the act passed on the 20th day of April, A.D. 1818, commonly known as the " neutrality law," the following acts are forbidden to be done, under severe penalties, within the territory and jurisdiction of the United States, to wit :

1. Accepting and exercising a commission to serve either of the said belligerents by land or by sea against the other belligerent.

2. Enlisting or entering into the service of either of the said belligerents as a soldier, or as a marine, or seaman on board of any vessel of war, letter of marque, or privateer.

3. Hiring or retaining another person to enlist or enter himself in the service of either of the said belligerents as a soldier, or as a marine, or seaman on board of any vessel of war, letter of marque, or privateer.

4. Hiring another person to go beyond the limits or jurisdiction of the United States with intent to be enlisted as aforesaid.

5. Hiring another person to go beyond the limits of the United States with the intent to be entered into service as aforesaid.

6. Retaining another person to go beyond the limits of the United States with intent to be enlisted as aforesaid.

7. Retaining another person to go beyond the limits of the United States with intent to be entered into service as aforesaid. (But the said act is not to be construed to extend to a citizen or subject of either belligerent who, being transiently within the United States, shall, on board of any vessel of war, which, at the time of its arrival within the United States, was fitted and equipped as such vessel of war, enlist or enter himself or hire or retain another subject or citizen of the same belligerent, who is transiently within the United States, to enlist or enter himself

to serve such belligerent on board such vessel of war, if the United States shall then be at peace with such belligerent.)

8. Fitting out and arming, or attempting to fit out and arm, or procuring to be fitted out and armed, or knowingly being concerned in the furnishing, fitting out, or arming of any ship or vessel with intent that such ship or vessel shall be employed in the service of either of the said belligerents.

9. Issuing or delivering a commission within the territory or jurisdiction of the United States for any ship or vessel to the intent that she may be employed as aforesaid.

10. Increasing or augmenting, or procuring to be increased or augmented, or knowingly being concerned in increasing or augmenting the force of any ship of war, cruiser, or other armed vessel, which at the time of her arrival within the United States was a ship of war, cruiser, or armed vessel in the service of either of the said belligerents, or belonging to the subjects or citizens of either, by adding to the number of guns of such vessels, or by changing those on board of her for guns of a larger calibre, or by the addition thereto of any equipment solely applicable to war.

11. Beginning or setting on foot or providing or preparing the means for any military expedition or enterprise to be carried on from the territory or jurisdiction of the United States against the territories or dominions of either of the said belligerents.

And I do further declare and proclaim that by the 19th article of the treaty of amity and commerce, which was concluded between his Majesty the King of Prussia and the United States of America, on the 11th day of July, A.D. 1799, which article was revived by the treaty of May 1, A.D. 1828, between the same parties, and is still in force, it was agreed that the vessels of war, public and private, of both parties, shall carry freely wheresoever they please, the vessels and effects taken from their enemies, without being obliged to pay any duties, charges, or fees to officers of admiralty, of the customs, or any others; nor shall such prizes be arrested, searched, or put under any legal process when they come to and enter the ports of the other party, but may freely be carried out again at any time by their captors to the places expressed in their commissions, which the commanding officer of such vessel shall be obliged to show.

Farther on is this passage :

And I do further declare and proclaim that it has been officially communicated to the government of the United States by the envoy extraordinary and minister plenipotentiary of his Majesty the Emperor of the French, at Washington, that orders have been given that in the conduct of the war the commanders of the French forces on land and on the seas shall scrupulously observe towards neutral powers the rules of international law, and that they shall strictly adhere to the principles set forth in the declaration of the congress of Paris of the 16th of April, 1856, that is to say: 1st. That privateering is and remains abolished; 2d. That the neutral flag covers enemy's goods, with the exception of contraband of war; 3d. That neutral goods, with the exception of contraband of war, are not liable to capture under the enemy's flag; 4th. That blockades, in order to be binding, must be effective, that is to say, maintained by a force sufficient really to prevent access to the coast of the enemy; and that, although the United States have not adhered to the declaration of 1856, the vessels of his Majesty will not seize enemy's property found on board of a vessel of the United States, provided that property is not contraband of war.

And I do further declare and proclaim that the statutes of the United States' and the law of nations alike require that no person within the territory and jurisdiction of the United States shall take part, directly or indirectly, in the said war, but shall remain at peace with each of the said belligerents, and shall maintain a strict and impartial neutrality, and that whatever privileges shall be accorded to one belligerent within the ports of the United States shall be in like manner accorded to the other.

And I do hereby enjoin all the good citizens of the United States, and all persons residing or being within the territory or jurisdiction of the United States, to observe the laws thereof, and to commit no act contrary to the provisions of the said statutes, or in violation of the law of nations in that behalf.

The sale of arms went on; not to the belligerent governments, at least not nominally so. Intermediate agents were easily found, and the number of arms bought by or for France was so large as to prove simply and plainly, without further demonstration, that they were purchased for the purpose of being used in the then flagrant war.

On page xvii of the report we find this passage:

Congress having, by the act of 1868, directed the secretary of war to dispose of these arms and stores, and the government being engaged in such sales prior to the war between France and Germany, had a right to continue the same during the war, and might, in the city of Washington, have sold and delivered any amount of such stores to Frederick William (correct names might perhaps have been used in so solemn a paper placed before so dignified a body as the senate of the United

States) or Louis Napoleon in person, without violating the obligations of neutrality, provided such sales were made in good faith, not for the purpose of influencing the strife, but in execution of the lawful purpose of the government to sell its surplus arms and stores.

It is useless to investigate what exactly the words " in good faith, not for the purpose of influencing the strife" may or even can mean. Nor is it of any importance for the present purpose to inquire whether it is correct to say that " the government being engaged in such sales prior to the war between France and Germany, had a right to continue the same during the war, and might, in the city of Washington, sell," etc. Vattel is quoted at length to support this view. Our opinion is that the fact that the selling of arms by a neutral government to a belligerent had begun previous to the breaking out of the war, does not make it lawful, in right and equity of the law of nations, to continue the sale. Whether the government of the United States was allowed to do so, or obliged to do so, its having done so creates the necessity of providing for the non-recurrence of the fact. A provision in a treaty concerning neutrality between the leading nations of the earth, having become necessary after the Alabama affair, a similar treaty, after the sale of arms at Washington, ought to contain a provision estopping any such sales by neutrals, *flagrante bello*, in all future times.

The unprofound ones—and they must always be the great majority—will ever be found, at the breaking out of any war, in one of the two extremes. They clamor either for a total abolition of neutrality laws, or for extending and strengthening them beyond all bounds of practical execution, or, indeed, of good service to humanity. Both are greatly mistaken. Neutrality is an idea natural and necessary to civilization; it has always shown itself in private as well as intersocial communion, and becomes more distinct and rational, as well as more and more indispensable, as our family or commonwealth of nations extends and unites more firmly at the same time. The idea of neutrality and the laws belonging to it, evolve themselves out of the ethical and social nature of man; indeed, there would be no ethics were there no social individuals, as blades and plants unfold themselves with the advancing season. They are not artificial nor arbitrary.

Too loose a definition of contraband of war, or too close a restriction; too lax an enforcement of the laws of neutrality, or too grasping, or lifting of the laws of a country above the requirements of the law of nations—all lead to international irritation, and increase that fevered disposition, into which a great war necessarily throws our whole Cis-Caucasian group of nations. Yet the laws of neutrality arise out of the desire to mitigate the severities of war, which needs must extend beyond the belligerents, and to prevent spreading conflagrations.

The supposed or real difficulty of neutrality laws is not put aside, as many have also imagined, by supposing that essential neutrality consists in granting equal chances to both belligerents. Not granting equal chances to both parties would, indeed, all but amount to a declaration of war, and certainly lead to additional war, but in far the greater number of cases the *equal chances* would be but theoretical. The principle, and therefore the law, is: If you are neutral and wish to remain such, abstain from participation in war, open or underhand; if not, join in the war, or you will soon be forced to join it, and, at any rate, you will increase the evil and duration of the war.

The two cases repeatedly mentioned, furnish, it is believed, a signal opportunity for a farther treaty.

Well would it be for our species if not only all privateering could forever be abolished, as it was honorably abstained from in the Crimean War, but if the private property of belligerents were acknowledged and respected on the seas as it is on land. How long shall we wait for this! First the sea disimpropriates all property, even during peace; and only special agreement with particular states could somewhat protect it. It was pretty much so in the times of Thucydides. Then property begins to be respected even on the seas during peace. Now we call for its protection even in war. The acknowledgment of property at sea always follows at long periods—of centuries —the acknowledgment of property on land.

The Washington treaty of May 8, 1871, contains this Article VI., namely :

> In deciding the matters submitted to the arbitrators they shall be governed by the following three rules, which are agreed upon by the high contracting parties as rules to be taken as applicable to the case, and by such principles of international law not inconsistent therewith as the arbitrators shall determine to have been applicable to the case.

RULES.

A neutral government is bound—

First, to use due diligence to prevent the fitting out, arming, or equipping, within its jurisdiction, of any vessel which it has reasonable ground to believe is intended to cruise or to carry on war against a power with which it is at peace ; and also to use like diligence to prevent the departure from its jurisdiction of any vessel intended to cruise or carry on war as above, such vessel having been specially adapted, in whole or in part, within such jurisdiction, to warlike use.

Secondly, not to permit or suffer either belligerent to make use of its ports or waters as the base of naval operations against the other, or for the purpose of the renewal or augmentation of military supplies or arms, or the recruitment of men.

Thirdly, to exercise due diligence in its own ports and waters, and, as to all persons within its jurisdiction, to prevent any violation of the foregoing obligations and duties.

Her Britannic Majesty has commanded her high commissioners and plenipotentiaries to declare that her Majesty's government cannot assent to the foregoing rules as a statement of principles of international law which were in force at the time when the claims mentioned in Article I. arose, but that her Majesty's government, in order to evince its desire of strengthening the friendly relations between the two countries and of making satisfactory provision for the future, agrees that in deciding the questions between the two countries arising out of those claims, the arbitrators should assume that her Majesty's government had undertaken to act upon the principles set forth in these rules.

And the high contracting parties agree to observe these rules as between themselves in future, and to bring them to the knowledge of other maritime powers, and to invite them to accede to them.

The principles in these *rules* ought to be embodied in the desired treaty ; for their being mentioned here proves the necessity of doing so, but it ought to be added, that no belligerent shall be furnished directly with any contraband of war, and no neutral government shall furnish a belligerent directly with money, unless, indeed, the loan had begun before the breaking out of the war.

No neutral government has the right to sell, or can owe the duty of selling arms or any other contraband articles to a belligerent; nor can it allow the sale of the same by private persons directly to the belligerent. If private citizens of a neutral power sell contraband of war to a citizen or subject of an equally neutral power, to be shipped on board of a vessel sailing under a neutral flag, the government of the country where the transaction takes place has nothing farther to do with it.

Contraband of war is everything necessary for the active and direct pursuit of hostilities, found on neutral ground and destined for or in neutral bottoms on their way to a belligerent, who, as well as the government against whom the latter carries on the war, is at peace and in amity with the government of the country where the transaction concerning the indicated war material is taking place. Contraband of war is farther all such material as is indispensable for the preparation of a material necessary for the pursuit of hostilities, and exclusively or almost exclusively used for that purpose under the conditions just mentioned.

Contraband of war of the first description are arms of any kind, men-of-war, or armed vessels of any sort, gunpowder, etc.

Contraband of the second kind is saltpetre in large quantities.

Material very necessary for the prosecution of war, but neither used for the direct infliction of warlike harm, nor, indeed, used exclusively for that purpose, ought not to be considered contraband of war. Flour, leather, coals (except direct for war steamers), cloth, etc.—most of these are indispensable for the carrying on of war, but they are not necessaries for the direct pursuit of hostility, nor are they exclusively used for the purposes of war.

Does the shipping of metal, say lead, or metals requisite

for artillery pieces, or timber for the belligerent's navy-yards, fall within the prohibition of contraband trade here given? I think not. I repeat that it is of the greatest importance to limit the war prohibitions for neutrals to as few rules and articles as possible, and to insist on the strictest possible carrying out of them.

A treaty ought to be concluded containing the mutual acknowledgment of international copyright peculiarly necessitated by our common and interwoven civilization, as well as by the most elementary principles and ideas of individual property. All human advancement turns between the two poles of individualism and sociality, and nowhere is this fundamental treaty more distinctly illustrated than in literary property. As our race advances and spreads—I mean the Cis-Caucasian race—the more nations will exist speaking the same language. The literary work and composition is surely as much an individual production, and has its exchangeable value, as the material book has. Within all printing countries it is now acknowledged; but some states, and unfortunately and undignifiedly we Americans are the foremost among them, require yet what the Greek interstatal law called the *asylia*—the protection of property of a foreigner, though he might be a Greek, against seizure of whoever might seize it. This protection was granted by special treaty between different states, and was called the *asylia*[1]—non-seizure. We speak, of course, of peaceful times; in war I dare say the Greeks acted towards the property belonging to a citizen of a belligerent state, as the French did with German property in the war of '70 and '71, two thousand years later, when, indeed, it had been believed that the law of nations had made some progress. Ought then, perhaps, the protection of the property belonging to an alien, and the alien himself, whose government is at war with the country in which they are, to

---

[1] The writer of this essay has long ago expressed his convictions on the subject of international copyright, and on the necessity of individual property, as well as his hostility to communism, in two works: On International Copyright, and Essays on Labor and Property.

likewise form a portion of such a pact and treaty? These
rights and privileges of high-minded civilization are so distinctly and plainly acknowledged by the modern law of nations that a treaty could hardly do it more distinctly.   Still,
since a nation in recent times has so significantly broken this
elementary law of war and peace, just as Napoleon I. did it
some sixty years previous, it may be well to add it to the
desired essence of a code in the shape of a treaty or international pact.   Ought not, also, in such an international covenant, the unrighteous pardoning of criminals on condition of
their leaving the country, or of going to a certain country, be
pointed out and provided against?   The more the Cis-Caucasians, first spread over the hemispheres, now reassociate in
the family of nations, the greater the difference of occupation
of land in Europe and here, and the more intercommunication
as well as criminal talent increases, the more urgent becomes
the necessity of abstaining from an international wickedness
in which, nevertheless, every now and then some European
governments have indulged, and continue to do so.   All penal
exile ought to be abandoned, except concerning political offenders; but more imperatively it is demanded by the laws of
the commonest morality and the plainest honesty, not to
smuggle convicted criminals into a foreign country.   The
rebels tried to infuse the smallpox and pestilence into the
United States.   We speak from a personal knowledge of the
so-called rebel archives at Washington.   Is not the introduction of professional and convicted criminals into a foreign
country very similar in its immorality and international infamy?

A prominent modern writer on the law of nations has sa-
tirically said that it almost looked as if treaties were made to
be broken.   Is it different with any penal or civil law?   We
might ask, is it better in the laws of morality and truth in
any branch, with our religion itself?   And is it not psychologically of great importance plainly to pronounce and distinctly to put forth a jural truth, as a great rule of action?
Opinion gradually shapes itself, and gains strength accord-

ingly, and despite the millions and millions of murders committed since Moses, it was not in vain to engrave it on stone: Thou shalt not kill.

If some six points were derived from the foregoing and embodied in treaties between the leading nations in Europe and America, and Russia, as well as Brazil, what a bold yet firm step forward in the path of civilization, and the application of the message, peace and good will toward men, would be achieved in the latter third of the nineteenth century!—

Let all privateering be done away with, and acknowledge private property of citizens or subjects belonging to belligerents on the high seas as it is acknowledged on land;

Adopt the essence of the *rules* given in the treaty of Washington;

Define contraband of war as it has been done in this paper, and adopt few but strict rules of neutrality regarding them;

Let it be proclaimed that the law of nations is the supreme law of our race, as indeed the American Constitution says, that "all treaties made, or which shall be made, under the authority of the United States, shall be the supreme law of the land;"

Protect internationally literary property;

Protect the persons and property of aliens though belonging to belligerents—a rule signally violated by the French at two memorable epochs, as our rebels infringed them during the civil war.

And the law of nations would draw a breath of relief and gain renewed vigor, after such serious acts as the English Alabama troubles, our sales of arms at Washington, and the French breach of the law of nations against the German aliens.

Once such a pact being concluded, the opinion of our race, perhaps, would soon ripen to an energetic conviction that arbitrators ought to be permanently appointed, to be ready to meet and act when called upon—not a permanent court of arbitration. This subject, however, cannot be entered into here.

What nation ought to take the lead in this great measure? To none, it seems, would it be more natural at this period (and—may not such a term be used in an international sense? —more graceful) than to the Germans, the English, and the Americans. The Italians would readily join; and all the other nations and governments would soon fall in and join the steady tramp of onward civilization.　　One alone might hold back, in the sullen discontent of smarting disappointment; but civilized nations cannot now keep long aloof from the gathering and binding law of nations.[1]

---

[1] GOVERNMENT SALE OF ARMS.

To the Editor of the Nation :

Sir,—Dr. Friedrich Kapp, in his letter of January 18, published in the Nation of February 9, repeats the charge against the United States government of having sold contraband of war, especially firearms, to the French. Would it not be well to say that this has been denied upon very good authority ? It is true that cases of arms, with the sign of the government factory on the cases, have been sold and shipped to France. Our government sold the arms then, as it always does, to private parties, who, in turn, sold them to the French. It was no surreptitious transaction, nor was it a feigned one.

I mention this simply to correct an erroneous statement made in good faith by the distinguished writer. Were we to discuss the law of neutrality as it stands, and as it ought to stand, it is very probable that I should be found more strict than Dr. Kapp, as it would appear from his very letter. Here we have to do with the simple question, Has our government sold arms to a belligerent, or has it made any extraordinary sales ? The answer, I believe, is, It has not.

I cannot help seizing upon this opportunity to say that, immediately after peace shall have been concluded, the subject of neutrality ought to be taken in hand, whether officially or by agreement, among international jurists, but in either case authoritatively, and ought to be brought nearer to a state agreeing with the growing interconnection of nations. The modern law of nations rests first of all on the principle of neighborliness ; and, as our civilization advances, so does good neighborhood become more important, and so, in turn, does the subject of neutrality grow in comprehensive importance.　　　　　　　　　　F. L.

New York, February 11, 1871.

D.　UNIVERSITIES IN INTERNATIONAL ARBITRATION.

A Letter to Hon. William H. Seward, Secretary of State.

. . . The United States have large claims upon Great Britain for the injury done them by the armed vessels fitted out against them in English ports contrary to the laws of neutrality. On the other hand it is understood that Great Britain exhibits counter-claims against the United States.

The subject is, in every respect, a serious one. How are such claims and counter-claims to be settled?

International disputes of a grave character can only be concluded in one of the following four ways:

The discussion may be drawn on for so long a time that greater questions arise in the course of events, and the original subject is dropped by its mention being omitted in a new treaty, which may be concluded. This has happened, indeed, but such a settlement by default as it were, is not likely to occur again, in modern times, when the parties at issue are large and powerful nations, and the subject in question is of commensurate magnitude.

Or, the contending governments may diplomatically settle their difficulties and seal the settlement by special treaty. It is not probable either that America and England will arrive at a conclusion of their differences by this means; certainly not within a reasonably short time. All protraction, however, of international difficulties, especially between great nations destined to have the closest intercourse, is both injurious and dangerous. It interferes with the international spirit of peace, without which a purely formal peace, that is, mere non-existence of war, amounts only to international quiescence shorn in a great measure of the best realities of peace. This is especially the case with all those nations who acknowledge that the first and perhaps the highest law of modern extending civilization is the commandment that there shall be an increasing and widening family of nations, bound together by the great law of nations. At any rate, this communication is written on the supposition that the present English-American disagreement will not be settled by diplomatic transactions, or cannot thus be concluded within any reasonable period of time.

The third way of stopping international discussions is war. A discussion may certainly thus be stopped for a time, but neither party can expect the settlement of pecuniary claims by rushing into a war, since new claims would necessarily arise, and each belligerent would be obliged to incur expenditures greater than any indemnities claimed of the opponent before the war. Neither ourselves nor the English would expect to indemnify themselves by conquest, which, moreover, is generally a poor indemnification, so far as the settlement of pecuniary claims is concerned. The enormous sums which Napoleon drew by way of "contributions," from the conquered countries, did not lessen the heavy taxation in France, made necessary by his wars. Going to war with England on account of our pecuniary claims would simply amount to the attempt to kill a fly, crawling on a costly piece of Sèvres, by throwing a stone at the insect, through fear that it may soil the precious vase.

There remains, then, arbitration only, as the fourth method of ending international differences. International arbitration, freely resorted to by powerful governments, conscious of their complete independence and self-sustaining sovereignty, is one of the foremost characteristics of advancing civilization—of the substitution of reason, fairness, and submission to justice, for defying power or revengeful irritation. It belongs to modern, indeed to recent times; yet although it is a noble characteristic of the more recent times, it still bears uncouth features of coarser periods, and demands improvement and development. The law of nations is awaiting them.

The administration of all law may be said to originate with arbitration, and all law, as it develops itself further and further, largely returns to courts of arbitration, justly and beautifully called, in French and German, Courts of Peace. The Roman civil law acknowledged arbitration. The courts of arbitration, with elected and non-professional judges, to whom parties voluntarily go to obtain equitable arbitraments, with the exclusion of professional counsel, have spread all over Prussia, Denmark, and other countries, settling annually immense amounts in litigation.

The ancient Greeks, with their many city-states and confederacies of the same language and religion, and with a similar culture, knew, if not of international, yet of *inter-statal* arbitration—temporary commissions appointed by contending cities, to whose judgment the parties swore to submit. For it will be hardly necessary to state that the characteristic feature of these arbitrations is the voluntary submission of the parties to a freely chosen judge, with a binding and solemn promise of the litigants to abide in good faith by his adjudication.

That international arbitrament, however, which consists in a sovereign power chosen by two contending equally sovereign powers, or by governments representing entire nations, rendering judgment, and this judgment being submitted to in good faith by two potent sovereigns—this arbitration belongs to the most recent times, and is considered by international jurists, and by the students of the history of civilization, one of the encouraging signs of real progress.

So far, however, monarchs have been almost exclusively chosen as arbiters, which is inconvenient on several accounts. It may happen that the parties may be unable to unite in the election of a monarch or government suiting both alike. The present case between the United States and Great Britain seems to be a case in point. We would probably select none but the emperor of Russia, if we were at all willing to submit our case to a European government, and if we were convinced of a sufficient acquaintance with the law of nations as well as with maritime law in the officials of that highly military government; while Russia, in all probability, would not suit Great Britain.

The other and great inconvenience, in selecting a monarch as arbiter, is the fact that the only one who is publicly known as the judge, is the very one who, in the course of things, does not occupy himself with the case, cannot do so, and is not expected by any one to do so.

When an international difficulty is brought before a monarch, or even before the chief representative of a republic, who is now always the chief executive, what is the course which things take? The minister of justice, or some similar high functionary, is directed to take the case in hand; he appoints some counsellor or other officer, possibly a committee, to make a report to him, which he lays before the nominal arbiter. Those who really decide the case are unknown, or at least bear no public, and feel no last, responsibility. There exists in many cases of this sort the grave inconvenience, and serious inconsistency, of handing over questions of the highest law and most elevated justice to an executive, and not to an authority of judicial renown and responsibility.

How much easier would be the acquiescence in the judgment, how much more becoming to civilized communities, and how much nobler in every way would be the selection of judges from among jurists of a high reputation for their comprehensive knowledge and unyielding loyalty to justice and jural truth! There is probably no fair-minded Englishman or American who would not submit the whole amount of the claims in question far more readily to a Hugo Grotius, than to the ruler of any empire now existing. Still, it may be observed that there is not always a Hugo Grotius at hand, nor can individuals, however unsullied in reputation and resolute in speaking out what is right, be expected, in all countries, to be able wholly to separate themselves from government pressure. It would be difficult, in the present state of our civilization, to make two contending nations agree on a single person, not a monarch, and assign to a living jurist that authority which the congress of Vienna granted, among others, to Grotius, freely quoted in that great international council.

Nor would it be easy to persuade a private individual to serve as umpire, could the contending parties be made to agree as to the desirable international judge; but could they not be induced to agree to lay the whole subject at issue before the law faculty of some foreign university, if both parties are sincerely disposed to obtain only what is due to them and what is strictly right? The members of such a faculty are generally men who have already made a name which they hope will go down to posterity in law and its literature; they know the whole weight and meaning of a grave decision in the highest regions of the law, and would be conscious that in an international case their decision, while probed and scanned by the foremost intellects of their race, would pass over as part and parcel into that law, which prevails between independent nations, which is enforced by equity and reason, and is gradually extending even beyond that race which happily created it: for I am writing this paper when not only Turkey, Egypt, and Persia have given in their adhesion to many of the main points of our law of nations, but when a translation of Wheaton's Law of Nations into Chinese has arrived in this country, and is now in the library of your department.

In the present case it is taken for granted that neither party desires nor hopes to be able to outwit the other. The American and the English nations are too great to descend to diplomatic artifice; and if there were no objection to such a course or to such attempts, on the ground of international high-mindedness and equity, prudence and expediency alone would dictate to abandon so unworthy a desire. The Americans and English are people at once too clear-sighted and too stubborn; too much on a level of intellect and civilization, and they agree too much in their knowledge and conceptions of justice, law, and fairness, to hope much from diplomatic cunning, or from successful overreaching. But if they really wish to settle their differences on the principles of law, it may be asked whether there is a single English-speaking man this side of the Atlantic, or on the eastern side, who would doubt that such a faculty of law as that of the University of Berlin, with the international jurist Heffter in it, or if Prussia were considered too much of a great power, the law faculty of Heidelberg or of Leyden, would be a fitter body to decide our differences than any emperor or any republic. A republic could not decide the case as a republic, but must hand it over to some commission. A law faculty, especially that of a renowned university in a minor state, seems to form a tribunal fitter than any other that can be imagined for many, perhaps most, of the great international cases. It would seem almost made for so high a function, and the selection of a law faculty as a court of international arbitration would be a measure worthy of being inaugurated by the two freest large nations, and whose governments are to be numbered, in diplomacy, among the least unreasonable and uncandid ones.

Let the United States and Great Britain agree upon the university; let them obtain the permission of its government to appeal to the law faculty, which would doubtless be readily granted; let the two powers distinctly settle the remuneration which each, in equal shares, is to grant to the faculty, excluding all other immediate or prospective presents or distinctions; let each contending party appoint its commissioners, as many as each party chooses, and nobody would doubt that a just judgment would be obtained.

The compensation, out of place, as it would seem, in an international case, is nevertheless taken into consideration here, for the reasons that the case at issue would occupy a very large space of time of the high judges; and in order to forestall every particle of that machinery which consists in part of ribbons and orders, snuff-boxes and titles, presents of money or land, direct or prospective. Not that such judges would be likely to be swayed, by means of this kind, in their judgment. That tribunal, with nations for its clients, would doubtless be conscious of standing, in turn, before a greater tribunal—before their profession in all history; but all seeming attempt, or faint suspicion, of an attempt at lowering so great a court to common diplomacy ought to be kept far away.

Great universities have been appealed to in former times, though it was generally in theological matters. Within the different countries, such as France or Germany, they have indeed been appealed to, and still are occasionally so, at least in the last-mentioned country, in civil and penal matters. Why should we not seize upon these institutions, themselves characteristic of our own civilization, in international matters? The adoption of the proposed plan would be a signal step in the progress of our race. There is no nobler sight than the strong—be they single men or nations—laying down their strength, like a sword by their side, saying, "We will abide by the judgment of the just; let justice be done."

This proposition does not interest my mind by the charms

of novelty. I communicated a similar one to a prominent statesman in congress as far back as the time of the Oregon question, and it was clearly elicited in my mind when the decision of King William, of the Netherlands, concerning the northeastern boundary, became known in this country. Circumstances did not call for a closer consideration, but I now venture to lay it before you, sir, in a more elaborate form, and try to attract the attention of the public to it through your eminent name.

Whether the two nations to whom the spread of civilization over the globe has been assigned more than to any other people will accept this way of settling differences in the present case or not, there is no doubt in my mind that the Cis-Caucasian race will rise, at no very distant day, to the selection of such umpires, far more dignified than a crowned arbitrator can be.

WASHINGTON, D. C., Sept. 17, 1865.

E. ON INTERNATIONAL COPYRIGHT.

A Letter to the Hon. William C. Preston.

. . . The subject of an international copyright law does not appear to attract that general attention in our country which fairness, justice, expediency, our own advantage, and our reputation, nevertheless, call for, and which, it cannot be doubted, they would command, were the subject more widely and more thoroughly understood. It is my intention, therefore, briefly to exhibit the most important points connected with it in as clear and popular a manner as the character of the subject may admit.

By international copyright is understood copyright acknowledged and mutually protected by various independent nations, so that a copyright having originated in one nation is of equal legal value among the people living under a different independent government; and by copyright is understood

the exclusive right of multiplying compositions and conceptions, which are represented upon paper ; in other words, of
multiplying original books, music, maps, and engravings.[1]
This exclusive right of multiplying the copies of a composition or conception is at least by far the most essential part
of that "property which an author, or his assignee, has in a
literary work," as Blackstone defines the term Copyright;
and the only one of great importance in political or civil intercourse.   Wherever laws have been enacted to acknowledge
copyright internationally, they are founded upon the principle
of reciprocity, that is, a state says : Such is the protection
which I grant to literary property of authors subject to my
government, and likewise to that of all foreign authors, whose
government grants to my citizens all the protection it affords
to its own respecting literary property.   By an act of parliament, 1 Victoria, c. 59 (July 31, 1838), "protection is afforded
within her majesty's dominions to the authors of books first
published in foreign countries, and their assigns, in case, where
protection shall be afforded in such foreign countries to the
authors of books first published in her majesty's dominions,
and their assigns."   The last paragraph of the Prussian copyright law of June 11, 1837, the most comprehensive law of
the kind, I believe, in existence, runs thus : "This whole law
shall have force respecting works first published in a foreign
state, if the laws of that state grant all the rights established
by them respecting works first published there, likewise to
works first published in our dominions."

We cannot correctly understand the question of international copyright, if we do not first clearly present to our

---

[1] The term copyright has not yet been extended, in England or the United
States, to statues, pictures, etc., and casts or copies of them on canvas, etc.   In
several other countries the corresponding term comprehends the right of multiplying by way of copy (whether in the same dimensions or not) any work of
science or the fine arts, and, moreover, whether this multiplication be in or upon
materials or not.   Thus the Prussian law secures the author of a dramatic composition against its unauthorized performance for gain, for this performance is
justly considered a publication or multiplication of the original.   The same is
the case in France.

minds the nature of literary property in general, on which, therefore, a few remarks will be offered, before we proceed to the main subject. Probably there exist, respecting no species of property, so radically erroneous notions, as those entertained with regard to literary property, partly because it is incorporeal,[1] as the law term is, and the foundation for the title of this property was for a long time imagined to exist where it actually does not exist; partly owing to other circumstances, peculiar to this species of property, as we shall presently see. It was, perhaps, natural that the human mind should not at once distinguish between the following several, nevertheless, totally different things: the property in the individual book, consisting of paper, the print upon it, and the binding; secondly, the possession and ownership of a manuscript; thirdly, the copyright, or in other words, the exclusive right freely to dispose of the conditions on which the composition or literary work shall be published, that is, multiplied; and, lastly, the thoughts contained in the compositions, and conveyed by the signs or characters printed (in colored ink) upon (white) paper. Hence the many erroneous arguments which we find in the history of literary property, drawn from the false position, that by the very act of publication the author deliberately resigns any particular right in his manuscript, except in the material itself; or those arguments drawn from the mere possession of a manuscript, which, however, as we all know, may be purchased, for instance, at auction, by a collector of autographs, without acquiring in any degree the right of publication, that is, of multiplying the work; or those arguments drawn from the perfect freedom of mind and thought, defying all limitation and circumscription by laws of property; or, lastly, those derived from the rightful possession of the book, that is, a single copy, the purchase of which, it was maintained, establishes a perfect right for its owner of doing with it whatever he chooses, and, consequently, also that of transcribing, reprinting, or multi-

---

[1] 2 Blackst., 4.

plying it in any way he thinks fit. It will presently be seen how untenable all these arguments are, because they are founded upon a false original view of the subject.

Whatever origin of individual property and its rightfulness speculative philosophy may establish, all those who maintain the justice and necessity of individual property, and the actual impossibility of eradicating it, (who form the overwhelming majority of mankind, from its rudest wandering stage to its existence in broadly organized states and refined societies, and from whom religious fanatics, shallow reasoners, or enthusiastic philosophers only, have formed, from time to time, comparatively speaking, inconsiderable exceptions) all agree, however unjust many specific titles, and doubtful in their character others may be, that the most undeniable title to individual property has ever been established, and must forever be so, by personal, individual production: that is, changing by personal labor, skill, ingenuity, or pains, with the aid of natural agents, the shape or substance of what exists; or giving value, that is, utility or desirableness, to what had none before; or increasing their degree of desirableness. The idea that the first individual of a future nomadic tribe, who catches an animal, tames it and makes it subservient to his peculiar wants, should not have the right to say that this is peculiarly his own, because he has had all the trouble of catching and taming, feeding and taking care of it; that the milk of the mare does not exclusively belong to him who caught and domesticated her; or that the industrious fisherman should not have the indisputable right of calling the fish or the seal which he has caught, by exposing himself to the dangers of the sea, individually his own, is so preposterous that no one would listen to this position, were it seriously advanced. The right of calling that my own which I have first appropriated, changed, fashioned, and improved, upon which, in short, I have first bestowed value, if it did not belong to some one else before I appropriated it to my particular use, rests upon that primitive and direct consciousness, which in every chain of argument must form the first starting-point, which we never can dispense with, not even in mathematics, and which, therefore, lies beyond absolute proof, and forms its foundation. To whom should the product belong if not to the producer? Individual property is absolutely necessary for society, peace, and civilization; and to some one it must belong. Property is so direct an effect of man's nature, that it precedes government, if we understand by the term Government those more stable institutions only which spring up when men begin to live in those societies called more particularly States, and if we do not designate by Government the existence of every sort of authority or of any superiors and inferiors. If we give to Government this latter meaning, in which indeed we must frequently take it in our philosophical speculations, man never exists without it, and government is as primeval an institution as property, both existing always and necessarily along with him, because they are the infallible effects of his nature. In this sense, family, property, and government are coeval.[1]

Stable governments and states proper, that is, political societies fixed in some sort or other, only grow up after men have begun to till the ground; when they have passed from the

---

[1] I have shown in the first volume of the Ethics why I consider the view that things, unappropriated by any individual person or by society, belong on that account to all, erroneous and leading to several very serious misconceptions. These things belong to no one; but not, therefore, to all. They are not yet property. The words property, or " Belonging to," have no meaning if they do not designate a particularization of ownership. An individual relation between the thing owned and the person owning is the chief element of the idea conveyed by the word property. In this alone lies the right of any one to appropriate things unappropriated. A fruit, on an island in the Pacific, never seen or touched by human eye or hand, and decayed before any one knew of its existence, has been as little the property of all as the stars of the heavens are property of all, although they belong to the material world, and are, nevertheless, unappropriated. What would render it so ridiculous to pronounce the heavenly bodies property of all mankind? Simply the fact, that every one is conscious that we have no control, no disposing influence over them. The same is the case with all things over which no disposing influence exists. They belong to no one, until this effect of appropriation begins. It is, likewise, thus only possible to show why property, beyond personal production, is not, on that account, spoliation. Property is the reflex of man's all-important individuality in the material world around him.

roving and nomadic life into the agricultural; when they begin to assimilate their labor and experience or knowledge with the soil; when they no longer merely gather but produce, with the assistance of the earth and other natural agents; when, in brief, they possess property in the soil and they perceive the urgent necessity of protecting this as well as the intercourse between the neighboring possessors of the soil, arising out of the possession of this property. It is the first species of property which very decidedly and palpably presents itself to the human mind, with the absolute necessity of its being protected by a stronger force than that of the individual, which, in a great measure, is sufficient to protect the little personal property of the earlier stages, such as arrows, cloaks, and tents.[1] Civilization, with each progress it makes, confers value upon subjects which had none before, because they were not wanted, not desired. Gradually a great variety of property arises which it is as necessary to protect as landed property. We see then that property is not the creature of government, as has been asserted. It is no more so than individual liberty or the right of existence are creatures of government. They exist, and government acknowledges them, because one of its greatest objects is to protect them. With far greater truth might it be maintained that government is the creature of property. There is indeed some property created by government; but it is but a minimum compared to the immense bulk of property existing all over the earth. It is not maintained that government cannot regulate the transfer of property, prune certain species of it, and influence it in various ways. For, there are other demands of primary importance, especially the one that men must and ought to live in society, which it is our imperative duty to reconcile to other demands. But it is, indeed, maintained,

---

[1] Hence the fact that landed property is called in English law "real property;" because, when the term came into use, this was infinitely the most important species of property; so much so, that it became necessary, in later times, to enact specific statutes in order properly to protect other property likewise, for instance, shares, stocks, etc.

that property is not held as a boon of government or originally as a boon of society, most especially not the property which is the product of personal skill, individual exertion, and particular knowledge. The sweeping remark that property is the creature of government, is as erroneous as the assertion would be that government makes crime by acknowledging certain wicked acts to be such, and therefore to be punishable, and that, on the other hand, it takes away guilt from other wicked acts by not acknowledging them as crimes, that is, by abstaining from punishing them. The family affords us instances for both cases. Most codes do not, for good reasons, acknowledge individual property of the members of the same family living under one roof, in the various articles of daily use; nor do they acknowledge that a minor, under such circumstances, can commit robbery against his parents or other members of the family. Yet we all know, that although the law does not acknowledge the crime, it remains a very grievous one, in the eye of every virtuous man, if a minor steals from his brother what belongs to him, although this property is not acknowledged by the government. History amply proves what has been here advanced. Nowhere do we find the original invention of property; everywhere government is in a process of acknowledging it; nowhere do people say let us have property; everywhere it exists already; it exists before society; nowhere does the law first enact the meaning of the word Property. It is found already, coeval with law. Even the origin of the laws of inheritance is an acknowledgment on the side of government, and that even a gradual one, of usages having grown up out of the feelings of men. When at a later period the state becomes more and more a distinctly political society, and its actions likewise become more distinct, many positive regulations are made, no doubt; but the process of mere acknowledgment is likewise all the time going on, and must be so, as long as society continues to be a living, therefore, a changing and transforming thing.

That property is the creature of government is the slavish doctrine of Asia, where it is a principle, universally maintained, at least in theory, that the prince is the original and absolute owner of all the soil, and the people are mere tenants at will; or of so degenerate periods as that of Louis the Fourteenth, who, indeed, advanced a theory not very unlike it.

We find, therefore, that the vast majority of all laws referring to property belongs, in all countries, to that bulk of laws which must ever form the large foundation of all enacted law; that law which spontaneously and necessarily springs up from out the intercourse of the people, in the shape of custom, usage, observance, and which at a later period becomes acknowledged by the government—the common law of the land; that law which in all regions, without exception, constitutes not only the vast basis of all statute law, but at the same time, that inexhaustible stock from which the unavoidable insufficiency of all statute law must and can alone be eked out. Nearly all the most important laws, all fundamental laws, are acknowledged, not invented by government. Lord Coke distinctly maintains that Magna Charta is a declaratory act; it did not invent or create the privileges and principles which it contains; it only declared, it acknowledged them, solemnly and distinctly. "Our custom," or "our usage," is the term with which all early free nations resist the encroachments of wayward or regardless power, or endeavor to give the appearance of legality to arrogations on their part. Nor can I omit mentioning here the wise and philosophic law maxim of the ancient jurist, that the right is not derived from the rule, but the rule is abstracted from (grows out of) the right, which exists already.[1]

It has ever been most amply acknowledged, that whatever a man righteously or lawfully produces by his own hands (which always includes their being directed by some skill or knowledge, that is, by his mind), and with his own sweat, is his, and his only; and it is not his and his only, if he has not the right of disposing of it according to his pleasure; for, possessing a thing in right of property, is "to have the sole right

---

[1] Ne ex regula jus sumatur, sed ex jure, quod est, regula fiat.

of using and disposing of it." There is no other meaning to the word of owning. Yet no man can create anything; it is a well-acknowledged truth that nowhere an increase of matter takes place. Production does not mean creation. But the greater man's own personal activity, skill, perseverance, exertion, trouble, or sacrifice have been, in order to produce a certain thing; the greater the share is which they have in the new product conjointly with other agents, made tributary by man's exertion and knowledge; the more clearly established is also his title of property in his product, and consequently the more unjust or cruel it is to deprive him of it. Hence no civilized government considers itself entitled to take part of a fortune which a man himself has personally gained; but considerable shares are often taken before a large property descends by way of inheritance to one that did not make it. It would be more cruel to rob a man of a hide, which he has dressed with much care and at considerable trouble, in order to use it for the protection of his body, than the depriving him of a fruit which he but that moment plucked from an unappropriated tree. It is more unjust to deprive a man of a cow, which he has bought with the savings of his wages, than to spoliate another of a grant of land given for no service. We must farther observe, that the more a producer unites with his manual labor intellectual exertion, the more, for instance, he directs his physical endeavors by a judicious choice of means, or by making the natural agents— light, heat, cold, wind, water, drought—subservient to his use by sound judgment, the more readily does the universal voice of mankind acknowledge his individual title of property in the product effected by this combination of judgment, agents, and material. Indeed, the more man's judgment and intellect are active in conferring value, the more he approaches to the creating of a new thing.

Both personal and intellectual activity appear clearest in a literary production; and if any product of individual activity has any claim whatever to an individual title of property, it is a literary composition; if there exists any species of property not made by government, but existing by its own spontaneous right, and which requires only to be acknowledged by way of protection on the part of government, it is literary property ; if there is any property which does not trench upon the rights of others, and exists without any sacrifice of theirs ; in brief, if there is any property peculiarly innocent and inoffensive in its character, it is literary property. It has always been held so, until untoward circumstances have warped and distorted the notions respecting it. In England literary property was considered property at common law, that is, it was believed that in order to make it good property no particular statute, mentioning this species of property, was any more necessary than that a particular variety of apples, or any species of fruit, cannot be considered individual good property, because no statute protects that variety or species.[1] We find the same view in Germany. Luther already writes : " What does that mean, my dear gentlemen printers, that one robs so publicly the other and steals from him what is his own ? It is a manifestly unfair thing, that we shall sacrifice labor and expenses, and others shall have the profit of it, we, however, the loss." [2] So he calls the piratical printing of his

---

[1] 4 Burr., 2303 ; and Holliday's Life of Mansfield, p. 215.

[2] Luther's Works, vol. xi., 34, quoted in Hitzig's pamphlet on the Prussian Copyright Law. Mr. Hitzig, at present one of the higher law officers in the highest court in Prussia, and one of the distinguished savans in Berlin, was thrown out of employment, with so many other officers, in the year 1806, when Prussia was conquered and reduced to a small part of its former territory. It was the time when the distinguished Hoffmann, at a later period member of the same court with Mr. Hitzig, became first a painter, and afterwards director of the opera at Dresden. Hitzig chose the book trade. His shop became the rendezvous of the most intelligent and patriotic men in Berlin during the time of the gloomiest oppression. When the French were expelled from Germany, Mr. Hitzig returned to the department of justice. The minister of justice communicated to Mr. Hitzig all the information which had been gathered preparatory to a new copyright law, with the bill itself, asking his opinion, which Mr. Hitzig was eminently calculated to give, both as a jurist and former bookseller, as well as on account of the high character he enjoys as a man and scholar. When the Prussian law was promulgated, Mr. Hitzig wrote the above pamphlet, giving the motives of each provision of the law.

translation of the Bible, in his Warning respecting the Witten-
berg Printing of the Bible, " a right great robbery, which God
assuredly will punish, and is ill-befitting for any honest Christian soul." The reader will remark, that these words were
written at the very outset of printed literature.

Although, however, the title in literary property seems to
be so just and clear, and a correct, or nearly correct view was
at first entertained, when, in the course of civilization, especially by the art of printing, this species of property received
a pecuniary value; it is nevertheless true, that its essential
character has been more obscured perhaps than that of any
other property. The reasons of this apparently surprising
fact are plain. When books were multiplied by transcrip-
tion only, their number was comparatively so very small, and
the process of multiplication so expensive, so slow, and, besides, so uncontrollable, that the work could not retain any
pecuniary value for the author.

This it could attain only with the discovery of the art of
printing, or some process of rapid and cheap multiplication.
Even then, however, the books were sold at first in so small
a number, and the whole process of multiplying was yet so
expensive, that no profit of any importance accrued to the
author. This simple fact had a twofold effect: on the one
hand this species of property received a pecuniary value at a
very late period only, when all other kinds of property had
already been acknowledged in some sort or other, either by
distinct laws, or by repeated judicial action, so that to some
persons it appeared as though it was no property because
there was no distinct law for it; on the other hand, the author
deriving no profit from the work, the publisher seemed generally to be the only person interested in this property, by
way of profit, and the author only by way of reputation, or
the correctness and beauty of the edition. We find this error
prevalent at an early period in several countries, and, consequently, meet with so many failures in establishing by sound
arguments the just title of literary property. For, while it
was evident that the publisher's business was only the making

of the *book*, not the producing of the literary *work*, it was felt at every stage of the discussion that no peculiar title of property could be retained in the individual book, or copy, so soon as purchased by another; yet it was felt likewise that the question of literary property necessarily resolved itself into the finding of a title enduring beyond the purchase of an individual copy. Hence all those arguments, which have been urged on the ground that by my fairly buying a book it becomes bona fide mine; consequently, I can do with it whatever I like, and, among other things, I may multiply it as often as I choose. Another and very strong reason why there should have been so much vagueness and injustice respecting literary property, is to be found in the peculiarity that its value consists chiefly in the right of multiplying the work. It is a right which can be easier infringed than almost any other right or property. Other property remains near its owners or his agents; this property, however, requires the more specific protection of government the farther society advances, and the cheaper, in consequence, the means of multiplying become, as well as the greater the demand for books becomes. Specific laws and privileges, exhibited to the public at the beginning of the book, were asked for at the hands of governments. When they had once been granted, the belief soon grew up as though they had first created this species of property; as though the whole title of property was a boon granted in that privilege as a gracious reward for the toil of the scholar, and an incitement for similar exertion to others. This was a fatal mistake, which in a very high degree indeed continues to be entertained by many people to this day. They consider the fact that a specific law protects literary property for a limited term, or that copyright is guaranteed by the constitutions, as an evidence that this property is the creature of grace, a thing made by society for some real or supposed benefit which it expects to derive from this gracious grant. This error has always been much promoted by the fact that literary property is not material; it cannot be grasped, or presented in bulk and size, but belongs to what Say would call the class of "immaterial products." It requires, therefore, more reflection and some power of abstraction to acknowledge it. Sergeant Talfourd distinctly stated, a short time ago, in the commons, that the act of parliament, 8 Anne, c. 19, for the encouragement of literature, has been of infinite injury to literary property, in the way I have just indicated. In Germany, where many of the Austrian booksellers lived for a long time chiefly by pirating German works, the fact, that specific privileges against literary piracy were granted by the German emperor, was actually claimed by those piratical republishers, justly excluded from the Leipsic book fair, as unfit to meet with their brethren engaged in honest trade, as a proof that they had a right to pirate the unprivileged books. The specific promise of protection was assumed as evidence that it made, created the property. Because the same emperor granted at times letters of safe-conduct to individuals, had, therefore, every highway robber or waylaying nobleman a right to plunder all others who were not provided with a safe-conduct? "What?" says Lichtenberg, a distinguished German author of the last century, "because privileges promise to some persons specific protection, is it on that ground lawful to pirate those books which are not furnished with this sign of protection? May I assault that man who cannot defend himself, or has not money, or lacks an opportunity of buying arms? May I rob that garden, at the door of which there is no sign with the words: Beware of spring guns? May I cut down the trees of an alley, because no sign-post near it threatens with public whipping, or steal the plough, because it lies unchained in the field?"[1]

An additional reason we find in another peculiarity of that property. Books affect the mind, the course of ideas. Wheat bread affords the same nourishment under a Titus as under a Caligula; woollen cloth warms as much, and no more, under a wise Elizabeth as under a puerile James. It is far different with books, and yet they are an article of trade, a commodity.

---

[1] Quoted in Hitzig.

They may be good, and yet be feared by tyrants; they may be wicked, and yet relished by a degenerate class of readers, and must be discountenanced by all good governments. Books may disturb the private or public peace. Some sort of peculiar action of government towards them has, therefore, at all times existed. This action, however, was more especially increased, when, in the sixteenth and seventeenth centuries, the power of the prince rapidly rose at the expense of the many aristocratic and corporative powers which had existed in the middle ages. This swaying power very naturally perceived the great importance of that new agent, the art of printing, which came into play nearly at the same time when the concentration of monarchical power was making rapid strides. The concentrated power of the modern monarchies found it necessary to establish a control over this new and vast agent, which seriously indicated that, within a short space of time, it would leave almost every other agent of society far behind, in vigor and irresistible activity. The censorship was established, and, in nearly all countries, books could not be issued at all, except with the specific permission or privilege of the prince. This permission or Imprimatur was frequently changed into a privilege. When this was once established, the next and very natural step was to designate the period for which this privilege should last; and this, natural enough, led to the erroneous idea that the whole privilege was a boon of that power which had the right thus to circumscribe its duration; in short, an act of grace on the part of the prince to the publisher.

It is, however, cheering to observe that, universally, with the advance of political civilization and a clearer perception of individual rights, the acknowledgment of literary property has likewise advanced, and the true basis upon which its justice rests has been more and more clearly perceived in countries where the true ground had been lost sight of. It was one of the early acts of the first French revolution to acknowledge literary property on a comprehensive principle; all modern constitutions acknowledge it. At least, I do not remember a single exception. If there are any, they must be in South America, and might be easily accounted for by the little attention which this property may have yet attracted in some of those states. Everywhere we find the period during which protection is guaranteed extended; in several countries to the end of the natural life of the author, as the minimum period. The Act of Union of the Germanic Confederacy, of June 8, 1815, provides in article 18, "that the diet (that is, the congress of the ministers of the various members) at its first meeting shall occupy itself with the making of uniform decrees (that is, for the whole of Germany) respecting the protection of the rights of authors." It will be observed that the "rights of authors" are fully acknowledged as already existing; the fundamental law speaks of protection only. Everywhere, indeed, we find the whole question more and more reduced to that point where the right truly centres. And where is this?

It has been said already that it is not the manuscript nor the individual book, as all the piratical publishers like to represent it. Thus the Austrian republishers[1] stated in their answer to the urgent memorial which the German publishers had addressed to the congress of Vienna, in 1815, where, among other things, the German affairs were remodelled, after the downfall of Napoleon, that "the publisher buys from the author, for whatever price they agree upon, the *copy* of the *manuscript* only, and not the right of publication. This his government grants him for its own territory; for foreign states that same government cannot grant it. The subject of a foreign state buys a *copy* of the *printed* edition, likewise for a certain price, in order to imitate this piece of manufacture, if his government permits it, and the *foreign publisher* has as little right to complain as the foreign trader in shawls, cloth, steel has, of any injury done to him there where government prohibits him from trading, in order to protect its own subjects."

---

[1] In Hitzig, as above.

"The book is no intellectual, independent thing, . . . it is a piece of manufacture upon paper, with signs of thoughts printed upon it. It contains no thoughts (*sic!*); these must be produced in the head of the intelligent reader." (Yes, and what is very strange, these thoughts may be, as in the case before us, the very opposite from those which the sagacious author desires to produce.) "It is an article of trade, which we obtain for money; every government, however, has the duty to stem the avoidable export of national capital (here we have the old beautiful theory of the balance of trade), "to encourage the domestic manufacture of goods first produced in foreign countries (*sic!*), and by no means to impede the industry of its own citizens for the enrichment of foreign manufacturers." (*sic!*)

"Whoever does not choose to see his book printed in foreign states, must abstain from printing and selling it in his own state." (Whoever does not choose to have his pippins robbed must not plant them in his orchard, but raise them in his closet. Whoever does not want his pockets picked must not put anything into them, or must sew them up, or not go abroad.)

This is Austrian philosophy and enlightened political economy. This is the Austrian view of literature; a literary work, a piece of Manchester calico, and a Connecticut tin pot are all the same. This is—we confidently hope it soon will be no more so—to this moment, likewise, American philosophy, political economy, and generosity with respect to the book trade! Many readers, indeed, will be startled at these gross views, thus concentrated; but let them be still more startled when they are told that, however hideous they may appear, they are nevertheless essentially the principles upon which we ourselves continue to act.

In reading these arguments of the worthy Austrian pirates, luminous ideas crowd so fast upon us, that we can hardly find room to express them. How is it if an author gives away an autograph manuscript to a collector of autographs, but retains a copy? Has the collector, who is the lawful owner of that manuscript, that is, of the paper with signs of ink upon it, on that account the right to give or sell it to a bookseller for publication? According to the above theory, he undoubtedly has. The book, they further observe with rare sagacity, is a thing, something white, called paper, with something black, called ink, upon it, and a man can do with it what he likes, except where the government prohibits it. So the whole right of literary property is a thing absolutely made and invented by government, a monopoly. Why government always grants the monopoly to the author, and not sometimes to some one else, when the author is living, or why, if this were done, it would be considered downright pillage, is not shown. Forsooth, even the Austrian piratical printer thinks it is fair that the author should have the monopoly; but why? Is there any other reason but because it is felt that his work is his own, and that, after all, it is no monopoly? But so far does their philosophy not penetrate. I suppose it has never been doubted that a man's body and all that belongs to it is his own, bona fide his own. Yet governments have at times ordained to cut the hair or trim the beard in a peculiar fashion. To some this may appear a little oppressive; "Oh," the Austrian pirate would say, "if you do not choose government to interfere with your beard, keep the hair back; but if you allow it to grow forth, you must not complain if government grants you permission to let it grow only on certain conditions."

It remains, however, to be shown whether the possessor of a book actually has the right to do with it what he likes, even according to the view of those whose opinion on literary property has just been given. With that single copy, which he has purchased, he undoubtedly has. He may cross, for instance, with ink a whole sentence, and write the contrary over it. Suppose he were to publish the book in that garbled manner, in a foreign country, still under the name of the first author, would not even the Austrian pirate confess there was some slight degree of unfairness in the proceeding? Yet why should it be unfair? Has not the defacer bought the book, and can he not do with it whatever he has a mind to do, where

government does not prohibit it? Perhaps even those gentlemen have here a dim and distant perception that there is
a difference between the book and the literary work or com-.
position; that the one belongs to the purchaser, who can do
with it what he lists, and though he were to make pasteboard
of Napoleon's work on Egypt, but that the other remains the
author's. How else is the whole case of plagiarism to be explained? Even there where government allows free republication to "stem the avoidable exportation of national capital,"
it is considered dishonorable if B copies a passage from the
work of C into his own work and gives it as his own. If the
Austrian doctrine be correct, that is, if there be no difference
between the book and the work, and the whole be but a piece
of manufactured good, which of course I have a full right to
cut and alter according to my fancy, B, the piratical author,
has acquired as full and extensive a right over every part of
the purchased book as the republisher. This is undeniable;
and if by buying a book we buy all and everything appertaining to it, or connected with it, B has as much right to give a
passage of C's book as his own as I have a right to eat the
fruit purchased for my money, although another has produced
it, because he has relinquished, for my equivalent, the whole
of the fruit; and not a particle to be called his remains in the
fruit.

Nor is it the thought in which the right of literary property consists. A thought, an idea, of itself is not a thing that
can be *owned*, and of course not be protected by government.
There is no command over thought. If it were so, the piratical publisher would have indeed a right to prosecute me, if,
in reading a publication of his, it should happen to convey to
me, besides the thoughts of the author, also thoughts on the
wretched printing, gray paper, or pale ink, because I did not
pay for these additional thoughts; I only paid for the thoughts
intended by him to be conveyed.

The right of the author's property lies in the composition,
the *work;* this is the *product*, in which the author has invested
his labor, skill, ingenuity, and accumulated knowledge (or

labor saved) of previous study, as we invest the same in all products; it is, as has been stated before, what Say calls an immaterial product, but not the less a real product for all that. It is "incorporeal," although the produce of it is not; as the father is entitled to the labor of his children under age. He does not own their bodies; he owns their labor; and his property is incorporeal, although its effects are not; for instance, when he sets his children to work in the field, which brings him grain. Thought is not marketable; but invested thought, ingenuity, calculation, combination, is daily brought to market. This literary *work* forms a separate independent product of its own, and is bona fide the author's own. It cannot belong to any one else. The author has truly and verily produced it; he is the owner; and he would not be the owner if he could not dispose of the work as he pleases. Many individuals may have, and actually have daily the same thought, but no two individuals can produce the same composition. The work, the composition, that immaterial or incorporeal product, has nothing to do with either manuscript or book. Casting the *work* into a *book* is only one way of publication; another is, for instance, the performance on the stage, and every well-regulated copyright law, for instance, that of France, as we have seen, protects the author against piratical publication of a dramatic composition in the shape of performance on the stage. If it were possible to impart a whole comedy from memory to the actors, who for a compensation have obtained the right of performing it, and other theatres were to perform it, they would in France be guilty of pirating the work, which work in this case would exist without manuscript or book. A professor might sell the permission of taking down his lectures while he is delivering them, and of publishing them, if he has a perfect confidence both in himself and the employed stenographer. Here would be a sale of a work without manuscript. The copyright laws of several countries distinctly prohibit the unauthorized publication of lectures, written down during delivery, for instance, that of Prussia. No abuse of manuscript or copy can take place in this case, still the unauthorized publication of the lecture is robbing the *work* from its owner, who is the owner because he is its producer. The purchaser buys the book, not the work; part of the rights over the work are bought by the publisher. With the book the purchaser may do what he likes; he may read it, he may read it to others, he may lend it to others. But this must not become a second publication. It might become a decidedly important question, whether the purchaser of a book would have the right of assembling multitudes and read to them the work, without additions or commentaries of his own. It would stand on the same ground with the performance of a drama in the theatre. Indeed, peculiarly skilled people do read in Europe, for money, dramatic pieces to assembled numbers. Suppose a professor should read only the book of his colleague to his hearers. The case of circulating libraries deserves attention in this point of view. Speaking in a strictly legal sense, there is in my mind no doubt but that the making a business of lending out books for money is publication. Still we do not prohibit the lending out of books for money of copyrighted works, either because we consider it an exception on the ground of sovereign expediency, or because the trouble of protection would in this case be greater than the advantage to be obtained; or, lastly, because it is no essential injury to the author, for it is generally found that by whatever means the perusal of a work is promoted, its sale will likewise be promoted.[1]

The philosopher Kant founds the justice of copyright—seeing the impossibility of attaching it to the book—in the fact that writing a book is communing, speaking by signs to the public; the author has a right to prescribe the conditions on which he may be heard. The publisher is the doorkeeper, who admits, for a stipulated fee (the price of the book), the hearer (*i.e.*, the reader) into the lecture-room. I think this

---

[1] Thus, indeed, it is frequently found that the gradual publication of novels in periodicals prepares only a greater sale when the novel comes to be published entire.

view is liable to some substantial objections; the circulating library, in particular, cannot well be disposed of by this theory, unless, indeed, it be said at once, that among the conditions for which the purchaser pays his money is this, that he may lend it to others for gain as well as gratis. At any rate, we stand in need of no comparisons or similes; the ownership in a literary work is as clear, direct, real, and sound as any existing, and more so than most others; it needs no metaphorical prop.

The essential difference between the book and the literary work may be strikingly shown in a popular manner. A young lawyer buys Blackstone's Commentaries; he writes his own name on the fly-leaf or the inside of the cover. No one, who opens the book, finds any objection, because these are the places where the owner of a book usually puts his name, so that the individual book may be distinguished from other *copies* of the same work. Let him, on the other hand, strike out the name of Blackstone on the title-page and put his own instead of it. Every one would laugh at the egregious folly, because this is the place where usually the author of the *work* puts his name, and although that identical book became the true property of the young lawyer, the work conveyed in or by that book, or of which the book is but a *copy*, continues to be Blackstone's, and cannot be affected by the purchase, nor can it ever become another's, although part of the disposal over it, that is, its multiplication, may be sold, while another part, for instance, the right of making changes, is not sold.

Of those who, of late, have denied the right of property in literary works, one of the most distinguished is Mr. Augustin Charles Renouard, in his work on the Rights of Authors in Literature, Sciences, and the Fine Arts, in French.[1] Some of the chief points of this work are, that property cannot be predicated of thought, and consequently the term Literary Property ought to be banished from the language of the

---

[1] The Jurist, of October, 1839, Boston, has a full article on Mr. Renouard's theory.

law; that, nevertheless, the sole right of multiplication ought to be secured to the author for a limited time, on account of his merit, the advantage he bestows upon society; and that, lastly, both theories amount pretty much to the same thing. Every one of these positions is directly or indirectly erroneous. Property can indeed not be predicated of thought; no one has ever claimed it, but it can be predicated of composition, of works. Mr. Renouard, and many others before him, maintain that a work (they mean the manuscript) is undoubtedly the author's property, but that by publishing it he deliberately abandons all specific right respecting his composition. This is begging the question, for it takes for granted the very point under discussion. We wholly deny it. Indeed, so far from conceding this position, I rather maintain that, if the author does not first acquire the title of property by his act of publication, he certainly avails himself for the first time of the value of his property by publishing his work; and for all civil intercourse, property is as though it had no existence, so long as the owner cannot affix exchangeable value to it.[1] Indeed, we do not call all things which are our own our property on that account. No one will doubt that his arms, his legs, are his own, but they are not called his property, because they have no exchangeable value; while a girl's tresses might be called her property, because she can cut them off and sell them to the hair-dresser. To say, then, that a composition is the property of the author so long as he chooses to keep it in his desk, but that he forfeits his ownership so soon as he publishes the composition, is saying this is your property, but the act itself of availing yourself of that property deprives you of it, which is absurd. Secondly, if the exclusive right of multiplication depends upon the merit of the work, the advantage which society derives from it, it becomes a very necessary and serious question before grant-

---

[1] This is another strong reason why we cannot speak of general or common property, belonging to all, before the great division took place. The chief reason for the desirableness of property is the exchangeable value of itself, or of that which we derive from it.

ing the exclusive right, whether the work has any merit, whether it be not injurious. Who would decide whether the majority of all books printed nowadays are beneficial or the contrary? Literary property is not protected on the specific ground of merit, but like all other property, because it is of essential importance to society that individual property should always be protected, very few and palpably injurious cases only excepted. Many sons of rich men are ruined because they inherit a large fortune, nor would it be in many cases difficult to predict that a rich inheritance will ruin a certain individual. Yet we do not interfere and throw the individual upon his own resources, which would be for his benefit, because general protection of property is incalculably more important. Most governments interfere when a female prostitutes her charms for money; but they do not interfere if a handsome woman sells her charms in obtaining a rich husband by means of them, although she despises him, base as the act is; because interference would be worse. So we must protect all works, bad, foolish, or good, on the general ground that they are property, and we can make exceptions only in cases of flagrantly immoral or palpably injurious books. Lastly, the ground upon which we base literary property is of the greatest importance respecting international copyright, as we shall presently see.

Property, or the means of acquiring it, must unite various qualities, in order to be fairly entitled to the protection of property. It must be capable of being protected, and the trouble of protection must not be out of all proportion to the value protected. Stray pigeons are unprotected in nearly all countries; yet, sometimes, they are of considerable value to pigeon fanciers, pairs having sold as high as thirty dollars.[1]

---

[1] These pigeons may be instanced as a species of property, unacknowledged by government, yet considered bona fide property by the persons interested in it. There was formerly, and in all probability there is still, a club of pigeon fanciers in the city of Berlin. At its meetings stray pigeons were valued, and the ownership proved. The owner had the right to claim the pigeon for payment of part of the adjudged value; others had to pay the whole value.

It must be lawfully gotten; which of course means that before property can forfeit protection it must be proved to be unlawfully gotten, or, in other words, not to be the property of its present possessor.

It must not work decided evil by its own tendency. The beauty of a young female may, in the light of political economy, undoubtedly receive value by prostitution, as any other natural gift, for instance, the talent for music; yet society does not only withhold protection from this trade, but discountenances it by law.[1]

"On the other hand, it is a general principle of the highest importance that the whole society is most deeply interested in the utmost protection of every species of property, which is not objectionable on the grounds just enumerated. For the greatest possible security of property and its pursuit is the greatest possible inducement to its accumulation, to industry, and civilization. Literary property, besides the plain justice of its origin, unites all the qualities of good and beneficial property for which protection is or may be claimed. It is capable of protection; it is just to protect it, because the pecuniary reward obtained by the author is, in most instances, but a very disproportionate return for the toil and labor invested in his work, and society is greatly interested in its protection, in order to offer an incentive to gifted men, who are not in easy circumstances, and ought to provide, like good citizens, for their families.

Indeed, among the various unreasonable arguments against copyright, and especially international copyright laws, we find

---

[1] Where prostitution stands under the police, and permission to keep houses of ill-fame is granted, as in Paris, it is avowedly only with a view of preventing still greater mischief; and it must be observed as a very striking fact, which we learn from the excellent work of Parent-Duchatelet on Prostitution in Paris, that the whole surveillance over prostitution in that city, with all the regulations most rigidly enforced, the police bureaus for that particular branch, the numerous clerks, physicians, etc., and the great restrictions to which the houses of ill-fame are subjected, does not exist by law, but by connivance of the whole society only. It is, perhaps, the most striking instance of the all-sovereign power of opinion.

even that which is believed to be founded upon the little reward which, after all, awaits, in most cases, the most laborious literary or scientific inquiries, in the shape of money for the sale of the copyright. It is, moreover, advanced that the author is rewarded by the reputation which he acquires. If this argument holds, a man who cultivates his garden or farm chiefly or partly for the sake of pleasure or health, must not be protected in the property which he may acquire by the sale of part of his produce, which may amount to far less than his experiments have cost him; or we would have the right to spoliate a day-laborer of his little savings, which he may have contrived to lay up at the end of the year, because they are but trifling, after all. The soldier, minister, physician, lawyer, and politician acquire likewise reputation along with their pecuniary rewards; so do many distinguished farmers, engineers, manufacturers, and machine-builders. Are they, nevertheless, not protected in the property acquired by their profession?

If, then, literary property is not a thing made by government, no monopoly, and the term for which protection is granted by the law is, notwithstanding, limited, whilst most other property enjoys protection *ad infinitum*, it must be proved that protection, after a certain period, becomes too troublesome; or that the property, in most cases, loses its value after a reasonable time; or that society, for some reason or other, is too deeply interested in debarring farther protection, in order to give any color of justice to the spoliation. For spoliation it always remains, because it was originally no boon of government, no grant, as little as the farm of the agriculturist is, which he first rescued from wilderness uninhabited and unappropriated by any one. Government does not say, You have had this farm long enough; your children shall have no benefit of it; we allow henceforth any one to plunder your fields, or take from you their produce when you carry it to market at home or abroad. On the contrary, if the cotton produced by our planter were unjustly seized upon in a foreign port, our government would protect the planter;

it would seek redress, and go as far as to make reprisals if redress were not granted.

I have dwelt so long on the essential character of literary property in general, and that in which it truly consists—the literary work—because the question of international copyright laws can only be solved if we keep this point strictly in view. It is no monopoly; it is the author's own, if ever anything could rightfully be called an individual's own. Now, it is one of the greatest and most beneficent effects of civilization, that we acknowledge rights beyond the limits of the state; that we acknowledge rights where we can no longer be forced to acknowledge them; that we acknowledge rights when we cannot acknowledge the citizen, but merely the man, in the interested individual. In the earliest times, all property of foreigners, met with on the high seas, is considered a perfectly fair subject of plunder. It is taken and carried away to be sold. The property of foreigners within the territory of a certain state must in those periods be protected by specific grants, charters, and treaties. The various Greek confederacies granted to single foreigners or whole states the asylia, or exemption from piracy, or any other forcible seizure. At present, however, a barrel of flour ground in Rochester, in the state of New York, is considered to be as fair property, and is protected accordingly, in the port of Lisbon as at home. In many countries a foreigner could formerly bring no action against a citizen of that country. Who was he? A mere foreigner; what has he to do with our laws? The Chinese government would say to an Englishman who should complain against an American, both residing at Canton: "Who are you, barbarians? Fight it out among yourselves." But a Frenchman may bring an action against an Italian in an American or English court, or that of any other civilized country. Nay, the very person of the foreigner was originally not acknowledged. Hostis (enemy) and Peregrinus (foreigner) were synonymes. Wrecks were lawful prize; first all wrecked goods were so, even those belonging to citizens of the same state. Then it became law that wrecked goods belonging to foreigners only should be lawful prize. The person of the unfortunate sailor wrecked on foreign shore was forfeited; he was made a slave. Have the civilized governments, who no longer pretend to so barbarous a right, made the personal rights of these sailors, or only acknowledged them in the progressive course of civilization? "In all that is good, of which we speak here, there is nothing more excellent, nor more comprehensive, than the tie of union among men, and as it were a society and communion of everything useful, and good will toward all men; which existed with the first origin, shows itself gradually more and more, first in the family and relationship; then comprehending the whole human species, which affection of the human mind is called justice."[1]

In an analogous manner we see, that the more the barbarous idea vanishes that the author is little better than a slave, who owns his property from no inherent right, but merely at the gracious pleasure of his own government, the more vanishes likewise the gross barbarous idea that his property may be forcibly taken from him, wherever we can lay hold on it in foreign parts. I have mentioned already three instances of international copyright law. The king of the French speaks of the necessity of such laws in his last throne speech. If the newspapers inform us correctly, there are now transactions going on between Belgium and France, the former having for centuries robbed and plundered the French authors to their greatest injury. Wherever the people of different sovereign states speak the same language, the question of international copyright law becomes as important as that of copyright law in general. For, the value of the work is founded in the language, which language extends beyond the state; just as the value of Michigan flour is founded upon the human organism, upon hunger, which hunger extends beyond the political limits of the state, and the value of the flour extends consequently likewise as far as hunger is felt.

---

[1] Cicero de Finibus, v. 23.

Man can produce nothing without certain agents, already existing, being seized upon by him; and existing wants, calling for it. The miller makes use of the water; the mariner seizes upon the wind; the farmer upon the rain; the bleacher upon sunshine. With the aid of these agents they confer value upon certain materials. The agent already existing, for the author, is the language; he seizes upon it, and confers value upon his conception by casting it in that language. He has an undeniable right, which civilization ought to deny no human being, to offer, directly or through some one authorized by him, his product in the best market, where it may obtain the highest price. If the advantage of authors is thus doubled and trebled by their being able to write for two nations at once, do they enjoy any greater advantage than civilization bestows upon every industrious man? Does the Sheffield knife-grinder not reap the advantage from civilization allowing the merchant quietly to carry his steel-ware to the best market? Is it not universally blessed as one of the most legitimate advantages of civilization, that it opens more and more distant marts? And who will say that it is not perhaps in the great plan, laid down for human progress, that increased reward and consequently increased literary activity resulting from the vaster public, extending over various countries, shall be substituted for the lessened literary production resulting from the lessened number of idioms? For it is an undeniable fact, that Languages pass through the various chief stages of literary production, not so much Countries. Languages, not countries, have their epic, romantic, dramatic periods.

But, it is objected, have we not the right to deny copyright to English authors? Are we not a sovereign nation? If right means that we have the power to do it, then we do possess the right, in the same degree as the Algerines did possess the right to plunder any Christian vessel. For they too were sovereign, and among other laws made this, that Christian property should not be acknowledged by them. If it be so, I do not know whence we could claim any right to chastise them; and if the Algerines were right, Decatur, or those that sent him, must have been butchers. We sent our ships to punish the Algerines, and demand our property, because we felt that no one has a right to plunder, or that every one has a perfect right to protect his own, whatever the laws of the plundering country may be; and, however inexpedient it might be, as to the absolute right I have no manner of doubt that a power would be perfectly justifiable to force another by reprisals, or any other forcible means, to respect the property of its own citizens in the shape of copyright. France would have the right to force Belgium to abstain from literary piracy. If right and power or advantage are confounded, we might waylay West India sugar, and possibly get it cheaper than we now do, when we have first to produce values, with which alone we can buy that sugar, and, when we have bought it, have for all this trouble no earthly advantage but the mean one of being conscious that we have obtained it in an honest way, while we might have sweetened our tea so cheaply for the little trouble of sending a fast sailing clipper, manned with a few desperadoes, to our neighboring seas.

In what does the value of a literary work for the author consist, besides the lofty pleasure of an active mind in conceiving and sketching out new thoughts and tracing truth? The pecuniary value consists in the exclusive right of multiplication; the other value, in his reputation; and in both we wantonly injure him. We rob him in the first, and we allow our republishers to bestow the least possible care upon the printing, or to curtail, mutilate, and deface works in order to make books of them more fit for a hasty sale. Those that have bestowed the least attention upon the subject can easily understand the grief with which Kant saw some of his lectures published by an unauthorized hand, in a garbled state; or the fervor with which Justus Lipsius calls for protection against unauthorized and mutilated publications of the lectures he had delivered.[1]

---

[1] We find at the beginning of Justus Lipsius's De Cruce Libri tres, Amstelodami, 1670, the following words under the inscription, Justus Lipsius ad Lectorem :

If the author has in any degree that love of truth, that enthusiasm of knowledge and noble ambition of rendering some substantial service in the advancement of learning and literature, without which either is deprived of its vital spark, and which it is the greatest interest of all society to foster for the sake of everything that is sacred to civilized men—if an author has any self-respect and has written his work to the best of his ability, and deposited in it the results of long and many meditations, weary research, industrious observation, and, perhaps, painful experience, or the fruits of his best and most inspired moments; then it is cruel, indeed, for him to see some one else who has no earthly claim upon him or the public, purposely mutilating or garbling, from niggard negligence, the work to which the author has staked his reputation and name, and to make which as perfect as his abilities would allow he has spared neither time, labor, nor the sacrifice of money and many enjoyments, perhaps of health. Does the author who asks protection against such injury claim anything more but what every human being has a right to claim, which you must grant him if he be your fellow-citizen, and which you ought to grant him because he is your fellow-man? Have we as men, and especially as Christians, a right to deny the plainest justice to foreigners solely because we may do

---

" Habes lector quæ de cruce scripsimus, sed germana. Antea atque alibi quæ edita (credes hoc nobis) non sunt nostra. Quid ergo? Non illa dictavimus? Fortasse, sed o imperitiam! quasi edendi illo fine. Reverentior posteritatis sum : et aliud scio esse schedia, aliud opera; nec subitaria hæc nostra dedicanda in memoriæ templo. Quid quod alii gravius etiam peccant? qui excipiunt aut intercipiunt dicta aut oratiunculas nostras, et in contumeliam mei divulgant. Aliter non accipio. Aevum hoc ut multis delictis fibulam, ita petulantiæ et licentiæ laxat : et quod avet procacissimus quisque, id etiam audet. Ego semel et serio testor, audite qui in Europa. *Nihil meum est, aut erit, quod non de autographo meo, et me volente, sit expressum.* Quicumque aliter, mihi injuriam facit, vobis fucum. Deus bone, hæc monenda publice esse? Ecce in bona opesque externas jus est non vivo mihi solum sed mortuo et solatium fati est voluntas ultra fatum : in istis animi et ingenii vere bonis non idem erit? Reprimite Principes qui potestis : et vos lectores qua potestis : illi puniendo, vos spernendo."

How true! How applicable to our case!

it with impunity, and, perhaps, imagine that some advantage accrues to our nation from it? "Those," says Cicero, "who have regards for their fellow-citizens only, and not for foreigners, tear asunder the great community of men, and if that ceases, benevolence, liberality, goodness, justice will be radically destroyed." [1] Let us consider a real case. Mr. Hallam has published his Introduction to the Literature of Europe. The work must have cost him many years' labor and study. It is an extensive work, which cannot command as large a sale as many trifling books. Hardly was it published in England, when an American bookseller advertised a republication, and a cheap edition appeared at Brussels. Is this a state of civilization, that is, of mutual, candid acknowledgment of justice, fairness, liberality? Or is it a state of barbarity, of pilfer and plunder, meanness and violence? Is this a state of things which gentlemen would like to exist between them? And what else is international law in its purity but the application of the principle of gentlemanliness, that is, of candor, fairness, liberality, and mutual respect, to the intercourse of nations? Barbarous or degenerate nations treat one another like ruffians or blackguards; civilized and elevated nations like gentlemen.

Utility or desirableness are the two things which confer value upon any product or exchangeable article. It is the just order of things, that he who has conferred this utility upon a thing, enjoys a proportionate share of those values which the consumers or those that desire the article give in exchange for it. It is the principle which lies at the bottom of all industry, the moving power without which all interchange between men would be at an end. Yet this fairest of all rewards is denied to the fairest of all producers, the author, so soon as we decline the grant of international protection of literary property. The consumer throws large profits into the laps of those who had no share in producing the desired

---

[1] Qui autem civium rationem dicunt habendam, externorum negant, ii dirimunt communem humani generis societatem, qua sublata beneficentia, liberalitas, bonitas, justitia funditus tollitur.—CICERO, De Off. iii., 5.

article, who employed neither labor nor capital in the product, that is, the work, whatever capital they may employ to
produce the book. If thousands in this country have derived benefit and pleasure from the perusal of Walter Scott's
productions, was he not fairly entitled to a share in those
values which the American readers were obliged and willing
to pay in order to obtain the pleasure and benefit of the books
which contained his works? It may indeed be convenient
for a few to "skim the cream of other people's wit," but the
question is whether it be right, whether it be just? whether
we ought, in conscience, to deny an honest class of society
those rights which we readily grant to all others?

Perhaps it will be answered here, that we derive great advantage by the reprinting of foreign works in two ways:
first, by keeping that capital which would go into a foreign
country to pay the foreign author in our own country, and
enriching with it our own republishers; secondly, by enabling
the public at large to buy the republished works cheaper.

Even though it were so, it would nevertheless be unjust,
and there is no greater truth in all politics than that the
shrewdest cunning and the merest expediency can never hit
upon a better means of essentially promoting their own ends
than, before all, essential justice towards all. It is the broadest,
safest, truest, and most enduring foundation of all prosperity
and success. It will always prove so in the long run, whatever the appearance to the contrary at the moment may be.
No sacrifice is ever made to essential and even lofty justice
which does not make returns with ample interest. Yet even
though it were not so, justice stands above utility; and we,
boasting of civilization and refinement, should not take a
meaner view than that which was pronounced two thousand
years ago by a profound statesman: Justice is to be cultivated
on its own account.[1]

With respect to the publishers in our own country, who
derive much benefit from republications without allowing a

---

[1] Cicero.

share of the profit to the lawful proprietors of the literary product, it is to be observed that but few share in this profit. These indeed may make large profits, but an overwhelming majority of our publishers do not share in it, and would have no objection against so just a law as one which should internationally protect literary property. I speak after having made some inquiry. I found not one bookseller among those whom I consulted in Boston who made any objection, provided the capital already embarked in republication, under the sanction of the law of the land, were properly protected, which is no more than justice requires. I found in other cities, where my inquiries, however, were not so extensive, numerous respectable publishers of the same opinion. I do not hesitate to say that an inquiry, conducted with any degree of care, would show the number of American publishers, who are anxious to see the present state to be continued, to be very small indeed.

What is the advantage the public derives from republications unauthorized by the authors? We are told that our people are enabled to purchase the books for a far lower price than they would do if the American republishers were obliged to pay for the copyright to a foreign author. This is but partly true. All those books which are largely and permanently desired by the public are, on the one hand, cheap where copyright is protected, because a profit, hardly felt by the purchaser on each copy, becomes a valuable revenue for the author, on account of its constant repetition. On the other hand, the book being in great demand, the unauthorized republisher raises its price as high as circumstances will permit, and almost the whole difference is this, that besides the fair profit which he would make on the investment of his capital, he appropriates also that profit which, if justice prevailed, he would have to pay to the lawful owner of the literary property. In addition to this fact, it ought to be remembered that the publishers, forming as they do a comparatively small class, there is far more understanding with one another among them than among the members of other trades. This is not only harmless, in all fair things, but desirable; in the case, however, which we consider, it prevents, in a very considerable degree, competition, so that the public are far from reaping the whole advantage of the fact that no copyright has been paid for, but the republisher alone gains it. As to the capital which would flow out of the country in the way of payment for the copyright, it would always be but a trifling sum, considered as part of the national wealth, and, moreover, does in no way differ from the money paid for any other desirable article. Value for value. The times of the once far-famed balance of trade it is to be hoped are past, at least in our country. The world lives upon exchange; what flows out of it must come back, if we only produce values with which to fetch it back. The work of an author is a value, else no money would be paid for it; thus one value flows in while another flows out. We shall presently see, however, that the law as it stands now, or rather the absence of law, forces likewise capital out of our country and prevents other capital from flowing into it, and thus counteracts the pretended advantages.

Respecting the second class of books, namely, those that are not largely desired, or are of a kind that they are reprinted in newspaper form, it is true with regard to some, or may be so as to most of them, that the public obtain them cheaper than they would otherwise: But there is a disadvantage connected with these publications, which does indeed not fall within the precise province of political economy, but is nevertheless great. The books belonging to this class are generally of a very light character; they are forced upon the public frequently in a slovenly and incorrect state, and, as to those published in newspaper form, on a very large scale. All these circumstances produce two results: they promote that mere reading for reading's sake, to fill out vacant time and vacant minds; to satisfy a craving for reading without reflection—a licentiousness of reading as it might be called, because it is a craving desire unguided by any judgment; and the books or other publications being in a shape not to demand any respect or desire of retaining them, they are naturally treated as mere means to satisfy the appetite of the moment. There is no reperusal, because the book is allowed to perish the moment after it has been gorged; there is no reflection, no purpose, and no profit of reading. It has been very hastily remarked that all reading is beneficial; for, however trivial the book may be, it will convey some information, and leave an increased desire for reading more. An unfounded remark, hardly worthy of being refuted. We might as well say all drinking, all eating is beneficial. When hurried, worthless, perhaps morally injurious reading interferes with labor, not only at the time when the reader is actually occupied with the book, but also by indisposing him for labor, and when injudicious and crammed reading renders the mind dull and heavy, instead of acute, fills it with a chaotic mass of indifferent matter, and unfits it for all sounder reflection—reading is not desirable. Inquiry, however, will show that such is actually the reading with some classes, especially with many working young women in our large cities. Do I then ask from government aid to direct judicious reading, to interfere with so private a subject? I am far from desiring so odious an interference; but I do desire our government to perform an act of justice, which, happily, will at the same time prevent, in a considerable degree, a great mischief; and I was desirous of showing that that, which many exhibit as an advantage and reason why we should continue to be unjust, is, on the contrary, a great disadvantage. In short, I do believe that by our denial of justice we additionally injure ourselves by inundating the country with the lightest literature offered in the least respectable form.

We have before considered the injustice done to foreign literary producers. The denial of an international copyright law operates with equal injustice, perhaps with greater, towards our own authors, and decidedly to our greater national disadvantage.

The author of the History of Ferdinand and Isabella informs us in his preface that as early as in the year 1826 he was occupied with his noble work. Ten years of very ardent and continuous labor, besides his talent and skill, are invested in that book. His reputation is now made, both here and in Europe. He is, as the papers have informed the public, engaged in writing the History of the Conquest of Mexico. England offers for some classes of books an infinitely better mart than our own country. Suppose that author has the legitimate desire of earning in some degree, at least in a pecuniary way, through this new work, the advantages of his reputation established by the first book. In doing this he would only do what every producer does, that is, the capital (in this case his reputation) gained by one product is invested in the second product to produce a greater gain, and so on with all successive productions. Suppose the author desired to offer the sale of his copyright in England, has he no right to do it? Yet he cannot do it; the English say, You will not grant copyright to our authors, so we will not to yours. Is this protecting our own citizen in a lawful and laudable pursuit, one that redounds to our honor and sheds lustre on our whole country? For such works as Ferdinand and Isabella add greatly to the respect paid by foreign nations to that of the author, and essentially promote esteem, good will, and easy intercourse among nations, while no citizen of the nation to which the author belongs, whose reputation transcends the barriers of states or languages, goes into foreign countries, in whatever pursuit, without enjoying a share of the good effects thus produced by an eminent mind. Is this the reward of gratitude? Is it judicious to prevent the value which he would have received for his copyright in England from flowing into our country?

The following is another striking instance. If a letter, under the signature of Mr. Catlin, published in the papers be correct—and there is no reason for suspecting its genuineness—this gentleman, who knows that a work such as he contemplates, with many costly engravings, finds a far readier sale in England, where there are more wealthy individuals, than with us, was obliged to go to that country in order to publish his work there. Otherwise he could not have obtained the

English copyright, without which he could not have made it worth his while to publish his work. Here, then, we have forced the production of much value out of our own country, because by denying international copyright we deny indirectly to our citizens that protection which every other producer enjoys, and which it is one of the primary objects and most sacred duties of all governments to bestow upon every one of their subjects.

Lastly, it is evident, in fact it is acknowledged by our republishers, that it is not worth their while to pay for literary home production in those branches in which England can produce as much or more than we can; because they find books with ready-made reputations in as large a number for republication as they wish, and their profit, of course, is greater upon those books than it would be upon others, for which they must pay copyright.[1] The consequence will be, that authors who can make it worth their while will go to England to publish their works in that country, while our own literature will remain in a languishing state. Some few highly distinguished minds will struggle now and then through these as through other difficulties; but an active, healthy, creative, and diffused national literature does not depend upon a few literary or scientific eminences alone, but upon a general state of mental activity, purity of taste, and mutual encouragement. It is so in the arts; it is so in

---

[1] Some American publishers have freely stated this fact to me. Mr. Washington Irving, in a letter to the editor of the Knickerbocker, January number, 1840, on the subject of the international copyright, says: "How much this (the American) growing literature may be retarded by the present state of our copyright law I had recently an instance in the cavalier treatment of a work of merit, written by an American, who had not yet established a commanding name in the literary market. I undertook, as a friend, to dispose of it for him, but found it impossible to get an offer from any of our principal publishers. They even declined to publish it at the author's cost, alleging that it was not worth their while to trouble themselves about native works of doubtful success while they could pick and choose among the successful works daily poured out by the British press, *for which they had nothing to pay for copyright.* This simple fact spoke volumes to me, as I trust it will do to all who peruse these lines." This rejected work is now one of the most popular.

all spheres. The flourishing state of any branch depends upon general activity, upon and out of which the lofty reputation of the peculiarly favored individual arises; and originality, without which no illustrious period of any species of human activity can be imagined, can never exist except where there is this diffused and united independent exertion. Raphael did not spring up single and alone; he is but the most prominent peak of a gradually rising mountain chain. Our own protection then, as well as justice towards others, demand the passage of a law, which, it ought once more to be observed, appears to many like a grant, because the law is passed, and the international acknowledgment of literary property does not exist without it. But so are many things of which men have been unjustly deprived, restored to them by specific law; yet that law does no more than do justice. The liberty of the press is as natural to man, after the invention of printing, as the liberty of speech; yet many nations are deprived of it, and many others enumerate it specifically in their fundamental laws, from which, indeed, not a few have actually inferred that it is a modern thing, made and granted by government. The Turks formerly levied an annual tribute of fine and healthy Christian boys, to be educated at Constantinople for the civil and military service of the Porte. This cruel practice has been discontinued, and cannot be renewed so long as the late hatti-sherif, protecting the property, person, and religion of all subjects to the Ottoman sceptre is a living law and not a dead letter. Will it be said on this account that the Christian father had no absolute right to his son; that he retains him in his family by way of grace, of a monopoly? The international copyright law in this respect stands upon the same ground upon which powers used to make particular treaties with piratical states, according to which the flags of the contracting powers and their property were mutually respected. Property ought to have been acknowledged without it; but since it was not, it was better to make a treaty and pass a law; yet this law grants no particular boon, it only grants what in justice ought never to have been denied. There are many things which unjustly have been denied for centuries, because he who denied had the power to do it; and it becomes necessary to establish the rightful state of things by positive law, yet that law does not on that account necessarily grant a favor.

Why should we deny to others that which we find many have established from a sense of justice alone ? The Germanic states, independent and sovereign, have established international copyright. Does the situation of the countries, their distance from one another, affect the principle of the question ? And do the steamships not bring us close to England ? Nor can it be objected that our position is peculiar in this respect, that England, publishing so much more and having so great a start of us in literature, our advantage in republishing is too great to give it up. Prussia grants free and unconditional reciprocal international copyright; yet every one knows that at Leipsic, in Saxony, a large majority of all German works are published, owing to the peculiar organization of the trade in that country. Prussia did not say: "I shall have the advantage, if I allow the republication of Saxon publications, although they may republish Prussian works," but she did justice as candor required it. Should we of all nations remain behind—we, who acknowledge no other master but Justice ? If we have denied justice so long, let us not assume this very ground for continuing longer, from fear of confessing our wrong. It is with nations as with private individuals; no nobler act than the manly acknowledgment of wrong by repairing it so soon as discovered. It is easy to be explained why this acknowledgment should not have been as rapid as many desired it. It is our happy lot that our laws must justly poise the interests of many. But it is high time that we should now willingly follow the voice of civilization, of national honor, of conscience, of justice, fairness, and righteousness.

SOUTH CAROLINA COLLEGE, March, 1840.

ANGLICAN AND GALLICAN LIBERTY.

NOTE.

THE following essay appeared originally in a newspaper published at Columbia, South Carolina, June 7, 1849, and is obviously suggested by recent events in France. Professor Mittermaier, of Heidelberg, caused the article to be translated and printed in the *Zeitschrift für ausländische Gesetzgebung*, xxi. Bd., 2 Hft. (1849). A few notes subsequently made by Dr. Lieber upon a copy partially prepared for republication are here subjoined to the essay as originally published. Reference should be made, in connection with this paper, to the author's remarks on the same subjects in his Civil Liberty.—G.

ANGLICAN AND GALLICAN LIBERTY.

IF the term Liberty, which always means unrestrainedness of action,[1] is applied to matters of civil society, it necessarily chiefly signifies protection of the free action of each member against the individual interference of any other member, and against society collectively, or public power.

Since, however, perfect freedom of action is impossible in any society, because every member claims the same freedom of action, and the society itself has its own important ends, as society collectively taken, it is obvious that civil liberty must always mean something relative. We designate, therefore, by civil liberty, the highest amount of that untrammelled and well-guaranteed action or absence of interference which is compatible with a social state and with the objects of a government established to obtain, by united energy, that

---

[1] Freedom, in its highest acceptation, means the faculty of willing, and the power of doing what has been willed, unrestrained by any extraneous influence —it means perfect self-determination. Absolute freedom, therefore, can be imagined only in conjunction with perfect power. The Almighty alone is perfectly free. To all other beings we can attribute freedom, but only in an approximate or relative sense. As to the synonyms freedom and liberty, the former is personal, individual, and relates to the whole being; the latter is granted, guaranteed, and, therefore, generally of a public character. The slave receives freedom, the captive liberty. We speak of the freedom of will, and of civil liberty. The same distinction is, I think, even traceable in the two expressions, freedom of speech and liberty of conscience; for freedom of conscience always exists, but when this freedom comes to be guaranteed by the laws of a country as a right to worship as the citizen chooses, we call it liberty of conscience, because it is an external guarantee of the internal freedom.

which is considered essential to each member, but cannot, or ought not, to be obtained by individual exertion. If, then, on the one hand, we never speak of liberty where we do not find a very high degree of well-secured independent action, it is natural on the other hand, that the idea of civil liberty varies with the different views which men may take, at the various stages of civilization, of that which is essential to man—in other words, of the essentials of humanity and the object and purpose of his terrestrial life. It follows that it is not inconsistent to speak of ancient liberty as contradistinguished to modern; for the ancients viewed man in his highest phase as citizen. The human being was, according to them, man, in the truest and noblest sense of the word, only as member of the state; but Christianity and modern civilization place the individual, with his individual responsibility, his personal claims, and his individual immortal soul as the highest object, and the state, law, and government, however vitally important to each person and to civilization, are for the moderns still but a means to obtain the yet higher objects of humanity.

It is equally clear, that for all practical purposes, we mean, by the word liberty, certain measures and institutions which secure the enjoyment of that which constitutes liberty in the opinion of men at any given period. Thus we find that Aristotle, when he speaks of liberty in his Politics (and not in his metaphysical works), means peculiar institutions. He goes farther: certain institutions serve him as tests whether liberty did or did not exist in the state which he had under contemplation; and in modern times we find that, while individuals might not easily agree upon the true import of the word liberty, if considered in a general sense, entire nations are agreed among themselves, with a remarkable degree of unanimity, upon the political principles and measures necessary for the establishment or perpetuation of liberty. There exist, of course, some differences. One civil society will consider a certain institution as a necessary element of substantial civil liberty, which may not appear in the same light to others;

perhaps because they have not yet arrived at the same degree of civil development; but, as it has been stated already, the unanimity of the Europeans and their descendants in America, upon this subject, is remarkable, and furnishes a very high degree of presumption that those institutions, established or struggled for, are in reality necessary for freemen.

These guarantees, the bulk of which, in modern times, is termed liberty, will be found to consist in the highest protection of the individual and of society, chiefly against public power, because it is necessarily from this power that the greatest danger threatens the citizen, or that the most serious infringement of untrammelled action is to be feared.

Civil liberty, then, consists, as the free modern nations understand it, according to the present standard of political civilization, in:

Protection of communion; liberty of the press; and what is called protection of the epistolary secret.

The right of the people, in the highest acceptation of the word, to adopt that government they think best; no extra governmental power, which yet deeply affects the government, except the sovereignty of the people; no divine right.

Full protection of person; no arrest except by law, and speedy trial after arrest; the *habeas corpus* principle, with a system of fair bailment.

Free choice of residence, and free locomotion; the right of emigration; free egress and ingress.

Full protection of every man's religion or worship; liberty of conscience.

Protection of free production and exchange, as the individual thinks best, and a high protection of property, acquired or acquiring; no taxation (which is a demand of part of property) without consent of the tax-payer (the owner of the property).

Submission to laws and lawful authority alone; the perfect right of resisting unlawful authority, or unlawful demands, though made by lawfully installed authority.

No submission to laws except those which the citizen has

contributed to form and pass, and an organism by which public opinion is gathered, settled, mutually modified, and passed into public will, that is law; and by which, on the other hand, public reason and carefully formed public opinion are secured against merely general and passionate opinion of society itself, or of the multitude.

Security against absolutism, that is, dictation by power, whether it be the dictation of one or of the unmitigated power of the multitude.

Popular control over public funds.

The right of peaceably meeting and discussing public matters; the right of petitioning.

A due share of the people in the administration of justice, and a guarantee against purely formal justice; trial by jury.

Certainty of a trial by common courts as established by law; no extraordinary courts or commissions.

A highly-protected penal trial, and especially a trial for treason, hedged in by the safest guarantees of the rights and safety of the individual against the prosecuting public power; defence of the accused by counsel.

The right of association for religious, moral, industrial, scientific, or political purposes.

Political equality or absence of privileges for the benefit of the privileged or privileged classes.

Protection of lawful opposition to the administration and protection of the minority against the majority.

Security that the people be well informed of their government; publicity of all administration of justice; of the finances and legislative debates, and of whatever may be public without injury to the public service.

Arming of the citizens.

Submission of the army to the law; no standing army, or a small one only, and votes of money supply for the same at short intervals; the mutiny-bill principle.

Security against the absorbing sway and domination of the central government; the communities, as towns, districts, etc., administering their own affairs.

Supremacy of the law over every one, crown or citizen; consequently no "power of dispensation."

Consequently, where enacted (written) constitutions exist, the authority of the proper courts to declare laws as conflicting with the fundamental law or constitution; security that the national sense ultimately prevail, and, consequently, dependence of the executive upon supplies—or, which amounts to the same thing—a government by parties; that is, men who stand pledged upon principles and measures of national magnitude, and not a government by the will of the executive, independent of the people; or by intrigues of individuals, or by administrations forming no homogeneous whole.

Responsibility of ministers; responsible officers, each of whom remains individually responsible for what he does, even though commanded to do so by rightful authority.

Security that the national sense control, whether directly or indirectly, yet truly, the power of making war and peace.

An independent judiciary and the independence of the law.

Protection of aliens and foreigners, no *droit d'Aubaine.*

Hence common law and the principle of the *precedent.* The last is at least acknowledged as indispensable to civil liberty by the English and Americans, but not yet on the European continent.

Generally the guarantee of all these rights in a constitution, that is fundamental law, superior to government. This is especially important; mere usage, as in England, does not stand instead of it.

In summing up these principles and institutions, it appears that they are guarantees of the security of individual property, of personal liberty, and individual humanity, of the security of society against the assaults or interference of public power, of the certainty with which public opinion shall become public will in an organic way, and of the protection of the minority. Many of these have originated, nearly all of them have first been developed, in England; but they are not confined to that country, nor have all of them, by any means, been developed in as high a degree in England as in America. In all countries where civil liberty is aimed at these principles have been adopted, more or less. We are justified, then, in saying, that when we speak in a practical sense of modern liberty, we mean these practical provisions and political contrivances. It is they that constitute the difference between this our modern, national, broad-cast liberty and the mediæval liberty, which was characterized by isolating political independence, by chartered freedom. "In the Middle Ages, governments chartered liberty; in our times, the people, or popular liberty, charters governments."[1]

It is obvious, that, where so many important principles are in action, one or the other may be more active than the

---

[1] Wherever modern civil liberty has been established, no matter in what country, we find the following contests; under whatever name, the principle is the same, for the contending agents are the same, namely, Power and Liberty:

The *lettre de cachet*, or general warrant—*i.e.*, arrest on the ground of its having been ordered by the executive. In England it began seriously under James I. The history of the general warrant is a most interesting thread in English history.

Proclamation, or pretence of power above law, and connected with this the dispensing power. Chief-Justice Fleming, when chief baron, in 1604, decided that the king had the undoubted right to levy whatever import tax he thought fit. This case is called "The Great Case of Impositions." Parliament had passed an impost of 2s. 6d. per cwt. upon currants, and James had added 7s. 6d. per cwt. Bates, a Levant merchant, went to law, and Fleming made a long, outrageous speech in favor of the king's power. Lord Campbell (Chief Justices of England, i. 234) says that if the British commerce had then been as important as now, there would have been an end to parliaments, for any government might have supported itself by import tariffs. He also expresses surprise that no historian mentions this solemn though outrageous decision. It is one of the many pieces of great good fortune in British history.

An army, independent of parliament and people. As now, in Prussia, the struggle *not* to let the army take the oath on the constitution. A standing army.

Taxation without a legislature, either entire or partially, and the ardent endeavor to rule without parliaments, which succeeded wherever the government was able to obtain a revenue without the consent of the legislature.

Extra courts of justice, commissions, etc.; arbitrary trials for high treason.

Extinction of the liberty of the press, and of discussion and opposition.

Whenever a new power grows despotic, these things are struggled for again. Thus the people first wrest them from the monarch; but where the popular power becomes despotic in turn, all these things are claimed again by the people, for instance, in France during the revolution, and by Cromwell in England. Wise men, therefore, leave these powers in the hands of no one.

rest, or may be developed even to the injury of some of the others; so that in the sphere of political freedom there arise, as in all spheres of unfettered action, different schools, to borrow a term from the province of philosophy and that of the arts. It is thus that we have in the province of political freedom an Anglican and Gallican school. The term Anglican has been adopted here for want of a better one. We stand in need of a term which designates characteristics peculiar to the Anglican race in Europe, here, and in other parts of the world. If they are not all peculiar to this race, they are at least characteristics, which form very prominent marks of its politics.

It is by no means the object here to show the gradual development of modern liberty and of the Anglican characteristics, their causes, and the circumstances under which they developed themselves, but rather to point out in what at this moment consist the striking features of these two political schools. With this view, it may be stated at once, that Anglican liberty distinguishes itself above all by a decided tendency to fortify individual independence, and by a feeling of self-reliance. The higher the being stands in the scale of nature, the more distinct is its individuality until it reaches in man its highest degree, and among men again we find the same principle prevailing. The higher, the more intellectual, and the more ethical the being is, the more prominent is also his own peculiar individuality. The same progress is observed in the scale of civil liberty. Individuality is almost annihilated in absolutism—whether this be of a monarchical or a democratic cast—while the highest degree of freedom (in the Anglican view of the subject) brings out the individuality of every one, and the individual activity of each, as best it seems to him, in its freest play. Independence in the highest degree, compatible with safety and broad national guarantees of liberty, is the great aim of Anglican liberty, and self-reliance is the chief source from which it draws its strength. At no period has the deplorable absorbing concentration of power, which characterizes the political systems of the continent of

Europe, during the seventeenth and eighteenth centuries, obtained a footing among the Anglican peoples, although it was several times strenuously attempted.   All the maxims of the common law, most dear to the people, and most frequently quoted with pride as distinguishing it favorably from the civil law, embody this manly feeling of individual independence.

Everywhere is liberty considered by the Anglican nations to consist, in a very high degree, in a proper limitation of public power.   Anglican liberty may be said to consist, essentially, in a proper restriction of government, on the one hand, and a proper amount of power on the other, sufficient to prevent mutual interference with this personal independence among the people themselves, so that order and a law-abiding spirit becomes another of its distinctive features.   No people of the past or present have ever made use of the right of association, even where it fully existed, equal to the vast, and at times gigantic application of this right, to great practical purposes of a social, as well as political, character among the English and Americans.   Public interference is odious to them.   Government with them, is not considered the educator, leader, or organizer of society.   On the contrary, in reading the many constitutions which this race has produced, and the object of which is to define the spheres of the various public powers, and to fix the rights of the individual, we almost fancy to read over all of them the motto, " Hands off."

This tendency of seeking liberty, above all, in untrammelled action, has produced among others the following great effects.

The untrammelled action or absence of public interference (which of course must in its nature be almost always of an executive character) has not been restricted to individuals, but as a matter of course, the spirit has extended to institutions and whole branches of power, so that time was allowed to them to grow, to develop themselves, and to acquire their own independent being ; consequently, we find the word law possesses a meaning very different from that which the corresponding words have even in their most comprehensive sense, with other nations; we find a common law rooted deeper in the people than any enacted law or constitution; we find a parliamentary law (no "*reglement*"); we find the indispensable principle of the precedent of greater power than minister or crown, even though it be worn by a Stuart, or a Henry the Eighth.

Secondly, a consequence of the principle of self-reliance is, that liberty is conceived far more essentially to consist in a great amount of important rights, than in a direct share in the government. The latter is sought after as a security and guarantee for the former.

Thirdly, Anglican liberty consists in or produces the utmost variety, as all untrammelled life and unfettered individual action necessarily does. Equality (if sought in aught else than in equality of freedom from interference, and if believed to consist in uniformity alone) is monotony, and becomes the opposite to life and action.

Fourthly, the Anglican race has mixed up subjects purely social with politics, far less than any other race, and it may be safely averred, has allowed itself to be less misled by phantoms, and adhered more to positive realities in the sphere of public life, than any other division of mankind.

Every great principle or movement of mankind has its own characteristic fanaticism, caricature, or mischievous extravagance. This applies to all movements, religious, social, or political, and Anglican individualism leads, if carried beyond its proper line, to selfish isolation and heartless egotism. The fanaticism of Anglican individualism is Utilitarianism as it has been taught by some. But it must not be forgotten that we speak here of civil liberty alone. No American, or Englishman, has ever maintained that we can do without patriotism, without devotion to the public, and it is a striking fact, admitted by all, that nowhere is shown so much public spirit, during successive periods, as by the Anglican people, although it might have been supposed that their individualism would have led to the opposite. The reason is, that Anglican liberty makes the people rely upon themselves, and not upon public power; they feel, therefore, that they ought to help each other and to depend upon their own united action, and not call for the aid of government at every step.

From a point of view, therefore, which belongs to Anglican liberty, the French device—Liberty, Equality, Fraternity, will appear in this light: liberty is aspired to by all; it is the breath of conscious man. If equality means absence of privilege, unfounded upon political equivalents, it is comprehended within the term of liberty; if it mean, however, social uniformity, it is rather the characteristic of absolutism, and not of liberty. For if liberty means unrestrainedness, it implies variety. Bating the monarch, there exists nowhere in Europe or America a degree of equality equal to that in all Eastern despotisms, or that which existed in the worst period of Athens, where democratic absolutism was consistently carried out, and where ultimately the principle of equality required the raising even of talent, fitness, and virtue, and the *lot* decided upon appointments, after the principle of equality had been established in a manner that Aristotle says, democratic liberty (or what we, according to modern terminology, would call democratic absolutism) consists in this, that every citizen is, in regular turn, ruling and ruled. Diversity is the law of all organic life, and despotism and freedom find their parallels in nature, in inorganic matter, and organic bodies. As to fraternity, it is the broad principle proclaimed by Christ; it is the divine principle of all social existence; it is one of the wells from which we shall draw, to irrigate our otherwise sterile life; it is like charity, like honesty, like forbearance, and to be true, ought to be infused into all our actions and measures, but it is no *right*, it is not *liberty;* nor does it necessarily indicate freedom. There is in some respects more political fraternity among Mohammedans than unfortunately among Christian people. Not that we put any slight value upon fraternity; Christians ought to have far more; but we merely mean to show that it is not necessarily connected with liberty. Fraternity exists often in the highest degree among the rudest tribes. That this device was adopted during the first French revolution was natural. It had a meaning in contradistinction to the utterly selfish and immoral state of things which had existed and which it was a settled purpose to destroy; but its resumption in the present third French revolution leads to misconceptions or rests on a confusion of ideas, which seems as great as if in America a political banner were raised with the motto, Liberty, Love of our Enemy, and Salvation, or Liberty, Production, and Daring. All these are excellent or sacred things, but used as distinctive political characteristics would either have no meaning or might easily be made to mean mischievous things.

Quite different from Anglican is Gallican liberty. The history of England distinguishes itself, from that of all the other nations of Europe, by nothing more than by the fact that, in that country alone, the nobility assimilated itself at a very remote period with the people. As early as in the year 1215 the noblemen did not wholly forget the people. The plodding husbandman was included in the Magna Charta; and repeatedly afterwards we find the knights siding with the citizens. The nobility of all other countries, however, were and remained selfish, oppressive, and rebellious barons. Louis the Eleventh and Richelieu greatly broke their power in France, and Louis the Fourteenth completed the work. No citizen-liberty having existed in that country, Louis found himself perfectly unlimited so soon as he had changed the baron into the servile courtier; and now a system of such absorbing centralization began that, when he died, he left France without institutions (if we take the term in the Anglican sense, meaning institutions with an independent and individual existence), as he left her without money and without morality in the leading classes. The absorbing centralization of power went on in all successive periods, and whatever changes of government have taken place, the process of centralization was only speeded on by it. The ball was ever rolling in that direction. The first French revolution, whatever benefit it otherwise produced, accelerated and perfected it much; Napoleon carried it still further, and a minister of the present provisional government, M. Ledru Rollin, lately declared, in one of his proclamations, that France should imitate the example of Paris, which he called the centre and representative of French virtue, intelligence, action, and patriotism.   How strange a similar declaration of an English minister, with reference to London, would sound in the ear of an Englishman, or of our President with reference to New York, or any state of ours ! [1]

Concentration of the most stringent kind existing, and it being neither disrelished nor suspected by the people, it is obvious that, coupled with the idea of liberty, in contradistinction to despotism, it can produce no other idea than equality— an equal change of "ruled and being ruler" ; and since equality, with this political meaning, is a practical impossibility with a nation so vast as the French, we have the further consequence that, practically speaking, equality means in France always the exclusive sway of a certain class.   He that seeks now to sway is the *Ouvrier*, and *Bourgeoisie* has actually become a name of shame or hatred, as the term *noblesse* had become in the first revolution.

Gallican liberty, then, is sought in the *government*, and, according to an Anglican point of view, it is looked for in a wrong place, where it cannot be found.   Necessary consequences of the Gallican view are, that the French look for

---

[1] The most remarkable fact in history, so far as centralization is concerned, is probably the last French revolution (of 1847).   A minority—but allow even a majority—of a single city changes a monarchy into a republic ; the republic is telegraphed into the provinces and France is a republic, without any attempt at resistance, any show of adhesion to the former government, any struggle.   If all France had been so thoroughly prepared for the republic (which we now know was not the case) that nothing more than the breathing of the name was necessary, the former government must long before have collapsed.   And if this was not the case, the so-called republic would not have been received so easily, were not the French accustomed to receive everything from Paris, fashions, pronunciations, and orders, and even now telegraphic despatches telling the prefect Monsieur so and so, that *Il n'y a plus de roi*, or some such thing.   Is not the people in a very abject state where such things can occur?   Is this not Russian ?   Does it not remind of the worst times of Rome ?   The French often, nay, almost universally, confound this submission to Paris with laudable patriotism.   But this only shows the more the absorbing centralization which exists in France.

the highest degree of political civilization in *organization*, that is, in the highest degree of interference by public power. The question whether this interference be despotism or liberty is decided solely by the fact *who* interferes, and for the benefit of which class the interference takes place, while according to Anglican views this interference would always be either absolutism or aristocracy, and the present dictatorship of the *ouvriers* would appear to us an uncompromising aristocracy of the *ouvriers*.

The universal acknowledgment of organization makes the Frenchmen look for every improvement at once to government.[1] Self-reliance does not exist in detail. While the

---

[1] All that I have said is exhibited in a very striking manner in a speech of Victor Hugo's, in July, 1850, on the new law of the press, a speech full of beauties and error, as almost all of his discourses are. I have added the chief passage having especial reference to the subject here treated.

" Messieurs, quoique les vérités fondamentales, qui sont la base de toute démocratie, et en particulier de la grande démocratie française aient reçu le 31 mai dernier une grave atteinte, comme l'avenir n'est jamais fermé, il est toujours temps de les rappeler à une assemblée législative. Ces vérités; selon moi, les voici :

" La souveraineté du peuple, le suffrage universel, la liberté de la presse, sont trois choses identiques, ou, pour mieux dire, c'est la même chose sous trois noms différens. A elles trois, elles constituent notre droit public tout entier : la première en est le principe, la seconde en est le mode, la troisième en est le verbe. La souveraineté du peuple, c'est la nation à l'état abstrait, c'est l'âme du pays ; elle se manifeste sous deux formes : d'une main, elle écrit, c'est la liberté de la presse ; de l'autre, elle vote, c'est le suffrage universel.

" Ces trois choses, ces trois faits, ces trois principes, liés d'une solidarité essentielle, faisant chacun leur fonction, la souveraineté du peuple vivifiant, le suffrage universel gouvernant, la presse éclairant, se confondent dans une étroite et indissoluble unité, et cette unité, c'est la République.

" Et voyez comme toutes les vérités se retrouvent et se rencontrent, parce qu'ayant le même point de départ, elles ont nécessairement le même point d'arrivée ! La souveraineté du peuple crée la liberté, le suffrage universel crée l'égalité, la presse, qui fait le jour dans les esprits, crée la fraternité.

" Partout où ces trois principes, souveraineté du peuple, suffrage universel, liberté de la presse, existent dans leur puissance et dans leur plénitude, la République existe, même sous le mot monarchie ; là où ces trois principes sont amoindris dans leur développement, opprimés dans leur action, méconnus dans leur solidarité, contestés dans leur majesté, il y a monarchie ou oligarchie, même sous le mot République.

" Et c'est alors, comme rien n'est plus dans l'ordre, qu'on peut voir ce phé-

British race seeks for one of the great applications of liberty in free trade, the French call for organization of labor, and M. Louis Blanc has proposed a plan, accordingly, which would appear to us as insufferable tyranny, and annihilation of individuality.   While we have seen, in the anti-corn-law league, a mighty private association coping with the most powerful interest that ever existed in a legislature, the British land-owner, and ultimately forcing government to fall into its own ranks, we do not find a solitary club in Paris pursuing one detailed practical measure, but all discuss the best *organization*, and to the minister of justice, and of worship, and others whom previous "organization" had already created, a minister of labor, and even one of progress has been added, if the papers have informed us correctly.   In Anglican liberty the movement not only begins with the people, but also the practical carrying out.   In France, liberty is expected to begin practically with government organization, and to descend to the people.

This is so true, that a large number of the French (we believe it to be a minority, but it is the active and loud minority) seem to have wholly discarded the idea that liberty is the main object to be striven for, and call for a *social* reorganization, and a very busy and wide-spread club at Paris has actually hoisted a banner on which the word Liberty is omitted, bearing the following device: Equality, Solidarity, Fraternity.   Here, then, we have the caricature of French liberty, as we have in ultra-utilitarianism that of Anglican freedom. Equality and solidarity are necessary elements of all politics. Without solidarity no nation could be a nation, no state a state.   Every one is obliged to bear with laws which he con-

---

nomene monstrueux d'un gouvernement renié par ses propres fonctionnaires. Or d'être renié à être trahi, il n'y a qu'un pas !

" Et c'est alors que les plus fermes cœurs se prennent à douter des révolutions, ces grands événements maladroits qui font sortir de l'ombre en même temps de si hautes idées et de si petits hommes !

" Des révolutions, que nous proclamons des bienfaits quand nous voyons leurs principes, mais qu'on peut, certes, appeler des catastrophes quand on voit leurs ministres !

" Je reviens, messieurs, à ce que je disais."

siders bad, or the consequences of a war which he condemns. It is the price we pay for living in a civil society; but if solidarity be elevated into a distinctive mark of a specific political or social system it is the death-blow to individualism, and a Spartan republic, destroying the family, must be the consequence. Here, too, is to be found the reason of the striking phenomenon, that at all periods the fanatics who have attempted the abolition of private property always made war against exclusive or individual marriage at the same time. Many communists have preached it, and many religious fanatics in the Middle Ages have attempted it.

The fact that Gallican liberty expects everything from *organization*, while Anglican liberty inclines to *development*, explains why we see in France so little improvement and expansion of institutions;[1] but when improvement is attempted, a total abolition of the preceding state of things—a beginning *ab ovo* —a re-discussion of the first elementary principles.

Anglican liberty produces variety, as was stated before, and demands absence of unnecessary restraint; Gallican liberty demands uniformity and even uniforms, so odious to Americans. A proclamation of the provisional government, dated April 30, actually begins with the words: "Considering that the principle of equality implies uniformity of costume for the

---

[1] Lamartine, in his famous speech on the law of election, May 23, 1850, speaks of this very thing. He calls it the French *impatience du mieux*. This is very true as far as it goes. I have spoken of impatience as a most dangerous element in politics, as in all else, in my Ethics; but Lamartine would have been more philosophical, would have gone farther back to the principle, as well as farther *on* to the practical results and mischiefs, had he seized upon the subject as I have done here. This impatience is both cause and effect of the fact that the French, whatever they may have been once, have been made, since the times of Richelieu and Louis XIV., an *un-institutional* people. Institutions—the idea of letting them grow, changing, amending, as the times suggest changes and amendments, and allowing them their own existence and expansion without continually having the executive and legislative finger on them—are founded upon and require the very principles of patience. In this the English have given the most illustrious example, although at times this principle, as all others, is carried to a degree of caricature, as illustrated in the lord chancellor's unsightly, untimely, and burlesque wig.

citizens called to the same functions," etc., prescribing a costume—coat, waistcoat, and pantaloons, to the members of the national assembly — that assembly which, according to the expression of the provisional government itself, is the highest representative of national sovereignty that has ever assembled, and into whose hands that same provisional government will lay down its power. Nothing can show more distinctly the difference between Anglican and Gallican liberty than that this order was possible.

In England and America, the principle of liberty dictates that all that can be done by private enterprise ought to be left to it, and that the people ought to enjoy the fruits of competition in the highest possible degree. In France, on the other hand, the provisional government made arrangements to buy up all the railways so soon as the king had been expelled.

All political changes, according to Anglican liberty, are intended more efficiently to protect the changes which society has worked for itself; according to Gallican liberty, the great changes are intended to be, not political, but social, organized by government: that is, according to Anglican liberty, forced upon society by the successful party, which, nevertheless, may be a very small minority, owing to the peculiar power which, in the great system of concentration, Paris exercises over France, and which all movable masses exercise over populous cities—an influence considered salutary according to Gallican views of liberty, and disastrous according to Anglican.

The object of this paper has been to show the difference of the two schools, and it would be foreign to the subject to dwell upon the generous enthusiasm which pervades at this moment large parts of the French people, and, coupled as it is with the fearful reminiscences of former days, has produced some very remarkable effects; but enthusiasm cannot last, and, if it could, it cannot become a substitute for individualism, an indispensable element of our ethical nature. Enthusiasm is a necessary element of all great actions of individuals as well as masses, but he who founds upon it plans of a permanent state of things, whether in worship or politics, deprives his system of durability. Nothing can insure principles against an early withering but institutions. No ruler, however popular or brilliant, no period, however glorious, and no enthusiasm, however generous, can produce lasting good if they do not lead first of all to the foundation of expansive institutions. Nations must neither depend upon popular rulers, nor trust their own enthusiasm. If they do, everything is frail and evanescent, and the continuity of the state, without which there is no law, order, strength, or greatness, is rendered impossible.

This remark leads us to the last observation we mean to make upon the difference of Anglican and Gallican liberty. The Anglican race is a decidedly institution-loving and institution-building race, as the Romans were, who built up the civil law. They are conservative as well as progressive, and believe that conservatism is as necessary an element as progression. The fanaticism of conservatism is a Chinese idolatry of the past and the old. The French, on the other hand, as they appear, at least in modern times, are philosophizing, often brilliant, organizers, and resemble in this more the Greeks, who built up no law but whose philosophers proposed invented governments. The fanaticism of this disposition is a restless re-beginning at every step and denial of the necessity of continuous progress.

It must have appeared to the reader that the writer of this paper is an advocate and lover·of the principles of Anglican liberty; that he believes the French are mistaking democratic absolutism for democratic liberty; that the whole continent will have to pass through long periods of ardent struggle before it can rid itself of the consequences of the unhallowed centralization, which absolute princes in their blindness mistook for power, and fastened upon the people; that he is a devoted friend to independence, and the liberty of the individual, which, in his opinion, need be as little connected with selfishness as Christianity is, although this religion, above all others, throws man upon his individual responsibility, thus raising him immeasurably; that, however dazzling the effects of democratic absolutism occasionally may be, it is still not freedom, which, like dew, nourishes every blade in its own individuality, and thus produces the great combined phenomenon of living nature; and that he would infinitely prefer a life in one of our loneliest log-houses to a barrack-residence of absolute equality, stifling his own individuality and that of every one of his fellow-citizens, however brilliant that barrack might be furnished.[1] But whether these are the views of the writer or not, is of little importance. The truth remains the same, that the difference pointed out by him exists between the two modes of liberty, that they differ widely, and that it behooves every sincere friend of liberty to reflect maturely on the subject and to come to clear results; especially on the European continent, where liberty is in a nascent state, and is of course exposed to be seriously injured in the tender age of her infancy; while a closer geographical connection with France often leads to the adoption of measures and views peculiar to that country, when no intrinsic reason for doing so exists. The European continental countries have had their periods of absorbing and life-destroying centralization. The principles of our liberty, therefore, are peculiarly necessary to the people of the European continent. Many of them seem to fall into the same unfortunate delusion of expecting everything from *organization* by public power.

---

[1] The writer is no admirer of the feudal ages. He has repeatedly given his views of that period, the essential principles of which with its graduated allegiance are wholly unfit for our nobler freedom. Whenever he has spoken of individual freedom in this paper, he has meant individual independence within *nationalized* societies, under the protection of broad, wide, organic, pervading civil liberty—the very opposite to mediæval spitefulness, arrogation, lawlessness, unnational and unsocial liberty.

NOTES ON FALLACIES

OF

AMERICAN PROTECTIONISTS.

NOTE.

FIFTH EDITION, PREPARED BY THE AUTHOR IN 1869, AND NOW PRINTED FROM HIS MANUSCRIPT.

A FEW notes originally jotted down for some lectures which I was in the habit of delivering yearly on the reasons given in favor of protection peculiar to America, in connection with a course of Political Economy, were ultimately published in three successive numbers of the New York Evening Post. Thence they were taken and published several times, always enlarged by myself, by the Free-Trade Society in New York and in the Boston Reform. I now offer the fifth edition, much enlarged, and for the first time with my copyright.

F. L.

390

NOTES ON FALLACIES

OF

AMERICAN PROTECTIONISTS.

No Right without its Duties.
No Duty without its Rights.

INTRODUCTION.

CERTAIN manifestations of elementary impulses and wants or reflexes of unfailing ideas and innermost urgencies are always found accompanying man in his normal condition, even though he be in the lowest stage, and they are never observed in the brute, though it be in the highest degree of development or have a degree of skill or cunning far greater than that of the surrounding human beings. The most brutish Indian by the side of the beaver—the pondering civil engineer of our forests—yet speaks, and the beaver does not.

There is, concerning these manifestations, no transition from the brute to man, such as undoubtedly exists, considering many other points and activities—transitions which induced many nations of antiquity to believe in the closest relationship between the animal and man, and modern philosophers to teach that "there is a difference in degree, indeed, between man and the brute creation, but not in kind." Animals build, gather and store, join, and, in a certain degree, show division of labor; but no brute animal ever speaks, if by speaking is meant the conscious combination of certain signs, especially oral signs, for the intentional conveyance of something thought or felt; no animal ever manifests a sense of the beautiful, not even a desire of mere ornamentation, without which the coarsest tatooing savage is never found. The most beautiful bird is nevertheless wholly unæsthetical, and no more conscious of its gorgeous plumage, which embellishes the deep foliage of the branch on which it rocks itself, than the water-lily is of its lovely white and gold resting on a stagnant pond.

We may call, then, these manifestations the Practical Characteristics of Humanity. There are seven or eight of these strictly dividing Practical Characteristics, and one of the most prominent among them is Exchange. Men always exchange, even the very lowest pappoose; and brute animals never exchange, not even the most sagacious beavers, nor the considerate elephant possessed of manifest imaginativeness, nor the most cultivated dog, while the relics of the prehistoric lake-dwellers prove that these beings produced and exchanged; for weapons and utensils are discovered of such materials as could only have been brought by exchange to the place where now found; and when human beings are physically prevented from exchange, such as the root-eating Indian whom Fremont found in the Western mountains, they are loathsomely low in their haggard brutality and in a far worse condition than the never-exchanging brute, so unnatural to man is not exchanging; while, on the other hand, exchange, which accompanies men through all stages, increases in extent, intensity, and importance the farther men advance in civilization and the higher culture. Money is a concomitant of exchange, for money is that most desired commodity which people are willing to take in exchange for their own commodity, although they do not want it for direct or personal use or consumption, because they know that they can soon re-exchange this money commodity whenever they stand in need of doing so. The consequence is that men are never met with, not even in the depth of Central Africa, without money commodity, while the brute animals, whether they live solitary, in clusters, or in herds, never have any money commodity, and, as a matter of course, still less tokens of money representing the money commodity.

Man, for these reasons, has been called an Exchanging Animal: it ought to have been *the* Exchanging Animal; he alone of all creatures exchanges, and his civilization is intimately bound up with this exchanging disposition and urgency.

The Practical Characteristics of Humanity must not be confounded with instincts. If we understand by instinct an unconscious impulse to that which has an important bearing toward the accomplishment of a thing or fact, of which the impelled being has no knowledge, in that case it must be observed that the lower the animal the more is its dependence upon strong and direct instincts; that man, therefore, depends less upon instincts than the brute animal; and that, having performed their offices, they become weaker as men advance, individually and socially, while each of the Practical Characteristics of Humanity increases in intensity and extensive importance as our species advances. Men always speak, but what a difference between the uncouth utterances of a savage and the developed language, oratory, and literature of a cultivated nation! Men always show a love of the beautiful, but what a difference between its manifestation in the hideous painting of our Indians and the production of a Phidias! Men always exchange, and the lowest barter of the South Sea Islanders is the beginning of the long chain which ends with the commerce which covers the globe.

Two laws, apparently cruel, but essentially beneficent, make exchange necessary from the beginning—laws which develop exchange more and more to world-wide comprehensiveness as men advance in the career of civilization. The first of these fundamental laws is that, as it seems, man is placed on this earth more helpless than any brute animal, and the cub of none is so frail and unprotected by nature as the child of man. The brute is always a *finding* or purely *gathering* animal. It finds what it wants, and the lower the animal is the nearer and readier round about it does it find all it needs. The oyster lives forever on one spot, in secluded self-sufficiency, more than a Diogenes of nature. It opens its valves, and nourishment floats into it. But man, not covered with fur, not provided with any claws, less swift than the running creatures, less agile than the monkey, with weaker and less direct instincts, has far more desires, wants, and urgencies than the *single-appetited* brute. Neither raiment nor shelter, nor even much food, is given him ready for use or consumption. He must skilfully catch his fish and prepare the deer-skin. He must cultivate his grain. Man is essentially not a mere gathering or finding, but a producing, being. No brute animal produces. But owing to different opportunities and requirements men produce of one kind of food or other needed things more than they want for themselves individually. The fisherman catches more fish than he wants for himself. He dries a portion of them and offers it for things which he desires, but has no opportunity of producing. Thus is man by nature a producing being, and production leads to exchange ; indeed, exchange is part of production. Production would very rarely answer were it restricted to the individual wants of the producer ; the lower men stand in the scale of civilization the more they produce for direct personal consumption, and the less they produce for exchange.

The first of the two laws, then, we will call the Law of Apparent Natural Destitution of Man, and the consequent Necessity of Production and Exchange.

The other law is the comprehensive Law of Inter-Dependence. The Economy of Civilization rests on this seemingly hard, but in truth kindly, law—that, with all the differences of races and climes, there is a pervading uniformity of the many human needs and likes, or of the Wants of Necessity, of Comfort, and of Culture, on the one hand ; and on the other hand there is the greatest diversity in the fitness of the earth and the conditions of men to satisfy these uniform appetitions. This is the civilizing Law of Inter-Dependence, and the farther men advance the more intense, as well as extensive, becomes its action, while the cravings of men multiply with every progress. First the members of the same family depend upon one another—not to forget that the organic law according to which the period of dependence of the children on the parents far outlasts the period of lactation, and does so with no other animal; then districts, then countries, and at last whole hemispheres, depend on one another,[1] until the most surprising exchange penetrates all regions.   Bordeaux dishes have long constituted the dinners of foreign merchants in Mexico, and Australian mutton has recently been consumed in London, at the opposite end of the earth.

For brevity's sake the second law may be called the Law of Uniform Wants, and diversified Fitness to satisfy them.   Barter, Division of Labor and Trades, Commerce, the greater portion of the Law and the whole Law of Nations, all Politics, and the Spread of Civilization are based on this Inter-Dependence.   Men were forced by it into the career of civilization, which they would never have entered had they been made for self-sufficient isolation—that grievously mistaken ideal of the anchorite of almost all ages and almost all wide-spread religions.

The uniformity of wants covers the whole globe; the spots fit to satisfy them can be easily marked on the map.   There are maps of the world which show the regions where, on the surface of the whole globe, rice or cotton is produced, or where iron or copper is found, where the grapevine flourishes or wheat is cultivated, and these regions are represented by spots far apart from one another, while those who desire these products or stand in need of them people the whole earth.

Iron, fish, fur, sugar, coal, cotton, rice, wool, silk, wheat, rubies, glass, guano, whalebone, fruits, tobacco, linen, indigo, cochineal, meat, wine, oil, drugs, copal, spices, salt, petroleum, hemp, timber, zinc, lead, cocoa, pepper, figs, tea, coffee, hides, copper, gold and silver, bamboo and pearls, and the thousand manufactured articles—all are desired by nearly all, but few spots only produce or manufacture them.   How can they be obtained?   In but one way—by Exchange; by the offer and exchange of one product for another product.   He who interferes with free exchange, and consequently with free consumption, interferes with the divine law of Inter-Dependence.   "Love"—not worry, still less hate—"one another."   All men stand in need the one of the other for food, health, comfort, and enjoyment; for safety, knowledge, skill; for justice and virtue, truth and religion; for the fine arts; for consecutive progress; and for the whole development of humanity; and as men advance, so does this mutual need increase and intensify.[2]

F. L.

New York, January, 1870.

---

[1] The Report from the United States of America to the International Statistical Congress at The Hague, Part I., 1869, by Samuel B. Ruggles, shows this magnificent fact in magnificent numbers.

[2] Pope in his Essay on Man says that God

"On mutual wants built mutual happiness."

PROTECTION FALLACIES.

FALLACY FIRST.—*Protection of American Capital against Cheap Foreign Capital.*

At the beginning of the American system, so called, the most favored argument of the protectionists was the American Capital argument. Capital, it was said, is dear in America— that is, high interest must be paid for it. In Europe capital is cheap, consequently the manufacturer can produce cheaper; therefore we must keep those cheaper products out of our country in order to give employment to our own American capital. It was the argument most popular in 1827, when I first landed in America. It was Daniel Webster's chief argument when he took the protectionist side. In 1824 he was still a champion of free trade, a statesmanlike and patriotic defender of unshackled exchange and free unstinted consumption.

The reply to this fallacy is, that no protection of capital is wanted, since no one assails capital or capitalists. The fact that higher interest is paid for capital here than elsewhere is sufficient proof that no privilege is required even were it justifiable, on the fundamental principles of politics, to grant a privilege of this kind. Whence is derived the right of granting prerogatives to the capitalists above other producers, workingmen and farmers, at a high cost to the latter? For, if products are kept out of the country because cheaper than they could be produced by American capital, in that case, of course, the consumers—that is, the people at large— of whom the straitened and needy are always the great majority, have to make up the sum given to the capitalist or to the monopolist. It was a simple matter of undue privilege, not in accordance with our public law, and inconsistent with the spirit of individual independence pervading our whole polity. It was adding privilege to fortune; for the fortunate possessors of capital received the additional privilege of having their high interest protected, and even increased at the cost of the consumers; while all this time the interest on capital in the new Southern States or Territories was almost as high as in the West Indies.

The name protectionist, claimed by those who openly proclaimed that their object was to favor American capital, was therefore, in this case, as it is in all others, chosen with peculiar lack of skill. Protectionist is a term which does not mean a person who desires to protect some thing or some one against some attack or injury, but it means exclusively a person who desires to favor one branch of business, or set of men, at the cost of the rest. The protectionist is always an assailant, and obstructionist would be the fitting name for him; but we must use the term as it is used in common language, though not without this protest, which the reader will presently find is not at all of a verbal interest alone.

When the argument founded on the protection of domestic capital was here in vogue, the favorite protectionist argument in England was that taxation in England was much higher than on the Continent, which, consequently, could produce cheaper than Great Britain; therefore, the cheaper productions of the Continent must be excluded from England—that is to say, from the English consumer, who is also made to bear higher taxation; at all events, the price of the articles he desires to consume must be raised, in order to benefit the comparatively small class of manufacturers, or actually to create a privileged class of manufacturers. This argument is now, when the heavy war debt is weighing on us, frequently used in our own country.

Fallacy Second.—*Hostility to Foreign Capital.*

If American capital was too dear for domestic manufacture in general, yet certain branches could be advantageously pursued in this country at that time, then, if it was not desired to grant prerogatives to the American capitalist, the question presented itself at once: Why do you not borrow foreign capital, which can be had at a much lower rate of interest than American?

It was answered, that it is bad to work with foreign capital; it makes the borrowing country dependent upon the lending country; the interest which must be paid for the capital is so much money leaving America, and therefore lost; so that working with borrowed capital is tantamount to impoverishing a country. General Jackson, in a message to Congress, the spirit of which was for moderate protection of certain branches by discriminating duties, within the limits of a revenue tariff, or a judicious tariff as it was then called, expressed himself strongly against working and producing with capital borrowed from the foreigner. When a conflagration had consumed the larger portion of Charleston, in 1838, and South Carolina allowed the city to borrow several millions, some would-be patriots blamed the corporation for preferring foreign capital, which could be had at five per cent. interest, to domestic capital, which could not be had at less than seven per cent. at the North, and eight, or even more than that, at the South.

Every merchant will admit that by far the greater portion of all the commerce in the world is necessarily carried on by borrowed or with anticipated capital. Every farmer in the West will testify that its magnificent agriculture begins with borrowed capital. Whether the lender of the capital is abroad or not makes no difference; it is a great benefit to a country if foreigners gladly lend their money. If loans can be made cheaper abroad than at home, it shows that capital finds better employment at home than abroad; that it is more productive in the country of the borrower. Was it or was it not a benefit to our country that foreigners readily bought our bonds, created by Congress to carry on our great war?

With reference to capital, as to every other economical question, there is no difference, in respect to honesty, expediency, or profit, between private and public financial questions; and the most comprehensive national transaction is only a vast multiplication of minor affairs, as, on the other hand, national wealth does not designate any wealth separate from private wealth, but simply the sum-total of all the wealth possessed by the individuals composing a nation, plus the productive property which the government may possess, and which is a mere minimum with all civilized nations. This latter is called public property, but also national property. The word national is taken in different meanings, but national wealth never means anything but the sum-total of all the wealth—of all the gardens, mills, roads, fields, manufactures, mines, houses, implements, goods, money, and what not—possessed by all the individuals. Whether the interest paid on borrowed capital goes out of the country is not the question, but whether we benefit by the loan. If we produce with the aid of the borrowed capital more than we have to pay for the borrowing, we profit by the transaction, just as, on the other hand, we are injured, economically speaking, by paying the interest of a public debt, although the interest remain in the country—that is to say, we must pay taxes to pay the interest all the same.

It used to be a fallacy, almost universally adopted in England, that there is no harm in a public debt so long as " England owed it to herself," and the taxation imposed to pay the interest of the public debt remained in the country. We, too, have had pamphlets with the title "A Public Debt a Public Blessing" scattered all over the land.

These are, philosophically speaking, simple absurdities. The word Owing requires two parties. No one can owe anything to himself in an economic sense. England as a unit may owe a sum of money to certain lenders, a part of whom, or all of whom, may be Englishmen, but they are individual lenders, not England, and must be paid the interest. For this taxation of all is necessary; and whether the English people at large benefit by the lenders being English individuals depends entirely on the conditions on which the loan has been obtained. If the English are annually taxed a million of sterling more because English people lent the money than they would have been had the loan been made abroad, in that case, of course, the English do not profit by "the interest remaining at home." In no case must "the English people" or England be confounded with a number of certain English people.

Borrowing from the foreigner does not make us dependent upon him. How should it? He cannot send us to jail. In international affairs it is the lender who is dependent upon the borrower, rather than *vice versa.* Spain and Mexico may serve as illustration. As to the presumed loss sustained by the interest of the borrowed capital being payable abroad, we shall say more farther on.

FALLACY THIRD.—*National Independence.*

Nearly as old, in our country, as the theoretical hostility to foreign capital is the argument founded on the desirable or necessary independence of this country. It was a favorite argument of John Quincy Adams. America—republican America—must not be dependent on Europe—monarchical Europe. What would become of us in time of war if we depended for every martial requisite on Europe? How shall we have cordage for our men-of-war if we do not protect Kentucky hemp?

The mixing up of monarchy and republicanism with iron, hemp, and cloth resembled much the demagogue's garniture of a poor argument misrepresenting Chinese seclusion and exclusion for civilized and dignified independence. We might as well speak of Baptist production or Presbyterian labor.

The whole economy of our species and of the globe on which it lives is founded upon mutual dependence—on that greatest of laws, that while all human beings have nearly the same desires, appetites, and wants, and while this agreement of wants becomes more manifest with the extension of civilization, the fitness of particular regions and the ability of particular people to satisfy the uniform cravings are infinitely varied, and become more exclusive with the progress of our kind. All men stand in need of iron, desire silk, are pleased with indigo blue; but very limited regions only produce them. This is the way the Creator enforces inter-dependence. This is the law which necessitates and more and more promotes international good-will, and leads to the great Commonwealth of Nations.

If protection, unfitly so called, enriches a few at the expense of the many, who must purchase the product they stand in need of by the labor of more days, it does not increase our national wealth, but diminishes it, and consequently diminishes our fitness to war with other nations if that becomes necessary. Even the ancients called money *nervus belli*, and Frederick II. of Prussia said, "He who can pay the last grenadier will remain master of the field." ("We must change this," said Joseph Bonaparte to me: "He who can pay the last newspaper," etc.)

If, then, in peace, we impoverish our country, we ill prepare it for the time of war. With plenty of wealth and brave sons to defend our country on land and sea, we need not feel nervous about the hemp for cordage. Besides, there is no nation whose soil produces all the various articles for war.

The martyr-patriot and greatest statesman of the Netherlands, Cornelius De Witt, showed in his paper, which bears, in the English translation, the title The True Interest and Political Maxims of the Republic of Holland, in the middle of the seventeenth century, that the Netherlanders, though producing a little wheat, ate the whitest bread in all Europe, and, though not producing a sheaf of hemp, a single plank, or any iron, had the best fleet which then ruled the sea, because Holland had wealth to pay for those commodities, and it possessed this wealth because its trade and all exchange was left unfettered, unimpeded, unlegislated upon, and by this free trade the Netherlands became both the most peopled and the richest country on earth, so that loans could be effected there for lower interest than anywhere else.

De Witt and his brother were murdered in 1672, and as early as 1621 Sir Edward Coke said in Parliament, taught by the prosperity of Holland on the one hand, and by the monopolies of James I. on the other hand: "Freedom of trade is the life of trade, and all monopolies and restrictions of trade do overthrow trade."

Although De Witt does not say so, I felt, when reading this forerunner of the whole free-trade literature, that a time will come when the bills of rights of advanced nations will contain a provision that no attack on free production, free exchange, and free consumption, under the name of protection, shall be permitted, for the reason that, men having been created exchanging beings, production and exchange are natural, primordial, indefeasible rights, because original and inherent duties.

Peace is the normal state, war the exception. Peace is the natural state, not war, Hobbes to the contrary notwithstanding; and it is not reasonable to sacrifice the entire normal state to the exceptional.

So far the martial independence only to be obtained by prohibition has been considered, but the protectionists extend this argument and maintain that national independence in general requires isolation; they call it "depending upon the foreigner," if products are bought of him. If, it is argued, we buy sugar of Cuba, we depend on Cuba. In what this dependence consists is not possible for us to discover. Does the buyer depend upon the seller in our common domestic intercourse? Do I depend upon my bookseller because I buy my books of him, any more than he depends upon me for buying his books? Buying and selling are two words differing in meaning for common intercourse; but there is no intrinsic difference between the two in a scientific sense. If A buys grain of B for ten thousand dollars, then B likewise buys ten thousand dollars of A for grain. All trade consists in exchange, in which both parties must be supposed to gain. If both did not gain, the trade could not be carried on for any length of time. All trade whatsoever, domestic or foreign, resolves itself into barter—goods for goods, products for products. If a cargo of coffee is bought of the foreigner for money, how is the money obtained if not by the sale of some product? When an American buys goods in Europe he pays for them in drafts on the holder of the money, which has been obtained by the sale in Europe of American produce, and which authority to draw he has purchased at home by the sale of goods which he had obtained by a similar process of exchange, and so on without end. Let a man not informed of the elements and details of these subjects follow step by step the history—that is to say, the origin, constant change, and end—of a common bill of exchange, and he will find that this simple study imparts to him much substantial information. No one, neither individual nor nation, can enter the market as purchaser without first having produced that with which he means to purchase, and the seller of the goods or products desired by the buyer is as dependent, speaking with scrupulous exactness, on the latter as the latter is on the former.

It is not flattering to the power of apprehension and analyzing capacity of the protectionists to suppose that when they urge the necessary independence upon the foreigner, they have an idea as though the foreigner might at any time shut up his shop and decline selling us his commodities ; it is not flattering, yet this idea is sometimes in the protectionist minds. What else can the independence on the foreigner mean ? But is the foreigner, the so-called seller, not as dependent upon us, the so-called buyer, as we are upon him? We are quite as much sellers to him as he is to us. All transactions are computed and expressed in money, but there is very little money in the world compared with the amount of commercial transactions ; and if really coin is sent to purchase foreign goods, that coin must first have been purchased by some commodity or product in foreign trade, as much so as in domestic transactions, and the so-called buyer is no more dependent on the so-called seller in international transactions than in domestic acts of exchange ; or, which expresses it more truly, in domestic as well as in international transactions of exchange both exchangers are dependent on one another in precisely the same degree, and the words domestic and foreign have very little meaning in economy, as they have none whatever in nature.

FALLACY FOURTH.—*Protection of American Republican Labor against European Pauper Labor.*

The argument that American capital must be protected against cheaper European capital did not long retain its hold on the Americans, if indeed it ever was popular. It came speedily, therefore, to be supplanted by what, for brevity's sake, we will call the Pauper Labor argument. This it is: Wages in Europe are miserably low—hardly sufficient to furnish sustenance to the workmen, whose labor, therefore, is called pauper labor. Now, the products of this ill-requited labor can be furnished for a far lower price than American products, because we pay higher wages to our workmen, and ought to do so, since our workman is a citizen of a republic, who ought to live in a fair degree of independence, and to be able to clothe and educate his children well; therefore let us prevent the competition of European pauper labor with our American labor by levying a high duty on the products of the former, or let us exclude them altogether. This argument became very popular, and is to this day one of the staple arguments of our protectionists. It was the favorite argument of the late benevolent and distinguished Dr. Channing. Daniel Webster, and all who have acted with him, left the American capital argument and adopted the anti-pauper labor idea. Nevertheless, it is mere fallacy; and possibly no other argument of our protectionists is so fallacious as this, their most popular because most insinuating argument. The errors and inconsistencies involved in it are so numerous that little more can be done here than barely to enumerate them.

All that is meant by American labor in this case is the manufacturing and mining labor, and that of the artisans— the workingmen, as they are styled. But is the farmer not a workingman? There are far more laborers engaged in farming than in manufacturing and handicrafts—I believe twice as many. All these citizens of our republic are left unprotected against the protected workmen; for the farmer has to pay a higher price—that is to say, he must work several days more—for what he stands in need of than he would had not our legislature privileged a particular class called workingmen.   The farmer cannot spend the product of so many days' labor, of which he is robbed for the supposed benefit of another class, on better schooling or more respectable dresses for his children, more comforts for his wife, more books for himself, or the improvement of his farm; and those to whom he would have paid that of which he is despoiled by the protectionist are arbitrarily deprived of that which would have come to them.   If left unprotected, the farmer might have bought an excellent English knife for the surplus of three days' labor, but must now, when protected, work five days to get a worse knife; in this case he is robbed of more than the value of several days' labor, and he of whom he would have bought something for these two or three days' labor, say sugar or a tract on drainage, is likewise despoiled; in short, mankind at large have been made poorer to the amount of two days' labor without any counterbalancing enjoyment or advance of civilization—a wilful loss and retarding, *pro tanto*, of progress or curtailment of the enjoyment of life.

If by aristocracy is meant a class privileged above and to the injury of others, then our anti-pauper labor theories create an aristocracy of the workmen; and if the American people consider anything odious, it is an aristocracy—a workman-aristocracy as much as any other.   Why should an aristocracy of workmen be better than an aristocracy of land-holders?   The modern protectionist aristocracies which the world has seen are these: first the English land-owners; then the American manufacturer; the French would-be patriotic exclusionist of everything and everybody not French; and lastly the American workingmen's aristocracy, joined by the miners producing coal and iron at an exorbitant rate.

But why do the manufacturers and mechanics lay exclusive claim to the title of workmen here and in Europe?   Not only is the farmer a workman, but the physician, the lawyer, the schoolmaster, the poor minister, all are hard-working men. I am sure that I have worked many more hours in my long life than any carpenter or printer. All men work at the same time with their hands and brains, and the difference lies only in the proportion of the one to the other. Now, will it be claimed that they are workmen only with whom the brains are a minimum in the performance of their work, and that *these* workmen shall form an aristocracy? Does the tailor cease to be a workman the moment he becomes a foreman?

Suppose, however, for argument's sake, that the products of the so-called pauper labor ought to be kept from competing with the products of our highly-paid labor, how is it that you allow the importation of the European pauper labor itself to compete with the American labor? Or has any protectionist ever waged war against immigration? Is there any one who would dare to do so? If not, then there is a great inconsistency in allowing the present vast immigration of our own race, which indeed is the modern and peaceful Migration of Nations on the one hand, and the exclusion of products of foreign, cheaper labor on the other hand. Mr. Frederic Kapp, in his recently-published work, Immigration and the Commissioners of Emigration in New York (New York, 1870), says that in New York alone, in the eleven years ending in 1860, three million immigrants arrived, and that from 1851 to 1860 the number of 179,721 mechanics arrived. This is importation of labor itself, and why is free trade allowed regarding "pauper labor" itself, but protection insisted upon concerning the products of pauper labor?

This argument, consistently carried out, would lead us logically to the times when there existed in England wide-spread hostility to machinery, but especially agricultural machinery, and would make us hostile to all labor saving, while in fact all civilized people are steadily engaged in finding out new processes of saving labor, therefore cheapening labor. The whole large edition of the Weekly Tribune, of New York, is most ingeniously folded and put in wrappers by a swift machine attended by a few young persons. How many hands were required to fold some 150,000 sheets before this machine came to interfere with these workingmen?

The whole name of pauper labor is wrong. Paupers are people who receive alms. The European workman produces, and receives wages; and if he produces certain articles cheaper, his labor, in point of political economy, is like the climate, which also produces certain commodities cheaper in certain countries. We have no right to deprive our fellow-citizens of the benefit of either. These arguments never fail to remind us of Bastiat's exquisite petition of the Parisian lamp-manufacturers to the chamber of deputies for the exclusion of sunlight, because, by furnishing light free, the sun very grievously interferes with the necessity of lamps, and consequently with the manufacture of them.

Even if the farming and fishing population were not far greater than that of the manufacturers and artisans, no one, and especially not our government, has a right to sacrifice the one to the other. Doing it on account of the imagined welfare of some one is the repetition of the argument in favor of slavery. The large laboring population, it was said, is deprived of its rights, even of the right of personality, for the general welfare, which *general* welfare was the presumed welfare of a few.

Our argument, however, does not stop here. Regarding production men are divided indeed; some produce by skill, some by accumulated values, called *capital*, some in this way, some in another. Regarding consumption, however, men are one undivided number. All men consume, and all consume the same staple articles. All must eat, all must dress, all must dwell in houses. The workman, therefore, in whose supposed favor the price of labor was raised, has, as consumer, to pay higher prices in the market for his clothing, for his books, for his recreations, and suffers along with the rest from the advanced prices.

The fallacy of protecting American labor is closely connected with that extravagant idea of "organizing labor," so dear to communists. Organizing labor! Why not organize agriculture? Why not organize vegetation? But more of this farther on; and I conclude my argument against the protection of American labor with a quotation from a passage in a speech of Daniel Webster's, delivered early in 1824, against Mr. Clay, then speaker. Mr. Webster said:

"Mr. Speaker seems to me to argue the question as if all domestic industry were confined to the production of manufactured articles—as if the employment of our own capital and our own labor in the occupations of commerce and navigation were not as emphatically domestic industry as any other occupation. Some other gentlemen in the course of the debate have spoken of the price paid for every foreign manufactured article as so much given for the encouragement of foreign labor, to the prejudice of our own. But is not every such article the product of our own labor as truly as if we had manufactured it ourselves? Our labor has earned it, and paid the price for it. It is so much added to our national wealth.

"There is no foundation for the distinction which attributes to certain employments the peculiar appellation of American industry; and it is, in my judgment, extremely unwise to attempt any such discriminations."

Summing up the argument against the popular Protection of American Labor, we have this statement:

1. Whence does the protectionist derive the right to interfere with the primitive right of free man to buy where he thinks best? To meddle with free consumption?

2. A workingmen's aristocracy would be as bad as any other aristocracy.

3. Interfering with free consumption and free exchange is presumptuous playing at Providence, and leads, like all unnatural things, to mischief.

4. The "protected" workingman suffers with the rest as consumer.

5. If the products of pauper labor are excluded, why is the importation of pauper labor itself allowed?

6. Protected labor—that is, artificially high labor—drives whole branches of industry out of the country, as at present no one comes to the United States to buy machinery and

engines, while formerly New York was a market for steam-engines.

7. If pauper labor, so called, produces cheaper, this cheapness is a fact of which we make use as we do of the warmer sunshine in the tropics, and we impoverish *pro tanto* the American citizens all round if we prevent them from buying cheap things.

8. Artificially excluding products needed by us surely leads in most cases to a degeneracy of our corresponding products. American steam-engines are no longer bought by the West India planter, because they have become much dearer and much inferior to English engines.

FALLACY FIFTH.—*That "Free Trade is good in Theory, but not in Practice; and if others would adopt it, we would."*

To judge by the frequent use of the following arguments, the one must be still very popular, the other must have been so.

Your free trade, we are constantly told, is true or excellent "in the abstract," or "in principle," but it does not answer in practice.

Our reply is: In political economy we know nothing in the abstract. That which is not true in practice is not true at all. The theory is necessarily false that is not verified in practice, or derived from reality and actuality. In one word, nothing can be true in theory without being true in practice. Can in medicine anything be healing in theory, but killing in practice? A theory founded on insufficient data, or only half-true premises, may be stated with that logical symmetry of words which, unfortunately, very many persons, in all spheres of thought, mistake for truths, but the theory is not true on that account. It were high time mankind had altogether done with odious Truth in theory, but Error in practice. It is anything but pleasant to be obliged to dwell on this subject, but it is necessary, and very necessary, nevertheless. Thousands of well-meaning people do not feel ashamed of using this seeming argument; consequently, it must be exposed—a task in which all lovers of truth, whether it be religious, scientific, political, or æsthetical, ought to unite.

The other argument was, that free trade would be very good if England would adopt it; but as long as England does not adopt it, we cannot. To this it is only necessary to reply that England has adopted free trade, and we have not adopted corresponding measures. On the contrary, we have rushed forward, we might almost say, with increasing frenzy in the career of isolating the United States and extending a kind of economical slavery over the whole land. But if England were plundering us a little, ought we, therefore, to authorize privileged classes here to plunder us more? What does the whole argument amount to, if not to this: Certain foreigners put a high duty on certain products of ours, and injure us so far; therefore let us injure ourselves still more by not allowing our people to buy certain articles they stand in need of of that foreigner. Whatever is written about offering the cheek, it is nowhere commanded that if a man receives a slap on one cheek, he shall forthwith himself slap the other cheek.

In addition, it may be said, and it ought never to be lost sight of, that free trade is no theory, no system, no conglomerate of whims and artificialities. By free trade nothing is understood but unclogged exchange. Free breathing is no theory, but a necessity. Man, born more destitute than animals, especially in proportion to his more numerous wants, and not having been made to live as a mere *finding animal*, is ordained to produce and to exchange. His Maker wants him thus; his very nature demands it. To let men have their exchanging course, especially when they have coalesced into political bodies, is called free trade. Protection, on the other hand, is a conglomerate of fancies, artificialities, theories, presumptions, miscalculations, and egotistic contrivances, some well meant, but mostly born in the brains and purses of men, not derived from the nature of men and the essential characteristics of things.

The enumeration of these many fallacies proves this. I am by no means sure that it would not have been better to call what we discuss Free Consumption instead of Free Trade, for trade is but a means to obtain consumption, the end and object of all production and exchange.

Since the foregoing was written, a party, if thus it can be called, has arisen in England, called by the formidable name of Reciprocitarians—workingmen who proclaim hostility to free trade with all foreigners who have not adopted free trade toward Great Britain. Our arguments are against all " Reciprocitarians ;" we have, therefore, nothing to add here.

FALLACY SIXTH.—*" All Countries have begun with Protection."*

" England, Germany, and France—all have begun with protection ; so must we."

Ought we, then, indeed, to begin with protection on that account? All the countries belonging to our family of nations, except ourselves, have had their Middle Ages, their Feudal System ; ought we to pass through the same because they have? All countries (except, indeed, England, which prevented internal " Evil Tolls" by her great charter of 1215) have commenced with provincial and city tolls, with intersection and interruption of domestic production and domestic trade of all sorts. Shall we, on that account, go through the period of internal " Evil Tolls," despite our Constitution, which, in Article 1, Section 9, most fortunately prohibits them, although it does not use the term of biblical grandeur " Evil Tolls" ? The essential law of progress is this—that one generation accepts the experience and results of the struggles of the preceding generations without sharing the errors which produced them. We justly accept the Greeks as our masters in sculpture without adopting the religion which, by imagining the gods in human form, led to that unrivalled sculpture.

What is actually observable as a uniform process, in the history of human progress, is a steady and universal removal of barriers and expansion of free intercourse between men. This is constant and uniform. We live now in the period in which internal or domestic free trade at least has conquered, and has at length been established, in all the great and lead-

ing countries—a period characterized, moreover, by the abolition of the many guilds and corporations which used to ham-
per production, and of prescribed maximum and minimum
prices. The protectionist wants, indeed, to force prices, believing that, by forced prices, he can increase value, and, along
with it, wealth; but the arbitrary prescription of prices, by
authority at least, is abandoned.[1]

And so is prescribed and enforced production, such as existed formerly in some countries, regarding certain agricultural
products, the government prohibiting the culture of some
products unless a certain amount of grain, say wheat, were
cultivated.

Domestic free trade and domestic free production, and consequently domestic free consumption, are obtained at any rate,
or are in the process of attainment everywhere, where there
is life and progress among men. The Californian may eat
New York salt, and Salt Lake lies "unprotected" between
San Francisco and Syracuse, N. Y. It took all the time since
the downfall of the Roman empire to the Revolutionary
period. We have free trade in our continental republic, at all
events; but even this some protectionists disrelish. And they
are right, if consistency of argument, from whatever error we
may start, makes right.

---

[1] The absurd tyranny of prescribing prices which was universal in the Middle
Ages, and which I have known in some instances in American towns, has been
illustrated in a recent work of great interest: Memorials of London and London Life in the Thirteenth, Fourteenth, and Fifteenth Centuries. Being a series
of Extracts, Local, Social, and Political, from the early Archives of the City of
London, A.D. 1276–1419. Selected, translated, and edited by Henry Thomas
Riley, M.A. Published by order of the Corporation of London, under the superintendence of the Library Committee. London: Longman, 1868.

In 1363 a proclamation, in Norman French, by the Mayor, prescribed "That
the best goose shall be sold for 6d.; the best sucking pig for 8d.; the best capon,
6d.; a hen, 4d.; the best rabbit, 4d.; a teal, 2½d.; a river mallard, 5d.; four
larks, 1d.; a *snyte* (snipe), 1½d.; a *woodcock*, 3d.; a *perdriche*, 5d.; a *fesaunt*,
2d.; a *spaude* (shoulder) of roast mutton, 2½d.; a *brusket* of roast mutton, 2½d.;
a capon baked in a pastry, 7d.; a roast goose, 7d.; the best carcass of mutton,
2s.; the best *loigne* of beef, 5d.; the best *pestelle* (leg) of pork, 3d.; the best
loigne of pork, 3d."

Our race is now going to enter the period of International Free Trade—that is, of International Peace and Good-Will. Indeed, it has already begun. The central portion of Europe, far the most peopled portion of the globe, is rapidly approaching this most desirable end, the close of short-sighted international selfishness and unneighborly ill-will. Free Trade is nothing else than the application of the gospel of good-will and love to protection and exchange, or to the material intercourse of distant societies which always precedes their intellectual intercourse.

Historically, however, it may be said that political societies do not begin with prohibition or protection. Men are exchanging creatures, and they begin *even* in childhood with exchanging. Interference with exchange comes in later, first merely to obtain money, just as in some countries people must pay a tax for marrying, or for entering as well as going out of the country. At a comparatively very late period vanity, ignorance, and greed combined to produce the mock-providential system of protection, which, as we have said already, vanishes again with the real progress of nations. Simplicity is the genuine stamp of real advancement in all things and thoughts; artificiality, the sure characteristic of ignorance, vanity, or barbarity.

If the protectionists were correct in their argument, it would logically follow that the addition of California and the whole Pacific Slope to our country was a calamity for the East, and free exportation of New England goods to what is usually called the West is, according to protectionist doctrine, a misfortune for the West—ay, and voices have been heard calling it such !

I am, indeed, no extensionist, simple and pure. Far from it. Mere bodily expansion is no more healthy to a body politic than to a fleshy body; and the wise emperor Adrian voluntarily contracted the limits of the Roman empire to make it stronger. But there are extensions both natural and wholesome. If Nova Scotia be added to our commonwealth—not by war, not by beggarly purchase, not by men-selling treaty, but by the manly action of the people, and by the equally manly resignation of the British government—it will be one of the most brilliant and most characteristic facts of modern, and indeed of all, history. Be this, however, as it may, we maintain that our protectionists, pressing heavily on our people by their coal tariff, quite as heavily as the English protectionists did by their corn laws, and consequent dear bread, on their people, must, might and main, object to the annexation of Nova Scotia, or to the abolition of the high coal duty now excluding Nova Scotia coal, after that colony should be annexed. Either they are wrong in their present tariff, or they would be inconsistent in not trying to retain the " Evil Toll" on coal after Nova Scotia should have become an American State, or two or three States. Else, where is the legerdemain work which makes a thing ruinous to us when Nova Scotia is called a colony of Great Britain, and painted yellow on my map, but makes it natural and right so soon as Nova Scotia is called a State of the American republic, and painted blue on my map?

Similar remarks apply to the discomfort which has prevailed among the gardening farmers near New York, during this spring and summer (1869), owing to the increased facility of bringing market supplies from distant portions of our country since the cessation of the Rebellion. Pears have actually been left ungathered. The New York market received them first from Florida; then from Georgia and South Carolina, from Virginia and Maryland, until the Jersey peaches came in, and the Long Island farmer found himself fairly forestalled. However sincerely we may sympathize with him, as with every honest and hard-working man whom unfavorable combinations despoil of labor's fair reward, we have no right to interfere with the facilitated intercommunication, and, had we such a right, would only make matters worse. Yet the protectionists are not consistent if they do not try to cut off the supply of our markets coming from a greater distance than a number of miles arbitrarily to be settled by them. Under the administration of Walpole, the gardeners around London indulged in

serious riots against parliament because it had passed acts facil-
itating the laying out of roads from distant points of the kingdom to London—roads which would bring vegetables to the
capital, and thus cheapen the commodity.   The protectionist
and his narrow policy can never be more truly symbolized
than by the London gardeners under Walpole.

Let one remark be added not unconnected with what has
been said—a very simple remark, but the truth of which seems
rarely to be considered by the protectionists: Do what we
may, occasional distresses cannot be avoided in this world of
toil and suffering; and one of the most unmanly mistakes which
men can commit is the constant resort to government for the
redress of all evils and inconveniences.   It produces moral,
legal, and material mischief.   That comprehensive and unfortunate phenomenon, Fashion, in the modern sense, is well
known by the economist as the occasional mischief-maker,
bringing hardships, suffering, hunger, and death to many who
have never risen above want, by a change in trimmings.   Yet
the mischief would be far greater were government to attempt—it never could be more than an attempt—to regulate
Fashion, or, as the communists would probably call it, to
organize Fashion.   Administrations are frequently made answerable for bad harvests.   Mr. Van Buren, it is generally
believed, lost his second election on account of the great
commercial distress at the time, and ancient German emperors
were obliged to do penance, barefooted and in the shirt, at the
cathedral door, because some plague was devastating the empire.   One of the stages of liberty last obtained is that of
collected self-reliance and of dispensing with constant government assistance.

FALLACY SEVENTH.—*" Is not the Great Object of all Government that of Protection ?"*

John Quincy Adams, sagacious though he was, asked in the
house of representatives, to which he had returned from the
White House, why any one opposed protection, and whether
the end and object of all government was not the protection

of all interests and persons. This argument is often repeated—a fact which imposes on us the obligation to enumerate it among the Fallacies, which otherwise would, doubtless,
not have been the case.

One of the main objects for which men live in political
societies is the protection of their persons, property, and
interests; but it is the protection of all, not the favoring of
some at the cost of the rest. There may be on record no
more striking illustration of the mischief resulting from using
an ambiguous word for what the logicians call the middle
term of a syllogism than this case. Protection is taken in
two entirely different meanings, even by so keen an intellect
as Mr. Adams was. Let everything good, essential, and right
be protected; above all, let every natural Right and Characteristic of Humanity be assiduously protected; let Production, Exchange, Consumption, Intercommunion be jealously
guarded; but do not call monopoly, or the favoring of some,
by the name of protection; do not give the name of protection to interests artificially created by legislation, and then
reason on this arbitrary term as though you had to defend
yourself against enemies. This argument is not even strong
enough for a postprandial speech or a newspaper turn.

FALLACY EIGHTH.—*" Look at the Lowells and the Busy Manufacturing Places."*

Strangely constructed, indeed, must be the man who can
sail down the Meuse, or fly along through the Elberfeld district, and along the valley of the Wupper, without being filled
with wonder at the human industry thus visibly, loudly, and
busily displayed before him. But the question always remains,
Is there poverty in the background? how many that are not
seen are forced to contribute to this activity? Or if all is done
in a fair and just way, such industry is a great good; but not
so if, by unjust laws, the farming community, and indeed the
population at large, the manufacturing people included, are
obliged to pay tribute to those establishments in the form of
enhanced prices. The manufacturing towns are seen, the

steam-driven spindles are heard, but no one hears or sees each time when a man, be he poor or rich, pays fifty per cent. more besides its value for an article he stands in need of.

Is there a nobler sight than a great and healthy forest? But the artificial forests which the English despots raised on the fields of civilization, doubtless, looked as fine as our Western groves, and the manly *Magna Charta* forced the king to disinforest these forests, beautiful though they were to behold.

There is no measure of extensive effort, however calamitous, that does not make the great fortune of some. Many bankers, most all of the contractors, became rich in the times of Napoleon, but his wars were certainly not productive of wealth. He himself pointed at the many millions of francs which he caused to flow into France from the conquered countries, when people complained of the impoverishing effects of his wars. As well might the Roman emperors have pointed at the enormous fortunes of some senators, to show that the wars of the empire were not pauperizing all Italy and the whole of the known world to an almost incredible extent.

Those vases filled with gold and carried toilsomely by rows of captives, in front of triumphal processions entering Rome, were no symbol of increasing wealth, but only of transfer of gold and of swelling riches of some, ruinous to the city and her dominion. How poor did Rome and Italy become with all that influx of gold!

The fact is, accumulated riches, busy towns, and astounding amounts of business done in single places, prove nothing of themselves. Real wealth is always greatly diffused and not easily visible. Great riches generally indicate wide-spread poverty. Not that the accumulated riches are necessarily withdrawn from the poor, but the great accumulations of a few do not, in any wise, indicate the improved condition of the whole people.

Let things branch forth in their natural way, and let consumers have Free Consumption, but do not force fortunes as fruits are forced in hot-houses, and do not take single busy manufacturing spots as a necessary indication of general welfare. Faulty legislation may have forced thousands of poor consumers to contribute their painful share to create this pleasing deception.

FALLACY NINTH.—*"Protection has a Tendency to make Things Cheaper."*

This fallacy would not have seemed to deserve mention here were it not very frequently urged in discussions on protection. It was not long ago one of the commonest arguments of the protectionists.

Protection, they said, raises prices, indeed; this leads to the invention of machinery; machinery saves labor and makes things cheaper. In the same manner it used to be argued in England, even by some prominent economists, that war had its good, economic effects, despite the enormous public debt, by driving the people to the invention of machines.

All that is necessary to reply to such an incoherent argument is, that if protection is recommended because it leads ultimately to cheapness, we prefer beginning with cheapness. That is all.

As to the specious war argument let no reader misunderstand us. War is far from being the greatest of evils, and blood may flow for things far nobler than itself, nor is physical well-being the highest of things we cannot do without; but we solemnly protest against all untruth and equivocation. It belongs to the *impossibilia* of this earth to increase wealth by war, directly or indirectly. When we must go to war, let us manfully present to ourselves the cost; provide, like honest men, for the expenses; and never listen for a moment to those men who recommend war to us for any economic reason, whether they are bungling thinkers or smooth-tongued self-seekers, nor to those who intend to repudiate solemn engagements, or gather their own harvest on the stony fields of a public debt.

FALLACY TENTH.—*The Anti-English Fallacy.*

"We hate the English," or whatever other words may be used; "the English are in favor of free trade; let us be for protection, for seclusion.   We don't want anything English."

In these or similar words a fallacy is expressed which is frequently made use of, however irrational it may be.

The difficulty in acting upon this principle seems to lie in the fact that we must begin with abolishing the English language, the Christian religion, and the practice of wearing the nose in the middle of the face; for we have all these in common with the English.

Even if the adherents of this doctrine think they do right in substituting " Hate thy neighbor as much as thou canst," for the command " Love thy neighbor as thyself," and for the first principle of the Christian law of nations " Peace and good-will toward man," even in that case they ought not to lay down the maxim, Hate thyself as much as thy neighbor ; and it does show disregard of self when the advantage which necessarily results from simple exchange is wilfully interrupted. But what can we say, when a leading protectionist actually stated, not in passionate speech, but in the considerateness of printed words, that a ten years' war with England would do us great good!   These men know better than the Creator, who made all things, beings, and climes, for Inter-Dependence and Inter-Beneficence.

Ashamed as a writer may feel in putting down the truth, it is a fact that this argument has been urged, and continues to be urged, in the latter part of the nineteenth century, and by people who profess a cosmopolitan religion of good-will and peace.

FALLACY ELEVENTH.—*The Balance of Trade.*

At length we arrive at what may be called a somewhat respectable fallacy after the four or five preceding ones.

By balance of trade is generally understood the balance between exports and imports; and the protectionists say, If more is imported than exported, it is clear that the balance must have been made up by money, so that the country has lost so much as the exported money amounts to.

Mr. Levi Woodbury, secretary of the treasury to General Jackson and President Van Buren, went so far as to show in a report, published with one of the President's annual messages, that ever since the establishment of this government the United States have imported more than they exported, and that thus they have been carrying on a losing business ever since. How the country managed to flourish and how national wealth increased, or why people continued to trade for nearly a century, while it was all the time a losing business, cannot be seen. This statement of Mr. Woodbury was made up from the books of our custom-houses. Now, if we carry on a prosperous trade, the books ought to show importation greater than exportation. If a thousand bales of cotton, valued at fifty dollars each in the port of Charleston, do not realize in Liverpool more than fifty thousand dollars and the freight, they had much better not be exported; but if they sold in Europe for sixty-five thousand dollars, and merchandise to the amount of this sum was imported, so that apparently fifteen thousand dollars' worth more was imported than exported, then it was most likely a profitable business. Yet the balance-of-trade protectionists would wish us to believe that in this case fifteen thousand dollars in coin went out of the country, and that, therefore, the country was by so much impoverished. Money, however, does not grow in the fields; at least, specie does not. In order to be able to purchase commodities in Europe we must first produce something to offer in exchange for it. (See Webster's words in Fallacy 4.) The figurative question much in vogue at one time, "How can a man expect not to get poorer from day to day, if he takes daily more money out of his breeches' pockets than he put in?" is utterly futile. There is no such thing as "the people's pocket." A pocket does not produce, except in the fairy-tale, and men must produce values to be able to exchange them for other commodities which they desire. An every-day process sufficiently illustrates this. A farmer carries corn and poultry to the market of the nearest town, sells them, and buys forthwith, for the money thus obtained, cloth and flannel—for winter may be approaching—also a book and some pairs of shoes for his boys, or a fine time-saving machine for his wife. These commodities consume all he obtained for his product. The question now is, Has he, or his house or family, village or county, become so much the poorer? He produced for this very purpose, and he brought home the equivalent. To the farmer it is worth more, else he would not have exchanged his values for what he purchased. Here, as elsewhere, we meet with the two truths which it were well for us had they never been forgotten.

He who interferes with exchange, natural and necessary, interferes with the essential welfare of mankind; and wealth cannot be increased but by production. It is the only way. Wealth can never be legislated into existence. Laws have indeed been passed, in the course of history, calling a half-dollar a dollar, but no law has ever been able to make two thousand dollars out of one thousand dollars.

If the people who carry on that peculiar and important branch of productive industry called commerce, and those people who furnish them with the commodities which by commerce are exchanged, are not to be trusted with their own interests, and if governments must regulate their exchange, and indirectly their production, and if disastrous years, like 1837 and 1858, are held up as terrible examples of unrestrained importation, we ask, Who are the government which is to play a sort of sub-providence over us? Are they not men like ourselves? Have governments never gone mad with ruinous speculations? What is asked of government on this point is directly hostile to the principles of self-government, which we cherish so highly. Why are all these government regulations insisted upon merely for foreign trade and foreign importation, and not also for New York trade with New Orleans or Oregon? May the people of San Francisco not overstock the market with Massachusetts goods, if left to themselves? Are these markets unimportant? Now, let a protectionist dare to propose government control in this case, and see how Boston and San Francisco would blaze up in a

fire of indignation. Yet why? If the government is expected
to regulate for us what we shall import and export, then we
must go farther, and let government (whatever that be) regulate, "organize" everything; in short, adopt communism at
once. Millions upon millions daily eat too much and injure
their health. Shall government regulate our meals on that
account, or shall we, like the Spartans, have regulation dinners? Protective tariffs are partial and slightly-veiled communism. The wider trade extends the steadier prices are, on
the same principle that averages, for instance of crime, become
steady in the same degree as the area of observation is extended. Perfect free trade in grain would impart an almost
unchangeable price to the cereals.

This idea of considering wealth to consist in the keeping of
money within our country, and which has led to the strangest
legislation in various countries, actually induced Mr. McDuffie,
senator of the United States from South Carolina, who had
been a fierce nullifier, and was a loudly-professed free-trader,
to declare in the senate of the United States that he must
own there was no harm in war, economically speaking, if all
the articles required for war can be obtained within the country of the belligerent, and the money can thus be retained
within the country. It is the exact argument of Louis XIV.,
that the many millions squandered by his mania for building
remained in the country, and that no harm was done. On the
contrary, he called the building of Versailles the method of
distributing charity appropriate for kings, and I must add that
I have heard educated persons in France say that Louis XIV.,
who nevertheless regretted on his death-bed his mania for
wars and building, was perfectly right, and that had not the
monarch put the many millions into these spacious fabrics,
which continue to stand, they would be lost and gone by this
time!

Spain, importing precious metals from her colonies for centuries, and having a law prohibiting all exportation of precious
metals, in order to "keep Spain rich," sank deeper and deeper
into poverty with every decennium, because it would not

produce.   So much for keeping " money" in a country.[1]   We
know exactly how many millions England has paid to Prussia
as subsidy in the Seven Years' War.   So many millions of
specie flowed into Germany, while the war carried off thousands of people, so that this money was distributed among
fewer persons; but was Germany richer after the peace of St.
Hubert?   She was lamentably poorer, and the Germans and
their governments knew it.   The Roman conquerors sent immense amounts of values to Italy in the shape of gold and
shares.   Did Italy become richer?   Poverty utterly ruined
the country, and in the same degree in which some senators
amassed immense fortunes the country and the people at
large sank deeper into pauperism.

" Money going out of the country" used to be considered,
and is still believed by many, to be simple loss of wealth.   So
long as the money being in a country was taken to constitute
its wealth this was consistent.   Montesquieu, again, says in
his immortal work that the amount of money existing at a

---

[1] Long after the Fallacy on the Balance of Trade was written down, after my
delivery in a lecture, I became acquainted with the speech which Daniel Webster made in the senate, April, 1824, on the Balance of Trade.   The Canon Law
allows an appeal *a papa male informato ad papam melius informandum.*   In
our case we must appeal *a Webster male informato ad Webster quandum melius
informatum.*   Mr. Webster said :

" Let us inquire, then, sir, what is meant by an unfavorable balance of trade,
and what the argument is, drawn from that source.   By an unfavorable balance
of trade, I understand, is meant that state of things in which importation exceeds
exportation.   To apply it to our own case : if the value of goods imported exceed
the value of those exported, then the balance of trade is said to be against us,
inasmuch as we have run in debt to the amount of this difference.   Therefore it
is said, that if a nation continue long in a commerce like this, it must be rendered
absolutely bankrupt.   It is in the condition of a man that buys more than he sells ;
and how can such a traffic be maintained without ruin ?   Now, sir, the whole fallacy of this argument consists in supposing that, whenever the value of imports
exceeds that of exports, a debt is necessarily created to the extent of the difference ; whereas, ordinarily, the import is no more than the result of the export,
augmented in value by the labor of transportation.   The excess of imports over
exports, in truth, usually shows the gains, not the losses, of trade ; or, in a country that not only buys and sells goods, but employs ships in carrying goods also,
it shows the profits of commerce and the earnings of navigation."

given time in a given country is tantamount to and represents its wealth. All this is now better understood, and the modern economist must acknowledge that, most happily, mankind at large may become, and at present does become, wealthier, which could not be the case if money alone constituted wealth. If wealth consisted in money, then one nation must needs get poorer as the other is rising, because the amount of precious metal is limited. This was firmly believed until Adam Smith taught a new statesmanship—namely, that with nations as with individuals, the richer your neighbors the better for you. Ever since the discovery of the sea-way round the Cape of Good Hope down to our own times, it has been maintained that, all money of Europe going to the East and the East not buying anything of Europe, one of two things must follow —either Europe must become bankrupt, or she must send conquering armies to Farther Asia to bring back the money.

How armies can bring back money from a distant country cannot easily be discerned; but let us pass on. The boot- and-shoe manufacture of Massachusetts produces, at present, over ninety-five million dollars annually. Suppose the rest of the New England States produce about twenty million dollars' worth. Comparatively few boots and shoes are consumed in New England or exported. Let us say that one hundred million dollars in boots and shoes are consumed by the United States minus New England. The question is: Do these States pay a tribute of one hundred million dollars to New England? Do they send their money to New England, and must they fetch it back some day? This was the opinion of Senator Hammond, of South Carolina, a loud "free-trader," who, nevertheless, insisted on preventing the millions from being sent to New England for "plantation shoes," forgetting that these very plantation shoes helped to produce the cotton which was the "money" purchasing among other things the plantation shoes.

This whole idea of money going to Asia was an anticipation of Mr. Woodbury's argument by several centuries. What, however, is the fact? Europe has not been broken; Europe has not sent armies "to fetch back" the money; and Europe is incomparably richer now than she was in the seventeenth and eighteenth centuries, when the lamentation about the money streaming Eastward was highest.

There is no other illustration of the error that money going out of the country is loss of wealth so astounding as that in a letter of Napoleon I. to his brother Joseph, who, as king of Naples, had complained that the emperor's policy stopped all commerce, and that the Neapolitans were sinking into greater and greater poverty. Napoleon, after having repeatedly told his brother, *frappez les*, with a sound taxation, actually scolds the king of Naples for his stupidity in not seeing that if the Neapolitans have no foreign commerce, the *numeraire* is kept from going out of the country, and if no specie goes out of the country, the wealth of the country is not dissipated or diminished. The authority for this almost incredible account is the Correspondence of Joseph Bonaparte, successively king of Naples and of Spain, published by order of the emperor of the French.

Advancing civilization requires increased consumption or expenditure. Popular school systems alone consume millions upon millions. If, therefore, mankind at large could not become richer, and one nation must always become poorer in the proportion in which another nation gets richer, then civilization at large could not advance, nor could its field expand; and territorial expansion, as well as increasing intensity, is a plain characteristic of European civilization from its Greek beginning.

FALLACY TWELFTH.—*The Rights of Labor, and " the Right to Labor."*

Some ten or fifteen years ago a pamphlet was published by Mr. Greeley, under the title The Tariff Question,[1] in which the rights of labor are discussed. Section 19 of that pamphlet is inscribed " The Right to Labor." The argument is pretty

---

[1] The whole title is: The Tariff Question. Protection and Free Trade Considered. By HORACE GREELEY.

much that of the communists to this day: "A man's trade is his estate," and he has a right to see it protected; which protection includes and requires a protective tariff or exclusion of products of foreign labor.

The brief space allowed us in these pages will limit us to simple indications of our views.

Of course, "a man's trade is his estate" if he lives by it, and for this very reason the trades of all ought to be most scrupulously protected. A blacksmith's trade is his estate. He must support himself and his family by it, wherefore no one, may he call himself king, kaiser, economist, congressman, or whatever else, has any right to invade his estate and make him work days and days more in order to buy his necessaries or luxuries, whose prices a despotic tariff may have raised, while at the same time the tariff has raised the price of iron, consequently diminished its consumption and lessened the fair income of the blacksmith. Nor can he lay by in the savings-bank for days of feebleness as much as he might have done without a protective tariff.

A farmer's acres surely are his estate; but let us suppose he insists on raising grapes on a soil unfit for the vine: shall the government protect this man's estate in this particular, and has it a right to force his fellow-citizens to drink wine, which, to use the words of a high and holy man of old, is ripened into vinegar without the transition state of wine?

If labor has any particular rights, and if they are natural and just, they ought to be protected by all means; not forgetting, however, that this applies to all labor, and also to the effects or results of labor—to saved and accumulated wages, to capital. That, too, has its rights. Or would a master-shoemaker like to see the capital which he has earned, and which has enabled him to set up for himself and carry on his business, refused protection so soon as he himself ceases to draw the wax-end?

Does protection of labor not include the right of production? What else is labor good for, if it is not productive? But protective tariffs seriously interfere with production. Has, forsooth, the present tariff not cruelly interfered with our ship-building labor, once so productively employed ?

If by right of labor is meant a special privilege of one species of labor—that, for instance, of the manufacturing or artisan labor over farming or trading labor—then we deny this right.

If by right of labor is meant that people have a right to produce what they like and in whatever quantity, without any reference to the question of demand, and that the commonwealth must purchase the undesired products, as the rights of labor were understood in France in 1848, and later, and as very many communists here understand it, then we wholly disavow it, as we disavow and abhor all communism, perhaps the most crushing of all absolutisms or despotisms. No liberty and life without individualism.

All that each man is he is in consequence of being an individual, and at the same time a social being. In politics, in law, in morals, in religion, in civilization, each man's life turns around an axis, the two poles of which are individualism and socialism ; or, each life is pervaded by the principle of individuality and the social element. Communism, however, annihilates individualism, as far as it goes, and is against our very nature. Protection is veiled communism, as far as it goes.

What has Spartan communism done for men by the side of Athens ? Furnished Plutarch with some fine anecdotes of dying soldiers. Modern grenadiers know how to die as well. Waterloo and Gettysburg prove that.

In the year 1844, Alexander Humboldt said to me : " You are wrong in your detestation of communism. People like you and myself, who write books which do not sell a hundredth part as well as many paltry and even bad books, ought to be communists. We write books that will not sell, poor books, no matter what books, and forthwith, according to ' organized labor,' the commonwealth ought to be bound to take them off our hands. To be sure, those who must pay for them may grumble, or we may grumble at being obliged to take bass-viols in our turn, though not playing the instrument; but what is that? *Vive le communisme!*" It made an impression upon me, as the reader may well imagine. On the other hand, he was amazed when I told him that American protectionists openly and publicly speak of the necessity of *protecting* American genius by putting a heavy tax on foreign, and especially on English, books.

John C. Calhoun, again, said to me: "Do you not agree that slavery contains all that is good in communism, and discards what is bad? Slavery in this, as in so many other cases, solves problems" (the statesman meant here, of course, the labor and capital question) "which cannot be solved otherwise."

All despots have a large element of communism. The fearful tyranny and absolutism "drawn" by Bishop Bossuet for Louis XIV. "from the Bible" is communistic in its doctrine of a community of property and rights of all in the monarch; and protective tariffs are, as far as their communistic element goes, despotic, often tyrannical in the extreme, and incompatible with essential civil liberty.

We say this, not challenging to disputation, but calmly to elicit reflection. Tyranny is a fearful thing, and stifles all loyalty; yet, of all governments, a republic stands most in need of citizens loyally devoted to it. The present oppressive, arbitrary tariff has a tendency to disloyalize our fellow-citizens. Would that the prominent protectionist who once acknowledged that he had been and still was a communist might ponder this serious question! Our tariff engenders dailygrowing discontent—a bitter rancor something quite different from a wholesome opposition.

Our forefathers plunged into the Revolution avowedly on these two principles:

We are Englishmen, and the mother-country denies us the liberties which are the birthright of every British subject; or, as Washington expressed it, they deny us the rights to which nature and the British constitution entitle us. And the home government will not allow us, the colonies, free exchange and free production.

This was the war-cry, and now we quarrel with free trade because it is called English, and insist on seclusion for ourselves and exclusion of all other countries, which means prohibition of Americans to trade, directly or indirectly, with whom they like. Our forefathers insisted on free commerce, and we have literally destroyed a fearless, searching, and remunerative maritime commerce by unfortunate protection, and then imagine we can help it on its keel again by the arbitrary payment of a few millions to some mail-packets!

FALLACY THIRTEENTH.—*The Vicinage Principle, so called.*

It was for many years one of the favorite arguments of Mr. Carey that protection was necessary, among other things, for this reason: that without it the factory could not be placed close to the producing cotton-field, and the immense cost of freight, first for carrying the cotton to Europe, and then the textile fabrics back to the producing country, could not be saved. A principle was thus attempted—namely, it is necessary to establish the manufacture close to the producing of raw material, and this was called the vicinage principle.

We briefly object to this the following points:

If the freight of carrying the substance to and fro enhances the price too much, why not leave it to the people to discover it, and why protect? Protection, in this case, would not be necessary.

There is nothing distant or near in political economy, except so far as the cost of transportation is concerned. Is, in point of economy, an expensive overland route to California nearer if you could carry the commodities cheaper round Cape Horn?

East India cotton is carried to Scotland to be woven into calico, which is carried back to the Ganges, there to be consumed by the Hindoos. Would he who should insist on erecting manufactories in Hindostan benefit the poor Hindoo?

If manufactories could be erected there, and work as cheap as the Glasgow manufactories, well and good. But in this case no forcible overriding of the natural turn of things would be necessary. So soon as we resort to forcible production we prove that we act economically and legally wrong.[1]

Thirdly : Suppose we can establish the manufactory close to the raw material, how is it with the consumers? In short, does the vicinage principle require that the wheat-field, mill, baking-oven, and the consumers with open mouths, all cluster together?

Fourth : It is simply impossible to carry out the vicinage principle. The raw material is gained, in most cases, where the transforming and industrial processes cannot be carried on.

And lastly : What becomes of the great principle of inter-dependence, inter-communication, inter-assistance? If the principle of vicinage were a true and a feasible one, it would lead to isolation rather than to inter-communication. The vicinage principle strives against the order of things, according to which men's varied appetites and necessities, increasing in number as civilization advances, can mostly be satisfied only from afar. Analyze a fairly appointed dinner-table of a common household. How many distant regions have contributed? What commerce has been necessary to bring it about by direct or concatenated exchange? Man is ordained not to find everything near him, as the brute does. Self-sufficient independence is not his destiny. All men are made for inter-dependence, which increases with our progress. What are miles in political economy? Our globe was not created on the vicinage principle—on the contrary, on the principle of mutual wants and reciprocal aid, near and from afar; on the principle of complementary neighborliness. To judge by this vicinage principle, we should suppose that the progress of civilization were marked by steady contraction, while in reality

---

[1] London journals of April, 1870, informed us that Bombay cotton sent by way of the Suez Canal has been returned to India from Hudderfield as yarn in forty-five days. The time usually required by the Cape of Good Hope is ninety days.

it is marked by, and in a great measure consists in, constantly widening means of intercommunication, saving time and space, and by a constantly expanding field, from the narrow theatre of little Greece to the drawing of hemispheres within the circle of intercommunication.

FALLACY FOURTEENTH.—"*The saving of the fertilizing elements of our soil would be immense by the establishment of protected industry, especially if established on the vicinage principle. Free Trade carries forever the fertilizing elements out of our country—for instance, by carrying so many million bales of cotton annually to England—and never returns any.*"

We are frankly desirous to state this argument as fairly as possible; and if we have not succeeded, we invite any protectionist to give it more agreeably to his mind. In whatever form it may be stated, we are sorry to say, we have given the substance, and, we believe, have thereby exposed its destitution of strength or vitality of sense.

Years ago, when we first saw this *fertilizing argument* urged in a protection journal, we felt pity for the editor, whom we could not help believing imposed upon by some waggish free-trader; later we found that it was urged by high protectionist authority, and down to this very day it is dwelt upon in the papers of our opponents as a choice bit in the catechism of their craft.

Possibly this fallacy arose in the imaginative mind of its first conceiver at the time when people, very properly indeed, came to discuss the possibility of preventing the frightful waste of fertilizing substance going on from hour to hour in a city, for instance, like London or New York. Of all the immense amount of matter which is daily carried into a large city, nearly the whole, building material and earthenware excepted, becomes wasted fertilizing substance. If the contents of the London sewers could be saved, it has been calculated that (I now forget how many) million bushels of wheat would be produced additionally in England; and they ought to be saved, provided the saving of the drainage would not cost more than the additionally produced millions of bushels would be worth—a condition which would hold good concerning the precious silt, carried by all the glorious rivers through thousands of years, since the day of creation, every second into the sea, where that becomes impediment, and even an injury, which was the very vivifier of human sustenance could it only have been utilized.

If such was the occasion of this hapless argument (chronologically the two agree), it is not possible to see an intrinsic connection. Let us, however, hasten as much as may be.

Waste of fertilizing matter! We had better look at our Mississippi—what amount of silt it carries down and wastes every hour!—to familiarize us with the idea of " wasted fertilizers." Can we help it? If not, let us drop the subject; if we can, let us save the silt.

But how is the fertilizing substance wasted when cotton is sent out of the country? Do we not receive other products for it in turn? Suppose not; are the advocates of this argument then really insisting on the necessity of agricultural producers, manufacturers, and consumers being all huddled together? What becomes of all commerce, domestic as well as foreign? Domestic commerce transfers fertilizing matter as much as foreign commerce does, and even more. What answer would it be if we were told that the fertilizer remains at least at home? How at home, when Carolina cotton is manufactured in Maine and sent to California, where the fertilizing rag may ultimately find resuscitation in peaches which are sent again to St. Louis, beginning a new series of disturbance of fertilizing order conceived by the protectionists. This is nothing less than trying daringly to imitate Providence. Once more, the carrying of a dozen eggs to market is a disturbance of fertilizers as serious, if the whole were serious at all, as the transfer of any given quantity of sugar to any number of distant coffee-drinkers. Nature knows nothing small or great.

Mr. Ruggles has recently shown the world that the United States, in 1868, produced 36 bushels of cereals—of vegetable food—to each inhabitant, and Europe, in the same year, only 16 bushels.[1] Still, our West is not yet developed. What is the meaning of this ? Simply that there is a gigantic power of feeding in our continent; let us carry our wheat and rye, barley and rice to the European weaver; he weaves for us and cannot produce cheap bread. " Stop," cries the protectionist, " by all that is sacred, stop ! or you carry the fertilizing matter away from our country. Stop, I beseech you, and do as the people of Bordeaux do, the producers of the claret, who drink themselves all the claret they produce, so that no fertilizer play the deserter !"

Agriculture has long ago found a remedy against the escape of fertilizers by manure, first from the stable, then from the Guano Islands. Liebig has proposed even the utilizing of the coprolites deposited in long-past geologic ages. Whether his advice will be followed, whether agriculture ever will cease to replenish our fields with fertilizing matter, and the West will send forth its population to unexhausted regions, who can know what may happen thousands of years hence ? But this we do know—that so long as men shall be, there shall be commerce too, and men shall act on the new fields, perhaps the centre of Africa, just as they did in the valley of the Mississippi and in the valley of the Rhine ; and there will be shifting of fertilizing substance from second to second for evermore. This is an order of things with which it is no more man's business to interfere than with the courses of the atmosphere or the influence of the heavenly bodies on one another. There are doubtless readers who consider the discussion of this Fallacy unnecessary, but they are mistaken. Men by no means below the average talent of our times speak loudly and scientifically, as it is called, in favor of this puerile argument.

---

[1] In the excellent Report mentioned in the prefatory words preceding these Notes on Fallacies.

FALLACY FIFTEENTH. — "*We are a young country; we are Americans; European Systems and Theories do not apply to us.*"

The positive fact that such fallacies are often heard can alone justify us in mentioning them here. Would that we Americans said of ourselves what the old Roman said of himself: "I am a man, and hold nothing human alien to me," and that we applied this saying in the sense : We are men, and no laws prescribed for men are alien to ourselves !

The " European systems" are manifold and contradictory, so nothing can be derived from the term European.

We are human beings placed on the same globe with other people, subject to the same physical and moral laws, liable to the same penalties for running counter to the dictates of wisdom, and bound by the same duties toward others and ourselves. There are no favorites in history, and God has no pet nations. If we are foolish, we must pay the penalty of folly like any other people.

Our country is no young country in the obscuring sense in which this is generally taken. It is not yet a century since we separated from England, but that does not make us *young* in every sense, as little as you create two *young* counties by dividing an old one. The substitution of *young* for *new* constitutes in most of the cognate cases a distinct and serious fallacy.

Europe, America, Asia, are names which, in many spheres of thought and action, have no meaning. The same mathematics for all ; the same physiology; the same facts. Divisions made for one reason lose frequently all meaning as soon as we speak of other subjects. The laws of production, exchange, and consumption do not alter any more than the laws of electricity change from one country painted red on a map to another painted blue. I have been called upon from Canada to join in the establishing of an American free-trade system, granting absolute free trade all over America (I suppose North America was really meant), to the complete exclusion of Europe.   What, let us ask, can be the meaning of the geographical word America in this discussion of values, of wealth, of exchange?

Does it affect the thermometer, that it was invented by an Italian? or the press, because a German invented printing? or the lightning-rod, because an American stole the fire from the heavens?

Patriotism consists in loving our country and being devoted to it in very deed, not in hating other countries nor in applying geographical names to regions of thought and action far beyond it.   Let us be Americans in the truest and widest sense, but as men, too, unnarrowed by provincial egotism, by —could I literally translate a German term, I would say— petty statishness.

If the youth of our country is urged in defense of prohibition, in order to show that we want it for the purpose of calling certain branches of industry into existence, we refer to previous remarks.   No one has a right to sacrifice the interests of the consumers by the forcing of certain branches of industry believed by certain men to be indispensable.   What if another set of men maintain that our incomparable country is made and destined to be the great feeding-country of the world, as Sicily and Egypt once were for Italy?   And very potent statistics might be adduced to support this assumption.

Let it be granted, however, for argument's sake, that so-called young countries ought to be *protected*, the question arises at once, How long does a country continue in the infantine state?   Lord March, now Duke of Richmond, declared in the commons, in the year 1846, that English agriculture and manufacture were still in their infancy, and, consequently, required protection.   The infancy cry has been heard in America from the beginning, near a hundred years; and as people now advance far more rapidly than in former times, it may be said that the protectionists have declared us to be in the state of helpless infancy during what would have amounted in past ages to centuries.   How long shall this last?

Again and again we repeat, that it is the first of duties, and

consequently the first of the rights, of man to produce and exchange—a duty and complementary right which no theorist,
no fancy economist, ought to be permitted to trifle with.

FALLACY SIXTEENTH.—*The Enforced Home-Market.*

Adam Smith, that man who first taught the glorious doctrine of a new statesmanship, that nations, like individuals,
profit and are not injured by the prosperity of their neighbors,
also said that domestic production and consumption far sur-
passes in amount the foreign trade of most or all large nations.
Therefore, the protectionists continue, let us make a home-
market.

Whatever be meant by that frequently-used term, home-
market—I suppose, chiefly, domestic production and consumption, and by *domestic*, again, is meant within the political
boundaries of a country—whatever be meant by the word
home-market, so much is sure, that however large and populous a country may be, its foreign trade is important, and increases in importance with the population; that nations are
no more destined for oyster-like seclusion and self-sufficiency
than individuals, but, on the contrary, are made for inter-dependence and inter-completion; that however important domestic production and consumption may be, it differs in no
essential from production and consumption in general, and
nothing good can be effected by enforced production and consumption on the one hand, and that on the other hand there
is great injustice in enforced home-markets to those who stand
in need of foreign commodities; that whatever difference in
some countries there may be in the amount of domestic exchange and foreign trade, yet that foreign trade is as important, as far as it goes, as the domestic, just as the olfactory
sense, carrying far fewer sensations to the brain than the eye
does, is nevertheless as essential in making up the being we
call Man as the sense of vision; and lastly, that we have no
right to meddle with the subject by that authority which was
not given for forcing people into wealth according to plans,
and by means which at the time may seem best to authority.

It has been calculated that the production of hay in the Northern and Western States is equal in value to the production of cotton. Be it so; it has nothing whatever to do with the production of cotton. On the other hand, it used to be maintained in the South that only the production of staples for export, like cotton, can increase national wealth. The idea of wealth consisting in money and of returns being made in money was always floating in the minds of men. This very fallacy was one of those which misled the South to believe in the complete dependence of the North on the South, was repeated year after year in speech and pamphlet by prominent men, and helped to inflate the pride which did so much to bring about the Rebellion. Nevertheless, the whole idea was an utter fallacy, devoid of any rational element. A writer on subjects of political economy of note maintained against the author that production alone was no source of wealth—that our wealth was only increased if we carried our products abroad and brought back specie! And he was a free-trader, a nullifier! Whither has common sense gone? Domestic and Foreign, when applied to production and trade, have no meaning essentially differing. It seems never to have struck the protectionists in Europe or America that the many interests which sprung up under the Roman empire—the cultivation of the vine in Gaul and Germany, the grain-culture, and so many others—had no protection in their infancy, as it is called. There was free trade in the Roman empire, that meant in the world. There were revenue tariffs in some provinces—for instance, for the province of Africa—but there was nowhere a protective tariff. An African tariff graved in marble has been found by the French in perfect preservation.

Home-market cannot mean anything else than an opportunity of selling at home—that is to say, within the limits of a given political society. Selling, however, is an act of exchange, requiring two parties; and if one of these parties is forced to buy of the other party what he would not have done had he been left, like a free being, to act for himself; if he must part with more of his own to obtain what he wants;

if he must work longer and produce more to obtain what after all is poorer stuff than what he would have gotten had he and his society been left alone to obtain their desired commodities where they thought best, being quite as capable to judge of the whole subject as the persons constituting the government,—then, indeed, the home-market is no benefit to the consumer or the country. Home-markets have nothing essential to distinguish them from foreign markets. It is exchange the producer wants, and no exchange can be effected except when he who desires to buy has first produced that which he can offer in the market. No buying without first producing, and the more the producer obtains for his products the better for him and for the whole race.

It would be better altogether to give up the word home-market. It is after all a figurative term, dangerous in all reasoning. So soon as the word home-market is heard, people imagine some place thronged with loud and busy buyers and sellers. The simple word exchange would be plainer and truer, although less picturesque.

The history of fairs is instructive in connection with this subject. Markets and fairs are very prominent in the history of antiquity. In the Middle Ages and in more modern times markets used to be established on the narrowest principle of home-market. Some fairs allowed wider scope, and those few which permitted the freest exchange of goods from all portions of the globe, like that of Leipsic, became the most extensively beneficent. The free-trader desires a declaration that the whole world be a Leipsic fair *en permanence.*

On the other hand, let us observe this, that fairs, however famous, and markets lose their importance in the same degree as security and facility of transportation increase—that is, as the ease and rapidity of exchange advances; and the principle of the home-market, strictly carried out, would reduce us again to the fairs of the Middle Ages.

What is Home in this case? Why does its meaning stop with the political confines of the United States? Why not apply it to the western slope of the California mountains?

Has not the gardener of this paradise of gardening a right, according to the protectionists, to call for a home-market for California apples against the New York pippins? To this very day *selling by samples* is prohibited in nearly all the Southern States, sometimes by a very heavy fine. This is nothing but the idea of the home-market again, very rudely carried out, but the idea is that strangers—*i.e.*, people from other States—shall not make engagements of sales of goods by samples to the injury of the home-seller, for there can hardly be a question about a home-producer.

FALLACY SEVENTEENTH.—"*Where are the Workshops of the World, there must be the Marts of the World;*" *therefore, let us erect our own Workshops, keep out Foreign Products, etc.*

Closely connected with the foregoing fallacy is that for which the words of Mr. Meredith have been quoted as a heading.

The report which Mr. Meredith made, when secretary of the treasury, on the state of the finances, December 3, 1849, has this passage, with which Section 3 concludes: "All history shows that where are the workshops of the world, there must be the marts of the world, and the heart of wealth, commerce, and power. It is as vain to hope to make these marts by providing warehouses as it would be to make a crop by building a barn." Indeed, it would; but it would be likewise as vain to hope to make people come to your workshops to buy what they want, when your workshops are like forcing-houses, and the people can buy what they want cheaper and better elsewhere.

The secretary saw the fallacy, but stopped short midway; he did not see that he condemned himself by his own words; yet the grievous error is neatly enough expressed, suited the protectionists, and the error had all the success which is almost sure to any neat formulation or pungent antithesis. To this day the World's Mart and Workshop Fallacy is popular with many not inferior minds, and the formula has acquired the weight of a dogma, however irrational it may be. Political Economists of a certain class have furnished us with illustrations of all the fallacies known in logic, and in induction as well as deduction, almost equalling the theologians of the Middle Ages in this respect.

Our objections are positive, and in no way equivocal. History does not show what she is here said to show. When the Cape of Good Hope had been discovered, and the chief trade concentrated in Lisbon, was Portugal the world's workshop? When Venice was the mart of the world, before Lisbon became such, was she the world's workshop? The Netherlands had very few workshops when they had the world's trade. But what is the world's workshop? These are big and uncertain terms. Nature is the world's workshop. In every product the natural agents perform far the greater part. Man is little more than the combiner, appropriator, and exchanger; God is, and ever must be, the Great Producer. The workshops of the world are not concentrated in one place, and never have been.

Nor is the tendency of advancing civilization toward creating "hearts of wealth, commerce, and power," any more than creating universal monarchy. Life, diffused energy, is the motto of modern times, not centralism in production or commerce, any more than in politics or religion. In ancient times there was always one leading nation, first in Asia, then in Europe. In modern times there are many leading nations forming a commonwealth of nations, or, as I have expressed it elsewhere, in modern times many nations draw the car of civilization abreast, like the chariot-horses in the Olympic games; and this is a distinct characteristic of modern times, as much so as the recuperative power dwelling in modern nations.

Suppose, however, that every word said here were erroneous, how did it happen that the treasurer of the United States did not perceive that he pronounced his own condemnation? Though it were true that workshop, mart, wealth, commerce, and power were always clustered in one golden grape, though it were true that the workshop—by which, of course, is meant the manufacture—were always the beginning of wealth, is it then not seen that you will not create wealth by calling up forcibly machine-shops and manufactures, and *impoverishing* people by obliging them to buy in those uncomfortable hot-houses? The serious error committed in this case is the common one of confounding cause and effect, and which had best be called Jack Downing's Fallacy, for in one of Downing's letters to General Jackson he says, that " Down East" the thermometer stood 20 degrees below zero, and the weather would have been much colder had the thermometer been longer. There is a great deal of wealth in England, and so there are a great many manufactories; therefore let us build as many of the latter as possible, by severe laws if necessary, and we shall accumulate proportionate wealth ! Dr. Franklin's " Build pigeon-holes, and pigeons will come," does not apply to all provinces of action. Buying pots and pans produces no dinner. There has been in the neighborhood of the writer for several years a spacious, light, and every way acceptable market-building, except people will not go there to buy: the pigeon-holes are there, but the pigeons refuse to come. We may indeed prevent our own people from buying foreign products, but how to force foreign people to buy here, and make this country a mart of the world, transcends our powers to imagine.

Experience shows, and it can be readily accounted for, that with very few exceptions so-called protection or enforced production (or prohibition of production) has the following effects :

It raises prices.

It deteriorates the commodity, or diminishes the value.

It blights exchange, or injures commerce, and

It lowers the standard of comfort and diminishes the means of progressive civilization, and increases pauperism.

The exception may take place, but on a limited degree only, when the government is a civilized people ruling, for instance by conquest, over a barbarous people. No American, it is hoped, will allow a difference of intelligence between his government and the people.

FALLACY EIGHTEENTH.—*A Judicious Protection within the Limits of a Revenue Tariff.*

A theory prevailing especially at the time of General Jackson's presidency, and which is an attempted compromise between free trade and protection, is this: We have no right whatever to raise more money by a tariff than what the government wants for its support; but within this limit it is fair to establish discriminating duties in order to help domestic manufacture.

If by this latter duty were meant so trifling a duty that none would feel it, the old law maxim, The law does not take notice *de minimis*, might be adduced; but a trifling tax does not do good to any one, nor does the subject lose in injustice by the fact that perhaps comparatively few are affected. For those few, that tariff is as injurious as a sweeping one is to all. We have no right to sacrifice any class, however small, to the supposed benefit of the whole. The argument is illogical. We have no right, it is said, to raise more revenue than what is wanted to support the government. So be it. If the support of the government is the object of a tariff, then whence is derived the right to discriminate within the limits of this tariff? That is to say, whence comes the right to sacrifice the wealth and well-being of certain consumers, not to the support of the government, but to promote the interest of a certain class at the expense of the others?

Shall, then, no regard be paid to those who, according to the laws of the land, good or bad, have invested large means? We mean no such thing. The state is a continuity, and we cannot otherwise but pay due regard to what has been done.

We can point out very briefly what we consider necessary according to moral and legal as well as economical principles, according to right, righteousness, and reason:

Acknowledge the right of free consumption in every one, and therefore free exchange in all. It is a natural—not an absolute, but a natural—right.

You have a right to establish a tariff for the support of

government and the discharge of its solemn engagements, and it is advisable to make use of this right, for a number of urgent reasons, in this country. But you have no right whatever to establish monopolies under the name of protection, nor to discriminate, within the limits of a revenue tariff, in favor of certain branches, excepting only those which your own misleading and unjust laws have called into existence, and then only with a view of speedy though gradual extinction of all protection, and forever.

FALLACY NINETEENTH.—*Protection is More Popular.*

" Three times have the people of America decided that they want protection ; why do you continue to trouble us with your free trade ?" Thus a leading protectionist said to me on a memorable occasion.

" Did you not observe that immediately after the expulsion of Louis Philippe, in 1848, the workmen of Paris expelled the English railway workmen and engineers ? It was the feeling of patriotic protection which made them act thus, so soon as free," said another prominent protectionist.

We are close to the conclusion of our remarks, and I must limit myself to the following suggestions, to which, nevertheless, the attention of the reader is invited :

The immediate profit on visible transactions is seen ; the vast advantage of unperceived transactions is not seen, but must be gathered by reflection. It was ordered by the town authority of the place I lived in, in the South, that no free negroes should be allowed to buy fowls for the Charleston market. Here the advantage of the chicken consumer of the place was seen ; the advantage to the chicken producer of getting the highest price was not seen, nor personally felt at once.

Even if the American people decided three times in favor of protection, which we doubt, that is no reason why protection should be right. How often did Rome decide against Christianity ? How often have the Law, the Church, and all the people decided in favor of the existence of witchcraft ?

How many centuries was interest on capital unanimously declared to be accursed usury, and legally allowed to the equally accursed Jews only? How many million times did mankind decide in favor of guilds, or in favor of devastating conquered cities and selling the conquered? The progress of mankind follows almost always this line—that a truth is suspected, proclaimed, a few adopt it, a minority struggles into a majority, and at last establishes the truth.

Truth is not settled by majorities. To this day far more dwellers on the earth believe in polytheism than in one God. Shall we worship, on that account, the Diana of Ephesus? But, in connection with this subject of majority, it ought to be mentioned that in no science or branch of knowledge has there been so large a majority, almost amounting to a unanimity of its distinguished votaries, as has been of the leading economists of all countries, from Bacon and De Witt, in favor of free trade.

Nor can plausibility always be taken as evidence of truth. What is more plausible than that the sun rises and our earth stands still? On which side is and has been the overwhelming majority of our kind from the beginning of things? And what is more erroneous? If a hat-maker receives twelve dollars for a hat, for which, before the tariff, he would have received five dollars, it is very plausible to him that the tariff makes him seven dollars wealthier; yet he is mistaken, for, as consumer, he loses more; if not, he becomes wealthy at the cost of his neighbors.

I hold it to be a verity, belonging to practical reasoning, that plausibility is, in all higher regions of thought and comprehensive generalization of action, *prima-facie* evidence of error. The greatest errors in religion, statesmanship, physical science, moral and political economy are plausible ; and whenever we find that a difficult question which has puzzled mankind is plausibly explained, let us be on our guard, and be almost sure that the reasoner before us is totally wrong. We could not possibly go through life were we not to follow plausibility in all simple, every-day cases, were we not to conclude that it rains because our friend enters with a dripping cloak; and we cannot err more grievously and miss truth more certainly than by allowing plausibility to guide us in inquiries of the higher sort. How plausible that fallacy was, which we will call the Titus or Vespasian fallacy, in the last century! The best government is a wise and virtuous prince, with absolute power and "no fools to discuss." It was in vogue at the time of Frederick the Great of Prussia. How plausible it still seems to many, because government is established for the benefit of the people, to throw all power into the hands of the people (meaning, practically, the majority), establish popular absolutism, and then to expect that the people will not act against their own interest! It was a favorite argument of Thomas Jefferson. Yet there exists no error more absolute, and, logically speaking, more absurd, than the Titus fallacy and the last-mentioned fallacy, which has come down to us from the period of Rousseau.

FALLACY TWENTIETH.—*The Labor Argument.*

The name given to this argument is not very distinct, nor is our idea of it very clear. Nevertheless, we find the argument frequently alluded to, and consider ourselves obliged to treat of this fallacy.

So far as we understand this argument, it is somewhat like this: Value consists in labor bestowed; let us therefore protect or cherish this labor (domestic labor, of course), and we shall increase the amount of existing value—that is, national wealth. We are not able to state this argument more rationally; all we can say is, that now, for at least forty years, we have found some such argument floating about. Perhaps this was the great truth symbolized by the protectionists of Hellas in the labors of Sisyphus, held, until now, to have been unproductive. Let us be brief. Labor is necessary for production, and productive labor is one of the means of putting a thing in a state of being desired, which leads to value; but labor is not indispensable for value: a *nugget* of gold found washed clear near the surface has greater value than the most laboriously mined gold-crystal of less weight and purity; nor does labor conferred constitute of itself value. It is, or at least used to be, the custom on board the British men-of-war to set the sailors, if nothing else could be found for them to do, to polishing the cannon-balls, piled up in mathematical correctness. Much labor was thus bestowed on the balls, but should they have come to be exchanged for something else they would have had no greater value than the unlabored balls. Is an Egyptian mummy valued by the labor bestowed upon it (not to speak of the interest upon interest of the capital invested in the body), or by the degree of desire to possess it which may happen to exist? Many products on which a painful amount of exhausting labor has been bestowed " fetch so little in the market"—that is to say, are of so little value— that the labor remains almost unrequited.

Be it repeated : nothing artificial is of service in anything that relates to exchange, and no value can be artificially created.

Great mischief has been done by the unsound, occasionally absurd, definitions given of value, of so-called real and fictitious value. A distinguished economist has defined value as being the cost of reproduction. Cost must mean what we give for reproduction—that is, therefore, value is the value we give for reproduction; but even if the definition was not " in a circle," the pyramids of Egypt would possess an immense value, since the cost of their reproduction would be enormous; and things which cannot be reproduced at all would be without value. Has the Kohinoor no value? If I am answered that it has no intrinsic value, I ask, What is intrinsic or real value? Surely not utility ?[1]

---

[1] I cannot forbear relating here a curious occurrence. In a conversation with a rich furrier, I happened to say that there was no such thing as intrinsic value, that gold which could not be exchanged had no value, and that the worst books sold best. " As to books," said the fur-trader, " they have merely imaginary value; but look here;" and he threw a sable fur on the counter. " This sable is worth one hundred and twenty dollars; there is real value. Books get value from mere fancy."

What is Value? Etymology is of as little assistance in ascertaining the true meaning of the term value as it is in a thousand other cases. Words travel curiously through successive centuries and various idioms. Value and Valor spring from the same root, and are shoots, equally close to it, while Valor is etymologically the same with the French *valeur*, which in turn means what the English word Value designates. The German word for value is *Werth*, which, etymologically, is the same with the English Worth.

It has been found difficult to define value, not because there is any mystery about the subject, but because value, as we shall see, indicates variable and reciprocal relations of exchangeable things, and also because value is one of those words with which a weighty though not accurate meaning is connected hundreds of years before an attempt at defining them is made, such as the words State, Money, even Property and Right.

Popularly speaking, it may be said that the value of an article is what people are willing to give for it, modified by what the possessors of the commodity are willing to receive for it, no matter about the reasons of the one or the other. A person selling apples in the market, if asked what is meant by the value of a barrel of apples, would answer: Value means what they cost. If asked again, What does this *costing* mean? he would hesitate. Cost, he would think; does it mean what I paid for, or what I wish the customer to pay, or what others have been willing to pay to my fellow-sellers of apples?—if, indeed, he would carry his analysis so far.

All definitions of value aiming at terseness are inaccurate, often false even to absurdity, and needs must be one or the other. If we are desirous to express ourselves with scientific accuracy, and do not shun a certain dryness of expression, then the following is the proper definition of value: Value, in Political Economy, means the desiredness of an exchangeable thing, expressed in exchangeable things possessed by the desirer, offered by him, and accepted in exchange for it by the possessor of the desired article; or expressed in a third commodity sufficiently familiar to the exchangers, called money. Value is the mean of Desiredness and Reluctance to part with the desired thing, expressed in money. Whether this money consist in gold and silver or "bricks" of tea, in cowries or quills filled with gold dust, in "ring money," arrows, cáttle, or skins, is indifferent.

Price is value expressed in current money; if not, it is what owners of offered articles ask.

Desiredness must not be confounded with desirableness. The least desirable things, injurious, vicious things, are often, unfortunately, more desired than wholesome, useful, or decorous commodities; and their price is determined by the degree of their being desired, not by their desirableness. The poorest books now generally sell the best, and obscene prints often sell better than religious representations. Mr. Say, in his excellent work on Political Economy, says that utility bestows value. Why, then, are things which minister to vanity of higher value, when supported by Fashion, though injurious, than simply useful and wholesome things? Some of the most useful or necessary things have no value at all, because they can be had for the mere appropriation, as water near its source.

Nor does desiredness alone impart value. The desire to possess must be supported by that which can be offered in exchange. The beggar's craving for a loaf of bread ·does not give value to it; a whole famished, and at the same time impoverished, province does not raise the value of grain, unless others who can pay for it step in and buy it for the sufferers. The occasional dearth of rice in China, when thousands perish, does not increase the value of rice.

If a barrel of flour is worth two barrels of apples, two barrels of apples are at the same time worth one barrel of flour; and if a barrel of flour is worth a certain amount of gold, called by law ten dollars, the barrel of apples in the given case is worth five dollars; but if, for whatever reason, the value of gold should sink one-quarter—that is to say, if it would require an amount of gold called by law one hundred and twenty-five dollars to purchase that for which, until then, one hundred dollars had been paid—in that case our barrel of apples would be worth six dollars and twenty-five cents. Flour, apples, gold, all are subject to change in desiredness, in value. There is not, there never has been, there cannot be, anything stable in whatever refers to value or to the comparison of values with one another. Whatsoever is connected with value is variable, and nothing absolute can be predicated of it.

There cannot be absolute value, and as a measure—*e.g.*, a foot—is an absolute magnitude, with which other magnitudes are compared, there cannot be a real or absolute measure of value. But a commodity desired by all may be, and is, used as an approximate estimation of value (valuation), and this is usually called money. But money is no real measure of value, since the commodity of which it consists itself changes in value. Nor does the fact of becoming money extinguish by any means the character of a commodity in the substance which has become money. When a substance is *demonetized*, it still remains a commodity. Nothing but a commodity can ever become money ; money always exists before regular governments ; and no money ever loses the character of a commodity, although it acquires additional characteristics.

Values were expressed formerly, in Virginia, in hogsheads of tobacco, and in West Pennsylvania, Canada, and other parts of America, in beaver-skins.

A similar definition applies to the value of service, labor, skill, valor, art, talent, knowledge, even virtue (such as integrity), and utility of land, rendered, given, or let, for consideration. The utility of the land does not constitute its value, but the desiredness of the utility. The finest lands bring very often nothing under peculiar circumstances.

Value can only be predicated of exchangeable things, or, in other words, value necessarily implies exchangeableness, and, consequently, requires at least two different commodities and two exchangers.

Things unappropriated have no value, because appropriation must precede exchangeableness, and without exchange there is no value. The pearl, the cod-fish on the banks, the herring, the medicinal herb in the forest, guano, the whale, the tusk of the wild elephant, have no value any more than the iron discovered in the sun, although they are desired by men, until they are appropriated. When appropriated, they become exchangeable. Water has no value where it freely flows unowned by individuals, but it receives value so soon as the water-carrier appropriates it and offers it for sale along the streets of the distant city. Water is all the time equally *desirable;* it is even *desired* by the thirsty; but before being appropriated, it is not an *exchangeable* thing : value, therefore, cannot be ascribed to it.

Value cannot be inherent, but arises out of exchange of desired articles. Rice has no value whatever with people who disrelish it, and Frederick the Great was obliged to protect the seed potatoes which he offered to the people by an escort of cavalry against the assaults of the people, in some of his provinces where potatoes were abhorred, because something new. The potato was introduced into Pomerania by an escort of dragoons. Potatoes had no value there. Black diamonds had, until lately, hardly any value, because they were undesired. Now, when used in mining, and for cutting a pathway through the Simplon, they have risen in value. Why? Because useful? No; their lustrous brethren, equally fit to cut through granite, are valued much higher, because personal vanity makes the jewel diamond more intensely desired. Utility, in this case, is indeed the cause of the desiredness of the black diamond, but the desiredness alone gives it value. Value is not worth. Worth stands infinitely higher. Woe to the people who consider value higher than worth !

The general worth, general utility, or desirableness of a commodity will procure for it general value ; but on the one hand so long only as desired, and on the other hand subject to everything which can influence the desiredness. The worth of wheat remains the same while additional wheat is pouring in, and makes it cheaper by changing its desiredness. Coffee may lie in store, and may become better all the time by age, and yet may lose in value, because its desiredness changes for some reason or other. Abundant crops may have increased the quantity in market and lowered the price. It happens daily. Even during the famine in Ireland, in the year 1847, the famished people could hardly be brought to eat maize, either as hominy or meal. Now the taste is changed; maize is desired and has value in Ireland. Fashion effects often terrible changes in value, because in the desiredness of certain things.

The following four elements, then, are requisite to constitute value. Without either of them value does not and cannot exist:

(*a*) Exchangeable and therefore appropriated things desired by a person.

(*b*) An owner of these things who can dispose of and has a right to exchange them.

(*c*) Things offered in exchange for the desired commodity.

(*d*) A desirer of the things spoken of under (*a*).

FALLACY TWENTY-FIRST.—*The Argument of Aspersion and Vilification.*

When the contest for free trade was going on in England, the land-owners were the protectionists, and the manufacturers were the active free-traders. Cheaper food for the laboring population was called for ; and when a statue of Sir Robert Peel, who carried English free trade, was erected, the inscription was proposed: "He gave cheap bread to the people of England." At the same time, if memory does not wholly deceive, it was the English free-traders who used the severer language against their opponents in their memorable struggle. Not, however, such scurrilous expressions as are not uncommon with American protectionists toward the American free-trader.

In America, the reverse of the English case takes place. Here it is the manufacturer from whom the clamor for protection first arose, and the vilifying invectives are, so far as my observation has shown me, chiefly, perhaps exclusively, made use of on the side of the protectionists. Reckless insinuations are freely resorted to, and unwarranted charges against free-traders are treated like evidence in favor of those who make the charges. Free trade is treated from the outset as a sin. It has thus been, at least ever since the renewed contest between protectionists and free-traders. The psychological phenomenon doubtless deserves a candid inquiry, but here we have sufficient space only to state the fact that want of knowledge, lack of common sense, " meanness," " cruel selfishness toward the poor," destitution of public spirit, of patriotism, and the charge of being hired by British gold, are the faults, the vices, and the crimes of which not only every free-trader is accused without shame or hesitation in America, but even those men who, upon the whole, are protectionists, but venture to express an opinion that our present tariff might be modified for the benefit of all. Protectionists and exclusionists of all kinds have always laid especial claim to patriotism, and provincial narrowness assumes the air of public spirit. Lord Shaftesbury and his associates fell into disgrace with the English landowners, whose patriotic indignation was roused by Shaftesbury's permitting Irish beef to be imported into England at a low duty.

The open charge of being bribed by British manufacturers has been repeated by leading American protectionists, when they knew it to be utterly unfounded, against prominent and deserving citizens of untarnished character. Times long past, when ribald terms were believed to strengthen an argument, when public men descended to calling their opponents by names, seem to have returned with our protectionists. Their virulence is surprising, and their boldness worthy of a good cause. The debates in Congress show a similar difference. It is a distinction greatly in honor of the American free-trader. He does not seem to think that abusive language or opprobrious insinuations prove anything, but are usually considered to indicate in the person who makes use of them an instinctive feeling or a secret conviction that all is not so simply clear and right as it is pretended to be.

It requires no gift of prophecy to foretell that, should the recent Japanese settlement in California be measurably successful in the production of tea, the following will take place in the order in which we give it:

First.—Tea-planters will clamor for high protection, as the Louisiana sugar-planters vehemently insisted on protection of their sugar, however loud many of these very planters were for free trade in South Carolina, even to nullification.

Second.—The forty millions of Americans will be told that it is no matter whether they have to pay double or treble the price for worse tea, although tea has become one of the necessaries of life. What is given to paupers in the alms-houses may surely be called a necessary; and tea is given to paupers in England and America.

Third.—We who shall protest against this invasion of a free-man's simplest rights, and who shall maintain that poor people have a right to drink their tea, as much as " poor people have a right to sneeze,"—we shall be indicted for having accepted bribes from the tycoon or mikado, whichever may be uppermost at the time.

Fourth.—We shall see it proved that tea produced four thousand miles from us, and distasteful to us, and very dear, still is *domestic* tea, and *therefore* is better, and that no patriotic man will hesitate to praise it above all Souchong pure.

May the American free-trader pursue his end with calm determination worthy of the cause of human progress, and not allow himself to be drawn into undignified disputes, however provoking the occasion may be!

FALLACY TWENTY-SECOND.—"*The very name of Free Trade shows that it is a System devised for the benefit of a few Merchants. Commerce is unproductive. We want increased Production, Highly-paid Labor, and a Busy Home-Market in General,*" *etc., etc.*

No fallacy, no error of any kind, has been imputed in this paper to the American protectionists which has not been used by them repeatedly and strenuously, and so has the fallacy at the head of this section been copied and not invented, startling as it may seem to the minds of indifferent persons.

It is in most cases dangerous, frequently unsound, to hang an argument on a name, an etymology, or a figure of speech. It can be readily shown how the name Free Trade came to be adopted; but it is not the best name that could be selected. Free Consumption would have been more philosophical, and would have expressed at once the rights and interests which we believe to be involved in this question. Men produce and exchange in order to consume, and everything in this world—life, progress, civilization, science and religion, education, nationalism and internationalism, comfort and æsthetics, literature and refinement, health and charity, government and law—requires increasing consumption with advancing civilization. Men produce and exchange in order to consume ; consumption is the end and object, so far as the material world is concerned, as a means for a higher sphere and life ; and to encumber consumption, to stint it by unwise laws, instead of aiding it to the fullest, is nothing less than interference with the sacred objects of humanity. To interfere with consumption is really as preposterous as an attempt would be to interfere, by sapient laws, with free respiration. All interference with production and exchange *is* interference with consumption. By unhampered exchange at home and abroad we increase production, and leave to every consumer the chance of obtaining the largest amount of the best commodities he desires for what he may have produced in his line of industry. However well meaning some protectionists may be in their grievous error, in reality they interfere with God's own laws and commands. They seem to think that the "sweat of the brow" with which the sons of Adam were cursed is not the effect of sin, but a divine object, and that the greater the "sweat of the brow" so much the better, while, in fact, our race is all the time engaged in finding new means of saving labor and of lessening the sweat of the brow.

The sacredness of the rights of production, exchange, and consumption does not exclude the right or the duty, as the case may be, of government to take the initiative in cases of production. A government is the agent of a community, and, among other things, it ought to do everything which is desirable for the community—if peaceable and not infringing natural rights—and which the individuals cannot do (*e.g.*, defending the country or measuring a degree), or ought not to do (*e.g.*, punish crimes), or will not do (*e.g.*, establish public schools for the poor and poorest). Prussia acted right when in the special treaty of 1815, between herself and Spain, she stipulated for the delivery of a certain number of merino rams, and established shepherd schools where young men might obtain, free of expense, the knowledge of raising merinos. Prussian wool, generally called in the market Saxon wool, forms now one of the important branches of production in that country. This, however, is very different from forcing the Prussian people to use such or such a species of domestic wool.

It would be better had the term Free Consumption been selected from the beginning instead of Free Trade, but the term is settled, and probably will not be changed, like so many thousand inappropriate terms; nor does any advantage arise out of the name Free Trade for the protectionist.[1]

---

[1] The term Free Trade has a curious history. Free Trade was used in England in the last century for trade in defiance of the custom duties, or smuggling, and the famous " Free Trade and Sailors' Rights" was not unconnected with this especial meaning. In Spain, on the other hand, *commercio libre* was officially used for the permission of the subject to trade between Spain and the Spanish colonies. See Reglamente para el Commercio Libre de España a las

Free trade is no system, no theory, no wicker-work of slender concepts; it is simply unencumbered exchange. The French name, Free Exchange, is better than our term, Free Trade. We want exchange of products, of values of all sorts, near and from afar. By commerce is generally understood a certain not well-defined branch or portion of the vast God-ordained exchange; but whatever may be its defining limits, it is, like all exchange, productive.

What is production? Not increase of matter. He alone that created it could increase it. Production means the creation of value or increase of value. When commerce fetches pepper from the coast where it is little wanted, and takes it to the consumer who desires it much, in that case commerce has added to the value of the pepper, and has been productive just as much as the miner is productively employed when he fetches the coal or the ore from the bowels of the earth, where it could not be exchanged, and brings it to light into the world of exchange, of formation, transformation, combination, constant re-exchange, and consumption.

All branches of human industry or activity are productive if they increase value. Appropriation is productive if our fishermen go to the banks and appropriate fish; agriculture is productive, commerce is productive, labor and service are productive, *if* they create additional value; the pavier is, at least, indirectly productive, as a good administration of justice or a peace-preserving government is, for they increase the value of things.

Protection, on the other hand, is waste; it imposes more labor on the consumer to obtain a needed commodity than would be requisite without protection. Frederick the Second of Prussia has always been commended for having cut off the third holiday of the great church festivals, adding thus four or five productive days to the year; the protectionists, on the contrary, enforce unproductive labor.

Indias di de 12 de Octobre, 1778. One of the gravest faults of the wretched system of colonization of Spain had been the prohibition of "free trade" between the mother-country and the colonies.

Why are modern times so immeasurably wealthier than the Middle Ages and antiquity? Why is Europe so much richer than Asia, with all its hoarded treasures in gold and jewels, despite the enormously increased expenses in some branches—in spite, for instance, of the standing armies which withdraw millions of men in their most vigorous age from production, and require the remaining producers to produce millions upon millions to support the purely consuming armies? We must not forget that, contrary to what was formerly believed, when money was considered to constitute wealth, and money alone, mankind at large are becoming richer; not one or a few nations at the cost of others, which become poorer. The following are the most prominent reasons:

Europe and her descendants in other parts, especially in North America, are far more active, more industrious. Idlers are decreasing.

There is greater security under the Municipal Law, as well as under the Law of Nations. The foreigner is no longer considered an enemy. Security is productive.

Money need no longer be secreted; it can be openly invested for production, and interest on borrowed capital has at length been acknowledged as lawful and righteous.

Capital has been accumulated and is used (as it is indispensable) for reproduction. Wealth no longer consists alone in land.

There is a far greater uniformity of ideas and concepts, of mail and money, dress and religion, and intercourse is, commercially, facilitated.

There is, consequently, a far more extensive as well as brisker exchange of things.

No religions as wasteful as many of Asia are, or as Christianity was in the Middle Ages, now exist. Empty but costly display has diminished, while the general standard has been much elevated.

Wasteful sumptuousness has greatly decreased, or frugality has increased, although the standard of comfort has greatly risen. The three factors of wealth are *security*, *industry*, and *frugality.* Religious liberty, going hand in hand with industry and manly activity, has greatly increased.

Knowledge is sounder ; education—the highest university education and the common-school education—is far more widely spread; printing has been invented; and by statistic proof sickness, the wasteful destroyer of production, is more limited. Skill goes with schooling; longevity with advance of civilization.

Not only individuals but nations live longer, and possess a recuperative principle. Accumulation, therefore, is easier, and unproductive hoarding has changed into productive accumulation.

Cleanliness has much improved, and cleanliness is important in more than one point of production. It aids in invigorating the body, and is an element of respectability, itself a stimulant to production.

Science is advanced, and the economical effects of this progress are twofold: it greatly aids in preventing waste, and it draws more and more natural agents within the province of protection. Waste is diminishing ; new materials are made useful. Hide chips are imported in New York from Manilla for paper sizing, and guano from the Pacific manures Cheshire fields, and Coburg toys spread over the whole globe.

The opportunities offering investment for the smallest savings are saving untold millions. The savings-banks are saving many a poor man, and graft the pleasure of laying by on real poverty.

Rational views concerning interest on money have been adopted, and the productiveness of capital has thus been increased.

Labor has come to honor and has been wedded to Knowledge.

Freedom has increased, and with increased liberty there has come an increased impulse and increased safety. Liberty and Commerce as well as manufacturing are found in history so often coupled together that the contrary is rather the exception.

Slavery, wasteful in all periods, except in the most barbarous, when the prisoner of war is allowed to live and turned into an agricultural slave, is fast dying out, and is extinct in the most productive regions—Europe and North America.

Even wars have become far less wasteful, and the Law of Nations stretches a protecting branch, named the Law of War, over hosts in hostile array against one another. Although science increases the destruction in battles, it is nevertheless a fact that modern wars, taken as a whole, are less destructive and wasteful than those of antiquity and the Middle Ages down to the most tragic of all contests—the Thirty Years' War.

And let us, lastly, mention, roads, navigation—in short, all means of intercommunication—have both been quickened and made safer, so that in this way, too, exchange has been promoted, and human inter-dependence has been developed more and more. Time is saved. The whole race works harder—quicker.

All these things have contributed to increase and intensify exchange. Exchange of what? Of products, of course. But of what products? Products which are wanted, desired. But is the desire of obtaining a product sufficient to create a demand? Does the craving of hunger alone create a demand for bread in the market? If it were so, why should so many fall victims to famine in a country famished as Ireland was in 1846 and '47? There was longing indeed for flour, but that craving created no market for it, because Ireland at the time had nothing to offer for the longed-for flour. Demand, in political economy, does not mean a mere desire to have, but a desire to obtain, certain commodities or values backed by values offered in exchange. Products alone can create a market. We cannot buy a single article in the market, be it large or small, a kitchen-market or a "World's Mart," except with or by a product of our own, or for money, which has been obtained by the exchange of some product for it. No artificial legislation or fanciful regulation can make people wealthier. Exchange and production go constantly hand in hand, and all the wisdom and knowledge about markets and free trade, commerce, production, and increase of wealth, may be put in the short and inexorable formula with which I shall conclude these notes, to make it possibly more impressive for some readers—namely:

PRODUCT FOR PRODUCT.[1]

[1] It is of great advantage, in the pursuit of any branch of knowledge, to define apparent synonyms, to distinguish between terms vulgarly confounded, or to disentangle confused ideas, met with in daily life, and which deeply affect the judgment of the people concerning subjects of comprehensive importance. In no branch does this fact deserve greater attention than in the study of Political Economy, because this science deals with subjects with most of which every one is partially and very often erroneously familiar, such as Money, Exchange, Production, Selling and Buying, Commerce, Wealth. Whether I studied a branch for myself or taught it, I have never found anything intellectually more profitable and more conducive to clearness of perception than the indicated process. The student of Political Economy will do himself an essential service if he presents to his mind clearly and impressively the difference of the following terms, related to one another in whatever degree they may be: Hoarding and Accumulation, Frugality and Parsimoniousness or Saving and Avarice, Liberality and Dissipation, Value and Worth, Wealth and Riches, Price and Value, Capital and Spoliation of Others, Money and Wealth, Representative of Money and Money itself, Profit and Cheating, Interest and Extortion, Production and Creation, Consumption and Loss or Annihilation, Appropriation and Robbing Others, Cost and Wages, Profit of A and Loss of B, Natural Agent and Spontaneous Nature, Consumption and Destruction.

THE UNANIMITY OF JURIES.

461

THE UNANIMITY OF JURIES.[1]

A LETTER TO A MEMBER OF THE NEW YORK CONSTITU-
TIONAL CONVENTION, REVISED, WITH ADDITIONS
BY THE AUTHOR.

OBSERVING in the papers that you have proposed in the
convention to abolish the unanimity of jurors as a requisite
for a verdict in civil cases, I beg leave to address to you a few
remarks on a subject which has occupied my mind for many
years, and which I consider of vital importance to our whole
administration of justice. Long ago I gave (in my Civil Liberty and Self-Government[2]) some of the reasons which induced me to disagree with those jurists and statesmen who
consider unanimity a necessary, and even a sacred, element
of our honored jury-trial. Further observation and study
have not only confirmed me in my opinion, but have greatly
strengthened my conviction that the unanimity principle
ought to be given up, if the jury-trial is to remain in harmony
with the altered circumstances which result from the progress
and general change of things. Murmurs against the jury-
trial have occasionally been heard among the lawyers, and
it is by no means certain that without some change like that
which I am going to propose, the trial by jury, one of the
abutments on which the arch of civil liberty rests, can be
prevented from giving way in the course of time.

The present constitution of our state permits litigants to
waive the jury, in civil cases, if they freely agree to do so.

---

[1] Now reprinted as published in the American Law Register, Boston, October,
1867.
[2] See Civil Liberty and Self-Government (3d ed. rev., Phila., 1874), p. 237.

This would indicate that the adoption of verdicts by a majority of the jurors, in civil cases, would not meet with insuperable difficulty; but it seems to me even more important and more consonant with sound reasoning to abandon the unanimity principle in penal cases. The administration of justice is a sacred cause in all cases, and the decision concerning property and rights and, frequently, the whole career of a man or the fate of an orphan is, indeed, sufficiently important not to adopt the majority principle in jury-trials, if it implies any lack of protection, or if there is an element of insecurity in it; and if there is not, then there are many reasons, as we shall see, why it ought to be adopted in criminal cases as well as in civil.

At the beginning of my "Reflections,"[1] I stated the different causes of the failure of justice in the present time. Circumstances obliged me to write that pamphlet in great haste, in which I forgot to enumerate among these causes the non-agreement of jurors. It would be a useful piece of information, and an important addition to the statistics of the times, if the convention could ascertain, through our able state statistician, the percentage of failures of trials resulting from the non-agreement of jurors in civil, in criminal, and especially in capital cases. This failure of agreement has begun to show itself in England likewise, since the coarse means of forcing the jury to agree by the strange logic of hunger, cold, and darkness has been given up.

In Scotland no unanimity of the jury is required in penal trials; nor in France, Italy, Germany, nor in any country whatever, except England and the United States; and in the English law it has only come to be gradually established in the course of legal changes, and by no means according to a principle clearly established from the beginning. The unanimity principle has led to strange results. Not only were jurors formerly forced by physical means to agree in a moral and intellectual point of view, but in the earlier times it hap-

---

[1] See supra, p. 183, etc.

pened that a verdict was taken from eleven jurors, if they agreed, and "the refractory juror" was committed to prison![1]

Under Henry II. it was established that twelve jurors should agree in order to determine a question, but the "afforcement" of the jury meant that as long as twelve jurors did not agree others were added to the panel, until twelve out of this number, no matter how large, should agree one way or the other. This was changed occasionally. Under Edward III. it was "decided" that the verdict of less than twelve was a nullity. At present, in England, a verdict of less than twelve is sometimes taken by consent of both parties. There is nothing, either in the logic of the subject, or the strict conception of right, or in the historic development of the rule, that demands the unanimity of twelve men, and the only twelve men set apart to try a cause or case.

At first the jurors were the judges themselves, but in the course of time the jury, as judges of the fact, came to be separated from the bench as judges of the law, in the gradual development of our *accusatorial* trial, as contradistinguished from the *inquisitorial* trial. It was a fortunate separation, which in no other country has been so clearly perfected. The English trial by jury is one of the great acquisitions in the development of our race, but everything belonging to this species of trial, as it exists at present, is by no means perfect; nor does the trial by jury form the only exception to the rule that all institutions needs must change or be modified in the course of time, if they are intended to last and outlive centuries, or if they shall not become hindrances and causes of ailments instead of living portions of a healthy organism.

The French and German rule, and, I believe, the Italian also, is, that if seven jurors are against five the judges retire, and if the bench decides with the five against the seven, the verdict is on the side of the five. If eight jurors agree against four, it is a verdict, in capital as well as in common criminal

---

[1] Guide to English Juries, 1682. I take the quotation from Forsyth, History of Trial by Jury, 1852.

cases. There is no civil jury in France, Germany, Italy, Belgium, or any country on the continent of Europe.

This seems to me artificial and not in harmony with our conception of the judge, who stands between the parties, especially so when the state, the crown, or the people is one of the two parties; nor in harmony with the important idea (although we Americans have unfortunately given it up in many cases) that the judges of the fact and those of the law must be distinctly separated. The judge, in the French trial, takes part in the trying, frequently offensively so. He is the chief interrogator; he intimates, and not unfrequently insinuates. This would be wholly repugnant to our conceptions and feelings, and may the judge forever keep with the American and the English people his independent, high position *between* and *above* the parties!

On the other hand, what is unanimity worth when it is enforced, or when the jury is out any length of time, which proves that the formal unanimity, the outward agreement, is merely *accommodative* unanimity, if I may make a word? Such a verdict is not an intrinsically truthful one; the unanimity is a real "afforcement" or artificial. Again, the unanimity principle puts it in the power of any refractory juror, possibly sympathizing more with crime than with society and right, to defeat the ends of justice by "holding out." Every one remembers cases of the plainest and of well-proved atrocity going unpunished because of one or two jurors resisting the others, either from positively wicked motives or some mawkish reasons which ought to have prevented them from going into the jury-box altogether.

I ask, then, why not adopt this rule?—*Each jury shall consist of twelve jurors, the agreement of two-thirds of whom shall be sufficient for a verdict in all cases, both civil and penal, except in capital cases, when three-fourths must agree to make a verdict. But the foreman, in rendering the verdict, shall state how many jurors have agreed.*

I have never heard, nor seen in print, any objection to the passage above alluded to, in which I have suggested the abandoning of unanimity, other than this, that people, the criminal included, would not be satisfied with a verdict if they knew that some jurors did not agree. As to the criminal, let us leave him alone. I can assure all persons who have investigated this subject less than I have that there are very few convicts satisfied with their verdict.

The worst among them will acknowledge that they have committed crimes indeed, but not the one for which they are sentenced, or they will insist upon the falsehood of a great deal of testimony on which they are convicted, or the illegality of the verdict.

The objection to the non-unanimity principle is not founded on any psychologic ground. How much stronger is the fact that all of us have to abide by the decision of the majority in the most delicate cases, when supreme courts decide constitutional questions, and we do not only know that there has been no unanimity in the court, but when we actually receive the *opinions* of the minority and their whole arguments, which always seem the better ones to many, sometimes to a majority of the people! Ought we to abolish, then, the publication of the fact that a majority of the judges only and not the totality of them agreed with the decision? By no means. Daniel Webster said in my presence that the study of the protests in the house of lords (having been published in a separate volume) was to him the most instructive reading on constitutional law and history. May we not say something similar concerning many opinions of the minority of our supreme benches?

By the adoption of the rule which I have proposed, the great principle that no man's life, liberty, or property shall be jeoparded twice by trials in the courts of justice would become a reality. At least, the contrary would become a rare exception. Why do all our constitutions lay down the principle that no one shall be tried twice for the same offence? Because it is one of the means by which despotic governments harass a citizen, under disfavor, to try him over and over again; and because civil liberty demands that a man shall not be put twice to the vexation, expense, and anxiety for the same imputed offence. Now, the law says if the jury finds no verdict it is no trial, and the indicted person may be tried over again. In reality, however, it is tantamount to repeated trial when a person undergoes the trial, less only the verdict, and when he remains unprotected against most of the evils and dangers against which the bill of rights or constitution intended to secure him. This point—namely, the making of the noble principle in our constitution a reality and positive actuality—seems to me a most important motive why we should adopt the measure which I respectfully, but very urgently, recommend to the convention. So long as we retain the unanimity principle, so long shall we necessarily have what virtually are repeated trials for the same offence.

In legislation, in politics, in all organizations, the unanimity principle savors of barbarism, or indicates at least a lack of development. The United States of the Netherlands could pass no law of importance except by the unanimous consent of the states-general. A single voice in the ancient Polish diet could veto a measure. Does not perhaps something of this sort apply to our jury unanimity?

Whether it be so or not, I, for one, am convinced that we ought to adopt the other rule, in order to give to our verdicts the character of perfect truthfulness, and to prevent the frequent failures of finding a verdict at all.

NEW YORK, June 26, 1867.

ON PENAL LAW.

469

NOTE.

PRISON discipline and the principles which should govern penal law were among the subjects to which Dr. Lieber devoted much study and thought, especially during the middle period of his life.

In the Appendix to the Encyclopædia Americana he published an exposition and defence of what is known as "the Pennsylvania system" of solitary confinement.

When the elaborate Report on American Prisons, by De Beaumont and De Tocqueville, was published, the authors requested Dr. Lieber to translate it into English, and this he did in 1833, prefixing an introduction, and adding to it the essay from the Encyclopædia and copious notes, for which he received the thanks of Chancellor Kent, Governor Marcy, and many other publicists.

In 1838 his views on Penal Law and kindred topics were published by the Philadelphia Society for Alleviating the Miseries of Prisons, in a letter addressed by Dr. Lieber to their President, John Bacon, Esq. Several years later he revised this pamphlet, but, so far as I am aware, he did not reprint it. His copy of the translation of the French Report is interleaved with copious notes, memoranda, printed slips, and letters from eminent men—intended doubtless to serve as materials for a treatise on Penology, or at least for revised statements of his views. Dr. Lieber retained his interest in this subject throughout his life, but the right occasion never came for a full and systematic presentation of the thoughts which he had worked out, and it is not easy for an editor to do justice, within a moderate space, to his matured opinions. Some extracts will, however, be given from the letter to Mr. Bacon, including several passages which he added to the original letter, and which seem to have been written about 1858.—G.

ON PENAL LAW.

Mild Laws: Firm Judges: Calm Punishments.

PART OF AN ESSAY WRITTEN IN 1838, WITH SUBSEQUENT
ADDITIONS BY THE AUTHOR.

THERE is no great movement in the progress of civilization which has not its flood and ebb tides until it leads to a broadly established reality. Even then the institution continues to attract more or less attention according to the peculiar character of each period. About twenty years ago prison discipline engaged the lively attention of many high-minded and practical men, both in Europe and here. Some thirty years ago prison discipline in America was one of the very ornaments of our country, which at that time was looked upon with longing favor by the highest intellects in Europe. It brought the De Tocquevilles and the De Beaumonts to our shores to observe and report to their governments. This and other things have sadly changed. At the present moment there is a lull in this movement, but so long as society consists of individuals who require rules of action that may be infringed, there must be the necessity of punishment, and the question, In what shall it consist, to correspond best to the welfare of punishing society and the punished offender, as well as to agree most with the progress of our race, will continually recur. Punishment is one of the standing subjects of mankind.

I have pronounced myself in the following pages clearly in favor of solitary confinement at labor, and all my observation and study since the essay was written, a period of twenty years, have had no other effect than to confirm my conviction

471

on all the principles and main points, although a variety of other systems have been tried and many attacks on solitary confinement have been made.

Quite recently a valuable testimony in favor of solitary confinement has been given. Mr. Schlake, after a six years' solitary imprisonment for participation in the rising in Baden, in the year 1849, has published his experience and penological views. He proposes improvements, indeed, but he is the advocate of solitary confinement. Until Mr. Schlake published his work I was, as far as I know, the only writer on penology who spoke in favor of solitary confinement from personal experience. I am glad that now, when I am descending the steps of life, another witness has stepped forward, among the younger generation, to take, with personal experience, which is a good and impressive teacher to those who are willing to observe and learn, the defence of a cause which I hold to be very important to our civilization.

May I not hope that the interest in prisons and prisoners is not so far abated as to make a translation of the work I have indicated impossible? The church of Christ prays everywhere for captives and prisoners, however guilty; let us also work for them. Praying without doing does not go far; it may recoil. The impulse first given by the church, and more clearly and practically acted on by Howard, will most assuredly never die out; but this means only that men will be found who take the subject earnestly in hand and impress their fellow-beings with its grave importance. Why shall our generation idly wait? We are not freed from the general obligation of society to punish; our period is not unstained by offences and crimes. On the contrary, increased activity, frequently rising to feverish restlessness, and the ill use of enlarged individual liberty, together with a morbid philanthropy in some and a reckless levity in others, to whom the administering of justice is confided, have fearfully increased, if not the absolute criminality of our own age, yet, assuredly, the number and heinous character of crimes, here as well as on the other side of the sea. Penology requires more than ever the attention of every citizen of leading influence, be he clothed with official authority or with the equally important authority which character and an acknowledged love of duty give to every citizen of a free country.

When the following pages were written, it was the intention of the author, as indeed he then indicated in the preface, to write a comprehensive work on penology, the art and science of punishing, for which then already many and valuable materials existed. They have much increased since that period, but no sufficient interest in the subject existed then, nor does it now, to warrant the publication. The work will be written, and the science will take its place by the side of Penal Law. An official offer was even made to the author in 1846, that a chair of penology, proposed by him, should be established in the University of Berlin, and that he should fill the chair with the name of his invention ;[1] but he could not give up his chosen country, and now he must leave all this willingly to younger hands and to abler minds.

[The essay begins with an inquiry into the sources from which the punitory power of the state is derived, and reviews a few prominent theories, namely, Expiation ; Necessity and Expediency ; Deterring; Special Prevention ; Warning ; Contrast ; Correction and Reform ; Retaliation. The author then gives his own view in the following words :]

Perhaps it is possible to give a more correct theory of punishment than either of these. In attempting to do this, however, it is necessary to state at once that every philosopher must be misled if he sets out with the idea that punishment is a subject which can be developed by a chain of abstract ideas. It is a subject derived from and applying to a compound of ideas.

All punishment, in whatever sphere resorted to, is an intentional infliction of some sufferance for some committed wrong.

Hugo Grotius says, Punishment is an inflicted evil for a committed evil ; but I think we ought to define it from a

---

[1] In German I have proposed the name Strafkunde. In English I could find no better word than penology.

point of view from which it is seen, not as an evil which we have no right to commit.

State punishment, or that punishment which society inflicts through its government, is a sufferance, intentionally or designedly inflicted by lawful authority (which implies in a lawful way) for a wrong, designated as such by the law, and responsibly committed (either by positive intention or with culpable neglect).

Whenever a punishment deviates from one or the other of the component elements here indicated, if it be inflicted for wrongs not designated by the law, or upon irresponsible individuals, or by unlawful authority, or by no authority at all, or for no wrong, it loses its character of state punishment and becomes revenge and crime in turn.

If the English term Right could be divested of the idea of privilege or claim of some sort, and if we could give it that one of the meanings which Jus has in Latin, according to which it means the result of a legal relation, and includes an amount of obligations as well as privileges, for instance, the Jus of the husband,—if I say the English word Right could receive this meaning, I would say that Punishment, from another point of view, is the Right of the offender, the obligation he owes to the state, with the privileges he is entitled to ; for a lawful punishment involves many and very valuable privileges and protections.[1]

---

[1] The state is a society founded on right, or it is human society, in as far as it constitutes itself and acts upon the principle of right. Right is taken here in its primordial sense, as that which gives the foundation of all single rights. It is the regulation and fixation of the use of individual moral freedom, which each man possesses as man, as rational and moral beings placed in society—that is, co-ordinately with others ; it originates out of the just demand each one makes to enjoy this freedom. All that the state, therefore, demands or gives, or all that the individual demands at its hands and yields to it—in short, all relations of the individual to the state—must be founded on right, or the idea of the just.

The difficulty of finding a firm basis for civil punition, and the great variety of opinions respecting this subject, have arisen from this very fact. We cannot do, or ought not to do, anything within the sphere of the state for which we do not at first establish the right we may have to do it. In domestic punition the same difficulty does not exist. No one can doubt the *natural* relation between child and

But definitions establish nothing; they merely epitomize what has been found or acknowledged. We have still to make good the right of punishing, for it must never be forgotten that all punishment implies the idea of a designed infliction of some sufferance, a very grave use of power which stands in need of justification.

---

parent. The child is naturally dependent upon its parents, physically, morally, and intellectually; or, in other words, for support and education. The object of domestic punishment is improvement. It arises out of the natural relation of the family. In the state, however, we have first to prove a right, we may have to improve morally or intellectually, in certain given circumstances or cases; for it is by no means the direct object of the state to educate or morally to improve every member of it. The general object of the state is, as I have said, the protection of that freedom which each individual has a right to claim as a moral being. Another difficulty has arisen out of an opposite error.

It is, moreover, a grave mistake of nearly all who have given a theory of the state and its attributes, that, as soon as they had construed, as they imagined, the state, they left society entirely out of view, as if merged in, absorbed by, the state. Yet society continues to exist with distinct attributes, even after all those which are founded on the idea of right are concentrated in and form the state; and not only does society continue to exist as such, but the closest connection between the two must forever remain. We find an instance in public opinion which is an attribute of society, when it passes over into the state and becomes public will. The state is the ægis of society, and it has likewise to redress toward individuals wrongs, which society may have committed or produced by its peculiar organization. This connection between the two is everywhere important, and not the least so in matters of punishment, as we shall see hereafter. Many jurors, I repeat, have fallen into errors, in treating of punishments, because they kept in view the state alone, and either forgot or did not suspect the connection of state and society, which is no fusion, but a connection of two distinct things. Yet the state is nothing artificial, nothing made, nothing that may be adopted. It is necessary, and therefore natural, grown, and indispensable. It is a necessary manifestation of society. If we now call right that which indicates man's relation to the state, or that which is the necessary consequence of his relations founded on the just, toward others, that which the state is bound to grant him, punishment is the right between society and the offender, or, however paradoxical it may appear at first glance, the right both of the society and the offender. But why is it so? Merely because it is necessary, and farther we cannot go? By no means. In order to prove that punishment be what we have asserted it to be, we have to show, first, that it be just; secondly, that it be necessary. All idea of the just is essentially founded upon equality; without it, as its first foundation, justice cannot be imagined. Every individual in the state must grant to others the right he claims for himself; if he interferes with the rightful state of others, he grants them the abstract right to interfere with his.

All reasoning must begin with a primitively acknowledged truth or fact; with a primordial conviction. In our case it is the conviction, felt and known by all mankind, that it is plainly just if injury is the consequence of injury. It is a law written in our hearts. Many things—ideas, truths, and aspirations—may come to modify this primary conviction and psychologic law, or wholly suspend it, but its original justice remains unchanged.

The lex talionis, therefore, starts undoubtedly from the right point, from perfect evenness, but it stops short of a most important item, without which we do wrong in inflicting injury.

The abstract principle of injury for injury, which is the principle of the lex talionis, pervades the whole sphere of human actions, from those between individuals, expressed in the homely alliteration "tit for tat," to the highest international actions. He who injures me gives me an abstract right to inflict injury on him. He who beats me gives me the abstract right of beating him. I speak here, as I am bound to do, of the abstract right, that is, of that which is founded on strict justice and on nothing else; not of actions which may be prompted by generosity, charity, prudence, or religion. Now, the principle of the law of retaliation, sufferance for sufferance, which exists between individuals, passes over into the state, for the state is a society in which every one individually owes certain duties to every one collectively. The principle of perfect evenness is retained, for man must, by his nature, live in society, otherwise he cannot live fully as man; that is, he cannot become that for which his maker has placed him on this earth. Society, again, cannot exist without the ægis of the state. It is, therefore, not at the option of the individual to consider himself insulated and independent, or as a member of the state. He is by his nature a member of the state, and the state, on the other hand, has a natural right to pay injury with injury, because each interference with the rights of the individual, is an interference with itself, or a wrong inflicted upon itself, as soon as the rightful state of things has been disturbed.

We have to mention two more points : first, the state being a society of moral beings, because right can only exist between these, each *public* immorality becomes as such an interference with the rights of the citizens, and gives the state a right to produce injury for the injury done, though prudence may dictate not to make use of the right. Secondly, every dangerous act, if knowingly done, becomes a wrong, an immoral act, interferes with the rights of the citizens, who demand protection from the state. If a man lets loose a tiger among men, it is certainly an immoral act, though he need not have absolutely intended to cause thereby the death of others. To injure a dyke in Holland is highly immoral, because highly dangerous to the lives and property of the community. To light a fire on the sea-shore is in itself an innocent act, but the danger for the mariners, who may mistake it for a light-house, makes it justly a highly penal act.

The important point, in which the principle of retaliation lacks, is this :

Punishment implies the idea of an application or infliction of some sufferance. In doing anything, however, which involves a sufferance of another, it is not sufficient that we have the abstract right of doing it, but we must have a good object in view, in making use of this right, else it becomes useless infliction of suffering—in other words, cruelty. The state stands, with regard to the offender, precisely on the same footing as to its right of punishing, as the parent stands respecting his child. The father or mother have a right to punish the child, but if no good object is kept in view in making use of this abstract right the act becomes cruelty. The Roman law already acknowledges that no one shall make use of his abstract right merely to the disadvantage of another, and without use or interest to himself. What would we think of an individual who would inflict injury, solely because injury had been done to him, for no use or benefit whatever to him, the injurer, or any one else? We would say that he is actuated by vengeance. How much more blamable, then, would be the state which, according to its true essence, is without vindictiveness or passion, if it were to inflict sufferance simply because it has the abstract right to inflict it! This is the reason why, frequently, we read of English judges pronouncing sentence, yet suspending the execution of it, and binding over the offender to appear whenever it should be found necessary to let the sentence take its course. It is done, for instance, when the meaning of some law has been considered doubtful, and the finding of a person guilty will settle the law for the future without the necessity of inflicting the sentence in the particular case.

We arrive, then, at this important point: that though equality and the idea on which the state is founded give us the abstract right of retaliation, we can make use of it only so far as it shall be found necessary.

The question occurs whether, in allowing necessity to form the ground of our use of the acquired punitory right, we do not, after all, fall into the theory of expediency, against which the strongest arguments were adduced. Is it not essentially the same? I think not. We acquire a right to punish on the primary principle of retaliation; the offender, at all events, cannot complain; and as he as well as every one else belongs to the state, a society always and essentially founded on the two polar principles—that of individualism and socialism[1]— and on whom the state has its claims of socialism, no injustice is committed if the state makes practical use of the right it has acquired. If this be so, the first question which presents itself is, How far is punishment necessary?

Man, as has been said already, is a moral being, *i.e.*, a being

---

[1] I take socialism in its philosophical sense, and, as a matter of course, not in the sense of political pedants who recommend community of property. I have given my opinion of this crudity in my Essays on Labor and Property.

Here I mean by socialism that principle which pervades the state as much as that of individualism, and is as necessary to form and bend any society. It is on this principle of socialism that I must pay taxes toward a war of which I may wholly disapprove; for it is God's will that men should live in society in order to obtain the ends of humanity, and it is on the same principle that, in my opinion, we have the right to make use of the acquired right of punition, so that we remain just.

endowed with a moral character. Wherever he goes, whatever institution he forms, he carries this attribute with him. Without it no relations of right, no rights themselves can exist between men. There are no rights between animals. He must, therefore, maintain this first of all attributes inviolate; and every committed wrong is not only the material wrong done to our neighbor, but the moral wrong of interference with the rights of others. A society in which every sort of wrong might be committed with impunity would necessarily lose its ethical character, and a community loses in its ethical character in the same degree as wrongs remain unpunished. The expression of public disapproval of wrong would be missing. The greatest injury suffered by a community, in which murders are frequently committed with impunity, is by no means the insecurity of life. After counting all the lives lost by bloody rencontres, it might be found that the number is far below the deaths occasioned in another community by imprudent exposure to a changeable climate. Would this justify the former community in continuing to leave murders unpunished? It is the lowering of the moral standard, a necessary consequence of trifling with the highest object in creation— with man himself, which forms the most baneful consequence of such a state of things. The state, therefore, has to punish all offences against its laws—for, according to its nature, it has no cognizance over others, no organ, as it were, to perceive them—likewise as offences against its necessary character, and must not become unjust by arbitrarily punishing some, and at other times omit punishment of the same offences. I wish not to be misunderstood as if I meant to assert that immorality alone can constitute the punishableness of an action to be visited by political authority. On the contrary, immorality without any other concomitant would form no ground for making use of the right of punishment which we have acquired as indicated already. Experience and science prove that nothing is more dangerous than the intermeddling of the state with private affairs; secondly, that no punishment can in justice take place where no violation of right has taken place.

This is now generally adopted by all the most profound jurists, and is, in fact, to be deduced from the principle of the right of punishment which I have just laid down, namely, reciprocity on the ground of equality. I shall speak, however, of the fact already alluded to, that immorality may become the ground of punishableness *when* and *because* it interferes with the rights of others.

It is on this ground, likewise, that the state has a right to punish shameful and offensive cruelty against animals, as, from sheer malignance, to the dishonor of man is sometimes practised. The animal, indeed, has no right, and therefore no legal offence against it can be committed ; but if the cruelty is committed publicly it is an offence against the rights of citizens who see it, for they have a right to claim that no such revolting acts be committed in their presence. The fact that the animal is the property of its tormentor does not excuse, for no citizen has a right to do with his property absolutely what he chooses. There are many acts which I am not permitted to do, though they affect directly my own property only. The danger is another ground on which we have the right and the duty to punish barbarity against animals, for, as has been stated, to do what is dangerous is immoral, and members of the state who can in cold blood torture an animal for the sake of torturing it are surely most dangerous to society.

Thirdly, immorality alone does not afford a ground of punishment, because the state would not reach it by its punishments. Immorality as such is to be reached by society, not by the state ; by public opinion, the many relations of respectability in the community, by religion, and is to be prevented by good, sound, and general education, and, if it has already acquired a character of danger with the young, by those excellent and benevolent establishments called houses of refuge, into which we acquire a *right* of placing the young offender, by the *danger* he offers to society, and *in* which we do not punish, but endeavor to correct and rescue, on account of the youth of the offender, which does not make him yet strictly accountable to the state, whose active member he has not yet become. The youthful offender, moreover, has a right to demand correction at the hands of society, because his youth is of itself a proof that he has become corrupt, in a great degree, by circumstances, that is, by unfortunate, yet perhaps unavoidable relations of society itself. What is the standard of punishment? This question is closely connected with the next: *What is the object of punishment?*

The first object of the state is the protection of its members—security. Security means that state in which the citizen is protected against any violation of his rights, and by which the great and general object of the state is secured. The object of the state, however, is the fully obtaining the ends of man as man. He cannot obtain them except in society. Man is absolutely made for society, and this society has to secure itself, and to remove all obstacles in the way of obtaining its ends, which forms the object of the state. Now this security is of twofold character: material and intellectual, direct or indirect. Direct security I call the positive protection against direct wrong, *i.e.*, interference with the individual rights of others. Indirect security I call that security which results from the maintenance of that general state of society, without which its ends cannot be obtained. Every immoral act, therefore, declared to be such by the state, is an act against this security, for without the moral state of society it cannot exist; it is, consequently, an interference with the rights of all its members. But this does not yet give us the privilege of making use of the general right of punishment thus acquired, because there may be other powers far more effective to repress it, as we have seen already, or the punishments possibly at the disposal of the state may not reach the evil, and thus punishment would be useless, *i.e.*, cruel, or the danger of interfering with it may be greater than the advantage to be derived from its punishment; or, finally, the wrong may not be sufficiently definable for the state, in order to bring it clearly under a category of punishable acts. Circumstances, moreover, necessarily connected with punishment, especially publicity of trial, may render the punishment a far greater evil to the security of the state than the punishable act itself. It is thus, for instance, the case according to the opinion of many, and for one, of myself, respecting certain vile offences, too vile to be named, which public opinion justly visits with far severer punishment than any human code could fix on them, and which on that account are committed in darkness and privacy, while the trial drags them into light and injures thus far more. Nay, several of these vile and disgusting acts are, as long as secretly committed, no violation of others—of human beings, which they could become only by being publicly done. If, however, at any time a part of society should sink so low that these unnatural vices should become general, society would have a right and, it may be, a duty to punish them.

The true standard of punishment, therefore, that is, the standard of the degree how far we are justified in making use of the previously acquired general right of punishment, is the danger, material or psychologic, to which the offence exposes society, and the effect which the punishment has on society or the punished individual himself. If it has no effect on either it is useless, though the desired effect is by no means merely the momentary one of deterring from crime, but also the general and far more important one of keeping up public feeling of right; that is, a public feeling that the state is a society of right, and cannot allow the violation of rights unpunished. If the punishment has any effect on the individual, we are likewise justified in applying it on the ground of security. We protect by punishing. To reform the inward man of the offender would, of itself, afford no right to punish, because that is his affair; but by his offence he has shown that his moral condition is of a kind that it becomes dangerous to society. We have, therefore, not only a right, but also the obligation to reform him, provided the state have means at its disposal to obtain this desirable end.

If, therefore, an interference with the rights of others has taken place, the danger of society affords the standard of punishment. Frequently the danger itself is, in turn, the sole standard of the interference with the rights of others, as I have mentioned already. A great historian[1] informs us, that it was a capital offence in the village of Ursern, in Switzerland, to cut a single tree of an ancient grove, high above it, because these trees alone protected the inhabitants from avalanches. Was it wrong in those people to fix the highest punishment to this act? Surely as little as the high penalties with which treason is visited, because it is an interference with the primary rights of the people—security in enjoying life.

Two reasons demand, moreover, that the punishment be just—*i.e.*, that offence and punishment stand, according to the moral views of the people, in proper relation. In fact, the principle of retaliation necessarily involves this; for, if the punishment be, according to the views of the society, too hard, it means nothing else than that retaliation has been exceeded. The two additional reasons are these: 1. The state is founded upon the idea of the just; destroy justice, and you destroy the essence of the state. Disproportionate punishments, however, whether disproportionately heavy or light, are unjust. 2. The effect of the punishment is destroyed. If too light, the offender as well as the community feel that there is no justice in the punishment, and the moral belief in the state, or public feeling of justice will be weakened or destroyed. If too severe, it will have the same effect with the addition that it alienates the offender still more from society, an effect which is, as we shall see hereafter, most diligently to be avoided, not by way of charity, but on strict grounds of justice on the part of the state. The necessity of punishment, before we acquire a full right actually to punish, leads us a step farther, and we find that not every illegal act is punishable; for instance, in those cases in which a restitution of the injury done, or a public declaration that no offence against the character of the injured person had been meant by the offensive words of the injurer, are entirely sufficient. Punishment in this case would go be-

---

[1] Johannes Müller, Swiss History, 2d Book, chap. i., note 159.

yond what is necessary, and therefore unjust. Punishment takes place when the avowal of wrong is not sufficient, when the protection of the rights of the offended demand it, or when rights have been violated which can never be re-established (*e.g.*, in case of murder), and the rights of others demand protection. Disproportion between offence and punishment is at once acknowledged as unjust. If the papers of the time have reported correctly, a lad, named James Death, aged fifteen years, was sentenced to death, in the year 1837, in England, by Mr. Justice Tolman, for having robbed on the king's highway another lad of buns, pork-pies, etc., with threats to kill the latter if he would not give up the edibles. The fact that no reader believes in the possibility of this sentence having been executed shows the injustice of the law.

I cannot pass over to the next point without once more referring to the meaning in which I have used the word effect. I do not mean the momentary and always accidental effect, but the general, or the belief of the community in the state, namely, that it is a society which rests on the idea of the just, which cannot exist without ethical ground. If wrong, however, does not meet with evil consequences, the moral character of the state is destroyed. To take the momentary and accidental effect, as the principle of gradation of punishment, leads to the theory of deterring, which is, probably, the very worst of all false penal theories; to tearing and pinching with red-hot tongs, cutting the tongue, and putting out the eyes; and lends the cloak of principle to unprincipled revenge.

As the effect of punishment is a necessary element of its gradation, it is clear that the latter must, in a great measure, depend:

Upon the material and intellectual state of society; upon the view society takes of the offence; upon the view society takes of the punishment; upon the general pyschologic state of the class of offenders; and upon the probable operation of punishment in other respects.

I have read, I believe in the Memoirs of Prince de Ligne, that Catharine II. related that Peter the Great changed some severe sentence against several noblemen into this, that they should receive a box on the ear, in the public market, by the hangman; and, added the empress, it was a wise and great principle which guided him; he wanted to impart the feeling of honor to his nobility, the offence having been a highly dishonorable act.

It will be seen that, the original right of punishment once settled, all the various objects, such as protection, warning, reform, expediency, from which it was believed possible to derive the first punitory right of the state, come in as *motives* of punishment, or, in other words, as reasons why we make use of the right of punishment already existing.

From the principles which have been ascertained, as from others laid down by the theory of penal law, or relating to human actions in general, we find that sound punishment must possess, among others, the following characteristics:

1. Inasmuch as punishment is a human action by which certain objects are to be obtained, the common rules of action are applicable to it:

We must strive to produce the greatest effect with the fewest means.

The means we use must effect the object we wish to obtain.

They must not defeat or counteract the object we strive for.

Still less must the means increase or generate the evil which we labor to counteract.

Finally, in order to obtain a 'general result we must act on a general plan, according to fixed principles.

2. All punishment must be founded in the right we have to punish, derived from the essential character of the state, as that society which rests on the idea of the just.

3. This right can be actually made use of only so far as is necessary and useful. Without this it is useless—cruel.

4. The great and final object of punishment is protection in its highest adaptation.

5. The principle of gradation of punishment is the danger of society, yet it must remain within the bounds of justice.

6. That punishment must have the effect it is intended to

have, is another reason why it must be just; and a principle which guides in the adaptation of the punishment to the offence. It must be just, therefore, according to the spirit of the age.

7. Punishment, in order to be just, must proceed from the state, and neither be left to private revenge nor to the private view of the judge. Those, therefore, err greatly who, with Sir Thomas More, in his Utopia, demand that the penal judges should have their hands entirely free, and assign punishment according to the combination of all the given circumstances, only guided by their virtue and conscience. Modern penal codes have been called by some, who dream of the perfection of patriarchic governments, penal price currents. No person acquainted with the subject has ever insisted upon an absolute fixation of punishments. Bodin was opposed to *tariffs* of punishments. The ancients acted on the principle adopted by Sir T. More. Lycurgus left it to the judges alone to settle the punishment; nor was the Areopagus bound by any law in assigning punishment; but we must not forget that penal law was then in its incipient stage, and that, according to the views of the ancients, the individual was all that he was, in and through the state alone, absorbed by it, while with us the individual is the object of the state. Protection, our great end of the state, requires fixed penal codes.

8. It is useless to talk against punishment as men like Coleridge have done (see his Letters and Conversations), and lately Thomas Walker, Esq., one of the police magistrates of the metropolis (London), because it will never abolish crime. They show that they have never thoroughly understood what punishment essentially is. If they assert that by education, removal of pauperism, etc., crime will be abolished, they forget that the human heart will always remain a focus of passion, and that the more civilized a nation is the more intricate are its relations, which will always induce some to commit offences, and that with increased variety of human activity increased opportunity of crime takes place. No physician ever pretended that medicine would eradicate disease among men.

9. If the punishment be just, it must be capable of graduation, and the more capable of graduation the better.

10. Yet that it be just and considered as such, it ought to be as even and uniform as possible. Uniformity and graduableness are two of the greatest desiderata in punishments.

11. The state knows of no revenge; by revenge it would lower itself to the offender. The state in punishing, protects, and not only the community at large, but it continues to protect the offender as long as he remains within it, *i.e.*, as long as he lives.

12. Punishment is not intended to atone; to wipe off and nullify the offence. This cannot be done, except by a repenting heart before a benignant deity, with regard to the immorality of the offence alone, and has consequently nothing to do with the state. What has been done is done, and cannot be undone as fact. "One thing," says Agathon in Aristotle, Ethics 6, ch. 3, "One thing even the gods cannot do, to undo that which is done."

13. Punishment ought to be calm in its character; it ought calmly to operate, and keep the true mean between trifling leniency and harsh cruelty. Cruelty is weakness. Strong governments, *i.e.*, governments which have grown out of and provide faithfully for the true wants of the people, can afford to be mild. A mild punishment strikes deeper than a cruel one, for it carries the whole weight of public opinion and that of the offender himself along with it.[1]

---

[1] When Damiens, who slightly wounded Louis the Fifteenth with a penknife, had been tortured and found guilty, "a consultation of physicians was held to determine by what form of death his agonies could be rendered most excruciating and most protracted, and this conclave devised for him the most barbarous cruelties ever recorded in history." (History of the House of Orleans, by W. C. Taylor, vol. ii. p. 182.) This happened in 1757. The execution lasted two hours. I remember nothing worse in Suetonius; indeed, I cannot bring to my mind, at the moment I am writing this, anything equally black. In reading such cruelties, which happened in our own race, at a period when elegance of manners, science, and what is generally called civilization, flourished in France, or at least in Paris, we almost peruse with blunted aversion the communication of Mr. Lynton to the Asiatic Society of London, in 1851, that a Chinese merchant

14. The state, being the agent of society, in punishing, and having the obligation of protecting even the offender, has the duty of aiding, as far as able, the possible reform of the offender, because society does not know by what fault of her own, *c.g.*, bad laws, neglect in general education, the offender has become such.

15. The state has the most solemn duty,

Not to make the offender worse than he was when he came within the sphere of its penal action.

To remove everything that, in the nature of things must, or probably will, make the offender worse.

16. The state has the right of turning the punishment of the individual to the greatest legitimate advantage of society provided punishment is founded on a previous indisputable right, and meted out according to justice. The state, therefore, acquires the right to use the punishment as example, as prevention of crime with the offender himself, etc.

17. The state, which has no right to interfere with the moral state of any loyal citizen, acquires it with regard to the offender, who, by committing offence, has fallen within its sphere of penal action ; for it is one of the means of prevention of crime, which the protection of society requires. By the offence the offender has shown that he is in a moral state dangerous to society.

18. The offender, who has not committed his offence from sudden passion, or prompted by powerful circumstances, as great misery of a parent, etc., considers himself at war with society, out of its pale ; he sees no reciprocal relation and obligation between the two. The state has few surer means of re-establishing this feeling of loyalty, without which an offenceless state of the individual is not imaginable, than by teaching him to work. It protects society and him by doing

---

was sentenced to die of sleeplessness for the murder of his wife. He lived for nineteen days without having slept a minute. At the commencement of the eighth day he implored his jailers to strangle him. Men have been far more ingenious in devising cruelties than in benevolence.

so. Labor and learning to work calms the mind and furnishes one of the requisites of an honest life.

19. The state, in endeavoring to reunite the offender with society, has carefully to obviate renewed irritation, which cannot but prevent the feeling of loyalty. If the punishment irritates, provokes, exasperates, it defeats its own object.

20. Far the greater part of crimes are committed from original thoughtlessness. Crime is prevented by making the criminal thoughtful.

21. If it be desirable that the offender should feel reunited to society, the state must avoid what would hinder this, for instance, acquaintance, even by sight, with other offenders.

22. The form of punishment, that in which it consists, must be regulated and influenced by the degree of social civilization; by the psychologic state of the offenders; by experience, including natural character; by our knowledge of man in general; and by the means at our disposal.

23. The state must not challenge by trifling punishments. Punishment must make a lasting impression. Nor must it defeat its own moral effect by disproportionate severity, still less by cruelty.

24. Certainty of punishment is more important than the degree of sufferance produced by it, because it flows from, and, in turn, maintains and diffuses a sense of justice, of the ethic character and importance of man, and a belief in the morality of the state. Respecting the transgressor, the fact that punishment will undoubtedly follow impresses the evil-disposed far more effectually than that the punishment will be severe, provided it does follow. Every man calculates chances in his favor, even the soldier scaling the breach.

25. If punishment ought to be certain, both in its being actually the consequence of transgression, and in its degree, it ought on the other hand to strike the offender alone, as much as this is possible in human society, in which all members are so closely interlinked. Hence exceptions are justly made of pregnant or nursing women respecting some punishments. This seems to be very simple, yet all the members of the

family of Damiens, mentioned shortly before, were banished from France, and all the family of the Chinese Keshen were executed, because he had been unsuccessful against the English. Sangermano's translation of the Damasat shows that the principle of punishing relations is regularly embodied in the code of the Burmese. Napoleon made parents and relations answerable for the desertion of soldiers. How great, then, is the following passage taken from the code of the Spanish Visigoths:

"*Omnia crimina suos sequantur auctores. Nec pater pro filio, nec filius pro patre, nec uxor pro marito, nec maritus pro uxore, nec frater pro fratre, nec vicinus pro vicino, nec propinquus pro propinquo, ullam calamitatem pertimescat. Sed ille solus judicetur culpabilis qui culpanda commiserit, et crimen cum illo qui fecerit moriatur: nec successores ant haeredes pro factis parentum ullum periculum pertimescant.*"[1]

26. Punishment ought to be, in its nature, as calculable as possible; that is, it ought to be so, that those who inflict it should be able to calculate its effects, or remain master over it as much as possible. Defamatory punishments, therefore, are bad, because they affect different individuals differently. Hence, likewise, should punishment depend as little as possible upon the prison keepers. They should not have it in their power much to aggravate or alleviate.

27. Punishment ought to be accommodable in its nature. By accommodable punishment I mean that which accommodates itself, by its own nature, to the given case. If an absolute fine be imposed for an offence, it is not accommodable, because the rich do not feel it, and it is heavy for the poor. If putting in irons and working on the high road be imposed, it is a far severer punishment to the well-educated than, to an uneducated offender, who had few ties with society, and yet the better education itself may have been one of the aiding

---

[1] One exception alone existed—the punishment for high treason. It was natural according to the views then, and in many countries now, taken. Conc. Tol. xvi. c. 10; Leg. Vis. L. ii., tit. 1, tit. 6. Lembke's History of Spain, vol. i. p. 226.

causes of the offence; for instance, in order to support a family in a decent manner. So the punishment ought to accommodate itself to sex, age, habit of reflection, keenness of honor, etc.

28. Punishment ought to be simple. Compound, accumulated punishments revolt and impress with the idea of vindictiveness. They are always undignified.

29. Punishment must be a sufferance of some sort, whether by way of privation or infliction; else it is no punishment. We shall see that privation is far preferable. English criminals, and even persons that had not yet committed any crime, used to inquire what crime was exactly requisite to *earn* transportation, and then committed it, because they lived better in Australia as convicts than at home without conviction.

30. Only accountable beings, *i.e.*, persons physically and intellectually free in their volition, are punishable. Insane persons, children, people in their second childhood, sleepwalkers, people who act by surprise, or under duresse, are either not at all accountable, or not so with regard to certain actions.

It is, therefore, degrading the woman, if a sickly feeling of vague honor or philanthropy prevents us from punishing female offenders, for we deny them, thereby, the degree of accountability they have an undoubted right to demand. First, woman was considered the slave of the parents or husband, or at least too much subjected to them to have any high degree of accountability of herself. The Christian religion aided powerfully in raising the rights of woman, as can be shown by history. King Magnus Erichson of Sweden decreed in 1335: "The woman must atone for all her crimes, like the man."[1] And now we begin again to deny them their accountability and to treat them like children, or as if they were too weak to be fully accountable, or as if they offered but little danger; while it requires no uncommon knowledge of criminal matters to be aware of the fact that, a woman once sunk to crime, and even only to vice, is one of the most dangerous

---

[1] Geijer, History of Sweden, in Heeren and Uckert, vol. i. p. 273.

members of the community.[1]   The reason why it should be
so, can be very clearly traced, though the limits of the present
lines do not permit me to do so.   Napoleon's opinions on this
subject, as given in O'Meara, coincide with this.

The Chinese law to this day contains the maxim, " A mar-
ried woman can commit no crime; the responsibility rests
with the husband;"[2] and the Japanese woman, although she
enjoys a high character in the house as well as in history,
cannot give legal testimony.

31. Correction can never afford us a principle for the duration of punishment; because reform is something on which
we cannot insist, nor can we measure it with distinctness, sufficient to ground acts of justice upon it.   If we cannot insist
on it, we become unjust toward those who do not reform and
are obliged to suffer longer.

32. Punishment ought to be founded first of all on a physical basis, because this alone affords a sure and safe basis; and
evenness of punishment can take place only when we have
gained that basis.   The moral state of the individual is not
directly tangible by the state.   But the punishment ought to
be so that it does not prevent moral effects, or positively produces bad ones.   It is desirable that punishment, though
founded upon a physical basis, as incarceration, do not consist in physical pain, because pain irritates.

33. Punishment presupposes an individual to be punished
within the sphere of the state, and who is accountable.   The
dead or the unborn are not accountable, because they cannot
account.   Hence all so-called punishments which are directed
against the dead, *e.g.*, disinterment and placing the body on
the gallows, or degradation of future generations, are inadmissible.

34. The state, in punishing, must never sink to the level of
the offender; hence punishments increased by cruelty are

---

[1] See my introduction to De Beaumont and De Tocqueville on the Penitentiary System in America.

[2] Davis, The Chinese Lord, 1836, vol. i. p. 282.

inadmissible, for they originate from wrath and hatred, not from justice.

35. Avoid even all appearance that you punish because the offender has *dared* to disobey, that is, as if you punished chiefly because your authority has been offended, not because the authority is for the common good, and *therefore* defying it, is an offence—is immoral. The very expression offending the authority is making it personal; a person, a moral individual may be offended, the state as such—its authorities cannot. They may be defied, disobeyed, but cannot be offended. Incalculable evil has flowed from this unhappy confusion of the ideas of personality and political authority.

36. It is impossible for the state to ascertain, with sufficient certainty to act upon, the psychologic state of the offender, and the entire relation between his whole inward man and the offence he has committed. God alone is that supreme and absolute judge who can do it, and who will truly deal out to every one according to his deeds. We mortal men cannot even frequently find out whether an offence seems to warrant in us a belief that it will be but the forerunner of many, according to the depraved state of the offender, or whether it was the sudden or peculiar action, provoked by a peculiar combination of circumstances. Yet the character of the offence depends greatly upon the individual within. How then shall we act? We have to ascertain a sort of punishment which will adapt, accommodate itself, even, to this circumstance as much as possible.

37. The offence must be punished; yet the offender alone should be punished. Who is the offender, the person that did the deed, or they who brought him up with all possible examples of vice and crime, as the children of offenders often are? Punishment, therefore, ought to enter as much as possible into the individuality of the trespasser. It ought to possess this quality in its nature.

38. He who has the right to dispose temporarily, or for life, of my personal liberty, has the undoubted right to dispose of my labor, for it is but a continuation and conse-

quence of the limitation of my volition, in which the essential character of imprisonment or privation of liberty consists.

39. Punition, considered with regard to the future actions of the offender, aims at political reform or outward loyalty. Let us remove, therefore, every thing from it which interferes with this subject, and connect with it every thing which promotes it, and which we have a right to connect with the punishment.

40. That punishment be certain, both in its being applied to each necessary case, and its effect on society, let it be so that those who have to apply it do it willingly, actively, and promptly, and those who are to benefit by it concur readily in its justice. (See 5.)

41. The state, in applying a punishment, which by its nature operates upon or appeals to the more essentially human qualities in the offender, has it in his power to raise him in his own estimation, and indirectly to raise the whole criminal community.

ESSAYS ON EDUCATIONAL POLICY.

A.—SUGGESTIONS FOR GIRARD COLLEGE, 1834.

B.—RELIGIOUS INSTRUCTION IN COLLEGES, 1850.

495

NOTE.

DR. LIEBER, having been invited by the Trustees of Girard College to submit a plan for the organization of that college, drew up an elaborate constitution, consisting of two hundred and sixty-nine articles, besides seventy-eight rules and regulations, which, together, extend through seventy-six pages octavo. He prefaced this constitution with voluminous introductory remarks, in which its principles are expounded and justified. The constitution, regulations, and report were printed by order of the trustees, and published by Carey, Lea & Blanchard (Philadelphia, 1834), 227 pp. 8vo. Only the first pages of the Report are here given, as the entire document is too extended to be included in this volume.

There is a letter of Edward Livingston's, written from Paris, in 1834, in which he acknowledges the receipt of this report, and speaks of it in favorable terms. He says:

"You have written three lines which ought forever to be impressed on the minds of all teachers, whether of science, politics, or religion. I know of no truth more happily expressed than that *There is a religion under all the variety of sects; there is a patriotism under all the variety of parties; there is a love of knowledge and a true science under all the variety of theories.*'

"The publication of your book will probably have a beneficent influence on a much wider scale than that for which it was originally calculated. It ought to be studied by all the law-makers in the different States."—G.

496

INTRODUCTION

TO A

REPORT ON AN ORGANIZATION

PROPOSED FOR

GIRARD COLLEGE FOR ORPHANS.

PHILADELPHIA, 1834.

MR. PRESIDENT, AND GENTLEMEN OF THE BOARD OF TRUSTEES:
YOUR predecessors had kindly invited, and you have charged me to draw up a plan for Girard College; I herewith lay before you the result of my labors. The confidence, of which you have been pleased to give me so signal a proof by this appointment, and the magnitude of the subject, have encouraged and animated me throughout my studies for this honorable task, and if the contents of the following pages fall far short of your expectation, I beg you to believe at least that no want of zeal, but deficiency of ability only, prevented them from becoming more worthy of your confidence; nor can any imperfection in all that I am going to propose to you have arisen from an inadequate appreciation on my part of the vast importance of Mr. Stephen Girard's munificent bequest. I consider it of an historical importance. In a country like ours, in which government cannot, according to its institutions, as profusely disburse the money of the people for the support of science, as the concentrated governments of some great European nations have the power to do—in a time when the rapid growth of some of our fairest cities warns us that, at some future period, a part of their population may grow up unprepared to dis-

charge the sacred duties of that full and entire citizenship which every one enjoys with us, if we do not wisely, and in time, provide against an evil, than which none can be imagined more directly at war with liberty—in an age when knowledge has taken a new start, many new sciences have been established, and the scientific activity of man is directed with peculiar vigor and a general energy not met with in any previous stage of the human family, toward the great aim of tracing out the laws of nature and of making her serviceable to us by the knowledge of these very laws, and when most institutions of education founded in earlier times or modelled after them, are not adequate to this characteristic trait of our time—in a period in which, in the natural growth of the European race, that part of society, inappropriately called the working class,[1] rapidly acquires an importance unknown be-

---

[1] The expression working class, or working men, must mean either those men who physically work, without thinking, in which case it will not be very acceptable to those who arrogate it, and a wind or water mill, working day and night, would be the beau ideal of a working man, or it must mean men who work and think. But if this is meant, who is not a working man and who is? Is the physician who follows his vocation at any hour of the day, the lawyer who sits up late at night, the scholar who sacrifices his health to his science, a conscientious editor, whose work never rests, are all these who rise much earlier and go to rest much later than those who call themselves working men by way of excellence, no working men? Is a Humboldt, who braves in the pursuit of his noble and chivalrous career, fever, beasts of prey, and insupportable insects, under a thousand privations; is a Champollion, who exposes himself to the burning sun of Egypt to learn the lessons of the past; is a Parry, a Ross, who dare the ices of the pole; a Davy, a Herschel, who enjoy no rest so regular, no health so sound as that of any farmer —are all these no hard working men? The division is entirely artificial and untenable, and therefore, if acted upon, highly mischievous. It is to be regretted, then, that so fictitious a thing is made, not unfrequently, a ground of political division, as though the interests of those who apply their mind to the changing and moulding of materials were separated from those who consume their productions or assist them essentially in discovering the best way of mastering the material. Where is the line of distinction between working and not working men? And if it were possible to draw it, why divide only these two classes? Suppose we should hear of a ticket of workmen in metal opposed to another of workmen in wood, coalesced with the workmen in leather, or a type founders' ticket in opposition to a printers' ticket. Yet all these divisions would be, as to politics, equally rational.

fore in history—in this great conjuncture, a fellow-citizen of ours, a single, private individual, hands us on his death bed the key to his vaults, where he had hoarded regal treasures, and says, "use them for the education of those who need support in it most, and for the diffusion of knowledge;" indicating, but merely indicating, by a few more words, the course he wishes us to pursue. There is a simplicity and grandeur in this event which cannot fail to inspire with enthusiasm all who shall be called upon to execute his great plan, and those who are engaged in preparing the way. Who, that contemplates but with a moderate degree of attention all these circumstances, must not be impressed with the momentous importance of the means which thus the testator has given into our hands, and can remain insensible to the imminent danger which must result from a negligent application of them. But I am confident I need not any longer dwell upon this point. I trust, gentlemen, that you are convinced of the uncommon value which I attach to the whole bequest of our benefactor.

The rules which I have laid down for myself in drawing up the following plan are these:

1. To consider the implicit directions of the testator, as the foundation and frame-work of the whole;

2. To follow conscientiously the wish of the testator, wherever it is clearly to be ascertained by fair interpretation of his testament, and to be guided by the spirit of his provisions in general;

And wherever he has left us entirely at liberty:

3. To provide for the great objects of education in general;

4. To provide for the wants of our time;

The French *classe industrielle* is by far more comprehensive and expressive, and late English writers have therefore adopted the expression *industrial class.* In this country we are all working men, and many individuals who do not belong to the industrial class are much harder working men, indeed, than those who do belong to it. If, therefore, I have spoken in various passages of the following pages of the great political importance which the industrial class has obtained in modern times, I wish by no means to convey the idea as if I consider their interest separated from the great interest of society in general. This would be aristocracy again.

5. To provide for the wants of our country in particular.

And here again I ought to observe, that though I may have erred in following these various rules, I have in no instance willingly and consciously deviated from them. It has been my anxious wish scrupulously to regulate my course by them alone.

I have therefore extracted from the will of the late Mr. Girard all that he implicitly prescribes; and this introduction will further show you how I proceeded to ascertain his wishes not implicitly laid down in his instrument.

His implicit directions, all of which you will find in the constitution, plan of education and regulations of discipline, are the following :

1. A college is to be established for poor male white orphans.

2. For such a number of these orphans as can be trained in one institution and can receive a better education as well as a more comfortable maintenance than they usually receive from the application of the public funds.

3. The college shall be permanent; with suitable out-buildings, sufficiently spacious for the residence and accommodation of at least three hundred scholars, and the requisite teachers, and other persons necessary in such an institution as the testator directs to be established.

4. The college and out-buildings are to be supplied with decent and suitable furniture, as well as books, and all things needful to carry into effect the testator's general design.

5. A library shall be established.

6. A room (of the college hall), most suitable for the purpose, shall be set apart for the reception and preservation of the testator's books and papers; and he directs that they shall be placed there by his executors, and carefully preserved therein.

7. Each building (of the college) should be as far as practicable devoted to a distinct purpose.

8. In one or more of those buildings, in which they may be most useful, he directs his executors to place his plate and furniture of every sort.

9. When the college and appurtenances shall have been constructed, and supplied with plain and suitable furniture and books, philosophical and experimental instruments and apparatus, and all other matters needful to carry the testator's general design into execution, the income, issues, and profits of so much of the said sum of two millions of dollars as shall remain unexpended shall be applied to maintain the said college according to his directions.

10. The institution shall be organized as soon as practicable.

11. To accomplish that purpose more effectually, due public notice of the intended opening of the college shall be given, so that there may be an opportunity to make selections of competent instructors and other agents, and those who may have the charge of orphans may be aware of the provisions intended for them.

12. A competent number of instructors, teachers, assistants, and other necessary agents shall be selected, and when needful, their places from time to time supplied.

13. They shall receive adequate compensation for their services.

14. No person shall be employed who shall not be of tried skill in his or her proper department, of established moral character, and in all cases persons shall be chosen on account of their merit and not through favor or intrigue.

15. As many poor white male orphans, between the ages of six and ten years, as the said income shall be adequate to maintain, shall be introduced into the college as soon as possible; and from time to time as there may be vacancies, or as increased ability from income may warrant, others shall be introduced.

16. On the application for admission, an accurate statement shall be taken in a book prepared for the purpose, of the name, birth-place, age, health, condition as to relatives, and other particulars useful to be known, of each orphan.

17. No orphan shall be admitted until the guardians or directors of the poor, or a proper guardian or other compe-

tent authority, shall have given, by indenture, relinquishment or otherwise, adequate power to the Mayor, Aldermen, and Citizens of Philadelphia, or to directors or others by them appointed, to enforce, in relation to each orphan, every proper restraint, and to prevent relatives or others from interfering with, or withdrawing, such orphan from the institution.

18. Those orphans for whose admission application shall first be made, shall be first introduced, all other things concurring, and at all future times, priority of application shall entitle the applicant to preference in admission, all other things concurring; but if there shall be at any time more applicants than vacancies, and the applying orphans shall have been born in different places, a preference shall be given —*first*, to orphans born in the City of Philadelphia; *secondly*, to those born in any other part of Pennsylvania; *thirdly*, to those born in the City of New York; and, lastly, to those born in the City of New Orleans.

19. The orphans admitted into the college shall be there fed with plain but wholesome food, clothed with plain but decent apparel, and lodged in a plain but safe manner.

20. No distinctive dress is ever to be worn.

21. Due regard shall be paid to their health, and to this end their persons and clothes shall be kept clean, and they shall have suitable and rational exercise and recreation.

22. They shall be instructed in the various branches of a sound education.

23. Among them reading, writing, grammar, arithmetic, geography, navigation, surveying, practical mathematics, astronomy, natural philosophy, chemistry, physics, French and Spanish, and such other learning and science as the capacities of the several scholars may merit or warrant.

24. The testator does not forbid, but neither recommends, the Greek and Latin.

25. He wishes the scholars to be taught facts and things rather than words and signs.

26. He especially desires that by every proper means a pure attachment to our republican institutions, and to the

sacred rights of conscience, as guaranteed by our happy constitutions, shall be formed and fostered in the minds of the scholars.

27. If any of the orphans become from malconduct unfit companions for the rest, and mild means of reformation prove abortive, they should no longer remain therein.

28. Those orphans who shall merit it, shall remain in the college until they shall respectively arrive at between fourteen and eighteen years of age.

29. They shall then be bound out to suitable occupations, as those of agriculture, navigation, arts, mechanical trades and manufactures, according to the capacities and acquirements of the scholars respectively.

30. In doing this the inclinations of the several scholars, as to the occupation, art or trade to be learned, shall be consulted as far as prudence shall justify.

31. The testator enjoins that if, at the close of any year, the income of the fund devoted to the purposes of the said college shall be more than sufficient for its maintenance during that year, the balance of the said income shall be forthwith invested in good securities, thereafter to be and remain as part of the capital; but in no event shall any part of the said capital be sold, disposed of, or pledged, to meet the current expenses of the said institution, to which the testator devotes the interest, income, and dividends thereof exclusively.

32. The testator enjoins and requires, that no ecclesiastic, missionary, or minister of any sect whatsoever, shall ever hold or exercise any station or duty whatever in the said college; nor shall any such person ever be admitted for any purpose, or as a visitor, within the premises appropriated to the purposes of the college.

33. It is the testator's desire that all the instructors and teachers in the college shall take pains to instil into the minds of the scholars the purest principles of morality, so that, on their entrance into active life, they may from inclination and habit evince benevolence toward their fellow-creatures, and a love of truth, sobriety, and industry, adopting at the same

time such religious tenets as their matured reason may enable them to prefer.

34. If application is made, as many orphans as can be maintained and instructed within as many buildings as the square of ground (designated and described in the will) shall be adequate to, shall be received, and additional funds shall be furnished by the final residuary fund expressly referred to in the will.

35. It is the design of the testator that the benefits of said institution shall be extended to as great a number of orphans as the limits of the said square and buildings therein can accommodate.

I have been obliged to mention here a provision of Mr. Girard's, which, I apprehend, has caused considerable anxiety in our community, and nevertheless is clear, implicit, and un-. conditional; I may, therefore, be permitted to interrupt, for a moment, the regular course of my introduction, in order to face at once this direction of the testator, which, if not properly understood, may have the tendency to render the whole college unpopular, however sound the scientific instruction which it will offer to the fatherless, or however thorough the discipline maintained in it may be.

Let us then ask at once, what can Mr. Girard have meant by the provision, given above, under number 32, and which excludes every ecclesiastic not only from any chair or station whatever in the college, but even prohibits their entry as visitors into the precincts of that institution? Had he the intention, as I believe some fear, to exclude, with the ecclesiastics and ministers, also religious education? He says distinctly, that "pains shall be taken to instil into the minds of the scholars *the purest principles of morality*," and even underlines these words in his will; at least thus I understand their being printed in italics in the copy before me. But who instils the purest principles of morality into the tender minds of youth without founding them on religious principles and without cultivating at the same time religion in their hearts? Is there a teacher who pretends to be able to do so? I know of none. We might, with equal justice, suppose Mr. Girard to have believed that " practical," or, as it is more frequently called, applied or mixed mathematics, might be taught without previous instruction in pure mathematics, because he does not especially mention the latter among the sciences which he wishes to be taught in the college. Can we ascribe an absurdity to him? He knew perfectly well that morals cannot be taught to youth without founding them upon man's relation to God—without religion. If we grant certain principles and fundamental truths, which can be conceived by religion alone, we may build upon them a logical system of ethics without farther assistance of religion, but we could not teach such a system to children; besides, there is a vast difference between teaching an ethical system like a science, which in its sphere has its great value, and " instilling the purest principles of morality into the tender minds of youth," so that " from inclination and habit they will evince benevolence towards their fellow-creatures, and a love of truth, sobriety, and industry." They shall love their fellow-creatures from *inclination*, and what shall *incline* their hearts to do so? how do fellow-creatures in the surest way evince benevolence towards each other? By considering themselves, what Mr. Girard calls us, *fellow-creatures*, which is, with other words, beings created by one common Creator, and by looking upon him and his great attributes. A time has existed when a Helvetius and other philosophers strove to found all morality on interest, to explain all virtue by egotism. The time has past, and should we suppose that Mr. Girard had this heart-chilling theory in view in the very moment when he provides for poor orphans, and when he uses an expression like that of " instilling the purest principles of morals," of which he well knew that no member of that society in which he lived, and to whom he intrusted the execution of his dearest project, would understand it thus? It is true the memory of Helvetius was cherished by him; he called a vessel after that distinguished writer, whose works, if we are justly informed, were found among the books constituting the small library of the testator. But a man may well admire the private character of Helvetius as a friend, a husband, a fellow-man, he may well be delighted by his style, and attracted by the acuteness and sometimes piercing consistency of his reasoning on untenable premises, and yet entirely differ from him in the conclusions he arrives at. Cannot a man even revere the stern probity of a Spinoza, standing the severest trials, and yet reject his icy philosophy?

When Mr. Girard says that the orphans, adopted by him, shall receive "a sound education," and knew that no one in this country has any idea of a sound education without the religious cultivation of those to be educated, would he not have used, had such been his intention, other language, more determinate words? There is in his whole will no expression of disregard toward religion; he calls the rights of conscience as guaranteed by our constitutions *sacred*. Surely, no right is called sacred which permits us to do something which is not of the highest importance to our moral well-being. Nobody speaks, even, of a sacred right of respiration. But I go farther. I maintain that, could we really believe Mr. Girard's intention to have been to exclude religious education from his college, we should have no right to let any orphan, dependent by poverty upon the support of society, profit by his bequest. Suppose a rich man should take it into his head to leave great treasures for the support and education of poor and parentless infants, on condition that their feet should always be tied as long as they were thus supported, and should be crippled for life, would any magistrate or guardian of those infants have a particle of right to expose them to this benefit? Yet this absurdity would be but slight in comparison to the prescription of crippling their souls—the souls of orphans, who more than any other beings stand in need of that comfort which alone can be derived from a knowledge of our relation to the Creator, the fountain of all knowledge and all morality. What teacher would degrade himself so far as to enter into a college on condition that he should ruin his pupils, should deprive them of the most precious knowledge, and answer to all their questions which go beyond the bare, sensible world, " I have promised to leave you ignorant, and to withhold from you the very props and staff which might support you in the sad vicissitudes of life into which all of us have to enter, and to suffer. I might, perhaps, give you some balm to heal, in years to come, painful wounds, which life will not fail to inflict upon you. Bereft of a father as you are, I might, before all, teach you to find another and still better one, and to lift up your innocent hearts to him— but I entered into a compact to make you unhappy."

Fortunately, Mr. Girard himself has dissipated every doubt on this subject. After having expressed his wish that the orphans should be brought up in the purest principles of morality, he says, "that they may adopt, on their entrance into active life, such religious tenets as their matured reason may enable them to prefer." He wishes then that they shall be prepared by the college for making a choice.

Now, there are but two ways in this world of making a choice between given subjects, trusting to chance or reflecting on the respective preference of the given subjects. In order to do the first, no knowledge of the subjects among which we have to choose is requisite, nor have we to exert our reason; to do the second, we must necessarily be acquainted with the nature of the given subjects, and must think. It is needless to say which of the two ways of choosing Mr. Girard meant, since he wishes that the choice should be made as matured reason may enable him who chooses. And, again, he italicizes the words "matured reason." He was, therefore, not only desirous that the orphans should receive a religious education, but that they should even be made acquainted with the chief truths of all religious sects, and how far they agree; otherwise, he might as well have demanded that the person or persons who should make the selection of books for the library which he wishes his college to be provided with should know nothing about their contents, in order to choose with an untrammelled mind. It is insulting his memory to assert any such incongruity. He wished to exclude dogmatics, and their variety—a bewildering confusion to a young mind—not religion.

But if we thus have shown what Mr. Girard did not intend, it remains to ascertain what he did intend. His will gives the answer. It says that the provision in question has been made because, "as there is such a multitude of sects and such a diversity of opinion amongst them, he desires to keep the tender minds of the orphans, who are to derive advantage from this bequest, free from the excitement which clashing doctrines and sectarian controversy are so apt to produce." He wished, then, the scholars of the college to be nursed up under the blessing and happy influence of knowledge and a religion pure and peaceful, and neither of a polemic·character nor disturbing the hearts of the youthful by perplexing dogmatics. In order to ensure this forever, he thought it necessary to exclude forever all ecclesiastics from the college. He knew, undoubtedly, of many ministers to whom he would have cheerfully entrusted the management of his beloved college; but he knew also that religious controversy has an enticing power, and leads but too frequently to agitations ill adapted to an institution which he wished to become and ever to remain an impartial seminary of knowledge to all sects and confessions. The framers of the constitution of the University of the City of New York had a similar exclusion of religious excitement in view, though, indeed, they did not resort to similar means to obtain their object. Mr. Girard thought that religious instruction and education might be afforded also by others than ministers; and, in fact, we see the same done every day in many schools; and he is not the first who thought it necessary to exclude the appointment of ecclesiastics, or ministers, in order to ensure for generations an undisturbed instruction in knowledge. Men often resort to strong measures if they wish to ensure a distinct character of certain institutions for all contingencies of future periods and the combinations of peculiar circumstances, which it is impossible to know and single out beforehand. I repeat it, our testator was desirous, in my opinion, to prevent his college from ever becoming either influenced by sectarian excitement or influential in it. Whether he has gone too far in his anxiety, praiseworthy in itself, by excluding ministers even from visiting the college, is another question. Many, and the writer of these lines for one among them, think that his zeal for liberality carried him even to illiberality in this instance, as Frederic the Great from a zeal to be just became unjust. But who is not subject to err thus? It is useless, however, to discuss this point; his provision is implicit, and it is beyond our power to change it. It is sufficient for us to know that he had no intention to exclude religion from his college; and I shall be happy if those provisions in the constitution which I have made in reference to this important point shall meet with your and our fellow-citizens' approbation. I believe that if they are adopted the scholars of our college will receive as much religious instruction, and a more truly religious education, than most other children. I shall have to return to this subject.

I now shall resume, gentlemen, the thread of my introduction.

The broad principles which Mr. Stephen Girard prescribes as the basis of the institution are then, according to the directions in his will, as given above, these:

- *a.* It is to be a college [he never designates it by any other name];
- *b.* For poor white male orphans;
- *c.* They are to receive a better education than they generally receive by the application of public funds;
- *d.* They are all to receive a sound education;
- *e.* A moral and religious one;
- *f.* An intellectual one;
- *g.* A political one;
- *h.* A physical one;
- *i.* Those who merit it shall receive a superior education, up to their eighteenth year;
- *j.* The chief and main sciences to be taught are, mathematics, pure and mixed or applied;

k. Physics and chemistry;

l. History and politics;

m. English, French, and Spanish;

n. Latin and Greek, or classical sciences, are not to be made the basis of the instruction;

o. The college shall prepare the scholars for those professions, arts, and occupations chiefly, which generally are not included in the so-called learned professions;

p. The instruction of each branch shall be a thorough one, not satisfying itself with words or signs; [hence, in chemistry and physics, experiments are indispensable; in mechanics, models; in astronomy, instruments and observations; in natural sciences, as mineralogy, specimens, etc.];

q. The college shall suffer in nothing; neither in a physical respect, nor in a competent number of teachers and agents, nor in the best qualified teachers, nor in instruments, apparatus, books, collections, furniture, or any other thing needful for a sound education;

r. He demands that all the sciences be taught, which those who have paid particular attention to education shall find, or which, in the course of time, may become necessary;

s. The college shall be planned in such a manner that it may gradually extend, and its sphere may gradually expand, without changing the original basis of the whole;

t. The college shall have undisputed power over the education of the orphans;

u. The discipline on the whole shall be mild, and the college on the other hand must have liberty to dismiss unworthy subjects;

v. The most scrupulous and conscientious choice of teachers, as well as of all other agents in the college, shall be made;

w. The teachers shall be adequately remunerated;

x. The scholars may, with the advice, and, if necessary,

the direction of their superiors, choose their future occupation; and consequently, their preparation for it in the college may vary accordingly, in those sciences which are not deemed necessary for the formation and education of every one;

y. The college shall never lack in funds, however much it may extend its activity;

z. No ecclesiastic shall ever be appointed in, or for the management of the college;

Mr. Girard demands, that the orphans admitted into his college shall receive a sound, and those who merit it, a superior education. [See, above principles, *c, i, j, k, l, m, p, q, r, s.*]

I have been told that some persons fear that the education which shall be offered by the college cannot be more than a common education, nearly such a one as our primary schools offer. It is evident that such individuals, if there exist any, judge from vague and incorrect impressions, not from the document which contains the outlines of the education which shall be given, because the testament contains, as we have seen, numerous and direct provisions to the contrary. It begins these directions by the expression of Mr. Girard's anxious wish " to provide for poor orphans a *better* education, and a more comfortable maintenance than they usually receive from the application of the public funds;" so that we see, that even those orphans whose talents do not warrant a longer stay in the college than to about their fourteenth year, an age indicated by the will, are to receive a better education. He allows others to remain, according to their merits, longer; and as long as to their eighteenth year; he prescribes certain sciences to be taught in the college, which do not belong to a common education, such as chemistry, physics, astronomy, navigation, surveying; he, after having enumerated a series of sciences, leaves the whole field open, as it may be found useful and judicious; he provides his college with apparatus of all kinds; he directs French and Spanish to be taught. He calls the institution to be established *a college,* and never a pauper-school, or even simply a school; nor does he use (if he had been in want of a better-sounding expression than pauper-school, yet one that was less distinct than college) the word orphan asylum.   In short, he demands a better than common, a sound, and, as circumstances may warrant, a superior education.   And, indeed, should we suppose that a man so intelligent in choosing his means for certain objects, so careful in wasting none, not even the smallest, had the intention to give two million of dollars, and as much more money as shall be wanted—for what?—to effect that which every day is obtained by means a thousand times smaller; and for which most, if not all, our communities have already provided years ago! Can a man like Mr. Girard be supposed to have been ignorant of the paramount importance of providing for poor white female orphans, when he tells us that he has "been for a long time impressed with the importance of educating the poor (he does not in this general introduction to the provisions for the college make any difference between sex or color) and of placing them, by the early cultivation of their minds and the development of their moral principles, above the many temptations to which, through poverty and ignorance, they are exposed"? He was not ignorant of the circumstance that poverty exposes the female child still more to moral ruin than the male, and that their education, as future wives and mothers, is of the most vital importance to society. He was not ignorant of the immense good which may yet be effected by a better education of the African race; nor can we, for a moment, believe him to have forgotten that by his vast treasures he might have assisted all of these in obtaining a common education even better than that generally afforded by public funds. But he preferred to limit his sphere of action, and to provide for a part of them only a sound, and, if warranted, a superior education, which object alone would require his treasures, great as they were. He wished to provide for the instruction in some sciences as yet generally neglected, and to raise the standard of education. He was desirous to provide, first, for the ruling part of the ruling race, and to set an example to be imitated by others, according to their means, for the other part of our poor and fatherless fellow-beings. Besides, he actually leaves considerable sums to other and already existing institutions; he bequeaths ten thousand dollars to the Orphan Asylum of Philadelphia; he gives an equal sum to the Comptrollers of the Public Schools for the City and County of Philadelphia; six thousand dollars to erect a school in Passyunk township, etc. He, therefore, wishes that an education different from that given in these establishments shall be offered in the college, which he calls his "primary object," otherwise he might have given his treasures to these schools, or simply ordered similar ones to be established. He wanted then a different education, and if the education is to be *different*, we know well, from numerous passages of his will, that it shall be a better, not an inferior one. Be it once more 'repeated, he demands a "better education than commonly is afforded to orphans;" he demands a "sound education" for all, and a superior one for the meritorious; and an orphan once received into the college, endowed with fair talents and conducting himself well, has a right and title to a superior education; which we dare not deny to the adopted child of the testator.

We live in a country in which knowledge and education is so highly and generally esteemed, and where political rights put every one, poor or rich, so perfectly on a par with his fellow-citizens, that it is unnecessary to refute an objection to the greatest possible diffusion of knowledge, which, in other countries, has not unfrequently been made. The injudicious remark that we have gone on so far without a certain knowledge, we may well go on for the future without it, is happily never heard here. The world also went on when all the commodities of Asia were brought by land to the Mediterranean, and *via* Venice distributed over Europe, yet the discovery of the way round the Cape of Good Hope was nevertheless all-important. England, already the most advanced country in industrial activity, yet has made for the last ten years the greatest efforts to enlighten her artisans and mechanics.

But there are, perhaps, some individuals in our country, I

know there are not many, who fear that a superior, a thorough
education, would produce in the scholars a distaste against
their future practical pursuits. I believe the contrary, and
experience bears me out. The scholars will learn how much
any honest occupation can be ennobled; how its whole sphere
can be expanded by knowledge, and at the same time how difficult it is to know too much for any kind of art or trade. The
excellent Polytechnic School in Vienna, which may be termed
a University for artisans, since all the sciences necessary for
them, and all the chief mechanical arts are studied and practised there, has never yet repented its imparting knowledge
to mechanics, but, on the contrary, it has been found to exercise the most salutary influence upon all the arts and trades,
to procure to the Austrian mechanic sources of wealth which
were unknown to him before, and to increase the national
wealth by the production of articles superior to those in neighboring states; and the celebrated *École Polytechnique* in Paris,
which affords so excellent instruction that Biot and Arago
could, when they had but finished their education in the institution, throw off their pupil's uniform and go forthwith to continue the great measurement of a degree, has never yet been
reproached with spoiling the scholars for the manifold occupations for which it prepares by giving a highly-scientific education. I cannot help believing that this fear arises almost
always from a very deficient acquaintance with the nature and
effects of knowledge and science, or, in other countries than
ours, often from a base anxiety to prevent their all-penetrating
effects. Men who entertain such views ought to read a work
which exhibits, in a masterly manner, the powerful effects of
knowledge on the whole class, which occupies itself with obtaining, fashioning, and subduing matter—Herschel's Preliminary Discourse on the Study of Natural Philosophy. We
must remember, too, that in all cases in which we wish to
apply knowledge we ought to be in possession of much more
than that which merely relates to the point in question. Surveying makes use of but very few and simple geometrical
truths; but he who does not know more of geometry and

mathematics in general than the solution of these few problems will make but a very indifferent surveyor.

I am convinced that Girard College will offer some branches of education superior to that which can now be obtained in any other institution in this country; and who would blame parents for regretting that their children cannot obtain an equally sound education if they have chosen for their future occupation an art for which the college prepares its scholars peculiarly well? but this can be no ground why we should withhold it from the poor and parentless. Should we, being possessed of adequate means for an extensive and sound education, abandon it because it is intended for orphans only? A distinguished writer of our country has justly observed that the college would be only so much more republican in its character if it were to offer a scientific education to meritorious and poor youths, which is as certainly true as that it is truly republican to pay officers well, so that the offices may not be occupied by the wealthy alone. But children who have not been bereft of their parents, or who are possessed of property, *will* profit by the college. Macchiavelli says, " after him who teaches men true religion, he is the greatest benefactor, who collects them into towns and villages and establishes governments among them;" and I would add, if I may add anything to the words of that great and noble man, that after him who thus civilizes man, he is the greatest benefactor of a nation who raises the standard of education. If you raise the standard of education for a certain class and certain branches by the system which you will establish in the college, it will have the most salutary effect on the whole community at large.

We cannot abandon the wise principle, true in education as everywhere else: obtain the best and greatest possible effect by the given means in the given time. It is our bounden duty to adhere to it.

Having, in my opinion, settled this point, the next question is, what is sound education? As regards morals and religion, necessary in a sound education, I have spoken already of them above, and you will find, gentlemen, various provisions respecting this subject, in my proposed plan. The final end of all moral education must be the same, whatever the system of education may be, though its method may greatly vary. But what is a sound intellectual education? I conceive it to be that which *trains* the mind well, and *stores* the mind well.

The mind is well *trained* when the education, adapting itself to the capacities and age of the scholar, leads him to think for himself, to judge and reason cautiously and correctly, to be ever awake to everything that surrounds him; when it imparts to him a true love of knowledge and inquiry, and a sincere love of truth which makes him willingly obey its voice, and give up prejudices for better information; which gives him the best rules and guidance for study, and its farther pursuit after he has left the school, and when all his faculties are harmoniously and in the highest possible degree developed. You will judge, gentlemen, whether I have proposed such means as to obtain best this end; more than general principles cannot be laid down in a constitution and regulations such as I have to lay before you; the selection of proper teachers, penetrated with these truths, and experienced in acting upon them, is of paramount importance to ensure success.

The mind is well *stored* if knowledge, the most desirable according to the means at our disposal, the allotted time, the wants of society in general, and the future destination of the scholars in particular is imparted to it.

We have here arrived at that point of our inquiry upon the correct appreciation of which the scientific character of our college depends.

That numerous class of men, which is occupied in producing, obtaining, fashioning, changing, transporting and exchanging material, and subduing matter by the application of knowledge, derived from experience and science, and which, as I have already stated, has been of late appropriately called the *industrial class*, has ever since the rise of free cities in the northern part of Italy, and the consequent and still more important growth of the free imperial cities and Hanse towns of Germany, steadily gone on increasing in importance, both

social and political, until we find it, in modern times, by far
the most important part of the population in all free countries.
To show how this great revolution was brought about, how
many great events were necessary to produce it, and again
how much time was requisite to allow these great events to
have their full effect, is one of by far the most interesting
subjects for the student of history, and, at the same time, one
of the richest in useful and salutary information; but it is
evidently not here the place to trace it out. You will all
allow the fact, which suffices for my purpose. This great
change in the European race,—the gradual elevation of the
industrial class, was much accelerated by a new power, which,
though of a totally different origin, joined the great current
of this movement in the sixteenth century, and operated
thenceforth toward the same end. From the time when
Copernicus and Galileo gave their momentous impulse to the
sciences which occupy themselves with the inquiry into the
laws of nature, after the discovery of America, and of the
passage round the Cape of Good Hope, had enlarged the theatre
of man's activity and inquiry, and when Bacon boldly drew
the sponge over the whole table of the physical sciences, to
have all written anew, as Pope Julius II. daringly ordered
the fine fresco-paintings of Pinturicchio in the Vatican to be
broken down to make room for the purer creations of the
immortal Raphael, all those sciences have developed themselves with increasing rapidity, and a proportionate effect on
everything that concerns man, until we have arrived at that
period when the investigation of nature, and the thousand-
fold applications of the knowledge thus obtained to the various
branches of industry, form one of its chief characteristics.
Science was originally rekindled among the modern European
nations by the revival of classical learning, and all institutions
for instruction were planned accordingly; but the increased
importance of the industrial class, and the new sciences
sprung up since that period, created a new want of learning,
and of adequate institutions to diffuse it, for which at last
numerous establishments have been founded. They are the

polytechnic schools in Paris, Vienna, Berlin, Hanover, Munich, Carlsruhe, St. Petersburg, and many others. The Prussian government, perceiving the necessity of providing for the new wants in education, and the inadequacy of the classical schools alone, has lately founded polytechnic schools in all provincial capitals, with a view to establish, as fast as possible, similar ones in all the other cities which now possess *gymnasia* only. They are the necessary effects of the development of civilization and the very offspring of the wants of our times.

I apprehend that many persons in this country are under the impression that a polytechnic school signifies an educa-tional establishment with more or less of a military character —a mistake owing to the circumstance that we read little of other polytechnic schools than the one in Paris, which has a military, and whose pupils even have much of a martial, char-acter. But this is merely accidental. When the plan of the polytechnic school was first laid before the revolutionary gov-ernment of France, it could then be recommended indeed only by showing the advantage which would accrue to the armies from teaching mathematics, chemistry, etc., by forming better engineers, directors of powder-mills, artillery, laboratories, etc. The whole attention of France was then turned toward her legions. The school itself, however, had no military organi-zation; Napoleon first gave it one, and most of its scholars entered the artillery or corps of engineers after they had fin-ished their course of education. In 1814 the pupils formed a corps, and fought nobly at Montmartre. Every one knows what a signal part they took in the revolution of 1830. (See the article *École Polytechnique,* in the *Americana.*) Yet all this has nothing to do with the essential character of polytechnic schools. The name signifies an institution in which a scien-tific and practical, not a classical education is given; thus the polytechnic school at Vienna has the very opposite of a mili-tary character, as the reader may be aware. It prepares young men for the various occupations of practical life for which no classical education is required. The expression *polytechnic school* will be taken in this work always in the latter and proper sense. Science and application are so intimately interwoven in our times that an artisan stands in a very different position from what he did in former ages. Civilization brings every day new principles into action, and he that applies them must have a proportionate knowledge of them. When all men were satisfied with hour-glasses, he that provided his fellow-citizens with instruments to measure time could carry on his occupation with a knowledge very limited compared to that of which he must be possessed who now provides the astronomer with a correct pendulum-clock, or a sea-faring man with a chronometer. A navigator of the earliest times was not required to know as much as the mariners who executed the noble plans of Prince Henry the Navigator, nor was a knowledge expected from them equal to what modern navigation teaches. If we consider one single department of modern industry only, machine-building, nay a mere subdivision of it, the building of steam-engines, what an extensive knowledge is not required in the artist merely to remain on a par with the progress of this branch. It is the same with all trades and arts. The Prussian government has even established a school for educating shepherds in order to provide the ennobled flocks with persons well prepared to take care of that important element of the national wealth of that kingdom. A modern nation that remains behindhand in diffusing knowledge among the industrial class sinks relatively in all its power. We have an instance in Spain. But a few years ago the Spanish government abolished the chairs of natural philosophy in the universities, and when, under Charles IV., Balthazar Sarmiento proposed to make the Spanish part of the Tagus navigable, the supreme authority of the Inquisition declared to the king, that "if God had wished that the Tagus should flow freely, he would have made of it that which he made of all navigable rivers,—he would not have thrown any obstacles into its course;" whilst Brindley, humorously asked by a committee of parliament for what purpose he considered rivers to have been made, is said to have answered, "undoubtedly to feed navigable canals." This is, we all admit, extravagant, but it nevertheless shows the spirit of the two nations, of which we clearly see the effects. The one industrious and consequently powerful in the highest degree, and diffusing every day more knowledge among the industrial class, the other torpid, and consequently insignificant,—a state in which it will remain just as long as it does not turn to industry, and open all channels to knowledge.

In our country, where industry is in so flourishing a state, and knowledge so much valued by all classes, we have not yet a polytechnic school, that is to say, an establishment which affords instruction to all those who intend to choose in active life an occupation belonging to that great and important class mentioned above. Let nobody say, I would repeat, "just because we are in a flourishing condition in industry without a polytechnic school, why should we establish one?" The answer is easy: in order to diffuse knowledge among all industrial classes, and to increase our national wealth, standing, and happiness, and extend the benign, refining, and purifying influence of knowledge to every class. Let us put the question quite simply, and every one will easily give himself the answer. Is it better for the dyer, when he brings a knowledge of chemistry to his trade; for the brass-founder, and any mechanic working in metals, a knowledge of the nature of metals, the effect of heat, their composition and decomposition; for the canal-builder, of statics and hydraulics; for the machine-builder, of mechanics, physics, and machine-drawing; the cabinet-maker, of the nature of woods, afforded by technological botany and of the most tasteful and approved ornaments of all ages; the merchant, of commodities of the produce of the various nations; the manufacturer, of the progress of manufactures among other nations, and of the manifold manufactured articles; the architect, of the many branches preparatory to his occupation; the navigator, of astronomy and higher mathematics, etc., etc., besides the instruction in so many branches useful to all practical men? and these are branches, a knowledge of most of which cannot be well obtained by private study, and a want of proper instruction in which leads to innumerable failures, and an experience bought at a dear rate, so dear that it ruins many before they arrive at it. There is yet another point which requires consideration here.

It would be a very mistaken notion were we to suppose that enough would be done if general information in our country were kept only on the same level and does not actually fall. Increased activity, as well as greater extent of our population, creates a greater variety of interests—interests which will clash with each other and deride us, if we do not actively search for a remedy there, where we have to look for all, and every support in our whole national life—the diffusion of knowledge. The *Union* requires us to keep pace with the progress of knowledge, and proud as the American must be if he contemplates this characteristic trait of his country, which gives it so lofty a station among the nations of the earth, it also acquires a greater activity and watchfulness, in the same degree as knowledge is superior and more refined than common force. We must be fully aware that it is not our lot ever to rest in security; we must *go on* in order to be safe; standing still, relaxation, would be with us ruin. A power founded upon brutal force may for a time rest, as a granite block remains unchanged and strong, but organic life must be active, or it dies away. The fate of our nation, trusting entirely to knowledge, is that of the mind—there is no standing still; either onward, or ruin.

Certainly if any country wants a polytechnic school it is ours; the establishment of such an institution would be to support and raise us in one of our most national branches of activity, and it would therefore meet at the same time with the greatest success. In addition to all this, it is, if I understand the testament right, the distinct demand of Mr. Girard to form a polytechnic school. The sciences which he enumerates as being desirable to be taught in the college, and the occupations which he mentions as those for which the scholars should be prepared in the same, are such as essentially constitute and require a polytechnic school. There is one institution in our country, justly fostered by the nation, which comes in some branches near to a polytechnic school; but excellent as the United States Military Academy at West Point is and much information as we may derive from it for our purpose, the object for which it was founded gives it a character much too limited for our purpose.

But the great diffusion of knowledge and the consequent demand for it, for they go always hand in hand, has created another kind of institutions in our time which we do not yet possess, and which yet are allowed on all sides to be highly desirable for us—for us perhaps more so than for those countries in which they already exist: I mean seminaries for the education of teachers. Our population extends daily further over vast territory, knowledge is so indispensable an element of our whole social and political condition, and the demand for teachers increases so rapidly, that we should—such is our humble opinion—ill fulfil our duty were we not to make at once of Girard College a polytechnic school and a seminary of teachers, for which it affords an opportunity not easily met with, since those scholars who wish to choose the honorable occupation of teacher, and whose merits warrant such a choice, may, under the guidance of proper professors, learn the art and science of education,—a subject requiring much study,—and the application of it with their younger fellow-scholars. We should act by such an arrangement in the true spirit of the testator; for two reasons. We cannot but suppose, from so judicious and careful a man as he was, that he desired to lay out his capital to bear the greatest possible interest—to produce the greatest effect by his college. Now, as a horticulturist who has the improvement of his country at heart is not satisfied with raising a few trees that bear improved fruits, or domesticating exotic plants, but distributes the new seeds and plants to his neighbors, so we ought to make of the institution before us a true nursery of knowledge, not satisfying ourselves with educating certain individuals, but sending the seeds of knowledge everywhere where wanted. Secondly, we know well how much the testator loved his country,—his whole testament is a continued proof of it,—and we know equally well that if knowledge is with other nations a power, it is with us the very life and soul of our whole national existence. There is nothing else among all possible things that a human mind can conceive of which can sustain us in the solution of our great political problem. It has been said so often that its very triteness proves how generally we acknowledge its truth, knowledge is our only safeguard. If you wish to render safe a remote part of a large city during the darkness of night, light its streets. Darkness and danger, light and safety—between these we have to choose. If we then can do so much for our country by the diffusion of knowledge through the education of teachers, our respect to Mr. Girard, and the duty to act in the spirit of his testament alone would demand it, did not our hearts dictate it; and the president of the board, whom I have the honor to address, pointed, perhaps, at this circumstance, when in his pertinent and eloquent speech on the fourth of July last, on occasion of laying the corner-stone of the college building, he dedicated the institution to Education, to Morals, to our Country.

The scientific character, therefore, which I believe it is necessary to give to the college is, that it shall be a polytechnic college and a seminary for teachers; two things which may be admirably combined, and I shall consider it as my happiest labor if the following constitution shall appear to you to provide for these wants, and I shall thus contribute my mite to assist our nation in fulfilling its great and proud task, imposed upon it by history.

THE NECESSITY

OF

RELIGIOUS INSTRUCTION IN COLLEGES.[1]

THE present professor of the theological branches in the South Carolina College has resigned his chair, and, it is understood, the question has been raised whether this chair ought not to be abolished. Under these circumstances it will not be considered presumptuous in one who must be supposed to be thoroughly acquainted with the whole operation of the college within, and its relation to the State at large, and who yields to no one in the deep interest he feels in the institution, if he states his opinion on a subject which appears to him of vital importance.

The writer of these lines is convinced that South Carolina College, as indeed every college in the Union, would be essentially defective without a chair for the evidences of Christianity, and biblical knowledge in general, and without an officer whose particular duty should be to preach regularly to the students, and by personal intercourse with them to enforce religious truth. His reasons are the following:

Christianity, considered purely as a branch of knowledge, constitutes an indispensable element of liberal education, because the Christian religion, taken solely as a historical fact, is incomparably the mightiest of all facts in the annals of

---

[1] This essay was probably written about 1850, when the author was a professor in South Carolina College.

human society. It has so tinctured and penetrated all systems of knowledge, all institutions, both civil and exclusively social, the laws, languages, and literature of the civilized nations, their ethics, rights, tastes, and wants, that without a historical and philosophical acquaintance with Christianity, it is impossible to understand any of them. There is not the historian in existence, whatever view of religion itself he may take, who denies that Christianity is at the foundation of the whole of modern history, that is, of history since the downfall of the Western Roman Empire ; in other words, of the whole civilization of the Western white race. It was on this ground, among others, that the author of these brief remarks insisted, many years ago, when charged with drawing up a plan of education for Girard College, upon the introduction of the Bible; although the founder had prohibited the very entrance of a divine into the precincts of the institution by stringent provisions in his testament.

Without a comprehensive knowledge of Christianity, and as a matter of course, of the Bible, an institution for the education of youth, in this country, would be as defective as a similar one in the East (even if such an one were established for the education of Christian youth only), which should omit the imparting of a proper knowledge of the Koran ; because all institutions of the country are based upon it, and without this knowledge the first key to decipher them would be wanting. Indeed, the student of any foreign nation is obliged, first of all, to turn his attention to its religion, because man is, among other things, a religious being, and religion will always shape and frame the whole course of his thinking, and tincture his feelings for better or worse. No man ever attempted to study Hindoo history or institutions without acquainting himself with the Veda, or Grecian history and literature without a study of mythology.

Nor will any one, acquainted with the actual state of things, venture to say that the majority of applicants for admission into our colleges bring with them a sufficient amount of this knowledge, so that all further instruction in it may be fairly dispensed with. Let truth prevail, though scandal ensue, is the wise dictum of St. Augustine ; and it is a fact that the youth entering this college are often grievously destitute of biblical knowledge.

Not only is it impossible to dispense with instruction in Christianity, in an institution for liberal education, on the grounds just stated, but even religion itself, and as such, forms an indispensable branch of all sound education. Man is, it has been observed, a religious being, as he is a political, an exchanging, a communicating being. As we find him nowhere, though he be in the lowest stage of civilization, without some language, some government, some system of exchange, some feeling of shame, some property, some consciousness of right and wrong, and some sense of the beautiful, in whatever incipient stages all these may be, so we find him nowhere without some religion. These are the characteristics of man, without which we never find him, however low ; and with which we never find the animal, however intelligent. If true religion be not imparted and cultivated, he will cling to a bad one. It is the office of all education to cultivate in the young whatever constitutes essential humanity, and religion stands foremost among these constituents. If proper language be not imparted, speak he will, though it be ever so incorrectly ; and if true religion be not imparted he will become the dupe of a bad one, of superstitions, fanaticism, or enervating indifference. Had the youth who are in the college remained under their parental roofs, it would have been the duty of their parents to guide them in the path of religion, and so long as they are inmates of the college, the trustees and professors stand in the place of parents. No one, it is conceived, has the right to deny them proper instruction in religion. It may be objected, indeed, that the professor of the theological branches is necessarily the minister of a certain sect, and that, therefore, he cannot avoid imbuing the students with a bias toward that particular denomination. But does the professor of divinity stand in this respect in any other position than all the other professors whose duty it is to teach branches in any way connected with the moral sciences? The constitution of the United States and that of our State are very properly explained to the students; is it, on that account, feared that the respective professors will imbue the students with party views? The professor of history, if he be a man at all worthy of his station, must have reflected upon many of the most momentous questions of mankind, religious as well as political, and must have come to some ultimate decisive conclusions; but is it impossible for him on that account to teach his science fairly and liberally without influencing his hearers in party or sectarian matters? The professor of moral philosophy must have come to some definite conclusions as to the first principles of morality and the ethical nature of man, which needs must be contrary to the opinions of some parents of students; shall moral philosophy be on that account stricken from the catalogue of our studies? If this view were consistently carried out, it would lead to abstractions such as would require professors to be no longer individuals; yet the very object of an institution like ours is to impart living knowledge by the living word of living individuals. Professors are not intended to be passive receivers of recitations. Else the perusal of books in the solitude of the closet might be advantageously substituted. It is for the trustees, no doubt, to make the appointment of a professor for the chair of Christianity with the utmost care; to select a pious, learned, moderate individual, of a high order of talent and of comprehensive common sense. This once done, they must repose confidence in him, as they must do with all the other professors, not a confidence without superintendence, yet without trammeling anxiety. The position of every professor is essentially one of confidence, which must be granted on a large and liberal scale, or withdrawn altogether.

It will be hardly necessary to mention that the chair of Christian knowledge must have its due influence upon the general discipline of a college; still more the regular preaching in the chapel. The students might indeed go to the churches of the town, but the important practical question is, Would they go? One-third of the young men would stay at home, idling away the precious time or doing worse things. Sunday would become in fact a day of reprehensible conduct in the college. This is no remark particularly applying to the youth of South Carolina; it applies to all young men the world over. But there is a stronger reason yet for regular preaching in the chapel. Students form a community of their own. They are of a similar age, a similar degree of intellectual development, with propensities, wants, and faculties peculiar to their age and station; and sermons ought to be closely adapted to both. This cannot be expected of sermons which might be occasionally delivered in the college chapel by ministers of the town. They cannot have that practical knowledge which their own teachers only can possess.

It has been stated, and often, I feel sure, in perfectly good faith, that the appointment of a professor of Christian knowledge in South Carolina College is unconstitutional. The constitution of this State, in unison with the pervading spirit of the general polity of this country, disclaims every support of any religious denomination from the public treasury, but does it discountenance religion in its general sense, or can it do so? If what has been stated at the beginning of these remarks be true, an attempt of this kind on the part of any political society is futile. The Christian religion is interwoven with all the institutions which surround us and in which we have our social being. The Christian religion has found its way into a thousand laws, and has generated a thousand others. It can no more be excluded than the common law, or our language. If the principle of separation between State and Church be extended to religion itself, consistency must lead to the exclusion of the Bible from every public educational establishment, as indeed short-sighted fanaticism has made the attempt in other parts of the country. Considering all these circumstances, I do not hesitate to express my opinion that I should view the abolition of the chair in question as a grievous injury to the college. It is but an individual opinion, and claims no other weight than that of being the result of long experience and attentive observation.

It has been said that the professor ought to possess, among his other qualifications, that of distinguished talent. It is not sufficient that he be a gentleman of unimpeached piety; for in a general point of view, it may be stated as a well established fact that the discipline of a college depends in a very high degree, and naturally, too, upon the respect which the students may have for the talents of their professor; and, in a more particular point of view, he must teach, foster, and cultivate, as well as defend religion with young men, who are assembled for the very purpose of intellectual culture; among whom there are always some of very superior talents, and who, owing to the daily appearance of the professor before them in many phases of intellectual activity, constitute a searching and not very compromising or indulgent tribunal. A vigorous and accomplished mind is a necessary condition of the success which a professor of the theological branches may hope to meet with in this or any other college; a pious and kindly character as well as learning are necessary indeed, but not sufficient for the station.

THE WRITINGS OF FRANCIS LIEBER.

[NOT INCLUDING MANY OF HIS MINOR COMMUNICATIONS TO THE CURRENT JOURNALS, WHICH WERE VERY NUMEROUS, SOMETIMES UNDER HIS OWN NAME OR ITS INITIALS, AND OFTEN UNDER OTHER NAMES, AS AMERICUS, CIVIS, ETC.]

1823.

TAGEBUCH MEINES AUFENTHALTES IN GRIECHENLAND IM JAHRE 1822. Leipzig: Brockhaus; pp. x. 186, 12mo. (Trans. into Dutch.)

1826.

VIERZEHN WEIN- UND WONNELIEDER VON ARNOLD FRANZ. Berlin: Riemann.

UEBER DIE LANCASTERISCHE LEHRWEISE. (Aus. No. 122 und 123 der Literarischen Blätter der Börsen-Halle.) Hamburg: Carstens.

1828–32.

ENCYCLOPEDIA AMERICANA, ed. Francis Lieber. Philadelphia: Carey; 13 vols., 8vo.

1833.

ON THE PENITENTIARY SYSTEM IN THE UNITED STATES, AND ITS APPLICATION IN FRANCE, ETC., by G. DE BEAUMONT and A. DE TOCQUEVILLE. Trans. with Introduction, Notes, and Additions by FRANCIS LIEBER. Philadelphia: Carey; pp. xxxv. 307, 8vo. (Trans. into German.)

1834.

A CONSTITUTION AND PLAN OF EDUCATION FOR GIRARD COLLEGE FOR ORPHANS, WITH AN INTRODUCTORY REPORT. Philadelphia: Carey; pp. 227, 8vo. Extract pub. in Misc. Works.

LETTERS TO A GENTLEMAN IN GERMANY ON A TRIP TO NIAGARA. Philadelphia, 8vo.—1835. Pub. in London under the title of "The Stranger in America." pp. 301, 310. 2 vols., 8vo. Extract pub. in Misc. Works.

1835.

REMINISCENCES OF AN INTERCOURSE WITH MR. NIEBUHR, THE HISTORIAN. Philadelphia. pp. 231, 12mo.—London: Bentley. (Trans. into German.) Repub. in Misc. Works.

A BRIEF AND PRACTICAL GERMAN GRAMMAR. Never published.

CASPAR HAUSER.

THE RELATION BETWEEN EDUCATION AND CRIME. (Letter to Bishop White.) Philadelphia.

1836.

INAUGURAL ADDRESS AT COLUMBIA, S. C., ON HISTORY AND POLITICAL ECONOMY AS NECESSARY BRANCHES OF SUPERIOR EDUCATION IN FREE STATES. Repub. in Misc. Works.

1837.

LETTER TO ALBERT GALLATIN ON THE IMPORTANCE OF THE STUDY OF FOREIGN LANGUAGES. Southern Literary Messenger. Repub. in Misc. Works.

LEGAL AND POLITICAL HERMENEUTICS; OR, PRINCIPLES OF INTERPRETATION AND CONSTRUCTION IN LAW AND POLITICS. American Jurist, Boston.—1839. 2d ed., Boston, 12mo.—1880, 3d ed., with author's additions, and notes by W. G. HAMMOND, St. Louis: Thomas; pp. xiv. 352, 8vo.

1838.

MANUAL OF POLITICAL ETHICS. Boston. 2 vols., 8vo.—1839, London.—1847, 2d ed. 2 vols., 8vo.—1875, 3d ed. by T. D. WOOLSEY. Philadelphia: Lippincott; pp. 472, 459. 2 vols., 8vo.

ESSAY ON SUBJECTS OF PENAL LAW AND ON UNINTERRUPTED SOLITARY CONFINEMENT AT LABOR, IN A LETTER TO JOHN BACON. Philadelphia. Extract from an enlarged edition repub. in Misc. Works.

1839.

RAMSHORN'S DICTIONARY OF LATIN SYNONYMES. Edited and trans. from the German by FRANCIS LIEBER. Boston, 12mo.

1840.

GREAT EVENTS DESCRIBED BY GREAT HISTORIANS. Collected and in part trans. by FRANCIS LIEBER. Boston.—1847, 2d ed., New York.—1862, 3d ed., New York: Harpers. pp. 415, 12mo.

LETTER TO HON. WILLIAM C. PRESTON ON INTERNATIONAL COPYRIGHT. Repub. in Misc. Works.

1841.

ESSAYS ON LABOUR AND PROPERTY. New York: Harpers, 18mo.—1854, 2d ed., 18mo.—1856, 3d ed., 18mo.

1844.

UEBER HINRICHTUNGEN AUF OFFENEM FELDE ODER ÜBER EXTRAMUREN UND INTRAMUREN HINRICHTUNGEN. Heidelberg Jahrbücher.

1845.

LECTURE ON THE ORIGIN AND DEVELOPMENT OF THE FIRST CONSTITUENTS OF CIVILIZATION. Delivered to the Senior Class of South Carolina College. Repub. in Misc. Works.

BRUCHSTÜCKE ÜBER GEGENSTÄNDE DER STRAFKUNDE BESONDERS ÜBER DAS EREMITENSYSTEM. Hamburg.

1846.

THE CHARACTER OF THE GENTLEMAN. Cincinnati and Charleston.—1847, 2d and enlarged ed. Columbia, S. C.: McCarter, 12mo.—1862, with preface by E. B. Shuldham. Edinburgh: Patterson, 12mo.—1863, 3d and much enlarged ed. Philadelphia: Lippincott, 18mo. Repub. in Misc. Works.

1847.

LETTER ON ANGLICAN AND GALLICAN LIBERTY. Repub. in Misc. Works. (Trans. by MITTERMAIER into German.)

UEBER DIE NATIONALITÄT DER DEUTSCHEN IN DEN VEREINIGTEN STAATEN VON NORD-AMERICA.

1848.

SOPHISMS OF THE PROTECTIVE POLICY BY FR. BASTIAT. Trans. by MRS. McCORD, with Introductory Letter by FRANCIS LIEBER. New York: Putnam, 12mo.

THE WEST AND OTHER POEMS. New York: Putnam, 18mo.

REMARKS ON MRS. FRY'S VIEWS OF SOLITARY CONFINEMENT.

ESSAY ON THE LEGISLATIVE SYSTEM OF TWO HOUSES.

UEBER DIE UNABHÄNGIGKEIT DER JUSTIZ. In einem Brief aus Amerika von FRANZ LIEBER. Heidelberg, 1848.

1849.

ABUSE OF THE PARDONING POWER. Pub. by New York Legislature. Repub. in National Intelligencer, 1851, and in Lieber's "Civil Liberty," 1874, as Appendix II.

1850.

A PAPER ON THE VOCAL SOUNDS OF LAURA BRIDGMAN. (Smithsonian Transactions.) Revised and repub. in Misc. Works.

RELIGIOUS INSTRUCTION IN COLLEGES. Repub. in Misc. Works.

1851.

ADDRESS TO THE GRADUATING CLASS OF SOUTH CAROLINA COLLEGE. THE NECESSITY OF CONTINUED SELF-EDUCATION. Repub. in Misc. Works.

LETTER ON THE GREAT LONDON EXHIBITION.

1853.

ON CIVIL LIBERTY AND SELF-GOVERNMENT.   Philadelphia: Lippincott, 2 vols., 8vo.—London: Bentley, 1 vol., 8vo.—1859, 2d ed., enlarged and corrected. 2 vols., 8vo.—1874, 3d and revised ed., by T. D. WOOLSEY. pp. 622, 1 vol., 8vo.

1855.

WAS NAPOLEON A DICTATOR?   Putnam's Magazine.

THE MORMONS. SHALL UTAH BE ADMITTED INTO THE UNION?   Putnam's Magazine.

1856.

A LECTURE ON THE HISTORY AND USES OF ATHENÆUMS. Repub. in Misc. Works.

1858.

INAUGURAL ADDRESS AT COLUMBIA COLLEGE, NEW YORK.   HISTORY AND POLITICAL SCIENCE NECESSARY STUDIES IN FREE COUNTRIES.   Repub. in Misc. Works.

1859.

ALEXANDER VON HUMBOLDT.   An Address delivered at a Meeting of the Geographical and Statistical Society, New York.   Repub. in Misc. Works.

DISCOURSE INTRODUCTORY TO A COURSE OF LECTURES ON THE STATE.   THE ANCIENT AND THE MODERN TEACHER OF POLITICS. Repub. in Misc. Works.

1861.

TWO LECTURES ON THE CONSTITUTION OF THE UNITED STATES, WITH AN ADDRESS ON SECESSION, delivered in 1851. Repub. in Misc. Works.

1862.

GUERRILLA PARTIES, CONSIDERED WITH REFERENCE TO THE LAW AND USAGES OF WAR. Pub. by U. S. War Department. Repub. in Misc. Works.

1863.

GENERAL ORDER NO. 100: INSTRUCTIONS FOR THE GOVERNMENT OF THE ARMIES OF THE UNITED STATES IN THE FIELD.   Pub. by U. S. War Department. Repub. in Misc. Works.

1864.

WASHINGTON AND NAPOLEON. Repub. in Misc. Works.

POEM—OUR COUNTRY AND HER FLAG. Loyal Pub. Soc., New York.

1865.

AMENDMENTS OF THE CONSTITUTION SUBMITTED TO THE CONSIDERATION OF THE AMERICAN PEOPLE. Repub. in Misc. Works.

THE STATUS OF REBEL PRISONERS OF WAR. Repub. in Misc. Works.

LETTER TO HON. W. H. SEWARD ON INTERNATIONAL ARBITRATION. Republ. in Misc. Works.

LETTER TO HON. E. D. MORGAN ON THE AMENDMENT OF THE CONSTITUTION ABOLISHING SLAVERY. Loyal Pub. Soc., New York.

1867.

REFLECTIONS ON THE CHANGES WHICH MAY SEEM NECESSARY IN THE PRESENT CONSTITUTION OF NEW YORK. Repub. in Misc. Works.

UNANIMITY OF JURIES. American Law Register. Repub. in Misc. Works.

1868.

FRAGMENTS OF POLITICAL SCIENCE ON NATIONALISM AND INTERNATIONALISM. (Trans. into Spanish.) Repub. in Misc. Works.

1869.

ALEXANDER VON HUMBOLDT. An Address delivered at the unveiling of the bust of Humboldt in the Central Park, N. Y. Pub. in report of Central Park Commissioners. Repub. in Misc. Works.

1870.

NOTES ON FALLACIES OF AMERICAN PROTECTIONISTS. 5th and enlarged ed., pub. in Misc. Works.

1871.

ON THE IDEA OF THE LATIN RACE AND ITS REAL VALUE IN INTERNATIONAL LAW. Revue de Droit International. Trans. repub. in Misc. Works.

DE LA VALEUR DES PLÉBISCITES DANS LE DROIT INTERNATIONAL. Revue de Droit International. Littell's Living Age. Repub. in Misc. Works.

DE L'UNITÉ DES MESURES ET ÉTALONS DANS LES RAPPORTS AVEC LE DROIT DES GENS, ETC. Revue de Droit International.

1872.

NOTE SUR LE PROJET DE M. MOYNIER, RELATIF A L'ÉTABLISSEMENT D'UNE INSTITUTION JUDICIARE INTERNATIONALE. Revue de Droit International.

SUGGESTIONS ON THE SALE OF ARMS BY THE U. S. GOVERNMENT DURING THE FRANCO-PRUSSIAN WAR. Revue de Droit International. Trans. pub. in Misc. Works.

THE RISE OF OUR CONSTITUTION AND ITS NATIONAL FEATURES. Now first pub. in Misc. Works.

INDEX.

THE END.

www.ingramcontent.com/pod-product-compliance
Lightning Source LLC
Chambersburg PA
CBHW022127020426
42334CB00015B/793